I0093327

ANCESTRAL RECORDS
AND PORTRAITS

—

VOLUME I

The University at Henrico
Destroyed in the Massacre March M.DC.XXII.

This medallion commemorates the destruction by the Indians of the First University in America, at Henrico, Virginia, A. D. 1619.

Chapter I., The Colonial Dames of America, caused it to be designed for the Johns Hopkins University, which bestows a replica from time to time upon an alumnus, or a graduate student, for work of especial excellence in early American history.

ANCESTRAL RECORDS AND PORTRAITS

A COMPILATION FROM THE
ARCHIVES OF CHAPTER I.,
THE COLONIAL DAMES OF
AMERICA

PREPARED UNDER THE DIRECTION
OF THE PUBLICATION COMMITTEE
BY THE EDITORIAL DEPARTMENT
OF THE GRAFTON PRESS

VOLUME I

CLEARFIELD

Originally Published
New York, 1910

Reprinted
Genealogical Publishing Company
Baltimore, 1969

Reprinted for
Clearfield Company, Inc. by
Genealogical Publishing Co., Inc.
Baltimore, Maryland
1997

Library of Congress Catalog Card Number 68-57950

ISBN: 978-0-8063-1969-8

Made in the United States of America

To

Our fellow laborers whom we have
lost, in recognition of their loyal devotion to the welfare of this Society and the services that ended only
with their lives, this tribute is dedicated in affectionate remembrance by

CHAPTER I.,

THE COLONIAL DAMES OF AMERICA

PREFACE

These two volumes contain a compilation of the more important and interesting portions of the records which have been collected during the past nineteen years by the members of CHAPTER I., THE COLONIAL DAMES OF AMERICA. When it is understood that herein is represented only one of the Chapters, the great historical value of the work of the entire Society may be somewhat appreciated.

It is especially interesting to notice how closely historic events have linked the lives of the descendants of the *Mayflower* and other New England Families, with the Huguenot and the Colonists of the Southern States, by proving their common ancestry.

For many years the records of this Chapter have been preserved in fire-proof vaults, and while they were there safe from destruction by fire they were also difficult of reference. The wish to put them into convenient form for the use of our scattered kinsmen, and to preserve them for posterity, resulted in the publication of these volumes.

The arrangement of the book has been made as simple as possible. The records are given in alphabetical order according to the name of the member contributing them. While the Society accepts membership claims for lineal ancestors only, and these are treated quite fully, the Committee has, so far as space permitted, allowed the addition of the record of such collateral ancestors as were distinguished in the early history of the country.

The names of the claim ancestors are indicated by

the use of capital letters, and are thus distinguished from other lineal ancestors, whose names are printed in italic type. There are many foot-note references to the Authorities for the statements given, and dates especially have been carefully verified.

At the end of the second volume will be found a reproduction of the badge of the Society. Each Chapter determines the requisite qualifications of a claim ancestor because, in different sections of the country, the same office may represent various degrees of service. Gold bars inscribed with the name of the claim ancestors may be observed on the ribbon, their use being optional and not obligatory. To safeguard these bars, a majority vote of the Board of Managers in favor of granting each one, and signed by the Treasurer, is the required certificate giving the maker authority to deliver them.

The Chapter committed their data and other material to The Grafton Press, of New York, giving it authority to edit and publish them according to the judgment of its president, Mr. F. H. Hitchcock. This has proved no small task, and the vast amount of material furnished will account for the omission of much that might have been included to amplify the pedigrees and contribute interest to the story of our ancestors.

THE COMMITTEE ON PUBLICATION:
ELIZA W. WILSON,   MARY B. AMES,
MARY F. JACOBS,   MARY GRUNDY MURRAY,
EMMA ELLIOTT JOHNSTONE,
MARY WASHINGTON KEYSER, Chairman.
Members of Chapter I.,
The Colonial Dames of America.

THE BOOK PLATE OF THE COLONIAL DAMES OF AMERICA

ILLUSTRATIONS

ILLUSTRATIONS

Illustrations

ANCESTRAL RECORDS AND PORTRAITS

I

PENHALLOW

CHIEF JUSTICE SAMUEL PENHALLOW, of the Colony
of New Hampshire, was born in England, and married
Mary Cutt, July 1, 1687. Mary Cutt's grandfather
was Richard Cutt, a Member of Oliver Cromwell's Parliament in the year 1654. Chief Justice Penhallow
held many offices of trust under the Colonial government of New Hampshire, extending over a period of
twenty-two years, and was successively Councillor,
Judge of the Superior Court, Chief Justice of the Supreme Court. He is also widely known through his
History of the Indian Wars. The Penhallow house,
an old colonial building, is still standing in Portsmouth,
N. H., and was the first brick dwelling erected in the
town. It contains an interesting collection of relics of
the past, and is still owned and occupied by the widow of
a Penhallow. *Hannah,* the daughter of Samuel and
Mary (Cutt) Penhallow, married James Pemberton.

PEMBERTON

The Court House in Boston was erected upon the site
of the family residence of the Pembertons, and Pemberton Square, in which it stands, takes its name from
them. Also the Pemberton Savings Bank, opposite
the Court House. Doctor Thomas Pemberton was
born February 17, 1652, and died July 26, 1693. He
was a distinguished surgeon, accompanying the expedition against Quebec, in the war waged between the Colonies and Canada in the year 1690. He married Han-

nah Phillips, daughter of Nicholas Phillips and Hannah Salter, his wife.

Their son James married *Hannah Penhallow.* They had three children, *Hannah,* Mary, and Samuel, the two former known far and wide for their beauty and accomplishments. The portrait of the son, Samuel Pemberton, painted when at the age of fourteen by Blackburn, in the year 1736, has been called "the handsomest of all boy portraits of Colonial days." [1]

The eldest daughter, *Hannah Pemberton,* married Benjamin Colman, of Boston.

Their daughter, *Mary Colman,* married Reverend Ephraim Ward.

Their daughter, *Mary Ward,* married *Thomas,* the son of Thomas and Abigail (Blodgett) Stickney; the elder *Thomas Stickney* was the son of John and Abigail (Wingate) Stickney.

WINGATE

COLONEL JOSHUA WINGATE was born at Hampton, N. H., February 2, 1679, married Mary Lunt November 9, 1702, and died February 9, 1769. He was distinguished for public and private virtues, according to the quaint chronicle, held many offices, civic and military, and commanded a company at the taking of Louisburg in the year 1645. Many interesting traits of Colonel Joshua Wingate are recorded in the genealogy of the Wingate family, edited and published in book form about ten years ago by Mr. Charles Wingate. The Colonel had numerous descendants, one of whom, Mary Ingalls, of Haverhill, Mass., married Comte François de Vépart, at a period when "international marriages" were an exception, and has had her memory embalmed in some graceful verses by Whittier entitled:

[1] Alice Morse Earle, "*Child Life in Colonial Days.*"

HANNAH PEMBERTON
Wife of Benjamin Colman

BENJAMIN COLMAN

THE COUNTESS

An exile from the Gascon land
Found refuge here and rest,
And loved of all the village band
Its fairest and its best.

For her his rank aside he laid;
He took the hue and tone
Of lowly life and toil, and made
Her simple ways his own.

Ah! life is brief, though love be long;
The altar and the bier,
The burial hymn and bridal song
Were both in one short year.

Her rest is quiet on the hill,
Beneath the locust's bloom;
Far off her lover sleeps as still
Within his scutcheoned tomb.

The Gascon lord, the village maid,
In death still clasp their hands;
The love that levels rank and grade
Unites their severed lands.

The daughter of Colonel Joshua and Mary (Lunt) Wingate, *Abigail Wingate,* married John Stickney.

Their son, *Thomas Stickney,* of "Mount Pleasant," Leicester, married *Abigail,* daughter of Hon. Samuel Blodgett.

Their son, *Thomas Stickney,* married Mary Ward.

Their daughter, *Elizabeth Ward Stickney,* married Thomas William Hall, of Culpeper, Va. Their daughters are:

Bertha Ellen Hall Ahrens,

Annie Amelia Hall,

Members of Chapter I., The Colonial Dames of America.

II

WILLIAMS

The Williams family, associated with Society Hill, S. C., are descended from a family in Isle of Wight County, Va., but the name of the colonist who settled there is not known. Some of the family crossed into Northampton County, N. C., and from thence found their way to South Carolina.

The earliest individual to have a definite record, George Williams, was born in Isle of Wight County, Va., and went to Northampton County, N. C., where his will, dated January 6, was proved in the May Court of 1750. This document shows him to have been a man of wealth. No light has been thrown upon his personal history further than that his wife's name was "Sarah," that she survived him, and that their family numbered nine children, viz.: Robert, George, Samuel, Jacob, William, Sarah, Mildred, Elizabeth, and Ann.

The eldest son, Robert Williams, was born in Northampton County. His removal to the Peedee District, S. C., about the year 1748, and his settlement "on the west side of the river opposite to the lower part of Welch Neck," places the history of the family thereafter, for the most part, within the State of South Carolina. He had abundant means, and a large landed property (most of which has been kept by his descendants). He lived and died on his plantation, called "Millwood," now called "The Mill," his house being a brick structure, which was torn down early in the nineteenth century.

In 1752 he was ordained minister of the Welch Neck

Baptist Church. In the sermon preached at his funeral, it was said of him: "He was kind to the poor, and remarkably so to the afflicted; a man of excellent natural parts, and a minister who preached the Gospel to the edification and comfort of souls, as many have testified to me." His official connection with the Welch Neck Church was of short duration. Owing to a disagreement over questions of discipline, he withdrew from the church, and on declining to return, was formally suspended and afterwards excommunicated. The differences were healed later, but he never resumed his duties as minister. His death occurred in the spring of 1768. His wife was a daughter of Francis Boykin, but her given name is not known. She died between 1761 and 1766. According to "The Old Cheraws," they had issue, two sons and two daughters:

John; there is on record a grant to him of one hundred acres on the Peedee, adjoining land of Robert Williams.

Anne.

Mary, married Arthur Hart, a prominent man of St. David's Parish, who married, second, Miss Irby. Had issue by second, but not by first, marriage.

DAVID WILLIAMS, the youngest son, was born in Peedee, Cheraw District, S. C., February 1, 1739. The Charleston Association of Baptist Churches appointed him in 1772 one of a committee to draw up a System of Discipline, which was adopted 1773. He was appointed one of the Committee of Observation of St. David's Parish, June 22, 1775. His premature death, January 1, 1776, removed him from a career of patriotic usefulness. "Cut off in his thirty-seventh year, his loss was one that his country could ill afford." He received his education in Charleston, where he met his future wife, Anne Rogerson, an English lady, who was there on a visit to her relations. They were married on Easter day, 1763.

After her husband's death, Mrs. Williams continued to live at "The Mill" plantation until the close of the Revolution, when, having means of her own, she moved to Charleston. Here she met and married a Mr. Brown of Providence, R. I., who was wealthy and came to Charleston in connection with his business. They moved to Providence; several children were born, but all died young. Later, she returned to South Carolina, and lived there until her death in 1812, at "Centre Hall," Society Hill, a plantation belonging to her son, David and Anne (Rogerson) Williams had issue:

Mary Ann, born April 16, 1772, and died December 18, 1834; married John Edwards McIver.

David Rogerson.

While living in Providence, after his mother's second marriage, *David Rogerson Williams*, born at Robbin's Neck, S. C., March 8, 1776, entered Brown University, but did not graduate. In 1801, however, he was given an honorary degree. While in college the remittances from his plantations failed him, and he went to South Carolina to investigate the cause, but returned to Providence, where he had known the beautiful *Sarah Power,* and their marriage occurred August 14, 1796. She was the eldest daughter of Nicholas and Rebecca (Corey) Power, of Providence.

Leaving college then, he went south with his wife to his plantations. In 1797, after the birth of their first child, Mrs. Williams' health compelled a return to her native climate, and they lived in Providence, while he studied law, and practised his profession for three years. Business interests required his return to South Carolina, and taking possession of his plantation, he built there the house now known as "Centre Hall." Captain Power, his father-in-law, when visiting them, suggested the embankment of his river lands at Robbin's Neck, the first work of the kind ever done in the State. With the invention of the cotton gin, his plantations became very profitable. He moved to Charleston later, where he lost his wife, February, 1803. He became the publisher of the *South Carolina Gazette and Advertiser,* later merged in the Charleston *Courier,* of which his brother-in-law, John E. McIver, was the editor.

Shortly afterwards, he returned to Society Hill, and in November, 1809, married, second, Elizabeth, the daughter of John and Mary (Conn) Witherspoon, of Peedee. Entering public life, he was a member of the U. S. House of Representatives from 1805 to 1809, and again from 1811 to 1813. He was most prominent in the debates which formed part of the preliminaries to the War of 1812. He was Chairman of the Committee of Military Affairs, and many references to his ability and activity are made in Adams' *History of the United States.*

On the breaking out of the War of 1812, President Madison appointed eight brigadier-generals, one of whom was David Rogerson Williams. This was on July 9, 1813. He was assigned to the Seventh District, including Louisiana, Mississippi, and Tennessee, but soon was moved to the North. He served for only a year, being invalided home immediately before the battle of Lundy's Lane, and resigned April 6, 1814. On recovering his health to some degree, he was given charge of preparing plans for the coast defense of South Carolina; and his drawings for the fortifications are now in the possession of his family. In 1814 he was elected

Governor of the State of South Carolina, and held office for the term of two years. After the expiration of his term as Governor, he represented his district for several terms in the State Senate, and was also trustee of the South Carolina College for many years.

In the industrial development of South Carolina, Mr. Williams' part, that of a pioneer, was vastly important. The first planter in the State to guard his fields against the floods, by banking the river, he also built, about the year 1812, a five-story frame cotton-mill, some two hundred feet in length, and established shoe and hat factories. In 1829 he erected a machine for the manufacture of cotton seed oil, and he made hemp cordage. His interest in building good roads was also active. His home near Society Hill, which was burned in 1873, was called "The Factory." His plantation at "Millwood" covered ten thousand acres and he had several other plantations. He had a house at Rocky River Springs, where his family lived in the hot weather.

Mrs. Williams owned a ferry across Lynch's Creek on the Georgetown road, about fifty miles from Society Hill, which had belonged to her uncle, Robert Witherspoon. General Williams determined to improve the facilities for crossing, by bridging this. In personally directing the work of erecting the trestles, which were to make the land approach, the timbers fell, he was caught by them and fatally hurt. Heroically he insisted that the negro workmen, also caught by the falling beams, should first be cared for. He died the next day, November 17, 1830. His interment was in the family cemetery four miles below Society Hill.

His most marked characteristics were fearless honesty, mental and physical vigor, and untiring energy. There are two portraits of him; one in the possession of

Gov. Stephen Decatur Miller

Burwell Boykin

David R. Williams

Sarah Power
Wife of David R. Williams
From a miniature by Malbone

his great-grandson, David R. Williams, III.; the other is in the Library of the University of South Carolina at Columbia. The inscription on the back of the latter portrait reads: "This portrait of David R. Williams, late Governor and Commander over this State, President of the Board of Trustees of Columbia College, and now Major General of the Militia of the State, was painted and presented to the Legislature thro' His Excellency, Andrew Pickens, to be suspended in the Library of the College,—by John S. Cogdell, on the 27th November, 1817."

His second wife, born 1784, died November 17, 1840; she was devoted to the church at Society Hill, as shown by the *Historical Sketch* of this church in which are many references to her. Her portrait, painted by David R. Williams, II., is owned by the family. Issue, first wife:

John Nicholas.

George Frederick, was born 1799, and died December, 1812.

POWER

ARMS: *Or, a chief embattled sable.*
CREST: *An antelope's head erased, the neck transfixed by a spear all ppr.*

"The Powers of Rhode Island [2] are descended from the family of the same name in Ireland; but by what line is not known. Tradition says that a Power went with Raleigh to Guiana in South America; and it is apparently certain that the Power family of Providence owned plantations there. The family of Poer is of Breton origin. They were settled at Poer-Hays

2 Austin's *Gen. Dict. of R. I.* Austin's *Narragansett Hist. Reg.*, Vol. vii, No. 1, p. 17.

in the parish of Budleigh, South Devon, where Sir Walter Raleigh was born. The first of the name there was Sir Bartholemy Le Poer; then Sir John Le Poer and Sir Roger Le Poer, whose daughter Cecilia carried Poer-Hays to John Duke of the adjoining parish. The estate passed to the Hayes family. A grandson of Sir Bartholemy, Robert Le Poer, was a marshal in the English army in the invasion of Ireland with Henry the Second of England; and the King in 1177 gave him ' a grant of Desies, or the entire County of Waterford, together with the city.' The Le Poers later became Earls of Tyrone. In *O'Hart's Irish Pedigrees* (second series), pp. 345-349, there is an interesting sketch of the Power family."

NICHOLAS POWER I., was one of the earliest settlers of Providence, R. I. Traditions concerning him are numerous, but most of them are false. His signature upon the compact of 1640 for civil government drawn up in Providence, is the first mention of him in the records. The disturbed conditions in Rhode Island, resulting partly from controversies between those known as " Gortonists " and the authorities in Massachusetts (who called the Providence Plantations " a nest of pestilential heretics "), brought many a good settler into trouble. Nicholas Power was one of these. He joined Gorton and his followers in the purchase of Indian lands at Shawomet (Shawmut), afterwards Warwick, on the west side of Narragansett Bay. The Gortonists were besieged and captured, and Power, with others, was taken to Boston for trial. Power was finally dismissed with " an admonition " and returned to Providence. His home was directly south of the present Power Street. He was Freeman 1655, Constable 1649, Surveyor of Highways 1656, and repeatedly chosen a Juryman and Commissioner. He died intestate August 25, 1657, and ten years later the Town Council disposed of his estate. His wife Jane, died 1667. Issue:

Hope, born 1650, married Rev. James Clarke, of Newport, who was born 1649, and died December 1, 1736.

Nicholas II., born in Providence.

"In 1672 he (*Nicholas II.*) and Thomas Field were fined £40 each at a meeting of the Governor and Council at Newport, for refusing to testify against Harris, accused of contempt of court in saying, 'Your Honors are wise'!"

He served as Constable of Providence 1671, and as a member of the jury 1673. He was killed December 19, 1675, in the Great Swamp Fight at Narragansett, a shot from one of his companions in the rear, taking fatal effect. His wife was *Rebecca,* the daughter of Zachariah and Joanna (Arnold) Rhodes. Issue: Hope, who died young; and an only son:

NICHOLAS POWER III., born 1673, and died May 18, 1734, was Deputy five years, from 1704 to 1730; a Member of the Town Council four years, between 1713 and 1730, and Assistant to the Governor, 1720 to 1721, 1724 to 1729, 1731, 1732, and 1733. As shown by the inventory of his estate, which was valued at £1,751, 13s, 3d, he was a prosperous merchant, and is referred to in the colonial records as Captain and later as Colonel.

He married, first, Mary Haile; second, *Mercy,* the daughter of Rev. Pardon and Lydia (Taber) Tillinghast; she died November 13, 1769, in her ninety-first year. A petition in the name of Nicholas Power, was made to the Town Council on December 13, 1708, for a piece of land between "my Ffather William his land

and mine."[3] This may imply that Mary Haile's father was named William. Issue, first wife:

Mary, married Daniel Cooke, of Saybrook, Conn.

Issue, second wife:

Hope, married James Brown, Jr.

John married Martha ——.

Joseph, married Jane Diana ——.

Anne, married, first, John Stewart; second, George Laws.

Sarah, married William Burrough.

Nicholas IV.

Lydia, married, —— Carr, of Newport.

Mercy, married Hezekiah, the son of Colonel Hezekiah Sabin.

The seventh child, *Nicholas Power, IV.*, was born in Providence, and died in Paramaribo, Surinam (Dutch Guiana), February 28, 1744, where he had gone to superintend the settlement of his estates.[4] On October 31, 1734, he married his first cousin *Anne,* the daughter of Philip and Martha (Holmes) Tillinghast, born April 13, 1713, and died 1770. Issue:

Elizabeth, married Joseph, the son of James Brown, Jr., and his wife, Hope Power.

Anne, died unmarried.

Mary, died unmarried.

NICHOLAS POWER V., born in Providence, R. I., April 5, 1742, and died January 6, 1808, was Captain in the Rhode Island Militia before the Revolution,[5] and appointed, December 17, 1774, as a member of the Committee of Inspection, to carry into effect the Association entered into by the Continental Congress. At

---

[3] *Early Records of Providence,* xvii, p. 248.

[4] *R. I. Tracts,* No. 15, p. 174, gives his death as February 27, 1743.

[5] Field's *State of R. I. and Providence Plantations at the End of the Century,* Vol. i, p. 444.

the town meeting in Providence, July 31, 1775, he was placed in charge of the construction of the town fortifications. 1784 to 1789 he was a Representative in the General Assembly.

He married, April 20, 1766, *Rebecca,* the daughter of William and Mary (Akin) Corey, who was born 1747, and died October 29, 1825. She and her husband are interred in the north burial ground in Providence. Issue:

Nicholas VI., married Anna Marsh, the daughter of Daniel and Susannah (Wilkinson) Marsh.

Sarah, married *David Rogerson Williams.*

Mary Ann, married Colonel William Blodget, Jr., the son of Major William and Amphillis (Chace) Blodget.

Rebecca, married, first, Charles James Air, of South Carolina; second, Hon. Joseph Leonard Tillinghast, of Providence.

RHODES

ZACHARIAH RHODES, born 1603, in England, was drowned "off Pawtuxet Shoare," Rhode Island, 1665. He settled in Rehoboth, but moved to Providence, finally going to Pawtuxet, where he remained. He held many public offices, being commissioner four years between 1659 and 1663, Constable 1660, Deputy 1664 and 1665, and Town Treasurer 1665,[6] besides other positions of public trust. He married *Joanna,* the daughter of William and Christian (Peak) Arnold, born February 27, 1617, and died later than 1692. Their daughter *Rebecca* married *Nicholas Power II.*

ARNOLD

WILLIAM ARNOLD, of Dorset County, England, was
6 Austin's *loc. cit.,* p. 364.

baptized there June 24, 1587. He "sett sayle ffrom Dartmouth in Old England the first of May, friday, and Arrived In New England June 24, Ano 1635," making his first home in Hingham, Mass. He became one of "the thirteen original proprietors" of Providence, going there April 20, 1636. He was one of four to found Pawtuxet in the year 1638. He again changed his residence 1651, moving this time to Newport. His part in the early history of Rhode Island was important, and he held many offices.[7]

His wife was Christian Peak. The distinguished Governor Benedict Arnold was their son (see p. 112), and their daughter *Joanna* married ZACHARIAH RHODES.

TILLINGHAST

PARDON TILLINGHAST was born at Seven Cliffs, Sussex, Eng., 1622, and died at Providence, R. I., January 29, 1718. He was the most prominent merchant of his day, and a very useful citizen, being Deputy six years, and Overseer of the Poor, a member of the Town Council, etc. In 1681 he became the pastor of the First Baptist Church, the building for which, as well as the land, he is said to have given.[1]

He married *Lydia,* the daughter of Philip and Lydia (Masters) Taber, on April 16, 1664, and died 1718. Issue, among others:

Mercy, who married NICHOLAS POWER III., and a son:

PHILIP TILLINGHAST, born at Providence, R. I., October, 1669, and died March 14, 1732, was a wealthy merchant, and took part actively in public life. He

---

7 *N. E. Hist. & Gen. Reg.,* Vol. xxxiii, pp. 427-438. Arnold's *Hist. of R. I.,* Vol. i. Austin's *loc. cit.*
1 Austin's *loc. cit.,* p. 203.

joined Captain Gallup's expedition against Canada, 1690; was a Deputy for twelve terms, Assistant to the Governor 1714, and a member of the Town Council for eleven years.[2]

His wife was *Martha*, the daughter of Jonathan and Sarah (Borden) Holmes, and they were married May 3, 1692. She was born 1675, and died March 10, 1729. Their daughter *Anne,* married her cousin, NICHOLAS POWER IV.

TABER

PHILIP TABER, born in England 1605, and died at Providence 1672, was a Deputy 1639 and 1640, and a Commissioner on many occasions.[3] He married Lydia, the daughter of John and Jane Masters. Issue:

Lydia, married PARDON TILLINGHAST.

Philip, Jr., married *Mary,* the daughter of John and Sarah (Warren) Cooke. Their daughter *Sarah* married *Thomas,* the son of William and Mary (Earle) Corey.

One of the earliest of the settlers of Watertown, Mass., John Masters, was admitted a Freeman 1631. He was "chosen to advise with the Governor and Assistants" about the raising of public stock in 1632.[4] He died December 21, 1639.

HOLMES

OBADIAH HOLMES was born in Preston, Eng., 1607, and died at Newport, R. I., October 15, 1682. He resided first in Massachusetts, but went to Newport in 1650. He was the leader of the Baptist church, and on one occasion severely whipped on Governor Endi-

[2] Austin, p. 203.
[3] Austin, p. 195.
[4] Prince's *Chronology*, Vol. ii.

cott's orders.[5]   He held several public offices, and was
one of the original patentees of Monmouth, N. J.[6]   He
married Catherine ——.

JONATHAN HOLMES, their son, who died 1713, passed
his later life in Newport, after living for a time in
Middletown, N. J., being elected Deputy 1668.   He
was a Deputy in Newport for ten years, and Speaker
of the House for seven years.

He married *Sarah,* the daughter of Richard and Joan
Borden.   She was born May, 1644, and died 1705.
Their daughter *Martha* married PHILIP TILLINGHAST.

BORDEN

RICHARD BORDEN, born 1601, died in Portsmouth,
R. I., May 25, 1671; married Joan ——.   He was
Assistant to the Governor 1653 to 1654; the next year
he was General Treasurer, and Deputy in 1667 and
1670.   He purchased land in Monmouth County, N. J.,
from the Indians in 1665, and many of his descendants
settled there.[7].

Their daughter *Sarah* married JONATHAN HOLMES.

COREY

WILLIAM COREY,[8] admitted a Freeman 1658 in Portsmouth, served as deputy three years, 1678 to 1680, and
was First Lieutenant and then Captain in the Militia.
His death occurred in 1682.   He married *Mary,* the
daughter of Ralph and Joan (Savage) Earle.   She
died March 22, 1718.

Their fifth child, *Thomas Corey* (1670-1738), inher-

5 Arnold's *Hist. of R. I.,* Vol. i, pp. 224, 225.

6 Austin's *loc. cit.,* p. 103.

7 Arnold's *loc. cit.,* Vol. i, pp. 250, 252, 255. Austin's *loc. cit.,* p. 23.
N. J. *Arch., First Series,* Vol. xxiv, p. 651.

8 Austin's *loc. cit.,* p. 56.

ited large estates at Tiverton, R. I. He is said to have
been educated in England. His first wife was *Sarah,*
the daughter of Philip, Jr., and Mary (Cooke) Taber,
born 1671. (*Philip Taber, Jr.,* was a brother of *Lydia
Taber,* who married PARDON TILLINGHAST.)

The eldest son of Thomas Corey, by first wife, *William Corey,* born 1693, and died April 13, 1779, was
educated in England. He married, third, *Mary,* the
daughter of James and Eliphal (Sanford) Akin. A
sampler worked by *Mary Akin* is in the possession of
a descendant. Their daughter *Rebecca* married NICHOLAS POWER V.

EARLE

RALPH EARLE was an early settler of Aquidneck, being admitted in 1638, where he held many places of
official trust.[9] He joined the first Rhode Island Troop
of Horse in 1667, becoming Captain of the company.
Captain Earle died 1678, his wife, who was Joan Savage, dying two years later.

His daughter *Mary* married WILLIAM COREY.

COOKE

FRANCIS COOKE (1597-1663) was one of the signers
of the "Mayflower Compact." Esther, his wife, came
over later on the ship *Anne,* with her daughters. Their
son:

JOHN COOKE came with his father on the *Mayflower,*
and had the distinction of surviving all the passengers
of that ship, dying 1695. For many years he lived at
Plymouth, being one of the Military Company. Taking part in the purchase of Dartmouth, he moved there
and was Selectman, also Representative to the General

9 *The Descendants of Ralph Earle,* by Pliny Earle.

Court for over twenty years. *Sarah,* the daughter of RICHARD WARREN, another signer of the "Compact" (see p. 122), was his wife.

Their daughter, *Mary Cooke,* married Philip Taber, Jr. She was in the third generation from two of the adult passengers of the *Mayflower.*

Their daughter, *Sarah Taber,* married *Thomas Corey.*

SANFORD

JOHN SANFORD, who died 1653, was an early settler of Boston. He was cannoneer of Boston and Surveyor of Arms there for several years. Removing to Rhode Island, he was Constable, Lieutenant, Assistant to the Governor, and in 1653, President of Portsmouth and Newport, having gone to Portsmouth at the time of Mrs. Hutchinson's banishment from Boston, in 1638.

His first wife was Elizabeth Webb; his second was Bridget Hutchinson, the daughter of William and Anne (Marbury) Hutchinson. His eldest son by first wife:

JOHN SANFORD II., born June 4, 1633, and died 1687, was General Treasurer, General Recorder and Attorney-General between the years 1655 and 1671, holding each office a number of terms. For sixteen years he acted as Deputy, three years as Assistant and was a member of the Council.[1] He married, second, April 17, 1663, *Mary,* the daughter of SAMUEL GORTON[2] and the widow of Peter Greene. She died in 1688.

Their daughter, *Eliphal,* was born February 20, 1666, and died 1726. She married James Akin.

Their daughter, *Mary Akin,* married WILLIAM COREY.

[1] Austin's *loc. cit.,* p. 171. Arnold's *loc. cit.,* Vol. i.
[2] *Life and Times of Samuel Gorton,* by Adelos Gorton.

GORTON

ARMS: *Gules, ten billets or, a chief indented of the second.*

SAMUEL GORTON, born at Gorton, Lancaster County, England, in 1592, where his family had lived for several generations, was a clothier in London. With his wife and children he emigrated to New England 1637, arriving in March of that year. In 1639 he signed the Portsmouth Compact; was at Providence 1640, and at Pawtucket 1641, when he became the leader of the company who bought the Warwick lands, and one of the corporators of the Government, now Rhode Island, under its first charter, 1644. Owing to religious differences, he had much trouble with Massachusetts, and in November, 1643, he was sentenced at Charlestown, Mass., but released the following March, when he was banished from Massachusetts and Warwick. The details of this controversy are fully set forth in the first volume of Arnold's *History of Rhode Island.* The same year he returned to England (being forced to sail from New York), to obtain redress from the attacks of the Bay Colony upon the Rhode Island settlement. Returning to Boston in May, 1648, he brought with him a letter of protection from the Earl of Warwick, and had won his cause, because the Commissioners of Plantations had given orders previously to Massachusetts, to allow him and his followers to live quietly on their lands at Warwick.

After this he held many public offices, being Assistant to the Governor 1649; Commissioner in the years 1651, 1656 to 1660, and 1663; President (or Governor) of Providence and Warwick from October, 1651, to May, 1652, and Deputy 1664, 1665, 1666 and 1670, dying in 1677. He was the author of several books, including *Simplicity's Defence against Seven Headed Policy,* which was published while he was in London, 1646; and was energetic in his disavowal of the belief in witches, and the earliest of slavery abolitionists.

His wife was Mary, the daughter of John and Mary Maplett, and a sister of Dr. John Maplett, physician to King Charles II. They had nine children; the fifth, *Mary,* who died 1688, married, first, Peter Greene, and had issue eight children; second, JOHN SANFORD II.

WILLIAMS (*Continued*)

The only son of David Rogerson and Sarah (Power) Williams, *Colonel John Nicholas Williams,* born at "Centre Hall," Society Hill, S. C., July 2, 1797, was graduated in 1816 from the South Carolina College. In 1832 was a member of the State Legislature, but declined to be a candidate for re-election. He held a very influential place in the social and political life of the "middle country," as one of the largest planters in the State, living at "The Factory" at Society Hill. As Colonel of the Darlington Troop, he was in command when it acted as escort to General Lafayette, passing through the State to Camden in 1825. His father, General Williams, rode in a coach drawn by four horses, with Lafayette beside him.

He married, first, December 3, 1820, *Esther Serena,* the daughter of Colonel James and Mary (Cox) Chesnut, of "Mulberry," Camden, S. C.; she was born September 29, 1797, and died October 27, 1822; married, second, September 29, 1831, Sarah Cantey, the daughter of John Dick and Elizabeth (Boykin) Witherspoon; she was born November 19, 1810, and died August 16, 1907, and was the sister of John Wither-

spoon, who married Colonel Williams' eldest daughter.
Issue, first wife:

Mary, Serena Chesnut, born November, 1821; died
1884; married, February 18, 1840, John Witherspoon,
of Society Hill.

David Rogerson II.

Issue, second wife:

Serena, born July 18, 1832; married, June 26, 1855,
James Douglas Kirkpatrick.

Elizabeth W., born 1833; died May 29, 1836.

John Witherspoon.

George Frederick, born May 6, 1836; died December
21, 1861; married, June 1, 1858, Frances Virginia Mc-
Iver.

Alice, born April 20, 1838; died November 6, 1898;
married, June 9, 1859, Thomas Frost.

Constance, born January 14, 1841; married, February 21, 1865, William Wood Finney.

Sarah Power, born March 14, 1843; married, June
15, 1864, Richard Henry Henderson.

CHESNUT

At an early age James Chesnut, who was born in
Ireland, went to Virginia with his parents, where they
settled in the valley of the Shenandoah. It is a tradition in the family that the name in Ireland was " Sars-
field." After his marriage and the birth of three children, he was killed in a border warfare with the Indians.
Mrs. Chesnut married Jasper Sutton and had three
children. The family moved to South Carolina and
settled at Knight's Hill, near Camden, then called
"Pine Tree Hill." Issue:

JOHN.

James, died unmarried; was the owner of "Mulberry" plantation.

Margaret, married Alexander Irvin.

COLONEL JOHN CHESNUT, the eldest son, was born in the Shenandoah Valley, June 18, 1743, being thirteen years old when he went to South Carolina. Soon after he entered the mercantile house of Colonel John Kershaw, in Camden, as an apprentice, beginning his career as a merchant at the expiration of his apprenticeship. By 1766 he was a member of the firm which had extensive and progressive branch stores throughout the State. In 1765 he was appointed Inquirer and Collector for St. Mark's. By the time of the Revolution his landed estates were very large.

A Delegate to the first Provincial Congress, which met in Charleston, January 11, 1775, and again on June 1 of the same year, he was later elected to the Committee of Continental Association. "He was appointed 'Justice of the Quorum' for Orangeburg District 1775, Justice of the Peace April, 1776," and was Paymaster, with the rank of Captain, in the Third South Carolina Regiment at the beginning of the Revolution, but a severe attack of rheumatism compelled him to resign. Recovering in about six months, he obtained a command in the militia, and served during the Georgia campaign. He was taken prisoner at the evacuation of Charleston, 1780, and was paroled to his plantation at Knight's Hill. Here his family remained during the war, and here his wife's mother, Mrs. Cantey, died and was the first to be buried in what is now the Chesnut family burying-ground. When the American army approached, August, 1780, Lord Rawdon, the British commander in Camden, called upon the inhabitants to take up arms against their countrymen. Many refused, among them Colonel Chesnut. He was put

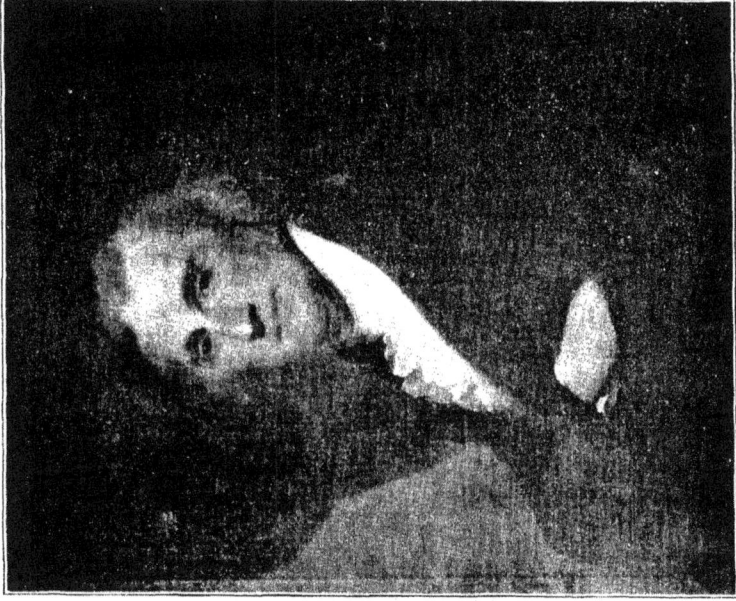

COL. JOHN CHESNUT
From a painting by Gilbert Stuart

SARAH CANTEY
Wife of Col. John Chesnut

in prison and chained to the floor.   To his grave he bore
the marks of these irons.

The war over, he was prominent in politics, and in
1788 a member of the Convention to frame the Constitution.   He went to the State Senate twice, and was
among the first selection of trustees for the new
South Carolina College.   His intimate friends were
leaders of their day, and among them were General
Charles Cotesworth Pinckney, Governor John Rutledge,
and Colonel Wade Hampton.   When General Washington visited the South in 1791, he was entertained by
Colonel Chesnut at Camden.

Gilbert Stuart painted the portrait of Colonel Chesnut, now owned by his great-grandson, David Rogerson
Williams III.   A very rich man, he lived in great state
at his different houses, giving a weekly ball and sup-
per, which pleased the young people of the community.
"He often travelled with coach and four to Charleston
or Columbia in the winter; and rarely missed a visit to
Virginia and Philadelphia or New York during the
summer, travelling with his servants and horses, taking
at least a month to make the journey.   He was well-
educated and had a fine library."

He married, in 1770, *Sarah,* the daughter of Captain
John and Mary (McGirtt) Cantey, of Camden.   She
was born at "Salt Lake" on the Wateree, February 15,
1753, and died February 12, 1786.   Colonel Chesnut's
death occurred April 1, 1813, and he was placed beside his wife in the family burial place at Knight's
Hill.   Issue:

Mary, married Duncan McRae.
James.
Sarah Cantey, married John Taylor.

Harriet, lived as a recluse for many years, never leaving the house, because her father refused his consent to a marriage which he considered undesirable.

Rebecca, died an infant.

John, died of yellow fever in Charleston, 1799, when about sixteen years of age.

Margaret Rebecca, married James Sutherland Deas.

The eldest son, *James Chesnut,* was born in Camden, S. C., February 19, 1773. As a boy of seven he accompanied his father on horseback to Charleston, and did many things for him when he was thrown into prison there after the surrender. He was educated at Princeton University, matriculating in 1788. A Member of the State Legislature in 1802, 1804, and 1808, Intendant of Camden 1806 to 1807, and a member of the State Senate, 1832, he was prominent in all the social and political life of Camden. His plantations near Camden were more than five miles square.

He married *Mary,* the daughter of Colonel John and Esther (Bowes) Cox, of Philadelphia, September 20, 1796. His portrait, as well as that of his wife, by Gilbert Stuart, belong to David Rogerson Williams III. Mrs. Chesnut said that when she met her future husband at Princeton, he was known as " The young Prince." On their bridal journey from Philadelphia to Camden, they drove a cream-colored coach with four horses and outriders. "Mulberry House," two miles south of Camden, was finished in 1820. Until then they lived at Camden.

Born at Trenton, N. J., March 22, 1775, Mary (Cox) Chesnut, as a girl of fourteen, was one who strewed flowers before General Washington at the reception given him by the people of New Jersey at Trenton Bridge, just before he was made President, April 21,

1789. She was appointed the first vice-regent for South Carolina of the Mount Vernon Associaton, April, 1860. She died at "Bloomsbury," March 13, 1864, and her husband survived her only two years, dying February 17, 1866.

A most pathetic account of James Chesnut's life after the death of his wife is given in a *Diary from Dixie,* written by his daughter-in-law, Mrs. Mary Boykin (Miller) Chesnut. "Bloomsbury" in Camden, the house which James Chesnut had built for his daughter Sally, called after Colonel Cox's house on the Delaware, was his last residence. The family moved there from "Mulberry" at the beginning of the Civil War. Mr. Chesnut and his wife were laid to rest at Knight's Hill. Issue, fourteen children, of whom seven died in infancy. The survivors were:

Esther Serena, married *John Nicholas Williams.*

John, married Charlotte Ellen Whitaker.

Mary Cox, married Dr. George Reynolds.

Harriet Serena, married William Joshua Grant.

Emma, was unmarried.

Sarah (Sally), did not marry, devoting her life to the care of her parents. Her home was "Bloomsbury."

Gen. James, Jr., married Mary Boykin Miller, the daughter of Governor Stephen D. and Mary (Boykin) Miller. He was a United States Senator, Brigadier-General, C. S. A., and led an active, useful life.

CANTEY

GEORGE CANTEY, the earliest colonist of the name to come to this country, "in the first fleet" sailing from the Barbadoes, reached South Carolina in 1670. His father and mother, Teige and Elizabeth Cantey, came to him at Charleston, from the Barbadoes, before

August 20, 1672, which is the date of a land grant to
the elder Cantey, whose will, dated September 21, 1678,
describes him as of Ashley River. The inventory of
his estate was filed May 7, 1679. In the report of his
executors the following items occur and bear witness
to his Irish ancestry: Funeral expenses, To three gal.
Wine. .9s; to three gal. & half of Rum. .14s; For board
for Coffin. .3s; Total £1, 6s."

A freeholder 1670 to 1671, George Cantey's name is
recorded the next year as one who might be called upon
for military service, "with two men able to bear arms."
At the first settlement on the west bank of the Ashley,
and at the new settlement where now is the city of
Charleston, he received allotments of land. Also grants
in Berkely County, on the north side of the Ashley
River; one, February 8, 1704, of one thousand acres.
For a residence on these plantations, he very early for-
sook the new town. From 1703 to 1704, he was a member of the Commons of Berkely, and in the first named
·year, was an Assessor for the north side of the Ashley.
In 1707, he was a Vestryman of St. James's, Goose
Creek. The last record of him is his deed of gift to
his granddaughter, Martha Ladson, 1714. His wife,
according to a number of deeds, was named Martha.
Issue:

John, born 1671, was twice married.
William.
Sendiniah, married James Boswood.
Elizabeth, married Thomas Elmes.

The second child, *William Cantey,* who died in 1729,
is always referred to in the early grants as William Cantey, Jr., or later, as of Craven. He died intestate, and
his estate was administered October, 1729. In 1715 he
was Commissioner of Taxes for "English Santee." He

aided to defend Charleston against the French and Spaniards in the year 1706.

He married, before 1703, Arabella, the daughter of JOSEPH OLDYS, who "was Deputy-Secretary of the Province of South Carolina 1688, and likewise Deputy Register."[3] Issue:

Josiah, married, first, Elizabeth Boswood; second, Susannah ——.

Mary, the only daughter, married General Richard Richardson.

William, Jr.

JOHN.

CAPTAIN JOHN CANTEY is first mentioned in the records as of "Pine Tree Hill," or of Craven County. The first reference is February, 1749 to 1750, when he is named as an executor of the will of Richard Middleton with William Cantey. At "Pine Tree Hill," which is now Camden, he was granted land as early as 1752, and owned extensive plantations. He was Captain of a company in Colonel Richardson's regiment, Littleton's expedition against the Cherokees, from October 8, 1759, to January 10, 1760. His official positions were as follows: 1762 and 1765, Commissioner for Roads and for the Wateree River, respectively; 1765, 1767 and 1769, one John Cantey was a Justice of the Peace for Craven County; "Inquirer and Collector" for the Waterees, 1767 and 1785; a member of the Grand Jury at Camden, December, 1774. Dying intestate, his sons James and Zachariah were appointed administrators of his estate, October 16, 1792, and the inventory was filed by them February 27, 1793. His wife was *Mary,* the daughter of Colonel James and Priscilla (Davison) McGirtt. Issue:

[3] *So. Car. Hist. Mag.,* Vol. v, p. 227.

Mary, married Eli Kershaw.

Sarah, married COLONEL JOHN CHESNUT.

James, married Martha Whitaker.

Zachariah, married Sarah Boykin.

McGIRTT

COLONEL JAMES McGIRTT, an early settler of South Carolina, was a cultivated man, with property, and is said to have had the best library in the colony. He was Commissioner for founding St. Mark's Parish, 1757, and a Lieutenant-Colonel in General Richardson's regiment of Provincial Militia, 1760. He was married October 12, 1732, to Priscilla Davison, and their daughter *Mary* married CAPTAIN JOHN CANTEY.

COX

ARMS: *Or, three bars, az.; on a canton, arg., a lion's head erased, gu.*
CREST: *An antelope's head erased ppr., pierced through the neck by a spear.*

"Copy of seal in ring belonging to John Cox and given to his grandson, James Chesnut, by Mary (Cox) Chesnut, daughter of John Cox, now in the possession of the great-great-grandson of John Cox, David R. Williams, of Camden, S. C."

THOMAS COX,[4] originally from Hertfordshire, Eng., came to America and founded the Monmouth County, N. J., family. First, he went to Marspath Kills, at the head of Newtown Creek, Long Island, and from there to New Jersey. In the year 1665 he settled at Middletown. He was a founder of the Baptist church in the settlement there, and one of the leading men in all affairs of interest in the community. Overseer for many years, he was also a Deputy and Town Agent.

[4] Stillwell's *Hist. & Gen. Miscellany,* Vol. ii.

COL. JAMES CHESNUT
From a painting by Gilbert Stuart

MARY COX
Wife of Col. James Chesnut

His wife was Elizabeth Blashford and they married April 21, 1665. After his death, she married Thomas Ingham. The will of Thomas Cox mentions six children: Thomas, John, James, Joseph, Samuel, and *William*. The records of the day give only five sons. Judging from family traditions and land records, the sixth child in this family was *William Cox*. He is found living at Middlesex in 1721, but New Brunswick was his later residence, where he was the owner of plantations, and saw and grist mills. These were offered for sale in 1745, and he moved to Shrewsbury, where he died, 1752. His will, which was signed January 3, 1750, was probated May 5, 1752. It mentions property left him by his "kinsman, Walter Cox, of Cheltenham, in Gloucestershire." Shrewsbury Churchyard was his place of burial, March 22, 1752. He married *Catherine,* the daughter of Cornelius and Mary (Greenland) Longfield. Issue:

William.

Thomas, married Mrs. Elizabeth Curlis (Corlies); (issue, Thomas).

Longfield, married Anne Sears, of Shrewsbury (issue, William).

JOHN.

Samuel.

Cornelius.

Mary, married Richard Allen.

Sarah, married Christopher Beekman (issue, William).

COLONEL JOHN COX, the fourth son of William and Catherine (Longfield) Cox, was born in New Brunswick, 1732, and died at Philadelphia, April 28, 1793. There are numerous recorded references to him as a Philadelphia merchant, as owning a house in Burlington, N. J., and being the "Proprietor and Conductor" of the furnaces at Batsto, Burlington County, and the forge and rolling mill at Mount Holly.[5] These supplied the Continental army and navy with cannon-shot and camp-kettles, as well as castings for the salt-works, so the workmen were exempt from military duty. An act of the General Assembly of New Jersey, 1776, provided for the organization of a company of iron-workers, not exceeding fifty, under the command of a Captain and two Lieutenants to be named by John Cox and commissioned by the Governor of New Jersey. February 8, 1775, he was appointed a Justice of the Peace in the counties of Burlington and Gloucester. Previous to the Revolution he was very prominent in public life. The Provincial Convention of Pennsylvania was held 1774, and he was elected a Deputy July 15, and again on June 23, 1775. He was appointed a Major in the Second Battalion of the Pennsylvania Associated Militia 1775, the Commander being Colonel Roberdeau. In the campaign of Washington, both before and after the army crossed the Delaware at Trenton, he was very active. In 1777, General Greene writes: "I hope the Committee of Congress will not lose sight of Colonel Cox; there is no man will serve their purpose better."[6] General Greene accepted the position of Quartermaster-General of the Continental army only on condition that Colonel Cox should be appointed Assistant Quartermaster-General, which was done by Congress March 2, 1778. This was the beginning of intimate relations between the two men.

[5] *N. J. Archives*, vii, 543; xii, 250, 330, 480; xix, 440, 479, 567; xviii, 525; 2d Series, I, 98; 409.

[6] *Life of General Nathaniel Greene,* by G. W. Greene. Johnson's *Sketches of the Life of General Greene.*

His first wife was Sarah Edgil, the widow of William Edgil, and they were married June 10, 1756, in Christ Church, Philadelphia. Legend says that Colonel Cox's brother William was engaged to Mrs. Edgil, who was a lady celebrated for her beauty and wealth. " The lovers quarrelled; John Cox tried to pacify them, and heal the breach, but to no purpose; they separated, and in time the unsuccessful peacemaker and the widow were united in marriage." She lived a year, and died, leaving all her fortune to her husband. There are still in the families of Colonel Cox's descendants many pieces of silver marked ' W. S. E.,' i. e., William and Sarah Edgil. By this marriage there were no children."

The second wife of John Cox was *Esther,* the daughter of Francis and Rachel (Le Chevalier) Bowes, whom he married November 16, 1760, in Christ Church, Philadelphia. She was born January 6, 1740, and died February 4, 1814. On the death of her father and the remarriage of her mother, she made her home with her aunts, her mother's sisters, the Mlles. Le Chevalier. She was well educated, played on the spinnet and organ, and was the only lady of the day who had mastered thorough bass.

"Colonel Cox never allowed his wife to do anything but fancy work, and to be well dressed, daily in her parlor. . . . During the Revolutionary War the French had their headquarters at Colonel Cox's, he being Assistant Quartermaster under Major Nathaniel Greene. Lafayette, Rochambeau and others were there. Their table was beautifully laid out. After each meal the silver was packed in their camp bag."

Such surroundings, however, did not protect against many discomforts. In 1777, commerce was entirely destroyed, and it was practically impossible to procure many of the conveniences of life. There was much ingenuity displayed in substituting unusual things for those that were missed in the daily economy. There were no pins, thorns were used; no candles, pine knots became the fashion. Mrs. Cox spun her own flax and wool, and all were dressed in linsey woolsey. To relieve the plainness of attire, hair was elaborately dressed high, on top of the head; coarse net, flowers and feathers were worn. On one occasion a bat found a refuge in Rachel Cox's headdress without her becoming aware of it. General Greene and Colonel Cox were intimate friends, and the General, in a letter to his wife, speaks of a letter from Mrs. Cox to her husband, and adds, "she desires him to prepare you to see an old-fashioned, plain woman, marked with age and rusticity among the pines. I believe there is no necessity, for everybody agrees she is one of the finest women of the age." On the occasion of the famous reception to General Washington at Trenton Bridge, April 21, 1789, Mrs. Cox was one of the matrons who, with their daughters, welcomed him.

Until her death, February 10, 1814, she wrote letters at regular intervals describing her life in Philadelphia, to her daughter Mary, who had married Colonel James Chesnut, of Camden, S. C. These letters are still in the possession of the family. Mrs. Mary B. Ames, a great-granddaughter, has in her possession a Negus glass which once belonged to Esther Bowes. It is marked on one side, "Suckcess to ye two Frinds, J.E.L.K." On the other, "1785 E.B." The history of it is not known. Mrs. Esther (Bowes) Cox gave it to her granddaughter, Miss Sally Chesnut, who in turn gave it to her great-niece, Mary Boykin Williams, now Mrs. Ames, the granddaughter of her eldest sister. It evidently was sent back to Mrs. Cox from Europe by some of the foreign officers of the Revolution.

It was at "Bloomsbury Court," Colonel Cox's home on the Delaware near Trenton, that Count de Rochambeau was entertained, the house being given up to him by Colonel Cox, as was the courteous custom of the time. He presented Colonel Cox "with a chaste and beautiful snuff-box, blue enamel, lined and mounted with gold." The snuff-box was left by Colonel Cox to his daughter, Sarah Coxe, who in turn left it to her son, Edward Jenner Coxe; the wife of the latter, Mary Louisa Coxe, leaving it to her son, John Redman Coxe, in 1891. "Bloomsbury" was at different times the headquarters of the French officers and of General Washington and General Greene. A delightful account of the life at "Bloomsbury the Beautiful," as "Bloomsbury Court" was called in the days of Colonel Cox's ownership, is given in Mills' *Historic House of New Jersey*. The house is described, the box-wood hedges, and the hundreds of roses tended by the "Demoiselles Chevalier, the French aunts of Mrs. John Cox." Another account says: "'Bloomsbury Court' during the Cox régime was a republican Hotel de Rambouillet in miniature." It was a stone house with large rooms, having an avenue of cherry trees leading to it. It was here that Colonel Cox retired after the Revolution. He remained only until 1790, when on account of failing health he moved to Philadelphia, where he died April 28, 1793. He was interred in Christ Church Yard. Issue:

Rachel, married John Stevens, of Castle Point, Hoboken.

Catherine, married, first, Samuel Witham Stockton, and second, Rev. Nathaniel Harris.

Esther, married Matthias Barton, the son of Rev. Thomas and Esther (Rittenhouse) Barton, of Lancaster County, Pa.

John Bowes, died in infancy.

Mary, married *James Chesnut.*

Sarah, married John Redman Coxe, M. D.

Elizabeth, married Horace Binney.

LONGFIELD-GREENLAND

An early settler of New Amsterdam, Cornelius van Langevelt (the name becoming Longfield in the next generation), came from St. Laurens in Flanders. He married, January 19, 1658, Marytze Jans, and died in the winter of 1662-63.

CORNELIUS LONGFIELD, their son, was born in New Amsterdam, 1658; baptized December 4 of that year, and died in New Jersey, where his will was dated February 5, 1733. He was in the House of Deputies 1698 and again in 1710, and was recommended for the Council by Lord Cornbury, 1708.[7]

He married in the old Dutch church of New York, September 16, 1680, *Mary Greenland,* " of London, but living up Kill Katway"; the daughter of CAPTAIN HENRY GREENLAND. Issue, *Catherine,* married *William Cox.*

CAPTAIN HENRY GREENLAND is first heard of at Newbury, Mass., 1662; later in Kittery, Me., and Piscattaway, N. J. He was an officer of the troops, Overseer, Justice, member of the House of Deputies, etc. He died in December, 1694.[8]

BOWES

FRANCIS BOWES, a prominent citizen of Trenton,

7 *N. J. Archs.,* Vol. ii, 340; xiii, 237 & 426.

8 *Whitehead's Contributions to E. Jersey Hist.,* p. 402; *N. J. Archs.,* Vol. i, pp. 300, 320, 364; xxi, pp. 192, 220.

N. J., was Justice in 1728, member of the Court 1739[9] moving later to Philadelphia. In his will he speaks of himself as a merchant and of "the many governments wherein I have lived." He died in Philadelphia, December 3, 1749.

His third wife was Rachel, the daughter of Jean and Marie (de la Plaine) Le Chevalier, of New York, and their daughter *Esther* married JOHN COX.

LE CHEVALIER

ARMS: *Or, an owl perched on a sword gules placed fessways in chief vert charged with a stalk of lilies proper.*

The colonist, Jean Le Chevalier, was the son of Jean, and both men were naturalized in England. The younger emigrated to New York, where he was a "joyner," and was admitted a freeman October 12, 1695.

He married Marie, the daughter of Nicholas and Susanna (Cresson) de la Plaine, and their wedding license was dated June 27, 1692. She was born in New York and baptized November 14, 1668. Her father, Nicholas de la Plaine, was a Huguenot "van Beersweer in Vranckryck," and was registered as a "small burgher" at New York, April 14, 1657. He married, September, 1658, Susanna, the daughter of Pierre and Rachel (Cloos) Cresson. Susanna was born in Ryswyck, Holland. Her father, Pierre Cresson, was born in Picardy, France. His Huguenot affiliations sent him to Holland, and later he emigrated to America. One of the founders of Harlem,[1] he was appointed, August 16, 1660, one of the three "schepens," and June, 1663, took command of the first company raised to repel Indian attacks.

9 *Snell's Hist. of Hunterdon Co., N. J.*, pp. 203, 238.
1 Riker's *Hist. of Harlem.*

The daughter of Jean and Marie (de la Plaine) Le Chevalier, Rachel, married FRANCIS BOWES, and their daughter *Esther* married JOHN COX.

WILLIAMS (*Continued*)

The only son of John Nicholas and Esther Serena (Chesnut) Williams, *David Rogerson Williams II.,* was born in Society Hill, S. C., October 3, 1822, and died in Camden, S. C., November 24, 1907. He was brought up at the home of his grandfather, because of the death of his mother when he was but a few weeks old. His father's second marriage, in 1831, brought him back to his home at " The Factory," but he afterward paid long visits to his grandfather's widow and to " Mulberry," the home of his mother's parents, near Camden.

In 1843 he was graduated from the South Carolina College, and shortly after built his house, called " Bellevue," on a hill near " The Factory." He owned extensive plantations on the river nearby; and these, as well as his house, he sold to his half-brother, George Frederick, in the year 1858, and moved to Florida, where he had previously bought plantations, near Gainesville, Alachua County, which were called " Serenola." He took his family, during the summer months, to Flat Rock, Henderson County, N. C., where he built a house in 1861. When the Civil War came he joined the army of the Confederacy in the 2d Florida Regiment, Company C, Fennigan's Brigade. His family went to their home, in Flat Rock. His marked skill in drawing caused him to be detailed to the Topographical Department, where he spent most of the time of his service. On the death of his mother's brother, General James Chesnut, in 1886, David Rogerson Williams II. inherited " Mulberry," and a large portion of the Chesnut plantation near Camden.

He married, December 22, 1846, *Katherine Boykin,* the daughter of Stephen Decatur and Mary (Boykin) Miller. She was born May 24, 1827, and died in Romney, W. Va., April 17, 1876. After the death of her father, which occurred in her eleventh year, she lived near Camden, with her mother, until her marriage. Many charming references to her may be found in *A Diary from Dixie* (written by her sister, Mrs. James Chesnut). Issue:

Serena Chesnut, who died in 1876.

MARY BOYKIN.

Stephen Miller.

David Rogerson, married Ellen Clarke Manning.

Katherine Miller, married James Douglas Kirkpatrick.

George Frederick, died in 1875, in his seventh year.

A son of John Nicholas and Sarah Cantey (Witherspoon) Williams, *John Witherspoon Williams,* born at Society Hill, S. C., June 26, 1834, was a planter near Society Hill until after the Civil War, when he moved to Baltimore. He married January 10, 1861, Augusta Rebecca, the daughter of Major Richard Lewis and Rebecca Augusta (Stockton) Howell of Philadelphia. Issue, six children, three of whom lived to maturity, viz.:

Alice Stockton.

John Nicholas.

George.

MILLER

Little of the early history of the Miller family of Lancaster County, S. C., is known, except what is given in a letter of Governor S. D. Miller, of date July 23,

1835, to his daughter Mary, who later became the wife of General James Chesnut. In this, he says, the ancestor of the family landed in Boston; and the family came south to Lancaster, S. C., by way of Maryland.

The earliest known member of the family in South Carolina is Charles Miller. There are land grants to him as early as 1772, and he was living in 1793, in which year, calling himself Charles Miller, Sr., he deeds to his daughter Priscilla certain tracts of land. His wife was Miss Lucas, the daughter of John Lucas, of Massachusetts, and, according to the letter referred to, he had issue, seven children, viz. (not arranged in order of birth):

Ebenezer, moved to Kentucky before 1790.

Jerome.

Stephen, married Hannah Webb.

William.

Jesse, through whom this line is descended.

Priscilla, married Andrew Kennedy, of York County, and moved to Tennessee; no issue.

Daughter, married Theodore Webb.

The fifth son, Jesse Miller, went to South Carolina with his father. He married Margaret, the daughter of William and Sarah White. Issue:

William, married Catherine Foster; she married again.

Priscilla, married William Hart.

Charles, married Margaret Miller.

Sarah, married John Porter; one daughter.

Hugh, died unmarried.

John Lucas, married Mary Simpson Doby.

Margaret Mary, married James Moore Harris.

Governor Stephen Decatur Miller was born in

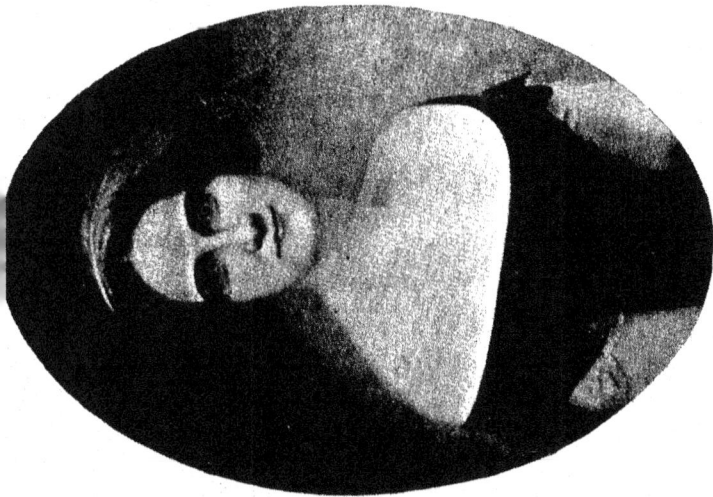

MARY BOYKIN MILLER
Wife of Gen. James Chesnut

COL. JAMES CHESNUT
A silhouette by
Mathieu

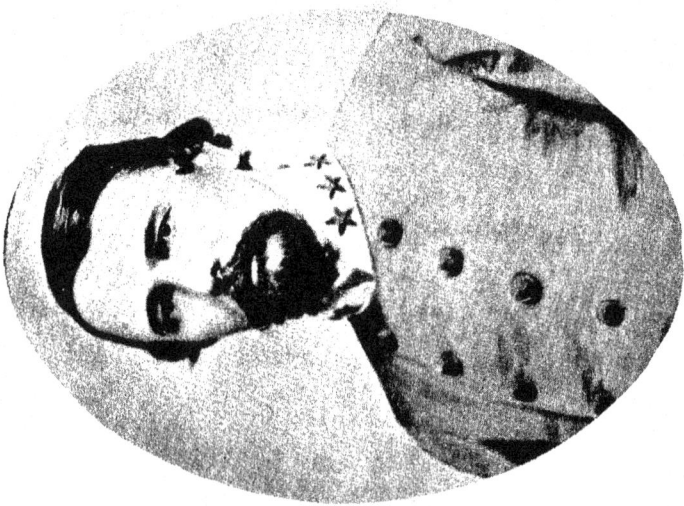

GEN. JAMES CHESNUT
Reproduced from a photograph by R. Wearn

the Waxhaws Settlement, S. C., 1788. His father died when he was quite young, and three slaves which he inherited were sold to provide for his education. He was prepared for college by the Rev. Mr. Conser, of Lancaster, and was well drilled in the classics and the Bible, being able to quote long passages. He entered the South Carolina College in 1804 and was graduated in 1808. He excelled in feats of strength and endurance, and was famed for skill in jumping. He assumed the additional name Decatur, and was always known as Stephen Decatur Miller. ,

On leaving college he studied law with John S. Richardson, of Sumter, and in 1811 was admitted to the bar. Richardson became attorney-general very soon, and moved to Charleston. Mr. Miller thus succeeded almost at once to this practice, and he had a large law business also in Camden, settling, however, in Stateburg, where the Sumter District records were kept. Entering the political field, Mr. Miller was elected to Congress in 1816 by an overwhelming vote. Owing to his wife's illness, he declined to stand for re-election. In 1822 he re-entered politics, and was elected to the State Senate, and at this term he introduced " the resolutions which first laid the foundations of the States Right Party." His colleague in the House, William Smith, joining with him, the two were largely responsible for this principle, which soon ruled in the State. He was Chairman of the Judiciary Committee in the Senate, and continued to serve in that body until he was elected Governor, 1828. As Governor he was the leader in the Nullification movement and his speeches and debates shaped public opinion. Not eligible for re-election as Governor in 1830, he was elected to the United States Senate. Poor health compelled him to resign as Senator in November, 1833.   During his two years of service, however, he highly distinguished himself.

In 1828 he removed to "Plane Hill," now called "The Terraces," only a short distance from "Pleasant Hill," the home of BURWELL BOYKIN, a few miles south of Camden.   He bought a plantation in the State of Mississippi in 1855, moving there with his family and a large number of slaves.   He showed as a planter the same energy and ability that he had displayed at the bar and in politics.   But his life was nearly closed, for he died at the home of his nephew, Major Charles Hart, Raymond, Miss., on March 8, 1838.   At this time, unfortunately, his family were in Camden, on a visit.

His portrait, painted after his health was impaired, is in the possession of his grandson, *Stephen Miller Williams*.   There is also a letter written July 23, 1835, to his daughter Mary, giving a sketch of his family. Numerous quotations from it have been made in this article.

He was twice married, first, 1814, to Elizabeth Dick, of Sumter, who died 1819; second, May 9, 1821, to *Mary*, the daughter of Burwell and Mary (Whitaker) Boykin, who was born March 3, 1804, and died February 9, 1885.   She was one of a large family of at least sixteen children, the favorite sister, and the dearly beloved aunt of the next generation.   Issue, first wife:

Elias Dick, who died in 1832 in his sophomore year at college; John Richardson, and William Smith, who both died young.

Issue, second wife:

Mary Boykin, married General James Chesnut, the son and heir of Colonel James Chesnut.   No children. During the Civil War she kept a journal, parts of which have been published under the title, *A Diary from*

Dixie. She adopted David Rogerson Williams III., her nephew, who inherited the personal effects of Colonel and General Chesnut.

Stephen Decatur, Jr., married Martha Whitaker Boykin.

Katherine Boykin Miller, married *David Rogerson Williams II.*

Sarah Amelia, married Thomas Edward Boykin, the son of Samuel and Fitzgerald (Ross) Boykin.

WHITE

The colonists, Moses White, Mary Campbell his wife, and their son William, came from the North of Ireland to Lancaster County, Pa., and were the progenitors of the White family of Lancaster County, S. C.[2] Originally from the west of Scotland, the family was one of many with similar descent, who came to America, not far from the middle of the eighteenth century. They were all strict Presbyterians. Moses White had a patent of land in Lancaster County, Pa., 1741.

As early as 1722 one Hugh White lived in Lancaster County, and was a man of note. There were also Moses, John, and Alexander White. Other White families moved south about 1750; some remained in North Carolina, and others passed over into South Carolina. Lancaster County, in this State, received its name because of the many settlers who came from the same county in Pennsylvania. The upper part of this southern State owed much to the White family, who were most active in regard to its settlement and who proved to be excellent men of affairs and noteworthy in their day.

2 *William and Mary College Quar.,* Vol. vi, p. 52.

So far as is known, there were six children of Moses White, all sons, William, Joseph, Moses, Henry, Hugh, and Stephen, the youngest, who went to the western part of North Carolina and had a large family.

The eldest child of the family, William White, had a grant of land in Lancaster County, which he sold in 1749. He then moved to the Waxhaws, S. C., and died there. He married Sarah ——. Ramsey's *History of South Carolina* says she died in 1806, at the age of ninety. But Governor Stephen Decatur Miller, who was born in 1788, says that she lived until he was about ten years of age. Issue:

Jean, married Major Robert Crawford of Revolutionary fame.

Hugh, married Mary, the daughter of Joseph White.

Margaret, married Jesse Miller, and they were the parents of Governor Stephen Decatur Miller.

Isabella, married Andrew Foster.

Christiana, married James Crawford, Jr., a first cousin of Andrew Jackson, who persuaded them to move to Tennessee, where they left a large family.

John, married, first, Nancy Ann Foster; second, Margaret Harper.

Moses married Jane Miller.

——, a daughter, married Captain John McClure; killed at Hanging Rock, 1780.

BOYKIN

The first of the Boykins in America, Edward Boykin, received a grant of land in Isle of Wight County, Va., 1685, this portion now being called Southampton County. In 1713, 1715, and 1724, he received other grants of land in the same locality. Edward Boykin died about 1728, leaving a wife named Ann, a son

John, and "other children." His will was written
January 4, 1725-26, and was probated May 27, 1728,
his wife Ann and his son John being appointed executors. John died early in 1729, his inventory being
filed on May 5. A report of Edward's estate was filed
September 28, 1730, by his executor (not named); and
the estate was closed on February 22, 1730-31, by Edward Boykin, Sr. (*i. e.,* Edward Boykin, of North Carolina). In various deeds Edward refers to his sons William and Thomas. Issue, as far as known: John,
through whom this line descends; Edward; Thomas;
William, and possibly others.

The eldest son, John Boykin, whose inventory was
filed May 5, 1729, died in Isle of Wight County, intestate, and therefore the names of his children are not
known. The evidence of wills, land transfers, etc.,
shows that he had issue (probably among others):

Francis, through whom this line descends.

Edward, married Mary —— (issue: Jesse, who married Sarah ——, and was living in Edgecomb County,
N. C., in 1769).

The eldest known son, Francis Boykin, was born in
Isle of Wight County, Va., and lived and died in
Northampton County, N. C., where his will is dated
August 1, and recorded in September, 1761. On August 3, 1727, he bought two hundred and forty acres on
the south side of the Meherrin River in North Carolina
from James Turner, and probably moved there soon
after. There are numerous deeds to him and by him,
and his wife Sarah; several of these last are to Richard
and Arthur Wall. Sarah was the second wife of Francis Boykin, as there is on record a deed in Northampton
County, 1748, in which Francis Boykin and Millicent,
his wife, deed to John Boykin two hundred and ninety

acres, which had been granted Simon Bryant November, 1723; William Boykin being a witness to the deed. In the will of Francis Boykin he refers to "wife and four children," son John Boykin, daughter Mildred Wall, son-in-law William Pace, and grandsons Samuel and Francis Boykin. Further, on December 13, 1766, "Robert Williams, of Craven County, and William Pace and Selah Pace and Richard Wall and Mildred Wall, of the Province of North Carolina, and of Northampton County," for "the true love and natural affection" which they bore John Boykin, deeded to him their parts of two tracts of land, one of old patent taken up by James Turner, the other of new patent taken up by Francis Boykin, "on the south side of the Cypress swamp in North Carolina and Northampton County." It is known that William Boykin, who moved to South Carolina about 1755, had a son Samuel and that there was a Francis (later major in the Revolution) living at this time. The latter's father was probably Francis Boykin, Jr. The issue, therefore, of Francis Boykin is as follows:

Francis, Jr.

John, married Sarah Wall (?).

William, through whom this line descends.

Mildred, married Richard Wall.

Selah (Celia?), married William Pace.

A daughter, married Robert Williams.

The third son, William Boykin, was born in Northampton County, N. C., and died in Camden, S. C., before 1761. He married Elizabeth Bryant. Issue:

Samuel (whose granddaughter married *John Nicholas Williams*).

BURWELL.

Francis, married Catherine Whitaker.

William.

Amelia, married Thomas Pace, and moved to Georgia with her brother Francis, and died there at an advanced age. Her name was originally Mildred.

John, married, first, —— Starke; second, Frances Inman.

The eldest son, Samuel Boykin, was a man of great strength and size, as well as of sterling character. He took an active part in the public life of Camden, after the Revolution. Before the war, he had been one of the "Regulators," and a leader among them, who were administering justice in the days when there were no courts outside of Charleston. He went as a Delegate to the Provincial Congress of 1775, and belonged to the committee who were to carry into execution the Continental Association. In 1776 he was Justice of the Peace for the Orangeburg District, and Commissioner of Elections October, 1778. He commanded a company of Catawba Indians in the Revolution "and did notable service." [3] When this company disbanded, as it did at times, Captain Boykin served under Taylor and Sumter. He was a Commissioner for clearing the Wateree and an inspector and collector for the district "to the eastward of the Wateree 1784," and Commissioner to open and improve the Wateree 1791. He presided as one of the judges at the first session of the County Court, February 28, 1791. December of that year he was injured by blows from some ruffians who encamped on his land, and died in consequence. His wife was Elizabeth, the daughter of John and —— (Bryan) Inman, of Virginia. (She married, second, Thomas Brown.) Issue:

[3] There are numerous references to this in the Minutes of the Council of Safety. See *Historic Camden*, pp. 116-120.

Burwell, died in college, aged eighteen.

Sarah, married General Zachariah Cantey.

Elizabeth, married John Dick Witherspoon, and their daughter married *John Nicholas Williams.*

Mary, burnt to death in childhood.

BURWELL BOYKIN, the second son of William, was born 1752. In 1775 he was appointed on the "Committee of Observation" for St David's Parish,[4] and took an active part in the Revolution, serving under Marion, Sumter, and others, and, according to his daughter Charlotte, was a Lieutenant in his brother Francis' Company of Militia. In 1777 he was a Commissoner of roads on the east side of the Wateree. In 1790 Burwell Boykin was a Member of the State Legislature. He was a most successful planter, and acquired an immense area of land south of Camden. In his will he says: "On no pretext whatever . . . must any portion of my land be sold." A great deal of his property is still in the possession of his grandsons. In 1812 he built his house at Pleasant Hill, still the home of his descendants. His nephew, Dr. Edward M. Boykin, in his sketch, *A Record of the Boykins,* describes the life at Pleasant Hill: "The stables full of horses, kennels filled with hounds, rooms filled with guests." In 1774 he was a Vestryman of St. David's Parish.

In 1782 he married Elizabeth Whitaker, born September 7, 1760, and died October 2, 1787, the daughter of William Whitaker; and after her death he married, 1792, her sister, *Mary Whitaker,* born December 5, 1776, and died October 7, 1838. She is said to have been a strikingly handsome woman, tall and slender, of a strong character and marked influence. After her husband's death, in 1817, she maintained his house at

4 Gregg's *Old Cheraws,* p. 227.

Pleasant Hill as a home for her family, and a centre of hospitality. Burwell Boykin's tombstone says, "He was the father of eleven sons and seven daughters." Of this large family, the names of sixteen are known. Issue, first wife:

Burwell.

Francis, married Mary James.

Elizabeth, married Henry Starke Hunter.

Issue, second wife:

Katherine, married William Wyly Lang.

Samuel, married Fitzgerald Glover Ross.

John, died unmarried; he was graduated from the South Carolina College in 1814; at his own expense he built the present Baptist church at Boykin, near Camden; he died on his knees in the church, and is buried in front of it under a large oak tree.

Thomas, married, first, Eliza Boykin, and second, Amanda Starke.

Lemuel Whitaker, married Mary English Hopkins.

Amelia, married Dr. John McCaa.

Mary, married Stephen Decatur Miller.

Sarah, married William Claiborne Clifton.

Elizabeth Tunstall, married Thomas Jefferson Withers.

Burwell, Jr., married Sally Wyly Lang.

William Whitaker, married Martha Whitaker Rives.

Alexander Hamilton, married Sarah Jones DeSaussure.

Charlotte, married James Madison Taylor.

WHITAKER

ARMS: *Sable, three mascles, argent.*

CREST: *An arm in mail armour, the hand grasping a flaming sword, proper.*

The Whitaker family, associated with the Jamestown

settlement in Virginia, is descended from the Rev. William Whitaker, who was master of St. John College, Cambridge. He was born 1548, and died December 4, 1595; married first, Miss Culverwell; second, the widow of Dudley Fenner. The most famous puritan divine in the Church of England of his day, he was distinguished as a scholar and preacher. His library was so large and well selected that at his death Queen Elizabeth desired to purchase it.[5] He belonged to the family of Whitaker of Holme, Lancashire. His pedigree is as follows:

Thomas Whitaker, of Holme, 1431.

Robert Whitaker, Esq.

Thomas Quitacre, aged thirty-four in 1492; died 1529.

Richard Whitacre, of Holme, living at Burnley 1543.

Thomas Whitaker, buried August 22, 1598; married 1530, Elizabeth Nowell (buried October 18, 1606), daughter of John Nowell, of Read, Esq., and Elizabeth Kay.

Their third son, the Rev. William Whitaker, a sketch of whom has already been given, had issue (order of birth not known):

Alexander, unmarried; called "The Apostle to the Indians," and was minister at Bermuda Hundred, Va., etc.

William.

Richard, a learned bookseller and printer of London.

Samuel.

Susanna, married —— Lothrup.

Marie, married —— Clarke.

Frances.

5 An excellent sketch of his life is given in *History of the Original Parish of Whalley*, p. 467, London, 1806, by Thomas Dunham Whitaker, and also in the *National Dictionary of Biography*.

Jabez Whitaker, from whom this line is descended, born shortly after his father's death, which occurred December 4, 1595, married Mary, the daughter of Sir John Bourchier.[6] "He emigrated to the Jamestown colony, Va. In the records of the Virginia Company for 1620 and 1621 there are interesting references to him. Thus, under date of June 23, 1620:

" Hee haveinge receaved notice of the good carriage of some psonns in Virginia was specially to recomend unto them one m[r] Iabez Whittakers Leivetennat of the Companies men who had given a good Accoumpt of the trust reposed in him." [7] And again: "Ffor so much as itt appeared y[t] m[r] Whittakers had obeyed the Companies orders in buildinge a Guesthouse for entertaynment of Sicke psonns and for y[e] releife and comforte of such cases as came weake from Sea and had allso begunn to plant vines, Corne and such good Comodities and rayled in 100 Acres of ground, itt was moved y[t] the Court would please to bestowe some reward oppon him for his better encourragment in soe good a course. Whereoppo itt was agreed and ordered that hee should have two boyes sent him when the Comp[a] shalbe able and that the reward of Tobacco allowed him by the Governor of Virginia shall be confirmed onto him." [8]

Bruce [9] says that this reference to Jabez Whitaker's railed land is the first evidence of the use of the " rail fence " now so well known. He was a Member of the House of Burgesses, which met March 5, 1623-1624,

[6] P. C. C. Admen. Act. Book, 1626.   "5 April, 1626, commission granted to Mary Bourchier, alias Whitaker, wife of Jabez Whitaker, daughter of Sir John Bourchier, late of the Parish of Lambeth, County Surrey, deceased, to administer the goods of the said deceased, Dame Elizabeth Bourchier, relict of the said deceased having renounced."

[7] Recs. of the Va. Co., Vol. i, p. 370.

[8] Ibid, pp. 508, 513.

[9] Economic Hist of Va., Vol. i, p. 316.

and a member of the Council 1626. He had at least one child, as is shown by the following quotation: [1] June 19, 1622, "Sir John Bourchier's request by letter for his Sonn Whittakers returne for England who (as he saith) intendeth not to staye here any longer from his wife and child, whome he means to leave behinde him, than he can furnish himselfe with necessaries." [2] Issue, as far as known, one son:

CAPTAIN WILLIAM WHITAKER, born in England, and died in Virginia after 1662.[3] His name first appears as "Viewer of Tobacco Crops," Warwick River County, 1639. From 1649 to 1659 he was a member of the House of Burgesses at all its meetings from James City County. He served on several of its most important committees. In 1659 he was a member of the Council. He is referred to as Lieutenant-Colonel, 1655, and as Captain 1658, and later.[4] There are land-grants to him in James City County, June 5, 1656, ninety acres; and March 16, 1662, ninety acres. He is referred to as an early resident of Martin's Hundred, and as sponsor for Edward Thruston's son, December, 1668. A William Whitaker is granted four hundred acres, part in James City County and part in York County, April 20, 1680. Issue, as far as known, one son:

RICHARD WHITAKER, who received a grant of land in James City County, one hundred and thirty-five acres, October 28, 1666, and stood "Sponsor (for another) for Edward Thruston's son, December, 1668, in company of William Whitaker." He held many public offices, being a member of the House of Burgesses,

---

[1] *Recs. of Va. Co.*, Vol. ii, p. 50.

[2] Neill's *Va. Co. of London*, p. 231. Stith's *Hist. of Va.*, Sabin's *Reprint*, p. 205.

[3] Stanard's *Col. Va. Recs.*

[4] *Ibid*, and Hering's *Statutes*, Vol. i.

November, 1685, 1688; April, 1691, and September, 1696, from Warwick County; a civil and military officer of Warwick County, 1680, and Sheriff of Warwick County, 1696. In 1676 he was denounced by Nathaniel Bacon as being one of the supporters of Governor Berkeley.

As far as known, Richard Whitaker had but one child, *John Whitaker,* who lived with his family in Warwick County, where he died before 1750, as in that year his widow, Martha (Gough) Whitaker, married John Drewry. About this time John Whitaker's seven sons all moved to North Carolina. The order of their birth is unknown.[5]

Richard, married Elizabeth Cary.

Gough, married Martha Cary.

John, married Olive Taylor.

Robert, married Sarah ——.

James, married Mary ——.

William.

Dudley.

Martha, married Thomas Cary, Jr.

The sixth child of this family, *William Whitaker,* was born in Warwick County. He went to North Carolina, and later to South Carolina, where he obtained some large land grants north of the city of Camden. His will was recorded September 18, 1789, and he must have died before May 19, 1789, when " power to administer oath to executors was granted," these being his sons Thomas and Lemuel, and his nephews, Willis and

[5] " In a deed to Dudley Whitaker (who was living in 1791), the order of the brothers' names is: Richard, John, William, James, Gough, Robert, but in a letter of Mrs. Sands, a granddaughter of Richard, she gives the names in the following order: John, Robert, Richard. William, Gough, James, Dudley."

James Whitaker. His large estate included forty negroes

His will names a wife " Mary," and therefore he must have been married twice, for the mother of most of his thirteen children was *Catherine,* the daughter of John and Catherine (Baker) Wiggins. John Wiggins was born in Surrey County, Va., but moved to Halifax County, N. C. His wife *Catherine,* whom he married before 1720, was a daughter of Henry Baker and his wife, Angelica Bray. Issue of William Whitaker:

Bythel.

William, died unmarried.

Richard, died.

Martha, married Colonel John Blanton.

Elizabeth, married BURWELL BOYKIN.

Thomas, married Mary Williams.

Catherine Baker, married Alexander Irvin.

Robert, died early.

Margaret.

Lemuel, married Elizabeth Brown.

Winifred, married —— Morse (?).

Edward, died young.

Mary, married BURWELL BOYKIN, as his second wife; their daughter *Mary* married Stephen Decatur Miller, whose second daughter, *Katharine Boykin,* married *David Rogerson Williams II.*

BAKER

LIEUTENANT-COLONEL HENRY BAKER, of Isle of Wight County, Va., had a prominent career between the years 1685 and 1705; a member of the House of Burgesses, Justice, Major of Militia and Lieutenant-Colonel. His will was probated in the summer of 1712. He was the son of Henry Baker, of Surrey County, who was a leading citizen and espoused the cause of Bacon. The elder Baker's will was probated in 1700. Colonel Baker's son:

HENRY BAKER, Sheriff at Nansemond, and a member of the House of Burgesses, married Angelica Bray. Their daughter *Catherine* married John Wiggins, whose daughter *Catherine* married *William Whitaker*.

WILLIAMS (*Continued*)

MARY BOYKIN, the daughter of David Rogerson and Katharine Boykin (Miller) Williams, was born May 18, 1851. She married, first, November 16, 1869, Thomas Bullitt Harrison; second, September 14, 1899, Joseph Sweetman Ames. Her daughter by her first husband, KATHARINE WILLIAMS, married, first, Gough Winn Thompson; second, Frank Gambrill Baldwin.

The third child and eldest son of David Rogerson Williams, *Stephen Miller Williams,* was born January 29, 1853. He married, first, February 25, 1878, Jane North Pettigrew; second, October 29, 1895, Mrs. Annie Caroline (Randolph) Rozier. Issue, first wife: SE-RENA CHESNUT, born February 7, 1879; married, November 23, 1909, Robert Mickle Miles.

The eldest child of John Witherspoon and Augusta Rebecca (Howell) Williams, *Alice Stockton Williams,* was born December 18, 1861. She married, in April, 1885, Charles D. Gaither. Their daughter is NINA WILLIAMS GAITHER.

MARY BOYKIN WILLIAMS AMES.

KATHARINE WILLIAMS HARRISON BALDWIN.

SERENA CHESNUT WILLIAMS MILES.

NINA WILLIAMS GAITHER.

Members of Chapter I., The Colonial Dames of America.

III

HARRISON

The Harrisons of Dorchester County, Md., are descended from Christopher Harrison, of Appleby, Eng., whose wife, Mary, the daughter of John Caile, of England, was born October 7, 1716, and died August 2, 1782. He was born November 17, 1717, died February 6, 1799, and is buried with his wife, in St. Lawrence church, Appleby. He was the son of Christopher and Janę (Gilpin?) Harrison. The elder Christopher died 1733. Although it cannot be substantiated, it is thought he was the grandson of Mr. Christopher Harrison, by whom there is an inscription on a choir seat, in the parish church at Brough.[1]

Two of the sons of Christopher and Mary (Caile) Harrison, Robert[2] and John Caile Harrison, came to Maryland shortly after 1750, and settled in Cambridge, where their uncle, John Caile, was already living. Governor Sharpe, under date of March, 1755,[3] mentions having received a letter from Mr. Hanbury in London, by the hand of Robert Harrison. The latter brought with him letters from Sir Thomas Abdy, and others in authority, asking Governor Sharpe to appoint him to office "on account of his alliance." The only office in Dorchester County at the disposal of the Governor in 1760, when this request was renewed, was that of sheriff, and he could not appoint Mr. Harrison to this, because John Caile already held the office.

[1] Mr. Chrisʳ. Harrison Parochuset Rectoriae Primarius S. S. fieri fecit Deo O. M., etc., 1682."

[2] Jones' *Hist. Dorchester County.*

[3] *Correspondence,* Vol. I, p. 185.

Finally, in March, 1767, the Governor appointed "Mr. Robert Harrison, Merchant, of Cambridge," to succeed to the office of sheriff at Martinmass of that year. Robert Harrison was a delegate to the Convention of June, 1774, a member of the "Association of Freemen of Maryland," in July, 1775; a Justice 1777 to 1781, and 1783; Judge of the Fourth Judicial District 1791; Colonel in the Continental Army, appointed May 20, 1778, and reappointed in February, 1781, and a Trustee of the poor 1785. He died in 1802, aged sixty-two. His wife, Milcah, the daughter of George and Elizabeth (Airey) Gale, was born June 20, 1751, dying in 1780. Their son, Christopher Harrison, was the first Lieutenant-Governor of Indiana. One of his daughters, Elizabeth, married Andrew Skinner, of "Fair View," Talbot County, Md., from whom are descended the families of Henry C. Tilghman, and Henry R. Wilson, of the Eastern Shore of Maryland.

JOHN CAILE HARRISON, another son of Christopher and Mary (Caile) Harrison, who came to Maryland with his brother, was born September 3, 1747, and died November 8, 1780. He was Register of Wills for some years, and then became Clerk of the Court of Dorchester County, from 1777 to 1780. At the beginning of the Revolution, on the organization of the Committee of Observation of the county, he was one of its members, and elected to be its clerk. In September, 1776, he was appointed an Ensign in one of the companies of the 19th Battalion. According to family traditions, he was so incapacitated by the hardships of the campaign, ending in the winter at Valley Forge, that he was invalided home, and soon after died.

He married, November 18, 1773, his first cousin, *Mary* ("Polly"), the daughter of Hall and Elizabeth

(Haskins) Caile. She was born September 10, 1756, and died February 24, 1812. (She married, second, Thomas James Bullitt, who died November 25, 1840, aged seventy-seven. She had three children by her second marriage, Thomas, d. s. p.; Elizabeth Haskins, married William Hayward, and Alexander C., who married Mary Dennison.) John Caile and Mary Harrison had three children:

Hall.

Hannah, born November 20, 1777; died, unmarried, November 4, 1799.

William, born July 7, 1780; died November 29, 1827.

CAILE

The Caile family, once so prominent in Dorchester County, Md., but where the name is now extinct, was of Swiss origin, it is said, and descended from John Caile of Howgate Foot, Westmoreland County, Eng.[4] He had nine children, of whom three were connected with families in America, viz.:

HALL.

Mary, married Christopher Harrison.

John, Jr., came to Cambridge, Md., where he was clerk of the court from 1745 until his death in 1767. He married Rebecca, the daughter of Henry and Mary (Hooper) Ennalls.[5] She was born July 26, 1717, and died August 28, 1750.

HALL CAILE was born May 28, 1733, in England,

---

[4] The will of "John Caile; Gent," was written Sept. 27, 1746, and proved in May, 1747. The will of his wife Margaret (Hall?) was written Mar. 17, 1746-7, and proved May 27, 1747.

[5] For a history of the Ennalls family see Baltimore *Sun,* issue of May 6, 1906.

and died January 3, 1761. He was High Sheriff of
Dorchester County, Md., from 1758 until his death.
He married, June 2, 1754, *Elizabeth,* the daughter of
Thomas and Mary (Loockerman) Haskins. She was
born May 25, 1733, and died November 3, 1805. They
had three children:

Mary, married JOHN CAILE HARRISON.

Margaret Hall, was born March 15, 1759, and died
July 2, 1826; she married, February 16, 1777, Gustavus
Scott.

John Hall, was born August 14, 1761; died February
14, 1783.[6]

LOOCKERMAN, OR LOCKERMAN

This family was represented in New Amsterdam by
three brothers, Jacob, Pieter and GOVERT, a sister Anneker, and Balthus, who was possibly a cousin.[7].

The elder, Jacob, married Tryntje ——, and settled
where now is the city of Albany, as early as 1657.
Pieter was at New Amsterdam in 1642, but in 1656 he
was living at Albany. Anneker probably came to New
Amsterdam in November, 1641, with her brother Govert, on his return to America. She married, February
26, 1642, Oloff Stephenszen van Cortlandt, the progenitor of that well-known family. She died May 14, 1684.
Balthus married, about 1660, Engeltje Hendricks.

GOVERT LOOCKERMANS was born in Turnhout, a village about twenty-five miles from Antwerp, about the
year 1616. He came to New Amsterdam in April,
1633, sailing from Holland with the Director-General,
Wouter Van Twiller, in the ship *Soutberg* (Salt Moun-

6 Jones' *History of Dorchester County.*
7 *N. Y. Hist. and Biog. Reg.* VIII, pp. 11-16. The *Dupuy Family.*

tain), but on the voyage they captured a Spanish cara-
vel, the *St. Martin,* to which Loockermans was transferred and on which he reached New Amsterdam.
Upon his arrival, he was taken into the service of the
West India Company, but soon left and engaged in
business for himself. He returned to Holland 1640,
where he married in Amsterdam, February 26, 1641,
Ariaentje Jans. They returned to New Amsterdam,
on the ship *Conick Davit* (King David), by way of St.
Christopher, arriving November 29, 1641. Their eldest daughter, Maria, was born on the voyage.

He bought the bark *Good Hope,* in 1642, and engaged in trade up the Hudson, along the Sound, and as
far as the Delaware River. He held many offices in
the colony, and was selected for many dangerous duties.
Thus, on the night of February 27, 1643, he and Maryn
Adriaensen, by order of Governor Kieft, led the attack of a company of citizens upon a party of Indians,
which resulted in the massacre of the Indians. He was
on the board of "Nine Men," from 1647 to 1650; Indian interpreter 1653; fire warden 1655; on the Council
of Schepens from 1657 to 1661; orphan master 1663
and 1664; a member of special commissions frequently,
and in July, 1670, Lieutenant of a Company of Foot.
He was deputed, with two others, in 1664, to arrange a
treaty of peace with the Mohawks, and at one time he
was in command of an armed vessel. He took a leading part in politics, was banished three times and as
often recalled. He carried on an extensive commerce
with Europe as his trading and shipping operations
grew. The site of his house was on the present Hanover Square.

"He possessed a superior education for the times in
which he lived. Bold, adventurous, enterprising, not

much troubled with scruples either in his trading intercourse with the Indians or the more extensive traffic in which he afterwards engaged with the Netherlands, he amassed a large fortune, and was, at his death, probably the weathiest citizen in New York."

It is recorded that Govert Aertsen, a small trader, was obliged to carry, in 1648, for his better protection when visiting the Connecticut settlements, a certificate from the magistrates of New Amsterdam, that he was not Govert Loockermans, for the latter " was a thorn to the English, who hated him for his influence over the Indians and his success among them."

His wife dying, he married, second, July 11, 1649, Marritje Jansen, the daughter of Tryn Jansen, and sister of Anneke Jans (of Trinity church fame).[8] He was her third husband, and in 1666, when he became a resident of Long Island, living near New Utrecht, his wife remained in New Amsterdam, where she kept a shop, a custom not uncommon with the prosperous Dutch settlers. He died in the fall of 1670. His Bible is now in the possession of the American Bible Society. He had two children by first wife, viz.:

Marritje, born November 3, 1641 (baptized Dec. 1), married, November 12, 1664, Balthazar Bayard, son of Samuel Bayard and Anna Stuyvesant.

Jannetie, born September 23, 1643 (baptized September 27), married, February 12, 1667, Dr. Hans Kierstede, the son of Dr. Hans and Sara (Roelofs) Kierstede.

Issue, second wife, an only child:

JACOB LOOCKERMAN, who was born in New Amsterdam 1652, being baptized March 17. In 1678, he was

[8] See *Anneke Jans Borgadus and her Farm*, Harper's Monthly Mag. Vol. LXX, p. 836; or Schuyler's *Colonial New York*.

obliged to leave New Amsterdam, on account of political difficulties. He applied to the General Assembly of Maryland for naturalization, and evidently lived for some time in St. Mary's County, but about 1681, he moved to Dorchester County, where he lived until his death.[9] He was educated as a physician, but apparently gave himself almost entirely to public life. He was a Commissioner of lands 1683, 1686 and 1706; Justice, 1685 to 1688, 1690, 1691, and 1702 to 1709; High Sheriff from 1694 to 1696; a member of the Assembly 1689, 1692, and from 1698 to 1704; a military officer 1696, and later, being in succession Major, Lieutenant-Colonel, and Colonel. He married, January 29, 1677-78, Helena Ketin. She died about 1699, and he married, second, one whom he named "Dorathy," in his will. Issue, seven children, the two elder being Jacob and GOVERT.

The eldest son, *Jacob Loockerman, Jr.*, was the clerk of various committees of the General Assembly, 1699 to 1701, High Sheriff 1701, Justice 1709, etc. One Jacob Loockerman was also a Justice in 1710, from 1712 to 1718, 1721, 1723, 1724 and 1725; and a Jacob Lockerman, "son of Jacob Lockerman," was Sheriff from 1728 to 1730.

GOVERT LOOCKERMAN II., was born in Dorchester County, Md., about 1681, and died before July, 1729. He was High Sheriff of Dorchester County, 1707 and 1708; Clerk of the Court 1710, and from 1716 to 1720; Commissioner of public schools; on the board of visitors of King William school at Annapolis (later St. John's College), and a member of the Assembly, from 1712 to 1714. He married *Sarah*, the

[9] Jones' *History of Dorchester County.* In Vincent's *History of Delaware,* this is given as Aug. 17, 1730.

daughter of Roger and Mary (Denwood) Woolford. She was born March 8, 1672. There were five children: Govert, Jacob, Sarah, Elizabeth and *Mary*.

The youngest daughter, *Mary*, was twice married; first in 1728 to Thomas Haskins (1699-1739?), who came to America from Bristol, Eng.; and second, to Joseph, the son of Henry and Mary (Hooper) Ennalls, who was born July 19, 1709, and died in October, 1756. Issue, first husband: William, Joseph, and *Elizabeth*, who married HALL CAILE. Issue, second marriage, six children.

WOOLFORD

ROGER WOOLFORD came from England to the Eastern Shore of Virginia about the middle of the seventeenth century, and soon after moved to Maryland. His seat was "Manokin," Somerset County. He was a Justice of his county, 1676, 1680, 1689, and 1694, and a member of the Assembly 1671, 1674, 1675, 1678,1681, and 1682. He died in 1701.

He married. March 1, 1661, in Hungars Parish, Va., *Mary*, the daughter of LEVIN DENWOOD, SR. (living in Virginia before 1633, and dying some time after 1665), and his wife Mary. (See p. 149 for Denwood line.) Issue, seven children: Elizabeth, Rosanna, Roger, *Sarah*, who married GOVERT LOOCKERMAN II., Ann, James and Levin.[10]

HARRISON (*Continued*)

The eldest son of John Caile and Mary (Caile) Harrison, *Hall Harrison*, was born in Cambridge, Md., October 13, 1774, and died in Baltimore, September 3,

10 Jones' *History of Dorchester County*.

1830, being buried in St. Paul's cemetery. When a youth he came to Baltimore and was apprenticed to George Grundy as clerk, and was brought up in the dry goods business. He lived in Mr. Grundy's family until his majority, when he went to England, and visited relatives for two or three years. He returned to America, married and lived in Baltimore until 1802 or 1803, when he moved to the Eastern Shore, and later was elected cashier of the bank at Easton, Md. In 1810 he returned to Baltimore, and formed a partnership with Govert Haskins in the iron business, on Bowley's wharf. This was dissolved the next year, and he formed a new one with Major Thomas Yates. On the death of Major Yates, after a year or two, he entered into business with Samuel Sterrett, under the name " Harrison & Sterrett, Vendue Merchants."

He married, March 17, 1800, Elizabeth, the daughter of Robert and Elizabeth (Thompson) Galt, of Coleraine, Ireland. She was born April 18, 1776, and died March 2, 1863. She had come to America on a visit to her uncle, Hugh Thompson, and was a lady of means and high position. Of their twelve children, four died in infancy. The surviving eight were as follows:

William Gilpin, married Anne Elizabeth Ross.

Thomas Bullitt, died unmarried.

Mary Caile, married Thomas Oliver.

Hugh Thompson, married Eliza Catherine Thompson.

John Caile.

Margaret Sprigg, died unmarried.

Samuel Thompson (1815-1857), a planter in Louisiana, married Emily, the daughter of Charles and Elizabeth Hestia (Yard) Kuhn, of Philadelphia. They had a daughter Emily, and a son Charles. The latter married Louisa Triplett, the daughter of Bolling Walker and Anne (Triplett) Haxall. Of their twelve children, ANNE TRIPLETT HARRISON, a Colonial Dame, married George Somerville Jackson. (See Haxall and Triplett families.)

George Law, married first Jeannette Bathurst; second, Helen Troup Davidge.

The fourth surviving son of Hall and Elizabeth (Galt) Harrison, *John Caile Harrison*, was born March 3, 1812, and died June 9, 1859. He was a commission merchant with his brothers, having their head office in Baltimore, and branches in New Orleans and Vera Cruz. For many years he was in charge of the New Orleans branch, and while living there he married *Sarah*, the daughter of Jacob and Elizabeth (Hazard) Barker, and their five children were: John Caile, *Thomas Bullitt*, Jacob Barker, William Gilpin, and Hall.

BARKER

This family, of Duxbury, Mass.,[11] was founded in America by Robert Barker, who was living in Massachusetts before January 20, 1632, on which date " Robert Barker, servt. of John Thorp, complayned of his Mr. for want of clothes. The complaint being found just, it was ordered that Thorp should either foorthwith apparell him or else make over his time to some other that was able to provide for him." He was later bound out as a carpenter's apprentice, and, as his time was out in April, 1637, he was probably born 1616. In 1641, he with others, bought a ferry and some land at Marshfield, and in 1643 he was a member of Lieutenant

11 *Barker Family.* By Barker Newhall, Ph.D.

Nathaniel Thomas' military company in that town. He
was surveyor in Marshfield, 1645 and 1648, a constable
1646, and admitted Freeman 1654. About 1650 or
1655, he moved to Duxbury, where he was surveyor for
many years. There is a tradition in the family that
he passed the first winter in Duxbury in a dugout, but
he prospered and left at his death, in 1691, an estate of
over £142.

He married Lucy Williams. The house he built
about 1650 at Pembroke, was standing until recently.
" The earliest portion of the structure was a single
room built of flat stones laid in clay, and covered with a
shed roof. It was about twenty feet square, and only
six feet high, with a huge fireplace that took fully a
third of the side wall." It served as a garrison house
during King Philip's War, and for several generations
was a sort of tavern. Issue, five children: Robert, Jr.,
Francis, Isaac, Abigail and Rebecca.

The third son, Isaac Barker, lived and died in Duxbury, where he was surveyor 1674, and constable 1687.
He married, December 28, 1665, *Judith,* the daughter
of Governor Thomas Prince (Prence) of Plymouth,
and his wife, Mary Collier. Issue, eleven children.

The eldest child of this family, *Samuel Barker,* was
born September 2, 1667, and died February 1, 1738-39.
He lived in Duxbury, where he was constable 1693,
but in 1714 he moved to Sandwich. He married first,
November 22, 1711, Deborah, the daughter, of John
and Mary (Perry) Wing, of Sandwich; second, January 21, 1718, *Bethiah,* the daughter of John and Mary
(Barnard) Folger of Nantucket. She was born 1692
and died 1774. Issue, first wife, one daughter Deborah; his second wife, had four children: Judith,
Robert, Samuel and Josiah.

The eldest son of this family, *Robert Barker,* was born in Sandwich, Mass., February 23, 1722-3, and died April 26, 1780, at sea. He lived on Nantucket Island, but seeing the Revolution was imminent, moved his family, in 1772, to Swan Island, in the Kennebec River. They were all Quakers, and they have been described as " averse to change of place, fond of society and good cheer, and attentive to woman, who from the beginning had equal rights and privileges, and shared not only in the property but in the opportunities of improvement at home and abroad."

He married first, February 16, 1744, Jedidah, the daughter of James and Rachel (Brown) Chase, of Nantucket, born 1723, and died 1762; second, in April, 1763, *Sarah,* the daughter of Abishai and Dinah (Coffin) Folger, of Nantucket, and widow of Hezekiah Gardner. She was born October 16, 1739, and died March 24, 1833. His first wife had eight children, and the second wife also had eight children.

The youngest of this second family, *Jacob Barker,* was born on Swan Island, December 17, 1779, and died in Philadelphia, December 26, 1871. He moved to New York when a mere boy, and began at once his wonderfully successful business career. By the time he was twenty-one, he was engaged for himself in the commission business, and owned five vessels. He became ultimately the second largest ship owner in the United States, employing chiefly Nantucket captains for his vessels. When Fulton built his first steamboat, Jacob Barker imported for him his engine, and advanced a large amount of money to enable him to complete his boat.

During the War of 1812, the British captured all of his ships, but in spite of these enormous losses he raised nearly $8,000,000 for the government, saying, "If the country breaks I want to break with it." He was never reimbursed for the money he advanced. In 1815 he founded the Exchange Bank, established a newspaper, and was among the first to urge the construction of the Erie Canal. He was a careful student of political economy, and a successful lawyer and politician. (He was an original member of Tammany Hall.) His strict honesty and unyielding nature caused him many lawsuits in New York, in which he defended himself with great brilliancy. In 1834, he moved to New Orleans, where he was admitted to the bar, and later engaged in banking. He opposed the secession of Louisiana, and in 1865, he was elected to Congress, but was not allowed to take his seat. Having lost his large fortune by the Civil War, he came to Philadelphia, and lived with his son Abraham.

He married, August 27, 1801, Elizabeth, the daughter of Thomas and Anna (Rodman) Hazard, of New Bedford. She was born December 2, 1873, and died September 18, 1861. Of their twelve children, the ninth, *Sarah,* married first, *John Caile Harrison,* and second, January 2, 1866, William H. Hunt, of New Orleans.

PRINCE-COLLIER

GOVERNOR THOMAS PRINCE (PRENCE), was born in Wiltshire, England, and died in Plymouth, Mass., 1673. He came to America 1621, on the ship *Fortune.* He was Governor of the colony for the years 1635, 1638 and 1658, and was also an Assistant for many years. He married three times, his second wife being Mary, the daughter of William Collier. Their daughter *Judith,* married *Isaac Barker.*

WILLIAM COLLIER, of Duxbury, Mass., died 1670. He was a merchant of London, and for many years one of the Plymouth "Adventurers," but not content with making profit by the enterprise of the Pilgrims, unless he shared their hardships, he came to Massachusetts in 1633. He was an Assistant twenty-eight years, between 1634 and 1665, and at the first meeting of the Congress of the United Colonies, 1643, he was one of the two Plenipotentiaries from Plymouth. In the alarms of 1642 and 1643-44, he was a member of the Council of War. His daughter *Mary* became the second wife of GOVERNOR THOMAS PRINCE, whose daughter, *Judith,* married *Isaac Barker.*[12]

FOLGER

The colonial ancestor of the Folgers of Nantucket, Mass.,[13] was John Folger, who emigrated from Norwich, England, in 1635, "aged about eighteen." He settled in Watertown, Mass., but about 1641, moved to Martha's Vineyard where he died some twenty years later. The name of his wife is not known.

His son Peter Folger, lived for some years in Martha's Vineyard, where he was surveyor and taught school, and where he learned to speak the Indian language fluently. About 1663, soon after his father's death, he moved to Nantucket, having been invited to come there to act as miller, weaver and interpreter. As a proper encouragement, a grant of land was made him. In 1667, he took charge of the first mill on the island, and in July, 1673, he was elected Clerk of Courts, an office which he held for many years. A poem written

12 Savage's *Geneal. Dict.*
13 *N. E. Hist. and Geneal. Reg.* Vol. XVI.

by him occasioned by King Philip's War, and called
"A Looking-glass for the Times, or the Former Spirit
of New England, in this generation," which was "written April 23, 1676," has been preserved. He married,
1644, Mary Morrill, who died 1704. Among other children were Eleazer, John, and a daughter, Abiah, who
was born August 15, 1667, and married Josiah Franklin, of Boston. They were the parents of Benjamin
Franklin.

The first named of these three children, Eleazer Folger, was born 1648, and died in Boston 1716. He moved
to Nantucket with his father, and for at least one term
was a Representative in the Legislature. He married,
in 1671, *Sarah,* the daughter of Richard and Sarah
(Shattuck) Gardner. She was born 1651, and died
October 19, 1729.

One of their children, *Nathan Folger,* was born 1678,
and died September 2, 1747. He lived on Nantucket,
and married, December 29, 1699, *Sarah,* the daughter
of John and Abigail (Severance) Church.

The eldest child of Nathan and Sarah, *Abishai
Folger,* was born September 27, 1700, on the Island
of Nantucket, and died January 22, 1788. He married,
at Hudson, N. Y., in September, 1735, *Dinah,* the
daughter of Stephen Coffin, Jr.; she was the widow of
Benjamin Starbuck, and was born July 23, 1713, and
died September 1, 1793. Their daughter, *Sarah,*
married *Robert Barker.*

Another son of Peter and Mary (Morrill) Folger,
John Folger, was born 1659, and died October 23, 1732.
He was a miller and farmer of Nantucket, and a member of the Society of Friends. He married Mary, the
daughter of Nathaniel and Mary (Barnard) Barnard,
of Nantucket. She was born February 24, 1667, and

died October 6, 1737. Among their children was Bethiah, who married *Samuel Barker.*

GARDNER

The Gardners of Salem and Nantucket, Mass., were descended from Thomas Gardner, who came to America in 1624, from Dorsetshire, Eng., settling at Gloucester, on Cape Ann, where he was overseer of the plantation. In 1626 he moved to Salem, Mass., where he died " 10th mo. 29, 1674." He was a prosperous merchant, a member of the General Court, 1637, and the holder of many town offices. He was married twice; first, to Margaret, the mother of all his children; second, to Mrs. Damaris Shattuck. His son:

RICHARD GARDNER, who died January 23, 1689, was living in Salem 1643, but moved to Nantucket 1667. On April 15, 1673, he was commissioned Chief Magistrate of the island. He married Sarah Shattuck, and their daughter *Sarah,* married Eleazer Folger.[14]

CHURCH-SEVERANCE

One of the early settlers of Dover, N. H., was John Church, active in many Indian fights, who was captured in the war of 1689, but escaped. He was finally killed by Indians near his own door, May 7, 1696. He married, November 29, 1664, *Abigail Severance,* who was born May 25, 1643.

JOHN SEVERANCE, who died April 9, 1682, was one of the original proprietors of Salisbury, Mass., and at one time Cornet of the Troop. His wife was Abigail Kimball, the daughter of Richard and Ursula (Scott) Kimball, of Ipswich. Their daughter *Abigail,* married

14 *N. E. Hist and Geneal. Reg.* XXV, p. 48.

John Church, whose daughter *Sarah,* married *Nathan Folger.*

COFFIN

TRISTRAM COFFIN, the colonist, was the son of Peter Coffin of Brixton Parish, Devon, Eng., and his wife, Joan Thember (?). From them the family of Nantucket is descended. (See pp. 262-263.)

One of Tristram's sons, *Stephen Coffin,* was born in Newbury, Mass., May 11, 1652, and died on Nantucket, May 18, 1734. He married Mary, the daughter of George and Jane (Godfrey) Bunker. She was born in 1652 and died 1724. Her father and mother died in 1658 and 1662, respectively. She was the granddaughter of William Bunker, of a Huguenot family living in England. The name was originally spelled " Bon Coeur."

Their son, *Stephen Coffin, Jr.,* was born on Nantucket February 20, 1676, and died 1725. He married, November 21, 1693, Experience, the daughter of Thomas and Elizabeth (Bunker) Look. She was born November 22, 1672. Her father was born in 1646, and her mother was a daughter of George and Jane (Godfrey) Bunker.

Their daughter, *Dinah Coffin,* married for her second husband, *Abishai Folger.*[15]

HAZARD

THOMAS HAZARD (1610-1680), the ancestor of this numerous family in America,[16] and one of the founders of Newport, was twice married. By his first wife, Martha, he had several children.

15 *N. E. Hist. and Geneal. Reg.* Vol. XXIV.
16 *The Hazard Family of Rhode Island,* by Caroline E. Robinson.

ROBERT HAZARD (1635-1710), his son, married *Mary,*
the daughter of THOMAS BROWNELL. (See pp. 100-102
for Hazard family, and p. 102 for Brownell family.)
They had eight children, the eldest of whom was
Thomas, and the third son, Stephen (from whom descends MISS SARAH RODMAN BALDWIN).

A large landholder, *Thomas Hazard* was born 1660,
and died 1746. His property, amounting to nearly four
thousand acres, was situated in what is called " Boston
Neck," near Kingston, R. I. His wife's name was
Susanna, and they had ten children.

Their third child and eldest son, *Robert Hazard,* was
born May 23, 1689, and died May 20, 1762. He lived
in South Kingston, and it is said that his farms were
the most extensive in New England. He married
Sarah, the daughter of Richard and Innocent (Wodell)
Borden, of Tiverton, R. I., and they had six children;
she was born July 31, 1694.

Their eldest son, *Thomas Hazard,* was born September 15, 1720, and died August 26, 1798. He entered
Yale College, but did not graduate, owing to his religious scruples—as a Quaker—concerning " degrees."
He was always called in the family "College Tom" to
distinguish him from his numerous namesakes. He was
one of the original " Fellows of Rhode Island College,"
now Brown University. In 1748, he was clerk of the
Council, and for forty years was a preacher of the
Society of Friends. He married, May 27, 1742, *Elizabeth,* the daughter of William and Martha (Potter)
Robinson. She was born June 16, 1724, and died February 8, 1804.

Their son, *Thomas Hazard,* was born November 15,
1758, and died July 24, 1828. Soon after his marriage,
Thomas Hazard moved to New Bedford, and amassed

a fortune. He took an active part in politics, being Postmaster, and in 1812, State Senator. Later, he moved to New York, where he engaged in many lines of business. He married, September 6, 1780, Anna, the daughter of Thomas and Mary (Borden) Rodman. She was born June 24, 1762, and died June 14, 1845. Their daughter, *Elizabeth,* married *Jacob Barker.*

BORDEN

RICHARD BORDEN, married Joan ——. They had issue, among others *Matthew,* JOHN and *Sarah.*

The first named, *Matthew Borden,* was born in May, 1638, and died July 5, 1708. He was the first English child born in Rhode Island, and lived in Portsmouth, R. I.; he married Sarah Clayton, born 1654, and died April 19, 1735.

Their son, *Abraham,* was born March 29, 1690, and married *Elizabeth,* the daughter of Joseph and Sarah (Freeborn) Wanton; she was born January 5, 1691. Their daughter, *Mary,* married *Thomas Rodman.*

JOHN BORDEN, another son of Richard and Joan Borden, was born in September, 1640, and died June 4, 1716. He lived in Portsmouth, and was a Deputy in 1673, 1680, 1700, 1704, 1705, and 1708. He married *Mary,* the daughter of William and Mary (Walker) Earle.

Their son, *Richard Borden,* married *Innocent,* the daughter of Gershom and Mary (Tripp) Wodell. Their daughter, *Sarah,* married *Robert Hazard II.*

A daughter of Richard and Joan Borden, Sarah Borden, married JONATHAN HOLMES. (See p. 18 for Borden, and pp. 17-18 for Holmes.)

WANTON-FREEBORN.

A ship-builder of Tiverton, R. I., Joseph Wanton

was born May 1, 1664, and died March 3, 1754. His father, Edward Wanton, of Scituate, Mass., was also a ship-builder. Joseph married *Sarah,* the daughter of Gideon and Sarah (Brownell) Freeborn; she was born January 14, 1667, and died July 10, 1737. Their daughter, *Elizabeth,* married *Abraham Borden.*

WILLIAM FREEBORN, one of the founders of Portsmouth, R. I., was born 1594, and died April 28, 1670. His son:

GIDEON FREEBURN, a Deputy from Portsmouth for the years 1675, 1690, 1703-04 and 1713, died February 28, 1720. He married *Sarah,* the daughter of THOMAS BROWNELL, of Portsmouth. (See p. 102.) She died September 16, 1676. Their daughter *Sarah,* married Joseph Wanton, whose daughter, *Elizabeth,* married *Abraham Borden.*

EARLE

CAPTAIN RALPH EARLE married Joan Savage. (See p. 19.) Their son:

WILLIAM EARLE, died January 15, 1715. He lived in Portsmouth, and was a Deputy in the years 1693, 1704 and 1706. He married Mary, the daughter of John Walker, of Boston and Portsmouth; he died 1647. Their daughter *Mary,* married JOHN BORDEN.

WODELL-TRIPP

WILLIAM WODELL, of Boston and Tiverton, Mass., who died 1693, was a follower of Gorton, and imprisoned by the government of Massachusetts. He was twice Commissioner, and a Deputy for sixteen terms, between 1664 and 1686, and was elected Assistant 1684, but declined.

His son, *Gershom Wodell,* who was born July 14, 1642, and died before 1683, was of Portsmouth, R. I. He married Mary, the daughter of John and Mary (Paine) Tripp. She was born about 1646, and died 1716. Their daughter, *Innocent,* married *Richard Borden.*

JOHN TRIPP (1610-1678), was of Portsmouth, R. I. He was Deputy for thirteen terms, between 1648, and 1672, and Assistant for 1670, 1673, 1674 and 1675. He was repeatedly a member of the Town Council. His wife, *Mary,* the daughter of Anthony Paine, died February 12, 1687. Their daughter *Mary,* married *Gershom Wodell,* whose daughter *Innocent,* married *Richard Borden.*

ROBINSON

The colonist, Rowland Robinson,[17] was born in Cumberland, Eng., 1654, and came to America 1675, settling in Rhode Island, where he was one of the largest landowners in New England, dying in 1716. He served the colony in many ways, and was Deputy 1705. He married 1676, Mary, the daughter of John and Elizabeth (Bacon) Allen of Newport. She was born February 4, 1653, and died after 1716.

WILLIAM ROBINSON, their son, was born January 26, 1693, and died September 19, 1751. He lived in "King's Town," R. I., and was elected to many offices of honor. He was Deputy ten terms between 1724 and 1742; Speaker of the House, 1735, 1736, 1741 and 1742; and in 1745 and 1748, he was Deputy-Governor. He married Martha, the daughter of John and Sarah (Wilson) Potter, and their daughter *Elizabeth,* married *Thomas Hazard* (College Tom).

17 Austin's *Geneal. Dict. of R. I.*

POTTER-WILSON

The Potters were very early represented in Rhode Island by Nathaniel Potter, (who died 1676), and his wife Dorothy, whose son, Ichabod, married Martha, the daughter of the first Thomas Hazard.

Their son, John, (1665-1715), was of "King's Town," R. I., and married Sarah, the daughter of Samuel and Tabitha (Tefft) Wilson, who was born 1666, and died after 1739. Tabitha Tefft was the daughter of John Tefft of Portsmouth, R. I., who died 1676.

Their daughter, Martha Potter, married WILLIAM ROBINSON.

RODMAN

The Rodman line of Rhode Island is descended from John Rodman who died in Barbadoes, 1686, where he went from Ireland.

His son, Dr. Thomas Rodman, (1640-1728), leading physician of Newport, R. I., was born in Barbadoes. He married, November 26, 1691, *Hannah,* the daughter of Governor Walter and Hannah (Scott) Clarke; she was born October 28, 1667, and died October 22, 1732. (See pp. 93-96 for Rodman family.[18])

Their son, *Samuel Rodman,* was born in Newport, July 23, 1703, and died there February 27, 1749. The only public office he held was that of Justice of the Peace 1739. He married, May 16, 1723, *Mary,* the daughter of Colonel Thomas and Helena (Stoothoof) Willett, of Flushing, L. I.; she died May 21, 1756.

Their son, *Thomas Rodman,* was born February 29, 1724, and died at sea, off Newport, November 16, 1766. According to one family tradition he was returning

18 The *Rodman Family.* Austin's *Geneal. Dict. of R. I.*

from England, where he had been to collect a large sum of money due him, and when his vessel was wrecked he could not save himself, being rendered helpless by an attack of gout. He married, April 5, 1750, *Mary,* the daughter of Abraham and Elizabeth (Wanton) Borden; she was born in May, 1729, and died February 18, 1798. As the Revolution approached, Mrs. Rodman became alarmed and moved with her family to Leicester, Mass., in 1770, where they remained until peace was declared. Her daughters were famous for their beauty and grace. One of them, *Anna,* married *Thomas Hazard,* whose daughter *Elizabeth,* married *Jacob Barker.*

CLARKE

JEREMIAH CLARKE came to America, after his marriage to Frances Latham. He was Lieutenant 1642, and later Captain. Treasurer of Portsmouth, R. I., 1644 to 1647, he was also Treasurer of the colony, 1647 to 1649, and Assistant and Acting-Governor 1648.

GOVERNOR WALTER CLARKE, his son, was born 1640, and died May 23, 1714. He was Deputy in Rhode Island four terms; Assistant four years; Governor 1676, 1677, 1686, 1697, 1698; Deputy-Governor from 1679 to 1686, and from 1700 to 1714; also a member of the Council 1686. His wife, Hannah, the daughter of Richard and Catherine (Marbury) Scott, was born 1642, and died July 24, 1681. Richard Scott was the first Quaker in Providence, and his wife, "an ancient woman," was imprisoned and whipped at Boston, for diffusing her opinions. Governor Clarke's daughter, *Hannah,* married Dr. Thomas Rodman.

WILLETT-STOOTHOOF

COLONEL THOMAS WILLETT, the son of Thomas and

Sarah (Cornell) Willett, was born 1645, being baptized
November 26, and died in September, 1722. He lived
in Flushing, L. I., where he was Sheriff from 1676 to
1678, and from 1683 to 1689, and for many years in
command of Queen's County militia; also a Judge
from 1702 to 1710. In the years 1690 to 1698, he was
a member of the Council. He married *Helena*, the
daughter of Elbert Elbertse Stoothoof. Their daughter *Mary*, married *Samuel Rodman*.

ELBERT ELBERTSE STOOTHOOF, of New Amsterdam,
was one of the " Nine men " in 1649, a Magistrate for
eight years, a member of the Convention of 1653 and
1664, and of the first Assembly, held in April, 1664.
In 1670 he is referred to as " Captain." His first wife
was Aeltje Cornelis, the widow of Garret Wolphertsz;
and his second, by whom he had no issue, was Sara
Roeloffse. His daughter, *Helena*, married THOMAS
WILLETT.

HARRISON (*Continued*)

The second son of John Caile and Sarah (Barker)
Harrison, *Thomas Bullitt Harrison*, married MARY
BOYKIN WILLIAMS. Their daughter, KATHARINE
WILLIAMS, married first, Gough Wynn Thompson;
second, Frank Gambrill Baldwin. (See pp. 6-55 for
Williams, Boykin, Miller, Cantey, Chesnut, Cox and
connecting lines.)

KATHARINE WILLIAMS HARRISON BALDWIN,
Member of Chapter I, The Colonial Dames of
America.

IV

BALDWIN

ARMS: *Argent a chevron, ermines between three hazel sprigs vert.*[1]
CREST: *A squirrel sejant or, holding a hazel sprig vert.*
MOTTO: *Je N'Oubliérais Pas.*

The All-Hallows Parish *Register* mentions Henry Baldwin, born in 1700, who died intestate, without inventory or administration account; also his wife Mary, who survived him, and their issue: Mary, Henry, Jr., and Edward, the eldest son. The latter was a planter of All-Hallows Parish, Anne Arundel County, Md.; born 1725, "10th month, 5th day," and died 1759, "8th month and 26th day." He was Grand Juror, 1756. In 1753, "9th month and 20th day," he purchased for £120,

[1] See arms granted Dec. 19, 1662, to Edward Baldwin of Wilton. *Baldwin Gen.*, p. 47 (Tomb of Samuel Baldwin in St. Leonard's).

of Charles Worthington, two hundred and forty-four acres, part of "Howard's First Choice, Howard's and Porter's Range and Howard's Addition." Edward acquired negroes and other personality, 1756 to 1758. He married, 1749, Deborah Weeks, who died, 1757. His will, probated September 10, 1759,[2] devised £70 sterling to each of his two daughters, and the lands herewith mentioned,[3] to his eldest son James and his youngest son:

LIEUTENANT HENRY BALDWIN, born in Anne Arundel County, 1754, and died 1792-93. He served in the American Revolution,[4] five years and five months, until the dissolution of the army, and was a Member of the Society of the Cincinnati from Maryland, and of the South River Club.[5]

He married, 1790, "1st month and 25th day," *Maria Graham,* the daughter of William Garrett and Dinah (Warfield) Woodward, who died in 1835. Issue: Eliza, and *William Henry* (see p. 84). Mrs. Maria Woodward Baldwin married, second, Augustine Gambrill.

WOODWARD

ARMS: *Two bars azure over all three bucks' heads caboshed or.*
CREST: *On a ducal coronet a boar's head couped argent.*
MOTTO: *Virtus semper viret.*

The colonist, William Woodward, a goldsmith of the Guild of London (1700-1774), was the son of Henry Woodward, of Newington, Butts County, Surrey, Eng., and his wife Mary, the daughter of James and Sarah Garrett. William Woodward came to Annapo-

---

2 Fol. 763, No. *Lib. B. T.,* No. 2, 1755-1760.
3 *Md. Arch.,* p. 519.
4 *Ibid,* p. 84.
5 All Hallows Parish *Register.*

lis by 1759, and was in Baltimore by 1770. He inherited a large landed estate in Anne Arundel County under the will of his uncle, Amos Garrett, a wealthy merchant. William Woodward's will, dated 1770, "1st month and 29th day," and probated 1774, "4th month and 5th day," mentions his son William, wife Jane, and daughter Maria Graham Edminston.

His son and executor, William Garrett Woodward, of Baltimore County, Md., was born 1725; will dated July 22, and proved August 28, 1799. He married *Dinah,* the daughter of Alexander and Dinah (Davidge) Warfield, who was born in March, 1742, and died before 1771.[6] Their daughter, *Maria Graham,* married, first, HENRY BALDWIN.

The first mayor of Annapolis, Amos Garrett (1661-1728), was the son of James Garrett, of St. Olave Street, Southwark, London, and his wife, Sarah ——. Amos Garrett is buried in St. Ann's churchyard, Annapolis, having died, according to the inscription on his stone, March 8, 1727-28, aged fifty-six. His will, dated September 4, 1714 (not found and probated till 1742), mentions among others his sister Mary, and her husband, Henry Woodward, the latter being his executor.

WARFIELD

CAPTAIN RICHARD WARFIELD, of England (1640-1703-04), emigrated to America in 1662, and settled west of Crownsville, Anne Arundel County. His estate reached back to "Round Bay on the Severn." The rent rolls show that he held during his life "Warfield," "Warfield Right," "Hope," "Increase," "Warfield Plains," "Warfield Forest," "Warfield Addition," "Brandy," "Warfield's Range." In 1689, then a cap-

6 *Deed of William G. Woodward,* 1771 and 1778.

tain, Richard Warfield signed as a military officer the address to King William. He was returned as first Vestryman of St. Ann's Church in 1696. He began the first westward movement of the early settlements to the unexplored frontier of Howard County in his old age.

He married, 1670, Elinor, heiress of Captain John Browne, of London, Eng., a direct descendant of Sir John Browne. She inherited "Hope" and "Increase," "taken up by Henry Sewall and John Winter, deeded 1673, to Captain John Brown, of London." In 1676 Richard and his wife were witnesses for Chancery contest over the will of Nicholas Wyatt. Issue: John, RICHARD, Alexander, Mary, Benjamin, Rachel, Elinor. Their second son:

CAPTAIN RICHARD WARFIELD, JR. (1676-1755),[7] was one of the first organizers of the public school systems of the county, in 1723. For many years he was "one of his Majestices Justices," and a Vestryman of St. Ann's Church, from 1710 to 1729; for a long time was a Representative of Anne Arundel County and one of the Magistrates; also a member of the House of Burgesses, from 1715 to 1735. He married, 1698, Ruth, the daughter of Thomas Cruchley. Their only son:

ALEXANDER WARFIELD, was born 1701, "1st month and 2nd day." His will, probated 1773, "6th month and 12th day," devises to seven sons and four daughters. He had settled, during his father's lifetime, upon "Warfield Contrivance" and "Wincopin Neck," during which time he extended his surveys along the Frederick turnpike from Cooksville to Lisbon. He inher-

---

[7] "Obituary notice of Captain Richard Warfield, Jr., the *Maryland Gazette*. On Sunday last died of pleurisy, planter of Maryland from town, in the 79th year—formerly representative of his county for many years, and many years one of our Magistrates. A gentleman of upright and unblemished character."

ited the homestead and became a Vestryman of St. Ann's Church.

He married, 1723, "12th month and 3rd day," *Dinah,* the daughter of Major John and Elizabeth (Hudson) Davidge, who was born 1705. Their daughter, *Dinah Warfield,* married William Garrett Woodward.

JOHN BALDWIN-DAVIDGE

In 1658, although a member of the Anglican Church, John Baldwin (1639-40), became a convert to the teachings of George Fox, and "made an open confession of his faith as a Quaker." He came to America in 1661, and settled at the head of the South River, on which, 1660, patents had been issued. Among them was "Baldwin's Addition," which, in his will, probated 1684, "6th month and 16th day," he devises to his daughter Margaret, who married Robert Davidge, whose son, MAJOR JOHN DAVIDGE, married Elizabeth Hudson; their daughter, *Dinah Davidge,* married ALEXANDER WARFIELD.

BALDWIN (*Continued*)

The son of Lieutenant Henry and Maria Graham (Woodward) Baldwin, *William Henry Baldwin,* born September 11, 1792, and died April 6, 1874, was a planter of Anne Arundel County, where he resided; Judge of Orphans' Court of that county; a Captain in the War of 1812, and a Union man in the Civil War.

He married, October 7, 1817, *Jane Maria,* the daughter of Captain Henry and Eleanor (Williams) Woodward, born at Bacon Ridge, Anne Arundel County, Md., November 12, 1798, and died March 7, 1866. Issue: *William Henry, Jr.,* Eliza Ann, Maria

Eleanor, Martha Elizabeth, Richard, Christopher Columbus, Summerfield, Reginald, Springfield, Charles Winterfield, Juliet Catherine.

WOODWARD

This line of Woodwards (see arms, p. 81), was descended from William Woodward, of London, Eng., who died there before 1744, and whose son, Abraham Woodward (1686-1744), settled in Annapolis, Md., prior to 1707. Will probated March 1, 1744.[8] He married, first, December 3, 1707, Elizabeth Finloe, and second, August 25, 1715, Priscilla (1690-1773), the widow of James Orrick and the daughter of Anthony Ruley, Gent.

Their son William, of Anne Arundel County, born December 6, 1716, and died April 16, 1790, married, 1744, *Alice,* the daughter of William, Jr., and Jane (Westhall) Ridgely. Their son:

WILLIAM WOODWARD, JR. (1747-1807), of Annapolis, Md., was drafted October, 1780, and served till December 10, 1781.[9] He married *Jane,* the daughter of Westhall and Sarah (Isaac) Ridgely, who was born 1750, and died April 21, 1817.

Their son, *Captain Henry Woodward,* of Anne Arundel County, Md., was born April 22, 1770, and died October 26, 1822. He was authorized by Governor Wright in 1809 to raise a company called the "Severn Rangers," to assist in protecting Annapolis in the War of 1812. He married, February 14, 1797, Prince George's County, Md., *Eleanor,* of the same county, the widow of Richard Warfield Turner, and the

---

[8] Annapolis Court Records.

[9] *Md. Arch.,* Vol. xviii, fol. 368. His gun is still in possession of descendant James T. Woodward.

daughter of Colonel Thomas and Rachel (Duckett) Williams. She was born September 29, 1774, and died August 15, 1850. Their daughter, *Jane Maria,* married *William Henry Baldwin, Sr.*

RIDGELY

Arms: *Argent on a chevron sable three mullets pierced of the field.*
Crest: *A stag's head erased.*
Motto: *Dum Spiro Spero.*

WILLIAM RIDGELY, of South River (1645-1716), came to the Province of Maryland in 1672. His first survey, 1697, was "Ridgely's Beginning," north side of South River, which in 1710 he and his wife Elizabeth sold to Amos Garrett, the Annapolis merchant. In 1690 he bought of James Finley a portion of "Abbington" at the head of South River, and made it his homestead. William Ridgely's landed estates were, "Ridgely's Beginning," forty acres; "Ridgely's Chance," three hundred and five acres, and "Abbington," two hundred acres. He died intestate.

His son, *William Ridgely, Jr.,* born at "Abbington," 1678, also died intestate, in 1719. He married, 1702, Jane the daughter of George Westhall, of South River. She was born 1682, "7th month and 8th day," and died 1748, the same year in which her will was dated. Upon a twelve-hundred acre tract of her father's estate, Colonel William Burgess laid out the once flourishing town of London. In his will of 1686 he named the tract as once the property of Mr. George Westhall. Upon the marriage of William Ridgely, Jr., his father and mother deeded to him and his wife their homestead tract, "Abbington." The tomb of a descendant of this family remains to this day on the land of the early Ridgelys. The monument has been removed to St. Ann's Church-

yard, Annapolis, Md., and bears the crest and arms of
the family.[10]   Issue: William, *Westhall,* John, Martha, *Alice* and Sarah.

Their son, *Westhall Ridgely,* born 1706 (will dated
1765, and probated in Frederick, Md., 1772), married,
1729-30, Sarah, the daughter of Richard and Sarah
(Pottinger) Isaac, born 1714.   They lived at " Ridgely's Rest," an estate containing two hundred and fifteen
acres, which he mentions in his will.[11]   Their daughter
Jane married *William,* the son of William and Alice
(Ridgely) Woodward.

ISAAC

The Isaacs were in Maryland by 1670, and deeds
and land records always mention them as " Gentlemen and Planters."   They intermarried with many of
the best old families.   Richard Isaac appears in the
records of Prince George's County.   Joseph Isaac was
a planter of Calvert County, and died in 1688.   He
married Margaret ——.

Their son, Richard Isaac, Gent., planter (1679-1759),
was a Vestryman of St. Ann's Parish, a Justice of the
Peace in 1753, and owned an estate in Prince George's
County.[12]   He married Sarah, the daughter of John
Pottinger, of England (who came to Annapolis in
1665), and his wife, Mary Beale, who was born at Col-
lington, Prince George's County.   Issue: Sarah, Jo-
seph, Richard, Mary, Rachel, Kezia, Drucilla, and
Jemima.   Their daughter Sarah married *Westhall
Ridgely.*

10 Riley's *Ye Ancient City,* 1649-1887, p. 19.
11 Lib. A. No. 1, Fol. 428.
12 Devised to son-in-law, Westhall Ridgely.

WILLIAMS

ARMS: *Argent a chevron between three boars' heads couped gules.*
CREST: *A boar's head couped argent pierced with an arrow.*
MOTTO: *Vincit qui patitur.*

The colonist, Thomas Williams, obtained a grant of six hundred acres 1664, "1st month and 7th day," for importing twelve persons in 1660.[13]

His son, Baruch Williams, of Calvert County, Md. (1665-1695), married, 1690, Eleanor Hilliary (1672-1724).

The will of their son, Thomas Williams (1693-1749), who married Eleanor ——, was probated in Prince George's County, Md.

His son, Thomas Williams, Jr. (1717-1770), was Justice of Prince George's Court, from 1752 to 1770. The inventory of his estate was filed 1770, "3d month and 20th day," and £2,221 were later distributed to his family. He married, March 3, 1744, *Cave,* the daughter of Francis and Margaret (Sprigg) King, who was born 1722. Issue, nine children.

COLONEL THOMAS WILLIAMS (1748-1785), their son, died in Prince George's County intestate. He was appointed Clerk to the Commission of Observation of Prince George's County, 1775; commissioned Major of the 25th Battalion of the same county, 1776; made Lieutenant-Colonel, 1777, and Colonel, 1778. His regiment fought at the battle of Germantown and took part in other battles of the Revolution. He was commissioned Justice 1777, also 1778 and 1779, in which latter year he was commissioned High Sheriff of Prince George's County.[14]

---

13 *Lib.* vii, 478, Annapolis.
14 *Md. Arch.,* Vol. ii, pp. 38, 260, 262; xvi, p. 532; Vols. xi, xvi, xviii, etc.; Vol. xxi, p. 242.

He married, 1771, Rachel, born 1749, the daughter
of Richard Duckett, Jr. Issue, four children.
Their daughter *Eleanor* married, first, Richard Warfield Turner; second, *Captain Henry Woodward.*

DUCKETT

The earliest of this family in Maryland was Richard
Duckett (1675, inventory 1754), who married, 1699,
Charity, the daughter of John and Anne (Cheney)
Jacob,[15] of South River, Anne Arundel County. Issue:
Mary, Elizabeth, Charity, John, Richard, Anne, Susan-
nah, Jacob, Margaret and Rachel, twins, and Sarah.

Their son, Richard Duckett II., whose estate was distributed in 1790 by son Isaac, married, first, November
13, 1729, Mary, daughter of John and Eleanor
(Sprigg) Nuthall; married, second, May 2, 1735, Elizabeth Williams. Issue, first wife:

Richard Jacob.

Issue, second wife:

Thomas.

Baruch.

Jacob.

Isaac.

Martha, married ―― Hall.

Anne, married ―― Hall.

Rachel, married THOMAS WILLIAMS.

Eleanor, married ―― Lyles.

SPRIGG

ARMS: *Chequy, or and azure a fesse ermine.*
CREST: *A laurel branch vert.*

LIEUTENANT THOMAS SPRIGG, Gent. (1630-1704),

15 John Jacob (1631-1726), married 1675, Anne Cheney (1660-1730).
All Hallows Parish Records.

was the first of the Sprigg family to settle in Calvert
and Prince George's Counties. He came from England, and in 1651 his residence was Northampton
County, western shore of Virginia, and there he signed
the submission to Parliament. He received a grant of
one thousand acres in Maryland from Lord Baltimore.
"Northampton," the old Manor House, encircled by a
plantation of eight hundred acres, the seat in America
of the Sprigg family, was built by him. A full length
portrait, which is still in possession of the descendants,
represents a handsome man in full court costume,while
the *Archives* of Maryland give abundant proof that the
original was a gentleman of official distinction and social
importance. The property was bought and is now
owned by the Fairfax family, of which Albert Kirby
Fairfax, twelfth Baron Fairfax of Cameron, is the
head. The portrait of Thomas Sprigg, the colonist,
hangs upon the wall. His name occurs among those in
the Province of Maryland "to sign the address to King
William III., congratulating him upon the escape from
conspiracy.[16] He fought against the Nanticoke Indians.[17] As early as 1661 he was Commissioner for
Calvert County,[18] and Justice,[19] 1668, 1669, 1674; Presiding Justice 1674; Sheriff 1668,[20] and High Sheriff
later. He was one of the first five gentlemen to be
made Justice and Gentleman Justice of Peace of
Prince George's County.

He married, 1667, *Elinor* (1648-1671), the daughter
of John and Elizabeth (Bacon) Nuthall. His will was
made May 9, and probated December 29, 1704. The
executor was his son Thomas. Issue:

THOMAS, JR.

16 *Md. Arch.*   18 *Ibid,* Vol. iii, p. 424.
17 *Ibid,* Vol. vii, p. 194.   19 *Ibid,* Vol. v, pp. 41, 61.
20 *Ibid,* Vol. xv, p. 37. *Ibid,* Vol. viii, pp. 490, 491, 493, 520.

Elinor, married Henry Wright.

Martha, married Thomas Prater.

Olivia, married —— Nuthall.

Elizabeth, married —— Wade.

Ann, married Philip Gittings.

Mary, married Thomas Stockett.

LIEUTENANT-COLONEL THOMAS SPRIGG, the eldest son, who received the estate "Northampton," was born in Calvert County, Md., 1668, and died in Prince George's County 1736. Like his father, he was in close touch with the Provincial Government. He was one of a committee composed of members of the Honorable Council, Justices of the Provincial Court, and Gentlemen of the Grand Jury, who were sent in 1697 to treat with the Emperor of the Piscataway Indians in Virginia. No will of Thomas Sprigg, Jr., has been found, but the land office at Annapolis shows that the inventory of his personal effects was filed May 28, 1736. He married Margaret Osborne, who died 1739. The inventory of Thomas Sprigg names "Mrs. Margery Sprigg" as administratrix. It was approved by Osborne and Edward Sprigg as nearest of kin, and about 1740 the inventory of Mrs. Margery Sprigg's estate was filed. The Osborne[21] name has long been handed down in the Sprigg family. Issue:

John.

Mary, married Jeremiah Belt.

Priscilla.

Edward, married Elizabeth Pile.

Margaret.

Osborne, married Rachel Belt.

The fourth child, *Margaret,* married, September 30,

21 Arms of the Osbornes of Kelmarsh and Doddington, Northamptonshire, are *Quarterly erm, an az, over all a cross engraved.*

1717, Francis King, and their daughter *Cave* married THOMAS WILLIAMS.

NUTHALL

JOHN NUTHALL, ESQ., of London and "North Hampton" (1620-1667), removed to St. Mary's County and bought there "Cross Manor," consisting of two thousand acres, in 1661; also, "St. Elizabeth's Manor," an estate of two thousand acres. He was a licensed Indian trader and a Justice of St. Mary's, 1663 to 1667.

He married, 1645, Elizabeth Bacon. In 1668, the Council ordered that the personal estate of John Nuthall, who died intestate, be divided among his three children, John, James and *Eleanor,* who married, 1667, THOMAS SPRIGG.

BALDWIN (*Continued*)

The son of William Henry and Jane Maria (Woodward) Baldwin, *William Henry Baldwin, Jr.,* was born April 17, 1821, and died October 20, 1902.

He married, November 10, 1859, *Mary Peckham,* daughter of Samuel and Mary (Peckham) Rodman, of South Kingston, R. I. She was born November 12, 1838. Issue: SARAH RODMAN and MARIA WOODWARD BALDWIN.

The latter married, November 27, 1900, Samuel McClintock, the son of Rev. Samuel McClintock and Matilda (Green) Hamill, born in Lawrenceville, N. J., March 27, 1858, died in Schenectady, N. Y., July 27, 1907. Issue:

Mary Baldwin, born November 29, 1901.

JOHN GREENE

THE HENRY BULL HOUSE

THE RODMAN MANSION HOUSE AT SOUTH KENSINGTON, R. I.

Matilda Baldwin, born October 30, 1902, died Novem-
1, 1902.

Samuel McClintock, born March 6, 1906.

RODMAN

ARMS: *Gules, a chevron argent between four cushions ermine, tas-
selled or* 22

CREST: *Out of a mural coronet or, a horse's head argent, maned or.*

MOTTO: *Garde la foy.*

The Rodmans were originally of Redman in Cumberland, Eng., now called Redmaine, formerly a joint
township with Isel-Radman, Redeman, Rodman, Red-
mund, Redmayn, Rodmund. All are variations of the
same name. The Redmans or Rodmans, obtained
Leven in Westmoreland (temp, Henry II.), and made
it their principal residence.

These same arms, granted in 1595, are now used by
the Rodman family of the United States of America,

22 *His. Arms and Gen. Mem. of the Family of Ducket from the Norman Conquest to the Present Time.* By Sir G. F. Ducket, Bart.

and were taken from an old seal ring belonging to Thomas Rodman, the first of the name to go to Newport, R. I. This seal was inherited by a great-great-grandson, Thomas Rodman.

One of this family, John Rodman (sometimes called Redman), of the north of England, was in good circumstances, well educated and a religious man. Although a member of the Anglican Church, he became a convert to the teachings of George Fox. He went to Ireland to dwell near his countryman and lifelong friend, William Edmundson. When about forty years of age (his oldest son being fifteen), John Rodman sailed for the Island of Barbadoes.[23] There he died in 1686. By his will he devised a plantation in the Parish of Christ Church in the Barbadoes, to his two sons, Thomas and John, "to dispose of as they think fit" after the death of his wife, Elizabeth. To his daughters, Anne Swayt and Katherine Brandreth, he gives land and negroes. His will was proved by Governor Edwin Stead and he was buried in Christ Church burying-ground.

His son, Dr. Thomas Rodman, a Quaker, was born December 26, 1640, and died January 11, 1728. He went to Newport in 1675 with William Edmundson, then on a religious visit to the Barbadoes, who, in his journal, says: "Thomas Redman, a Friend and Doctor, went with me." Thomas Rodman was an "eminent physician and surgeon," a prominent member of the Society of Friends, and a clerk of the Monthly, Quarterly and Yearly Meetings of Rhode Island for thirty years. He was also the first clerk of the New England Yearly Meeting, which position he held until 1718. He built the house at the corner of Thomas

[23] *Notes on Rodman Genealogy*, by Wm. W. Rodman.

and Ann Streets (now Touro). Dr. Thomas Rodman
bought property in Burlington, Hunterdon, and
Gloucester counties, N. J.; a grandson, Thomas, held
a portion of this as late as the time of the Revolution,
1776-83. He is buried in the Clifton Burying-Ground,
Newport, R. I.

His first wife died in the Barbadoes; his second wife,
Patience, the widow of Robert Malines, and the daughter of Peter and Ann (Coggeshall) Easton, was born
in 1655, "11th month, 20th day," and died 1690 or
1691 (as Thomas Rodman married Hannah Clarke in
the latter year).

Their son, *Dr. Thomas Rodman, Jr.* (1683-1775),
was a physician and surgeon, and moved to South Kingston, R. I., where he built the old Rodman mansion
house. September 20, 1706, he married *Katherine,*
the daughter of Thomas and Mary (Griffin) Fry, of
Newport, born December 23, 1683, and died May 4,
1740.

Their son, *Samuel Rodman,* was born March 22, 1716,
and died in 1776. His plantation, "Romanda," in
South Kingston, contained a thousand acres; he had a
large number of slaves, all of whom were freed at his
death. He and his wife, who was Penelope Halloway,
of Westerly, R. I., belonged to the Society of Friends
and were buried in South Kingston.

Their son, *Robert Rodman,* born November 28, 1745,
in the old Rodman mansion house (still standing), and
died January, 1806, married, July, 1768, Margaret,
the daughter of Daniel and Renewed (Smith) Carpenter; born September 1, 1749, and died December
13, 1800.

Their son, *Robert Rodman II.,* born May 18, 1774,
and died April 1, 1838, married, July, 1799, *Elizabeth,*

the daughter of Stephen and Elizabeth (Carpenter) Hazard, born in 1773, and died May 6, 1870.

Their son, *Samuel Rodman,* was born May 3, 1800, and died May 9, 1882. From his youth he was engaged in the manufacture of woolen goods. An anti-slavery Whig, representing his town many terms in the General Assembly, he built the village, which he named Rocky Brook. He married, July 15, 1821, *Mary,* the daughter of Benjamin Taylor and Abigail (Oatley) Peckham, who was born September 25, 1803, and died February 16, 1853. Their daughter, *Mary Peckham,* married *William Henry Baldwin, Jr.*

FRY

THOMAS FRY, born in Newport, R. I., 1632, and died June 11, 1704, was buried in the Newport cemetery. He was a Freeman in Newport, 1669, and served as General-Sergeant a number of years. October 31, 1677, with forty-seven others, he was granted five thousand acres to be called East Greenwich. He represented East Greenwich as Deputy, 1684 to 1690, but his residence there was only temporary. He was on the Grand Jury, 1687.

He married Mary Griffin, who was born 1649, and died March 12, 1717. Their daughter *Katherine* married *Dr. Thomas Rodman, Jr.*

EASTON

GOVERNOR NICHOLAS EASTON, was born in Lymington, Herts County, Eng., 1593, and died August 15, 1675, in Newport, R. I. He embarked at Southampton for New England, with his sons, Peter and John, March 25, 1634. His first tarrying place was at Ipswich, Mass., September 3, 1634. He was chosen overseer of the powder, shot, etc., in Newbury, Mass., 1635, and November 20, 1637, he and others were warned to deliver up all guns, pistols, swords, shot, etc., because "The opinions and revelations of Mr. Wheelwright and Mrs. Hutchinson have seduced and led into dangerous errors many of the people here in New England." He was in Hampton, N. H., 1638, and in Portsmouth, R. I., the same year, among the inhabitants admitted to the Island of Aquidneck, May 20 1638, Governor Winthrop writes:

"Those who were gone to Aquiday fell into new errors daily. One, Nicholas Easton, taught that gifts and graces were the Antichrist mentioned (in) Thes. and that which withheld, &c. was the preaching of the law, and that every one of the elect had the Holy Ghost, and also the devil indwelling."

April 28, 1639, he and eight others signed the following compact preparatory to the settlement of Newport:

"It is agreed by us whose hands are under written, to propagate a plantation in the midst of the Island or elsewhere, and to engage ourselves to bear equal charge, answerable to our strength and estates in common; and that our determination shall be by major choices of Judge and Elders, the Judge to have double voice."

The judge was William Coddington, and Nicholas Easton signed as one of the elders. November 25, 1639, he and John Clarke were appointed to inform Mr. Vane by writing of the state of things here, and desire him to treat about obtaining a patent of the island from his majesty, and likewise to write to Mr. Thomas Burwood, brother to Mr. Easton, concerning the same thing.

A Freeman, March 26, 1641, Nicholas Easton[24] was Assistant in the years 1640, 1642 to 1644, and 1653;

[24] *R. I. Col. Recs.,* Vol. i.

President 1650 to 1651, and 1654. May 18, 1653, he and seven others were appointed a committee "for ripening matters that concern Long Island"; in the case concerning the Dutch, 1660; Commissioner 1664. He was named in the Royal Charter of King Charles II., 1663; Deputy 1665 to 1666; Deputy-Governor 1666 to 1668, and 1670 to 1671; and Governor 1672, 1673 and 1674.

He married first, in England, name of wife unknown; second, 1638, Christiana Beecher, the widow of Thomas Beecher and the daughter of —— Barker; third, March 2, 1671, Ann Clayton (who afterward married second, Henry Bull). His son:

PETER EASTON, born in England 1622, and died February 12, 1694, was Deputy eight years, between 1666 and 1681; also Attorney-General three years, 1674, 1675, 1676. He married, November 15, 1643, *Ann,* daughter of Governor John and Mary Coggeshall. Their daughter *Patience,* the widow of Robert Malines, married Thomas Rodman, Sr.

CARPENTER

ARMS: *Argent a greyhound passant a chief sable.*
CREST: *A greyhound's head erased per fesse sable and argent.*

In 1576 William Carpenter was born, at Harwell, Berkshire, England, and came to Weymouth, in New England, 1638.

One of the thirteen original Proprietors of Providence Plantation, William Carpenter signed the agreement of 1640 for a form of government. He was Commissioner to the Court of Commissioners four years, 1658, 1660, 1662, 1663; Deputy five years, 1664, 1665, 1675, 1676, 1679; Assistant eight years, 1665 to 1672.

ABIAH CARPENTER, born April 9, 1643, died 1703, was of Rehoboth, Mass., and Warwick, R. I. In October, 1652, his father bought land in Warwick of Benedict Arnold, upon which Abiah subsequently settled. April 1, 1669, he was living in Warwick, and was Deputy, 1682, and on the Grand Jury, 1687.

His son, *Solomon Carpenter,* (1678-1750), was living in "Kings Towne" May, 1705, when he exchanged lands with Ephraim Bull. His will was proved October 8, 1750. He married, March 18, 1703, *Elizabeth,* the daughter of Samuel and Elizabeth (Jenckes) Tefft; she died in 1750.

Their son, *Daniel Carpenter,* was born December 28, 1712, and married, April, 29, 1733, Renewed, the daughter of Ephraim and Margaret Smith.

Their daughter, *Margaret Carpenter,* married *Robert Rodman, Sr.,* whose son, *Robert Rodman,* married *Elizabeth Hazard.*

JENCKES

JOSEPH JENCKES, born 1632, and died January 4, 1717, was of Lynn, Mass., also of Providence R. I., where he bought land and also received a grant October 10, 1671. A Freeman 1677, he was a Deputy, 1679 to 1680, and 1691, and Assistant thirteen years in the period from 1680 to 1698. He was chosen by the Assembly to run the eastern line of the Colony, July 2, 1695. He married Esther, the daughter of William and Elizabeth Ballard.

Their daughter, *Elizabeth,* (1658-1740), married Samuel, son of John and Mary Tefft of Boston, whose daughter, *Elizabeth,* married *Solomon Carpenter.*

HAZARD

ARMS: *Azure two bars argent on a chief or three escallops gules.*
CREST: *An escallop gules.*
MOTTO: *Sinceritus.*

THOMAS HAZARD, (1610-1680), the progenitor of the Hazard family in the United States, is first recorded in Boston, Mass., 1635, where he was admitted Freeman, March 25, 1638.   Two years later he was Freeman of Portsmouth, R. I.   April 28, 1639, he signed, with eight others, the compact which was drawn up preparatory to the settlement of Newport, R. I.   He married first, Martha ——, who died 1669, and second, Martha, (widow of Thomas Sheriff), who died 1691.   His son:

ROBERT HAZARD, (1635-1710), was admitted Freeman of Portsmouth, R. I., in 1665.   He sold all his interest in Canonicut (now called Jamestown) and Dutch Island in Narragansett Bay, to John Roome of Portsmouth, 1658.   The Court of Plymouth in 1667 ordered, with reference to a controversy between the English and the Indians about bounds, that if Robert Hazard could be secured, he should run the lines.   He was Juryman in 1670.

He bought, 1671, five hundred acres of land in Kingston, of the Pettaquamscutt purchasers.   He built his house in Moorsfield, South Kingston.   In 1695 he gave to his son George the larger part of the Pettaquamscutt purchase, and in 1710 sold the remaining part of the farm, with the manor-house, to his son Robert, for £300, current money, who gave it by will to his son Robert, three Roberts thus owning and occupying the place in succession.   Previous to the deed of gift to George, he had given his son Stephen rights and interest in land belonging to Point Judith Neck, "being ye seventh part of ye same, excepting one hundred acres, so-called

Boston Neck." His son, Jeremiah, also received two hundred acres in Tiverton. These deeds to his sons show the ownership of more than a thousand acres of land. He served the government on various committees and was Commissioner to the Court of Commissioners, 1662-1670, and Deputy five years,[25] 1664, 1665, 1667, 1670, 1671. Robert Hazard married *Mary,* daughter of Thomas and Ann Brownell.[26] In an old copy of the Boston *Gazette,* dated February 12, 1739, is the following:

"Newport, February 9th, Mrs. Mary Hazard, widow of Mr. Robert Hazard of South Kingston, and Grandmother to the deceased George Hazard, Esq., late Deputy-Governor of Rhode Island departed this life 28th day of January last, in the Hundredth year of her age."

STEPHEN HAZARD, their son, born 1660, and died September 20, 1727, was admitted Freeman in the Colony 1696, but was taxed in 1687 at Kingston. He was Deputy five years between 1702 and 1715, and Assistant for five years between 1707 and 1722; was Justice of the Peace for Kingston 1707, which office gave him the title of Judge, and he is thus known by his descendants. Very early in the century he saw the possibilities for water power in North Kingston, and bought large tracts of land so situated as to control the power near Bissell's Mills. This in addition to the land received from his father, about three hundred acres, made him a large land owner. Stephen Hazard, married Elizabeth, daughter of Rouse and Mary Helme. She was born 1671, and died 1727. Stephen Hazard gave to his sons Stephen and Robert, three

25 *R. I. Col. Recs.,* Vols. i and ii.
26 See line of George, one of their sons, p. 111.

hundred acres, by his will; Samuel, two hundred acres, and Thomas, three hundred acres, in North Kingston.

His son, *Thomas Hazard,* was born July 28, 1707, and died 1741; admitted Freeman 1730; in 1741 he moved to South Kingston. He married, February 22, 1727, *Hannah,* the daughter of Samuel and Hannah (Carr) Slocum, born April 5, 1710, and died January 24, 1737.

Their son, *Stephen Hazard,* was born May 10, 1730; died October 24, 1804. He adhered to the cause of the Crown during the war of the Revolution.

He married, 1760, *Elizabeth,* daughter of Daniel and Renewed (Smith) Carpenter. Their daughter, *Elizabeth,* married *Robert Rodman, II.*

BROWNELL

THOMAS BROWNELL of Portsmouth, R. I., was a Freeman 1665; a Commissioner 1661, 1662 and 1663, and a Deputy 1664. His wife was Ann ——. Their daughter, *Mary,* married ROBERT HAZARD.

SLOCUM

One of the purchasers of the territory which was incorporated March 3, 1639, under the name of Taunton, in New Plymouth, Anthony Slocum, had married before he left England —— Harvey, sister of William Harvey. Giles Slocum[27] was born in Somersetshire, England, and died in Portsmouth, R. I., 1682. He married Joan ——, who died June, 1679. Their son:

EBENEZER SLOCUM,[28] born March 25, 1650, and died 1715, married *Mary,* daughter of Edward and

[27] J. O. Austin.
[28] Newport Hist. Soc.

Elizabeth (Mott) Thurston, born February 1, 1657, and died November 16, 1752. Their son:

SAMUEL SLOCUM, born March 2, 1684, and died in 1741, married January, 1708, *Hannah,* daughter of Edward and Hannah (Stanton) Carr, who was born October 13, 1691. (She married second, Samuel Watson). Their daughter, *Hannah,* married THOMAS HAZARD.

THURSTON-MOTT

EDWARD THURSTON, born 1617, in England, and died at Newport, R. I., March 1, 1707, was a Freeman 1655, Deputy for Newport and Governor's Assistant, holding each office several years, in the period between 1667 and 1691. He signed an address, with others, from the Quakers of Rhode Island to the King, on August 26, 1686. His marriage to Elizabeth, daughter of Adam Mott, took place in June, 1647. She was born 1629, in Newport, R. I., and died September 2, 1694. Adam Mott was born in Cambridge, Eng., 1596, and his will was dated and proved 1661. He was a sailor and came as a passenger in the ship *Defense,* July 2, 1635. Became a Freeman and a member of the First Church in Roxbury, and then removed to Hingham, where he had a grant of land. In 1638 he was in Portsmouth, R. I., and a Freeman there 1641. He was clerk of the Military Company 1642. *Mary,* daughter of Edward and Elizabeth (Mott) Thurston, married EBENEZER SLOCUM.

CARR

The Carr coat of arms is a copy of the original which was brought to this country by George Carr 1620, and

has been handed down in his line. It bears the partly
obliterated signature of one of the Carrs of the house of
Somerset. Its exact counterpart was brought over by
William Carr, a brother of George, 1621, and has come
down through his line to the present time.[29]

In the year 1635 two orphan boys came to their uncle,
William Carr, who lived at Bristol, R. I., and afterwards at Newport. They were Robert and CALEB
CARR, minors, the sons of Benjamin and Martha
(Hardington) Carr of London, Eng., deceased. They
sailed on the ship *Elizabeth Ann* commanded by Captain Roger Cooper, May 9, 1635.

GOVERNOR CALEB CARR, second son of Benjamin and
Martha Carr of London, Eng., was born 1624, and died
December 17, 1695, by drowning; will proved January
6, 1696. He lived in Newport, R. I., and was Freeman 1655; Commissioner 1654, 1658, 1659, 1660, 1661,
1662; General Treasurer, 1661, 1662; Deputy, twelve
years between 1664 and 1690; Assistant ten years between 1679 and 1691; Justice of General Quarter Session and Inferior Court of Common Pleas; Governor
from May, 1695, to December 17, 1695. He was
buried with his first wife in the family burial-ground.
He married first, Mercy Vaughn, who was born 1631,
and died September 21, 1675. Their son:

EDWARD CARR, was born 1667, and died October
14, 1711. He lived in Jamestown and was a Freeman 1698, and a Deputy from 1699 to 1702, and
for five years afterward. He was on a committee to
audit the accounts of the Colony. His will, dated
December 22, 1711, was proved January 22, 1712.
Edward Carr married October 6, 1686, *Hannah*,
daughter of John and Mary (Harndel) Stanton. She

29 *Carr Family Records.*

was born November 7, 1670. Their daughter, *Hannah*, married SAMUEL SLOCUM.

STANTON

ROBERT STANTON, born 1599, and died August 29, 1672, was admitted, with others, inhabitants of the Island of Aquidneck, 1638. He was a Freeman of Newport, March 16, 1641; Sergeant Junior 1642; Sergeant 1644; Freeman 1655; Deputy 1670, and Juryman 1671. He married Avis Almy.

JOHN STANTON, their son, born August, 1645, and died October 3, 1713, lived in Newport. He was Freeman 1666, and Deputy 1696. He married first, Mary, daughter of John Harndel, and their daughter *Hannah* married EDWARD CARR.

PECKHAM

" The family from which the colonist, John Peckham came, have borne the same arms in Kent and Sussex Counties from the time of Archbishop John Peckham of Canterbury, 13th century, to the present time." [30] James Peckham, Esq., "dyed Anno. 1500. Buried at Wretham in Kent where is ye tombstone." [31] He married Margaret, daughter of Thomas Burgoine of Portiper in Kent. Their son, James, of Galden in Wretham in Kent, "dyed 1532; buried at Wretham." He married Anne, daughter of Thomas Ifley. Two John Peckhams were ancestors of Edward Peckham, Lord of the Manor of East Hampnett in Sussex near Chichester, who married Grace Lamburne of Berkshire. Their son, Henry, of the same Manor, married

[30] *The Herald's College Records* concerning the confirming of the original grant of Arms borne by the Peckhams of Nyton, which was the estate last owned by the Peckhams of Kent and Sussex.

[31] From Monumental Brass.

Elizabeth, daughter of Robert Badger of Winchester. The second son of this marriage, John, Captain to the Earl of Hertford, was baptized April 8, 1595. John's elder brother, Henry, was a member of Parliament for Chichester from 1654 to 1659 and was in possession of the Manor of East Hampnett in 1634. At Tunbridge are the ruins of the Castle of Tunbridge of which Hugo de Peckham was constable in 1199. At Wartham in St. George's Church are several memorial brasses to Peckhams. At Uckfield lives Harry J. Peckham, who has the portraits of the nieces of John Peckham, the colonist,—Mary and Elizabeth—in very exaggerated ruffs, and in a beautiful state of preservation, painted by the Dutch artist, Daniel Myrtens, in 1570. At Chichester, in the Council Chamber, is a portrait of Sir Thomas Peckham (who built the Peckham house at Chichester) by Romney, and one of his son, Robert, (who died in 1742, aged 25), by Holbein.

Abstracts of wills and chancery suits in Suffolk County, Eng., led to the identification of John Peckham, the colonist, as belonging to the Sussex family. He was among the first settlers of the Island of Aquidneck, in 1638. There, on May 20, 1638, his name is on a list of those who were admitted as inhabitants of Newport. In 1640, the bounds of his land, thirty-six acres, were established. March 16, 1641, he was admitted a Freeman and he was one of the ten male members of the First Baptist Church of Newport, in full communion, 1648. Soon after the first settlement of Rhode Island the Peckhams bought a tract of land one mile square at Little Compton, on which they built a house in 1640, which stood two hundred years, and in which six generations of Peckhams were born. Their purchases also extended into Dartmouth, Mass., to the

Acushnet River, where a part of the city of New Bedford now stands. John Peckham married Mary Clarke, born 1607.

Their son, John Peckham II, (1645-1712), lived on the Peckham estate at Little Compton and was one of the original proprietors of East Greenwich, R. I. He married, 1667, Sarah Newport.

Their son, Benjamin Peckham, was born in Newport June 9, 1684; will recorded June 21, 1769. He married 1708, *Mary,* the daughter of Caleb and Phillippa (Greene) Carr and the grand-daughter of GOVERNOR JOHN GREENE; she was born 1687. Issue among others:

BENJAMIN PECKHAM, JR., born March 22, 1715, and died February 27, 1792, settled at South Kingston, R. I., and had extensive landed estates which he cultivated in a large way. He was town clerk from 1736 to 1743; member of the Legislature 1768; on a Committee of Correspondence, 1774, and Moderator of the South Kingston Convention 1784. He married, June 2, 1737, *Mary,* the daughter of Lieutenant-Governor George and Sarah (Carder) Hazard, born July 16, 1722, and died April, 1805. Issue, seven children recorded; a daughter, Mary, married into the Perry family from which sprang Commodore Oliver Hazard Perry.

A son, *George Hazard Peckham,* named for his maternal grandfather, was born April 14, 1739 and died November 29, 1799; married January 7, 1763, *Sarah,* the daughter of Robert and Rebecca (Coggeshall) Taylor; she was born 1747, and died June 16, 1795.

Their son, *Benjamin Taylor Peckham,* was born October 27, 1773, and died December 16, 1853; married

January 28, 1799, *Abigail,* the daughter of Benedict and Elizabeth (Ladd) Oatley, who was born July 7, 1767, and died November 9, 1821. *Abigail Oatley* was descended from several families of colonial importance, among them the Churches, Bulls, and Warrens.

Their daughter, *Mary Peckham,* married *Samuel Rodman.*

GREENE

ARMS: *Azure, three bucks trippant or.*
CREST: *A buck's head or.*
MOTTO: *Nec timeo, nec sperno.*

The Arms which were borne by this ancient family are still used by the descendants. In King's Chapel burial ground, Boston, Mass., they are to be found on a family tombstone. Gardiner Greene, (1635-1753), used these arms as a book-plate. There are two crests; the one used by the New England Greenes is a Buck's head erased.

"The family of Greene, originally written 'de la Greene', derive their name from their ancient possessions in Northamptonshire where they were 'seated' " in the time of Edward I. In 1320 Thomas de Greene succeeded to the estates and was Lord of the Manor of Boughton and Norton, afterwards Greene's Norton, from whence branches of the family went out into surrounding counties. One of these branches[32] was " seated " in Dorsetshire in the early days of Henry VIII, "when Robert Greene of Gillingham, from whom an unbroken line of descent is traced, was assessed to that King's subsidy." [33] He had three sons and two daughters. His son Richard, heir to the estate of Bowridge

---

[32] Verified by the similarity of arms recorded in the *Herald's College.*
[33] *Rolls of the Exchequer,* 1545.

Hall, had two children. One, also called Richard, had five sons, of whom:

JOHN GREENE (1597-1658), came from Salisbury County, Wilts, the first of the name in New England. He sailed from Southampton, April 6, 1635, in the ship *James* and reached Boston June 3, 1635, with his wife and seven children. He was a surgeon in Salisbury, Eng., where he married his first wife, Jean Tattersale, November 4, 1619. For a short time John Greene lived at Salem, Mass. August 1, 1637, he (then called of New Providence) was charged with speaking contemptuously of the authorities in Massachusetts and was fined and "enjoined not to come into the jurisdiction of Massachusetts."

From his refuge in Rhode Island, he wrote a letter to the court at Massachusetts charging them "with usurping the power of Christ and the Churches and Men's Consciences," etc. He was one of twelve, to whom Roger Williams deeded land bought of " Canonicus " and " Miantonomie "; also one of the twelve original members of the First Baptist Church. In 1642, John Greene bought land called " Occupassuatuxet " of Miantonomie. This land remained in the family until sold to John Browne, and now is owned by the Browne family. January 12, 1644, John Greene and ten others bought of the Indians for one hundred and forty-four fathoms of Wampum the present town of Warwick. September 12, 1643, he with others of Warwick were ordered to appear at Boston on complaint of some Indians. They all refused to obey, and in consequence, soldiers besieged the settlers in a fortified house, and several men were taken prisoners. All were carried to Boston for trial, except John Greene, who escaped. He was one of the thirteen original proprietors of Provi-

dence Plantations; went as Commissioner to England
in 1644; to the Court of Commissioners from Warwick
for a period of five years, 1652 to 1657, and was Magistrate at the General Court of Trials, 1655 to 1656.
One of his sons:

JOHN GREENE, JR. (1620-1708), was Commissioner
for Warwick to the Court of Commissioners for twelve
years, 1652 to 1663; General Recorder three years,
1652 to 1654; Attorney-General four years, 1657 to
1660; Deputy four years, between 1664 and 1677; Assistant twenty-five years, between 1660 and 1690; Major
for the Main seven years, between 1683 and 1696, and
Deputy-Governor for ten years, 1690 to 1699, which
appears to have been his last public service. He was
one of those named in the Royal Charter granted by
King Charles II., 1663. He was sent on a special mission to England in 1670 with John Clarke; was one of
the council of Governor Sir Edmund Andros, 1686, and
took a leading part in all the important affairs of the
colony, sitting on a council 1676, with Benedict Arnold,
etc.

He married, 1648, Anne or Annis (1627-1709), the
daughter of William and Audrey Almy. Their daughter *Phillippa,* who was born October 7, 1658, and died
after 1708 (another record says 1690), married Caleb,
son of Robert Carr, the immigrant brother of GOVERNOR
CALEB CARR. Robert was a Freeman of Newport, 1641,
and one of the original purchasers of the Island of Canonicut. He gave by will (probated October 4, 1681)
all his land on the Island to his son, Caleb Carr. The
latter's will was probated March 30, 1690, and names
therein his wife "Phillis," four sons and daughter
Mary, who married Benjamin Peckham, Sr.

ALMY

WILLIAM ALMY, the American ancestor of all who bear the name, was born in Belinden Parish, Kent, Eng., 1601. He came to New England with John Winthrop and his associates, but made two journeys back to England before he brought over his wife Audrey and their son Christopher and daughter Annis, in 1635. He lived in Sandwich, 1637, but sold his property there to Edmund Freeman in 1642. He had a grant of land at Portsmouth, R. I., 1644; was a Juryman, 1656; Commissioner, 1656, 1657, 1663; and Foreman of Jury, 1668. He was a member of the Society of Friends, and died in Portsmouth, February 28, 1677, his wife having died earlier. Their daughter *Anne* or *Annis,* married JOHN GREENE, JR.

HAZARD

COLONEL GEORGE HAZARD (1662-1743), a grandson of the American progenitor, THOMAS HAZARD, and the son of Robert and Mary (Brownell) Hazard (see p. 100), was first admitted a Freeman of the Rhode Island Colony in 1696; was Deputy 1703 and 1704, Assistant 1713, and one of a committee appointed by the Assembly to make public roads throughout the colony. In 1719 he was Lieutenant-Colonel of the Militia for the main. Through inheritance and purchase he came into possession of the original Pettaquamscutt purchase of his father, and the manor house in Moorsfield, South Kingston, where he kept a large establishment until his death. In the inventory of his personal estate there are seventeen slaves. He was interested in the first woollen mill of South Kingston, giving land for the same. His wife was *Penelope,* daughter of Caleb and Abigail (Wilbur) Arnold, and they were married in 1688.

She was born August 3, 1669, and died in 1742. Their son:

GEORGE HAZARD, born October 9, 1700, died June 24, 1738, was Freeman, 1721; Deputy, 1729 to 1735; Speaker of the House of Representatives, 1733; Deputy-Governor, 1734, and re-elected four successive years, dying in office. He married *Sarah,* the daughter of James and Mary (Whipple) Carder. Their daughter *Mary* married BENJAMIN PECKHAM, JR.

ARNOLD

GOVERNOR BENEDICT ARNOLD, son of WILLIAM ARNOLD, the colonist (see p. 15), was born December 21, 1615, and died June 10, 1678. He signed the agreement of 1640 for a form of government. Removed to Newport November 19, 1651, and was made Freeman of that town; was a Commissioner, 1654 to 1663; Assistant, 1655 to 1656, 1660 to 1661; President of the four towns, 1657 to 1660, 1662 to 1663, and the first Royal Governor of Rhode Island, 1663 to 1666, 1669 to 1672, and 1677 to 1678. He was on a council with fifteen others, appointed by the General Assembly, to advise with the Assembly. In the will of Benedict Arnold, probated in Newport in 1677, the testator says: " I devise that my body shall be buried near the path leading from my dwelling house to my stone windmill in the town of Newport, and that the lot shall forever be reserved for my kindred." He left the stone windmill to his wife, with lands and mansion house, for life. At Governor Arnold's funeral nearly a thousand persons were present. He married, December 17, 1640, *Damaris,* the daughter of Stukeley Westcott, of Warwick; she died 1678.

Their son, *Caleb Arnold,* was born December 19,

1644, and died February 9, 1719. In 1671 and 1680 he was Deputy. August 24, 1676, was of the court-martial at Newport for the trial of certain Indians charged with being engaged in King Philip's designs. He was at this time called Captain, having served through the Indian war of 1676. In 1684 he was elected Deputy from Portsmouth, but refused to serve on account of his profession (physician), and another was elected in his place. In 1707 he was again elected from Portsmouth, which established his residence in that place. He styled himself "Practitioner of Physic." In old public documents he is called "Doctor." At the time of his death he had considerable landed estate. His father left him one-fourth of all his land in Newport and one hundred and sixty acres in Canonicut to be held until his eldest son was of age, when he should possess it.

His marriage to *Abigail,* the daughter of Samuel and Hannah (Porter) Wilbur, took place June 10, 1666. She died November 17, 1730. Their daughter *Penelope,* to whom in his will he left a silver tankard and ten shillings, married GEORGE HAZARD I.

WESTCOTT

STUKELEY WESTCOTT, died at Portsmouth, R. I., January 12, 1677, aged eighty-five years. He was Freeman at Salem, Mass., 1636; Providence, R. I., 1638; Warwick, 1648, and later at Portsmouth, where he signed the agreement of 1640 for a civil government. He was Commissioner, 1651 to 1653, 1655 and 1660; Surveyor of Highways, 1652 to 1656, and etc.; Assistant, 1653; Freeman, 1655; Deputy, 1671. His daughter *Damaris* married GOVERNOR BENEDICT ARNOLD.

WILBUR-PORTER

SAMUEL WILBUR, died September 29, 1656. He lived in Boston, Mass., Portsmouth, R. I., and later in Taunton. He was Freeman March 4, 1633, and admitted to the church with his wife Ann, December 1, 1633. He went to Rhode Island in consequence of his sympathy with Wheelwright, and was at Portsmouth by 1638. He was clerk of the train-band that year and Constable 1639; was a Freeman again, 1641, and Sergeant, 1644. He returned to Boston, but was again at Portsmouth in 1655. His will was dated at Taunton, April 30, and proved November 1, 1656. His son:

SAMUEL WILBUR, JR., was Freeman of Portsmouth, 1655; Juryman, 1656; Commissioner six years, between 1656 and 1663; Deputy four years, between 1664 and 1670; Assistant, 1665 to 1669, 1677 to 1678. He enlisted in the Troop of Horse, August 10, 1667, and was Captain, 1676. His will was proved November 7, 1679. He married *Hannah,* daughter of John and Margaret Porter, and their daughter *Abigail* married *Caleb Arnold.*

JOHN PORTER, was one of seven purchasers of a large tract of land in Narragansett County, called the "Pettasguansett Purchase." His wife was Margaret Odding, a widow.

CARDER

RICHARD CARDER, of Boston, Mass., Portsmouth and Warwick, R. I., was one of the eighteen original proprietors of Aquidneck, who settled Pocasset (afterwards Portsmouth), in 1638. He was one of the twelve purchasers of Warwick in 1642, and Commissioner to the Court of Commissioners for that place for three years, 1659 to 1663; also Deputy eleven years, 1664 to

1674 inclusive. He died in 1676, and his second wife, Mary ——, in 1691. His son:

JAMES CARDER, born May 2, 1655, and died April 25, 1714, married *Mary,* the daughter of John and Mary (Olney) Whipple, who was born March 4, 1665, and died October, 1721. James Carder was Freeman in 1678; Constable, 1688, and Deputy four years. Their daughter *Sarah* married GOVERNOR GEORGE HAZARD.

WHIPPLE

JOHN WHIPPLE, died May 16, 1685. He was of Dorchester, Mass., and Providence, R. I., and received as a purchaser at Providence, July 27, 1659, where he was Deputy for eight years, between 1666 and 1677. "He was one of those who 'staid and went not away' in King Philip's War." His will was proved May 27, 1685, and he was buried on his own land, with his wife, Sarah —— (1624-1666), whom he married in 1639. Subsequently, their bodies were removed to the north burial-ground. Their son:

JOHN WHIPPLE, JR., was born 1640, and died December 15, 1700. *Mary,* daughter of Thomas and Mary (Small) Olney, was his first wife, and their marriage occurred December 4, 1663. He was Town Treasurer of Providence, 1668; Town Clerk, 1670 to 1672, 1678 and 1681; Deputy six years, between 1670 and 1690, and one of the Town Council four years, between 1674 and 1687. His will being declared void by the Town Council, the estate was divided among the heirs in 1701.

His daughter *Mary* married JAMES CARDER, and their daughter, *Sarah Carder,* married GOVERNOR GEORGE HAZARD.

OLNEY

THOMAS OLNEY (1600-1682), born in St. Albans, Hertford County, Eng., embarked with his family in the ship *Planter* from London, April 2, 1635, bound for New England. His age was called thirty-five, and he had two young children, and a wife, Mary Small, whom he had married in England, born 1605. Thomas Olney was one of the thirteen original proprietors of Providence Plantations, and Town Treasurer from 1638 to 1669, signed the agreement of 1640 for a form of government, and acted as Assistant for nine years, between 1649 and 1667; was Commissioner for Providence to the Court of Commissioners for six years, between 1656 and 1663, and Deputy for four years, between 1665 and 1671. He was one of those named in the Royal Charter granted by King Charles II., in 1663.

His daughter *Mary* married JOHN WHIPPLE, JR., and their granddaughter, *Sarah Carder*, married GOVERNOR GEORGE HAZARD.

TAYLOR

The colonist, Robert Taylor, was a Scotchman, born 1688, and died at Newport, R. I., November 26, 1762. He was associated with Ralph Chapman as master shipwright on what is now known as Commercial Wharf. He represented Jamestown in the General Assembly, 1720. In 1730 he engaged in the West India trade with Daniel Ayrault, Jr. Much of the elegant furniture owned by the Taylors is still to be found in the homes of his descendants.

SARAH RODMAN BALDWIN, a lineal descendant of Robert Taylor through his daughter Sarah, inherited a clock which belonged to the Taylor family. The frame is of teakwood, with Japanese figures in old lacquer work, of which the art of making is said to be lost. The old key handle is of ebony.

Between 1721 and 1747, Robert Taylor bought of Godfrey Malbone a large tract of land on the "Neck" in Newport, comprising a part of the original grant by the town in 1641 to Thomas Braun. This land, called in Taylor's will his "farm," he gave to his sons Nicholas and Joseph. It was rented until about 1827, when a yellow ochre was found there which gave the modern name of "Ochre Point" to the former Taylor's Point. Robert Taylor married first, Patience, the daughter of Oliver and Phoebe (Cook) Arnold, and second, in 1740, Elizabeth, the daughter of John and Elizabeth (Clarke) Stanton, who was born in 1714, and died August 21, 1742; and third, *Rebecca,* daughter of Benjamin and Sarah (Easton) Coggeshall, who was born December 14, 1721, and died April 15, 1782. Robert Taylor's will was dated August 30, 1758. In it he leaves, among other things, £2000 to be put at interest for his fourteen-year-old daughter, *Sarah* (by his third marriage), the principal to be paid on her eighteenth birthday, or at her marriage. She married *George Hazard Peckham.*

COGGESHALL

ARMS: *Argent a cross between four escallops sa.*
CREST: *A stag lodged sable attired or.*
MOTTO: *Nec sperno, nec timeo.*

" The arms [34] here given are taken from a seal affixed to a letter written by John Coggeshall, Secretary of the Colony of Rhode Island (1677). . . . They are

[34] Burke's *Gen. Armory;* Austin's *R. I. Gen. Dict.,* 1886; *Heraldic Journal,* ii, 45; *Newport, R. I., Hist. Mag.*

the same as those used by the family of 'Cockshall,' of
Essex, Eng., the Coggeshalls, of Milton and Bengall,
County Suffolk, Eng., descendants of a younger
brother of Sir John de Coggeshall, of the manor of
Codham, Wethersfield, Essex, knighted by Edward,
the Black Prince, in 1337. The common ancestor, Sir
Thomas de Coggeshall, held the manor of Little Cog-
geshall Hall, Essex County, in the reign of King
Stephen."

JOHN COGGESHALL, the colonist, born 1591, in Essex
County, Eng., died in Newport, November 27, 1647.
He was the son of John Coggeshall, Gent., who was
born July 24, 1576, and his wife Ann of Castile, Hed-
ingham (her will has been found in England, dated
1648), and grandson of John Coggeshall, who died in
England 1600. John, the colonist, with thirty-two
others, signed the oath of allegiance before leaving England. His wife, Mary —— (born 1604, died November 8, 1684), and three children, JOHN, Joshua and
Ann, came with him. They arrived in Boston on the
ship *Lyon,* September 26, 1632. He was admitted
Freeman April 20, 1634; was a member of the First
Church, and afterwards a deacon. One of the original
proprietors of Aquidneck, who settled Pocasset (later
Portsmouth), 1638, he was also one of the three elders
of Aquidneck, and one of the nine who settled Newport,
1639. For four years he acted as Deputy, 1634 to 1639;
Assistant five years, 1640 to 1644, and was President of
the colony under the patent of 1647. He had three
hundred and eighty-nine acres recorded in Newport
by 1640, and was buried on his own land, now Coggeshall Avenue, in his fifty-sixth year. "With his labors
and fortune he had assisted in founding two States.
He had lived to see Rhode Island, the child of his heart,

a corporate power under a Parliamentary charter, and
a regularly organized government of which he stood at
the head. . . ."

MAJOR JOHN COGGESHALL, his son, born in England
1618, and died October 1, 1708, was already beginning
to take an active interest in the colony at the time of
his [35] father's death. Later he became General Treasurer for Portsmouth and Newport two years, 1653 to
1654; General Treasurer for Providence and Warwick,
1654; General Treasurer for four towns nine years,
1664 to 1672; one of those named in the Royal Charter
granted by King Charles II., 1663; Assistant ten years,
between 1663 and 1686; General Recorder four years,
between 1676 and 1692; Major for the Island two
years, 1683 to 1684; and Deputy-Governor three years,
1686, 1689 and 1690. His father left him a portion of
his farm at the southeast of Newport, where he continued to reside until his death. His house with its
stone chimney was standing early in the present century, but was pulled down to give place to a modern
villa. He held a large amount of real estate at the
time of his death. An inventory taken by order of
the court shows him to have owned five hundred and
ten acres of land, a portion of which embraced the
well known "Portsmouth Grove." The point at the
northern part is now known as "Coggeshall Point."

He married, first, June 16, 1647, Elizabeth, daughter of William and Charlotte Baulstone; second, December 2, 1665, *Patience,* daughter of John Throckmorten,
born 1640, died September 7, 1676; and third, Mary
——, who was mentioned in his will. Issue, second
wife, among others:

LIEUTENANT BENJAMIN COGGESHALL, born in New-

35 *R. I. Hist. Mag.,* Vol. v, No. 2.

port, July 27, 1672, and died in East Greenwich, April 16, 1739, was admitted Freeman for Newport 1707; and was Deputy in the General Assembly, as such being called "Lieutenant."

He married, December 22, 1709, *Sarah,* daughter of James and Miriam (Allen) Easton; she was born September 29, 1689, and died 1726. *Rebecca,* their fourth child, married Robert Taylor, whose daughter *Sarah* married *George Hazard Peckham.*

THROCKMORTEN

JOHN THROCKMORTEN, embarked at Bristol, Eng., in the ship *Lyon,* and arrived at Boston, Mass., February 5, 1631, soon going to Salem. His wife's name is unknown. May 18, 1631, he was Freeman. He was in Providence, R. I., October 8, 1638, where he was Moderator, 1652; Freeman, 1655; and Deputy between 1664 and 1675, for ten years. He took the oath of allegiance May 31, 1666; was on the town council, 1667, and Town Treasurer, 1677. He died in Middleton, R. I., where he is buried, and where some of his children lived, in 1687. His daughter *Patience* married MAJOR JOHN COGGESHALL.

EASTON

GOVERNOR JOHN EASTON, born 1624, and died December 12, 1705, was Attorney-General for Portsmouth and Newport, R. I., 1653 and 1654; Commissioner eight years, from 1654 to 1663; Freeman, 1655; Attorney-General for the colony sixteen years, between 1656 and 1674; deputy four years, between 1665 and 1672; Assistant during the period from 1666 to 1690; Deputy-Governor, 1674 to 1676, inclusive; Governor, 1690 to and including 1695. He was buried in the

Coddington Burial Ground. He married, first, January 4, 1661, Mehitable, the daughter of Peter Gaunt. Their son, *James Easton,* born February 23, 1662, and died March 23, 1697, married Miriam, the daughter of Mathew and Sarah (Kirby) Allen. Their daughter *Sarah* married BENJAMIN COGGESHALL.

GRAY

EDWARD GRAY, with his brother Thomas, came to Plymouth, Mass., in 1643. His baptism, April 15, 1623, is recorded in Stapleford, Tawney, Eng. He was Freeman May 29, 1670; on the Grand Jury, 1671; Deputy four years, 1676 to 1679, inclusive. The oldest stone on Burial Hill reads as follows:

"Here lyeth ye body of Edward Gray, Gent, aged about 52 years, and departed this life ye last of June, 1681."

This stone is roughly made of a common blue native slate, rudely cut and carved. It does not give his age in harmony with the recorded baptismal date.

He married, second, Dorothy, the daughter of Thomas and Ann Lettice.

Their son, *Samuel Gray,* died March 23, 1712; will dated March 20, and proved April 7, 1712. He married, July 13, 1699, *Deborah,* the daughter of Joseph and Mary (Tucker) Church. Their daughter *Lydia* married *Joseph,* the son of William and Elizabeth (Tompkins) Ladd.

CHURCH

JOSEPH CHURCH, was born 1638, died March 5, will proved March 11, 1711; the son of Richard and Elizabeth (Warren) Church, who were also the parents of the Indian fighter, Colonel Benjamin Church. Richard was a Sergeant in the Pequod War. Joseph was on the Grand Jury at Little Compton, R. I., and he took the oath of fidelity June 1, 1680; was Freeman, June 6, 1682; Selectman, 1683 to 1686; Ensign, June 4, 1686; authorized to solemnize marriages, October 2, 1689; Deputy, 1690; Court Associate, 1690 to 1691.

He married Mary, daughter of John Tucker, born 1641, and died March 21, 1710. Their daughter *Deborah* married, first, *Samuel Gray.*

WARREN

RICHARD WARREN, who came to New England in the *Mayflower,* married in England Elizabeth Marsh; he died 1628. His short career in the colony was "marked by great usefulness." Issue:

Nathaniel.

Joseph, married Priscilla Faunce.

Mary, married Robert Bartlett.

Ann, married Thomas Little.

Sarah, married John Cooke.

Elizabeth, married Richard Church. She came in the ship *Anne* with her mother.

Abigail, married Anthony Snow.

BULL

GOVERNOR HENRY BULL, born in England 1610, died in Newport, R. I., January 22, 1694, was one of the eighteen original proprietors of Aquidneck, who settled Pocasset (later Portsmouth), 1638; joined in the settlement of Newport, 1639, and was Commissioner for Newport to the Court of Commissioners, 1655 to 1657. He was Deputy for Newport eight years, between 1666 and 1690; Governor's Assistant, 1674 and 1675; Governor of Rhode Island, 1685, 1686, and 1690.

The Friends' records make the following mention of his death:

"Henry Bull aged about eighty-four years, he departed this life at his own house in Newport (he being the last man of the first settlers of this Rhode Island), ye 22, 11 mo. 1693-4." He was buried in the Coddington ground.

He joined the church at Roxbury in 1636, with his wife Elizabeth. He married, second, March 28, 1677, Ann, the widow of Governor Nicholas Easton.

A daughter of Governor Bull's first marriage, *Elizabeth*, born 1635, married John Allen, October 14, 1650.

Their daughter, *Elizabeth Allen*, was born July, 1651, and died March 24, 1714; she married, June 15, 1671, Nathaniel Tompkins, who died in 1724.

One of their daughters, *Elizabeth Tompkins* (1675-1729), married, February 17, 1696, William Ladd, born 1670, in Portsmouth, R. I.; will probated October 21, 1729.

Their son, *Joseph Ladd*, was born October 19, 1701, and married, August 25, 1731, *Lydia Gray*, who was born October 16, 1707, the daughter of Samuel and Deborah (Church) Gray.

Their daughter, *Elizabeth Ladd*, born July 9, 1735, at Little Compton, R. I., and died November 27 (or 21), 1814, married, in 1755, Benedict, the son of Jonathan and Deliverance (Cleveland) Oatley, who was born December 25, 1732, and died in South Kingston, R. I., August 1, 1821.

Their daughter, *Abigail Oatley*, was born July 7, 1767 (or 1768), and died November 9, 1831; she married, January 28, 1799,[36] *Benjamin Taylor Peckham*.

[36] These dates are taken from the Oatley Bible, bought from Thomas Hennah, September 26, 1734.

Their daughter, *Mary Peckham*, married *Samuel Rodman*, whose daughter, *Mary Peckham Rodman*, married *William Henry Baldwin, Jr.*; their daughters are:

SARAH RODMAN BALDWIN,

MARIA WOODWARD BALDWIN HAMILL,

Members of Chapter I., The Colonial Dames of America.

V

BAXTER

It is known that several Baxter families came from Shropshire, Eng., to Massachusetts, in 1631, were excommunicated with John Throckmorton, and went with him to Rhode Island, and when he removed to Westchester, N. Y., two of these families went with him, in 1643. One branch of Baxters moved to Bucks County, Pa.,[1] 1682.

JOHN BAXTER, born 1702, moved to North Carolina from Pennsylvania. His son:

MAJOR ANDREW BAXTER (1725-1781), Lieutenant and Captain in the Provincial troops, lived in the section called the "New Acquisition," near Fort Mills, in 1781. This section was part of North Carolina until 1762, when it was adjudicated to South Carolina. The inhabitants were constantly engaged in partisan warfare, and Andrew Baxter was killed on the porch of his own house, 1781, tradition says by Cornwallis' men, but probably by Tories. He married Frances ——.

Their son, *Andrew Baxter II.*, was born December 21, 1759. Shortly after the Revolution he moved to Greene County, Ga., where he died October 4, 1816. In 1784, he married *Elizabeth,* daughter of Charles and Elizabeth (Thompson) Harris, born 1764 and died 1844.

Their son, *Thomas W. Baxter,* was born in December, 1781, and died August, 1844. He removed to

1 From *N. Y. Gen. Reg.,* January, 1905, p. 32.

Athens, Ga., in 1831, and married *Mary*, the daughter of Moses and Ann (Jack) Wiley, who was born November 25, 1798, and died March 27, 1869. Their daughter, SARAH C., married, February 24, 1848, William Edgeworth, the son of James Wilson and Frances Pamela (Casey) Bird.

Their son, *Wilson Edgeworth Bird*, married, February 8, 1877, IMOGEN, the daughter of Andrew and Fanny Brooke (Gwathmey) Reid, who was born October 3, 1854, in Baltimore. SALLIE BIRD, their daughter, was born June 23, 1885. (See pp. 129-141.)

SAIDA BIRD, their daughter, married Victor Smith. (See pp. 650-660.)

HARRIS

JOHN HARRIS, emigrated to Pennsylvania 1719, and lived on the site of the present city of Harrisburg. He died 1748, in which year he was captain of the Pennsylvania troops.

His son, *Charles Harris*, died in 1776, having moved to North Carolina. He married a widow, Elizabeth, the daughter of the Rev. John Thompson, and the widow of —— Baker. Her father was born in Ireland, and was licensed by the Donegal Presbytery; came to New York in 1715 with his family, moving to the Valley of Virginia, 1744, and that year was sent by the Presbytery of Philadelphia as missionary to North Carolina. In 1751 he settled near his daughter, Mrs. Baker, in Mecklenburg County, where he died, and was 'buried in Baker's graveyard, one of the oldest in that region. His daughter's first husband died a few years later.

Their daughter, *Elizabeth Harris*, married *Andrew Baxter II.*

ALEXANDER-SHELBY-WILEY

ADAM ALEXANDER, was Sheriff of Mecklenburg
County, N. C., before 1771, and Captain of the North
Carolina troops, 1771. His wife *Mary* was the daughter of EVAN SHELBY, who was Captain of the Rangers,
1772.

Their daughter, *Susan Alexander,* married James
Wiley II., the grandson of David Wiley, who died in
Scotland (his widow coming to Pennsylvania with their
children, one of whom, James Wiley, went to Virginia).

Their son, *Moses Wiley,* was born in Mecklenburg
County, 1768, and married, 1789, *Ann,* the daughter
of John and Mary (Barnett) Jack, born February,
1774, and died 1858. They moved to Bibb County,
Ga.

Their daughter, *Mary Wiley,* married *Thomas W.
Baxter.*

JACK

PATRICK JACK, a grandson of William Jack, a Presbyterian minister of Ireland, was born there, emigrat-
ing to Pennsylvania. He moved to North Carolina
shortly after 1763, and settled in Mecklenburg County,
dying in 1780. He was Lieutenant in the third Lancaster Battalion. His wife was Lillis McAdoo. Issue,
two sons, James and *John.* Captain James Jack carried the Mecklenburg Declaration of Independence,
May 20, 1775, from Charlotte, N. C., to the Continental
Congress in Philadelphia, on horseback through a
country infested with tories.

The younger son, *John Jack,* married Mary, the
daughter of John and Ann (Spratt) Barnett, and
moved to Wilkes County, Ga., soon after the Revolution.

Their daughter, *Ann,* married *Moses Wiley.*

BARNETT-SPRATT

The father of Mary (Barnett) Jack, John Barnett, was born in Virginia 1720, and moved to Mecklenburg County. He married Ann, born 1725, the daughter of Thomas Spratt, one of the earliest settlers of Mecklenburg County, going there from Virginia 1724, and was still living in 1770. The first Court in Mecklenburg County was held at his house about two miles from the present city of Charlotte. His daughter, Ann Spratt, was the first white child born between the Yadkin and the Catawba rivers. She married John Barnett, and their daughter, Mary, married *John Jack.*

Their daughter, *Ann Jack,* married *Moses Wiley,* whose daughter, *Mary,* married *Thomas W. Baxter.* Their daughter was SARAH C.

SARAH C. BAXTER BIRD,

SAIDA BIRD SMITH,

SALLIE BIRD,

Members of Chapter I., The Colonial Dames of America.

VI

LEWIS

ROBERT LEWIS I. settled in Gloucester County, Va., early in the seventeenth century and received a large grant of land. Family tradition says he was a native of Brecon, Wales.

JOHN LEWIS I. settled on Pametank River in Virginia, 1653. Authorities differ as to whether he was the son of Robert or his brother. He married Lydia ——.

JOHN LEWIS II., a son of either Robert or John, I.,[1] was Captain of New Kent Horse 1680, and married Isabella ——. Their son:

JOHN LEWIS III. was born November 30, 1669, and died November 14, 1725; married *Elizabeth,* the daughter of Colonel Augustine and Mildred (Reade) Warner. She was born November 24, 1672 and died 1719. Issue, fourteen children; of these John IV,

---

[1] The relationship of these three men has not been determined.

Robert and Charles Lewis founded important branches of the family.

COLLATERAL LINES OF ROBERT AND CHARLES LEWIS

The eldest of these brothers, Robert Lewis, settled at "Belvoir," Albemarle County, Va., and married Jane Merriwether. Among his descendants was the distinguished explorer, Captain Merriwether Lewis (1774-1809).

The younger brother, Charles Lewis, settled upon the "Byrd," a small stream in Goochland County, Va., and married Mary, the daughter of John Howell of King and Queen County. From him are descended the families of Howell, Lewis, Cobb, Kennon, Taylor, Worsham and others in North Carolina and Georgia.

WARNER-READE-MARTIAN

CAPTAIN AUGUSTINE WARNER, born October 9, 1611, died December 24, 1674; came to America before 1630. His son:

COLONEL AUGUSTINE WARNER of "Warner Hall" born October 20, 1643, and died June 10, 1681, married *Mildred,* the daughter of Colonel George and Elizabeth (Martian) Reade. His daughter *Mildred* married MAJOR LAWRENCE WASHINGTON, and his youngest daughter *Elizabeth* married JOHN LEWIS III.

COLONEL GEORGE READE (1600-1671), was son of Robert Reade, Secretary of State, England, who married Mildred Windebank. George Reade came to Virginia 1637, and married *Elizabeth,* the daughter of Captain Nicholas Martian. Their daughter, *Mildred,* married COLONEL AUGUSTINE WARNER.

CAPTAIN NICHOLAS MARTIAN settled in York County. His daughter, *Elizabeth,* married COLONEL GEORGE READE. (See pp. 436-440.)

Col. Fielding Lewis

Betty Washington
Wife of Col. Fielding Lewis

LEWIS (*Continued*)

The eldest son of John III and Elizabeth (Warner) Lewis, *John Lewis IV*, was born in 1694 (some say 1702), and died January 17, 1754. He resided in Spottsylvania County, Va., and was a lawyer of distinction and a member of the Council in 1748. He owned part of the land on which Fredericksburg was built, and with Colonel Willis laid out that city in 1727. He married *Frances*, the daughter of Henry Fielding. She died in 1731. Their son was COLONEL FIELDING LEWIS.

HENRY FIELDING, of King and Queen County, Va., was the son of Madame Frances Fielding. He married a widow, Mrs. Howell. His will, proved in 1712, mentions two Howell children.

COLONEL FIELDING LEWIS, third son of John IV and Frances (Fielding) Lewis, was born July 7, 1725, and died December, 1781 (or January, 1782), and was buried in the vestibule of St. George's Church. An active citizen of Fredericksburg, the official annals show that he owned nearly half the place. Commissioned county Lieutenant 1758; Commander-in-chief of the Militia of Spottsylvania County, 1761, and a Burgess from Spottsylvania 1773. During the Revolution (being unable to enter the army because of a defect in his eyes), he advanced a considerable portion of his large fortune in the manufacture of arms at the "Gunnery," established by the State at Fredericksburg. For this outlay he was never repaid except in depreciated money,[2] with which he bought largely of Western lands in the hope of offsetting his losses.

He married first, Catherine, the daughter of Major

[2] Value 6 pence in the pound; letter of General Washington to Captain Fielding Lewis.

John Washington; she died February, 1749-50.   Issue:
John, born 1747.

Frances, born 1748, died s. p.

Warner, born 1749, died young.

He married second, May 7, 1750, *Betty,* the daughter
of Augustine and Mary (Ball)Washington, and sister
of General Washington; she was born June 20, 1733,
and died March 31, 1797.   Her husband built a residence for her in Fredericksburg, which was named
"Kenmore" by a later owner.   Colonel Lewis' will,
which was proved January, 1782, gave to his wife, for
life, the use of all his land in Spottsylvania County,
except certain rented tracts.

The Washington ancestry of Betty (Washington)
Lewis was as follows:

John Washington of Whitfield, England.

Robert Washington of Wharton, England.

John of Wharton, son of Robert, married Margaret
Kitson.

Lawrence, son of John Washington, Gentleman,
married Aimée Pargiter.

Robert, son of Lawrence, married Elizabeth Lighte.

Lawrence of Sulgrave, son of Robert, married Margaret Butler.

Rev. Lawrence, son of Lawrence of Sulgrave, married Amphillis Roades.

JOHN, the emigrant, son of Rev. Lawrence, married
Ann Pope, of Virginia.   (See p. 435.)

LAWRENCE, son of John, married *Mildred Warner,*
of Warner Hall.   (See pp. 436-437.)

AUGUSTINE I., son of Lawrence, married second.
Mary Ball.   (See p. 137.)

Betty, daughter Augustine I. and Mary Ball, married
COLONEL FIELDING LEWIS, of Fredericksburg.

(For the Washington family see pp. 407-435.)

What is known of *Betty,* the only sister of George Washington, is of a fragmentary character. She is said to have been so strikingly like her brother that it was a matter of jest for the younger people to throw a cloak about her and place a military cap upon her head. She was domestic in her tastes, and after her husband's death capably managed his estates. When her husband died, in her fiftieth year, she went to live with her daughter Betty, (who had married Charles Carter) at "Western View," Culpeper County, Va. The following letter was written by her to her brother George, June 5, 1796:

"My Dear Brother: I expected your coming threw Baltimore that you would ascertain Mr. Park's fortune, tho' I believe he would not tell anything false on the occasion. Harriot's brother wrote her a letter from Baltimore and likewise one to Mr. Parks congratulating them on their intended union. My love to you and to my sister Washington concludes me your affectionate sister Betty Lewis."

"We can infer that General Washington's inquiries were as satisfactory as they were diplomatic for 'my niece Harriet Parks' appears in his will. She was the daughter of Samuel Washington."

Colonel Fielding and Betty (Washington) Lewis had issue:

Fielding, born February 14, 1751.

Augustine, born January 22, 1752, died in infancy.

Warner, born June 24, 1755, died in infancy.

George, born March 14, 1757.

Mary, born April 22, 1759.

Charles, born October 3, 1760.

Samuel, born 1763, died in infancy.

Betty, born February 23, 1765, married Charles Carter.

Lawrence, born April 4, 1767, married Washington's adopted daughter, who left them two thousand acres of land, in his will, including part of Mt. Vernon.

Robert, born June 25 1769.

Howell, born December 12, 1771.

POPE

COLONEL NATHANIEL POPE settled in Westmoreland County and took up large tracts of land on the stream named for him, "Pope's Creek." He represented Virginia during the troubles with Maryland in 1645 over Kent Island, and was agent to that Island 1647. His daughter, *Ann*, married COLONEL JOHN WASHINGTON. (See p. 435.)

BALL [3]

ARMS: *Argent, a lion passant sable, on a chief of the second three mullets of the first.*

CREST: *Out of the clouds, ppr., a demi lion rampant, sable, powdered with etoiles, arg. holding a globe or.*

MOTTO: *Coelumqui tueri.*

COLONEL WILLIAM BALL of "Millenbeck," Lancaster County, Va., born 1615 in England, emigrated to Virginia about 1650, and died November, 1680, in Lancaster County. He married Hannah Atherold in London. He was the fifth William Ball in succession. With him came his wife and three children, William, Joseph and Hannah. In March 1675-6, "Coll William Ball and Lieut-Coll John Carter, or either of them, in the County of Lancaster" were empowered by the Virginia Assembly to raise soldiers for the defence of the County against the Indians. His title of Colonel

[3] *Wm. and Mary Quar.*, Vol. i, p. 114. Prior to 1776. *Ball original parchment copy.* Hayden's *Gen.*, Vol. iv, p. 178. *Lee of Va.*, p. 545.

BALL

at that time would indicate his being County Lieutenant, or commanding the forces in active operation. The following is the original wording:

"Att a committy (by order of ye Grand Assembly) for laying Levy in the Northern Neck for ye charge in raisinge ye forces thereof for suppressing ye late rebellion mett at Capt. Beales ye 14th of August 1677, being present: Coll. Wm. Ball. Coll. Jno. Washington and others.

"Itt is by them ordered, y^t ye County of Rapp^k and Westmoreland, pay for 802 tythabls at 31^{lb} of Tob° and poll 25025^{lb} (sic) Tob° to ye sev^{r}all psons hereinafter pticularly menconed."[4]

For the transportation of his wife, children and other persons, Colonel Ball received sixteen hundred acres of land. Captain William Ball, the eldest son, was three times married and left a large family.

COLONEL JOSEPH BALL, the second son of the immigrant, born in England 24th of May 1649, died at his

[4] *Wm. and Mary Quar.*, Vol. ii, p. 48.

estate "Epping Forest," Lancaster County, June 1711. This estate had its name from the English home. He received a grant of land. In 1702, his name is on the list of Burgesses for Lancaster County. In 1704, was a Vestryman of his parish and was Lieutenant-Colonel of the County, being commissioned by Governor Alexander Spotswood under the royal authority.

Among the letters written to George Washington we find the following from Joseph Ball, Jr., Esq.:

Stratford 5th Septr. 1755.

It is a Sensible Pleasure to me to hear you have behaved your Self with such a martial Spirit in all your Engagements with the French nigh Ohio. Go on as you have begun; and God prosper you. We have heard of General Braddock's Defeat. Every Body Blames his Rash Conduct. Every Body Commends the Courage of the Virginia and Carolina men: which is very Agreeable to me. I desire you, as you may from time to time have opportunity, to give me a short account how you proceed. As I am your Mother's Brother, I hope you can't deny my Request. There is no War Declared yet, either by the French or us; though it is expected there soon will. The King is not returned from Hanover yet; but is looked for very soon. The Yachts are gone for him. I heartily wish you Good Success, and am

Yr Loving Uncle,

Jos. Ball.

Please to direct to me Stratford by Bow nigh London.

Since the writing the Letter above, there are six more French vessels brought in. Though they pretended to be bound to the West Indies, they are really bound we found to Louisburgh.

Please deliver the Inclosed to your Mother. —

To Major George Washington at the falls of Rapp[k] River or Elsewhere in Virginia.

By favour of Mr. Butler.[5]

Joseph Ball's second wife was Mrs. Mary Johnson, of Lancaster County, Va., whose daughter, *Mary Ball*, married AUGUSTINE WASHINGTON. They were the parents of George Washington, his three brothers, and his sister *Betty*, (Mrs. Fielding Lewis).

Little is known of the early life of *Mary*, the daughter of Joseph Ball by his second marriage. She was born 1708 and died August 25, 1789, aged eighty-two years. An interesting word picture of her is given in a letter dated in the year 1722:

"Mama thinks Molly, (Mary Ball), the comliest maiden she knows. She is about sixteen years old, taller than me, very sensible, modest and loving, her hair is like unto flax, her eyes the color of yours, her cheeks like May blossoms."

When she married Augustine Washington they lived at "Wakefield," the Washington Homestead on Bridge's Creek, and occupied with the cares of a Virginian matron upon a large plantation of a thousand acres, she led a busy life. She was a widow for more than forty years, living in Fredericksburg from the year 1770 until her death. In 1833, the corner-stone of a monument over her grave was laid with great ceremony, by the President of the United States, but it remained unfinished for more than half a century, when a society of patriotic ladies completed it.

LEWIS (*Continued*)

The youngest son of Fielding and Betty (Washington) Lewis, *Howell Lewis*, was born December 11, 1771 in Culpepper County, Va. He married September 26,

5 *Letters to Washington*, Vol. i, p. 85.

1795, Ellen Hackley, the daughter of Robert Pollard of Richmond, Va. She was born December 7, 1776, her mother being Jael, a daughter of William and Ellen (Hackley) Underwood. Robert Pollard belonged to the business firm of Pickett, Pollard and Johnston, who acted as financial agents of the State of Virginia in the early part of the nineteenth century. He went to Richmond from Culpeper County and was a vestryman of St. John's church. Too young to take even a subordinate part in the military career of his uncle, or in all his political career, yet, as he approached his majority, *Howell Lewis* received this gratifying evidence of General Washington's confidence and esteem sent through his mother's hands:

"Philadelphia, April 8, 1792.

"My Dear Sister,

"If your son Howell is living with you and not especially employed in your own affairs, and should incline to spend a few months with me as a writer in my office, if he is fit for it, I will allow him the rate of $300. a year, provided he is diligent in discharging the duties of it, from breakfast until dinner, Sundays excepted. This sum will be punctually paid him, and I am particular in declaring beforehand what I require, and what he may expect, that there may be no disappointment or false expectations on either side. He will live in the family in the same manner his brother Robert did; if the offer is accepted he must hold himself in readiness to come on immediately on my giving him notice. . . . Mrs. Washington unites with me in best wishes and love for you and yours, and I am, my dear sister, your most affec. Brother, G. Washington."

This letter was written during the last year of Washington's first term as President, when he was residing

(1792) in the only house then obtainable in Philadelphia, which was considered a suitable residence for the first President. It was situated on High street, one door east of the southeast corner of High and Sixth streets. On April 24, 1792 (not by return mail), Howell Lewis sent this answer to his uncle's letter:

"Fredericksburg, April 24, 1792.

"Dear Uncle,

"I should have done myself the pleasure of replying to your letter on its receipt, but was at that time engaged in business in Frederick. I consider myself extremely favored by your proposal of a berth in your family, and shall accept it provided my probation is deemed satisfactory. I lament that I have not been more attentive to the improvement of my writing tho' I hope that I shall soon be qualified to do the business for which you mean to employ me. With best wishes to my Aunt, I remain most respectfully yours,

Howell Lewis."

In 1812 he took possession of a tract of land of thirteen hundred acres, left him by General Washington, in West Virginia, on the Kanawha River in Mason County, near the mouth of "Big Buffalo" Creek. He carried with him twelve male and six female slaves and their children. He had also inherited a half interest in twenty thousand acres of land in Kentucky, and other land from his father. He died in Kanawha December 26, 1822, and was buried there. His widow lived in Kanawha six years after his death when she moved to Marietta, O., where she resided until her death, June 15, 1859, with her daughter Betty, who had married Joseph Lovell in 1818.

The fifth child of Howell Lewis, *Frances Fielding*, married *Humphrey Brooke Gwathmey*, and their daughter, *Fanny Brooke Gwathmey,* married Andrew Reid. (See Reid).

GWATHMEY

The colonist, Owen Gwathmey, of Wales, came to Virginia between 1680 and 1690, and settled in Gloucester County. He married there a resident of the County, Mrs. Clevins. Their son, Richard, married —— Moore, between 1720 and 1724.

Their son, Owen, was born between 1725 and 1730, and married *Hannah,* the daughter of Joseph and Ann (Arnold) Temple.

Their son, *Temple,* married *Ann,* the daughter of Robert and Molly (Brooke) Baylor.

Their son, *Humphrey Brooke,* was born March 29, 1794, in Canterbury, King and Queen County, Va., and died October 22, 1852. He married, June 27, 1822, in Richmond Va., *Frances Fielding,* the daughter of Howell and Ellen Hackley (Pollard) Lewis. She was born February 11, 1805 and died May 28, 1888.

Their daughter, *Fanny Brooke Gwathmey,* married Andrew Reid.

TEMPLE-BAYLOR

JOSEPH TEMPLE, a Captain of the Rangers, in 1758, and also a member of the Committee of Safety in 1774, married Ann Arnold, and was the father of ten children, among them *Hannah,* who married Owen Gwathmey, II., whose son, *Temple,* married *Ann Baylor.*

JOHN BAYLOR, born 1650, was Burgess of Gloucester, afterwards moving to Essex County. Issue:

Robert, who had issue *Robert II,* who married before 1746, *Molly,* the daughter of Humphrey and Elizabeth (Brayton) Brooke. Their daughter *Ann* married *Temple Gwathmey.*

FRANCES FIELDING LEWIS
Wife of Humphrey Brooke Gwathmey

ELLEN HACKLEY POLLARD
Wife of Howell Lewis

HOWELL LEWIS

BROOKE-BRAYTON

ROBERT BROOKE of Essex County, married *Katherine,* daughter of HUMPHREY BOOTH. Their son: HUMPHREY BROOKE married *Elizabeth Brayton.* Robert Brooke, Jr., a brother of Humphrey, was a Knight of the Golden Horseshoe. (See Brooke line pp. 553-558.) Issue: *Molly Brooke,* who married *Robert Baylor II.*

GEORGE BRAYTON (1677-1746) was a Burgess from King and Queen County 1720 to 1722, and the father of George Brayton the Signer. Also of *Elizabeth,* who married HUMPHREY BROOKE.

REID

A native of Scotland, George Reid came to Virginia, and settled in Norfolk 1801, where he died 1849. He was the son of William Reid of Farfar, Scotland. The old mansion of the Reid family in Farfar, is one of the residences of the Earl of Grey. George Reid married Elizabeth, the daughter of John Taylor of Scotland, and his wife Margaret Carr, who was of Aberdeen. Elizabeth Reid was born April 12, 1777, and died, in Baltimore 1862.

Their son Andrew Reid, was born October 28, 1818, and died in Baltimore, Md., January 4, 1896. He married in Richmond, Va., December 8, 1853, *Fanny Brooke,* the daughter of Humphrey Brooke and Frances Fielding (Lewis) Gwathmey; she was born September 8, 1835, in Norfolk, Va. Their daughter is:

IMOGEN REID BIRD, whose daughter is:

SALLIE BIRD,

Members of Chapter I., The Colonial Dames of America.

VII

MURRAY

OF TULLIBARDINE AND STORMONT

MANSFIELD

The Murrays of Tullibardine and Stormont, trace their ancestry to one of the most ancient and loyal houses of Scotland. In the reign of David II., 1330-1370, there was granted a charter of the lands of Tullibardine etc., to Sir Walter Murray, who died 1390, leaving a son David, who was knighted in 1424 by King James I.[1]

Sir William Murray I., of Tullibardine, was a favorite of King James III. and James IV., and employed by the latter king in concluding a treaty with England in 1495. His son, Sir William II., of Tullibardine, married Margaret, the daughter of John, Earl of Athole or Atholl; he had also a second son, Sir Andrew Murray, from whom descend the "Viscounts Stormonts"

[1] Burke's *Peerage. Md. Heraldry.* By E. E. Lantz, who quotes Martin's *Geneal. Coll.* and MacFarlane.

and "Earls of Mansfield." Sir William Murray was created Earl of Tullibardine, 1606, by King James VI., and died 1609, leaving three sons. Eleven baronetcies have belonged to the powerful "clan of the Murrays."

The colonist, James Murray, who was said to be the son of the Marquis of Tullibardine, born in Elgenshire, Scotland, was banished, 1715, and his estates confiscated in consequence of his loyalty to the house of Stuart. He fled to Barbadoes with his wife, Sarah (Thomas?), and three children, where he lived "with considerable reputation," for some years.

DOCTOR WILLIAM MURRAY I., (1708-1769), their son, after the death of his parents, settled with his sister,[2] who married Mr. Calder, in Chestertown, Md. Having received his education at the University of Edinburgh, he took up the practice of medicine, in Chestertown, and was most successful. He was Justice of Kent County Court, 1750. His death is thus recorded in the family Bible: "The most affectionate of Husbands, the most indulgent of Fathers, and the best of Friends." He married, 1740, *Anne,* the daughter of James and Anne (Hynson) Smith. She was born 1720, and died 1807. They had three daughters and three sons, one of whom was *James.*

SMITH

CAPTAIN JAMES SMITH, of Chestertown, Md., who died 1760, was Justice of Kent County, Md., 1697, Burgess, 1719-1721, and 1728, and Clerk of the Court

[2] Her granddaughter, named Banning, married Benjamin Chew, of Philadelphia. A younger brother of Dr. Murray, Alexander Murray, returned to England, married into a noble family, and was supposed to have died soon after, as they never heard of him again.

for many years. He married *Sarah*, the daughter of
Colonel John and Ann Hynson.[3] Their daughter
Anne, married DR. WILLIAM MURRAY.

HINSON

ARMS: *Azure; a chevron between three suns or, and a bordure ermine.*

CREST: *A fleur-de-lis, per pale azure.*

In the twenty-third year of the reign of Henry VI.,
William Hinson, of Fordham, at the Damside, is registered as living there, in the County of Cambridge, Eng.

These arms were granted in 1644 to Thomas Hinson,
a descendant of William, by Ulster, King at Arms in
Ireland, for services done in that kingdom, which patent is registered in the Herald office, London.

LIEUTENANT THOMAS HINSON (1620-1667), a cadet
of the family of Fordham, arrived in the Province of
Maryland 1650-51, accompanied by his wife Grace and
three children, Thomas, JOHN and Charles. He was
promptly appointed to one of the most important offices, that of Clerk of Isle of Kent County, 1652, and
in a few years was High Sheriff " for ye county " 1655,
and Burgess 1654 to 1660.[4] He was a lawyer by profession, and a man of means, and bore the same arms
as those of his English forbears.

COLONEL JOHN HYNSON, his son, who died 1705,
remained in Kent. The spelling of the name with the
letter " y " instead of " i " was purely a Maryland
method, as the Fordham family and the emigrant wrote
the name with an " i." Colonel John was Justice of

[3] *Side lights of Md. Heraldry.* By Mrs. H. Dorsey Richardson. *Md. State Colonial Dames.*

[4] *Md. Society of Colonial Dames of America.* Mrs. H. Dorsey Richardson.

"Rockburn," the Residence of Daniel Murray

The Chestertown Residence of Dr. William Murray I

Kent, 1674, Burgess 1681 to 1683, 1694 to 1697, and High Sheriff 1670. His wife's name was Ann. Their daughter *Sarah,* married JAMES SMITH, whose daughter *Anne* married WILLIAM MURRAY.

MURRAY (*Continued*)

The eldest son of William and Ann (Smith) Murray, Dr. *James Murray,* of Annapolis (1741-1820), was born in Chestertown, Md. In 1755 he went to Edinburgh to be educated and study medicine. After graduating in 1769, he returned and settled in Annapolis. He married *Sarah Ennalls,* the daughter of the Rev. Daniel and Mary (Murray) Maynadier, and the widow of John Rider Nevitt. Their son was *Daniel.*

COLLATERAL LINES OF
WILLIAM AND ALEXANDER MURRAY

The second son of William and Ann (Smith) Murray, was Dr. William Murray II. (1752-1842), of Woodstock, West River, Md. He married Harriet, the daughter of Henry and Mary (Young) Woodward, and the widow of James Brice, of Annapolis. A letter has recently been discovered which was written by a daughter of Dr. William Murray of Woodstock, to her cousin, Mrs. Mason, a daughter of James Murray of Annapolis, in which she says:

"My father tells me that the ' Arms ' of our Grandfather are the same as borne by Viscount Stormont[5] (the Scotch Murrays), but owing to a mistake of Mr. James Burke in England (when yr. dear Father sent to him for the Family Arms) he sent out those of Lord Elibank (the Irish Murrays).'." [6]

[5] For arms see Earl of Mansfield, Burke's *Peerage.*
[6] *Nat. Gazette Biog.* Notes.

A brother of William Murray II., Commodore Alexander Murray (1755-1821), was of the United States Navy. He was in command of the *Montezuma* and the *Constellation,* in the war between the United States and Tripoli, and at the time of his death was in command of the Navy Yard in Philadelphia, where the grief displayed at the time of his decease, showed the esteem in which he was held by those under his command.

He married Mary, the daughter of Magnus Miller.

MAYNADIER

After the revocation of the Edict of Nantes, Rev. Daniel Maynadier, a French Huguenot, fled from Languedoc in the south of France, first to England, and thence to this country, landing in Annapolis in 1686. He finally settled in Talbot County, Md., and became Rector of White Marsh parish. He married a widow, Mrs. Parrott, of Talbot County.[7]

Their son, Rev. Daniel Maynadier II. (1725-1774), studied and practiced law, but finally, in accordance with his father's wishes, went to England, and took holy orders. On his return, he settled in Cambridge, Md., and was Rector of Great Choptank parish, for many years, until his death. He married, May 11, 1746, *Mary,* the daughter of William Vans and Sarah (Ennalls) Murray, and their daughter, *Sarah Ennalls,* married first, John Rider Nevitt, and second, *James Murray,* of Annapolis.[8]

7 Jones' *Hist. of Dorchester Co., Md.,* p. 304.
8 Family Recs.

MURRAY

OF THE HOUSE OF ATHOL

DOCTOR WILLIAM VANS MURRAY (1692-1759), the son of William and Mary (Vans) Murray, born at Castle Tullebardine, Perthshire, Scot., was of the House of Murray, Earl of that estate.[9]

He was the youngest of seventeen children, and being implicated with his family in the trouble which arose about the succession to the throne of Scotland in 1715, he was obliged to fly for his life. He escaped to France, and from there emigrated to Maryland, finally removing to Cambridge, Md., 1739. On his arrival he had but fifty guineas in his pocket. He purchased from the original patentee of Lord Baltimore, one-third of the land forming the present site of Cambridge. By this means he accumulated a large fortune. A practitioner of medicine until his death, he enjoyed the love and respect of the entire community. He was cousin and ward of the Duke of Athol of his day, chief of the Murray clan, and his sister Marguerita, a widow, who came with him to Maryland,

JAMES MURRAY'S BOOK PLATE[10]

9 *Family Recs.*

10 The arms bear the name of James Murray, who was the ancestor of William Vans Murray. They were engraved upon the book plate shown above, carried by the Murrays of Cambridge since their colonization in Maryland.

was a member of that household.[11] He married *Sarah,*
the daughter of Colonel Henry and Mary (Hooper)
Ennalls. Their daughter, *Mary,* married Rev. Daniel
Maynadier II.

ENNALLS

It is said that this family was of Dutch origin, emigrated to Scotland in the sixteenth century, and from
there went to Suffolk, Eng.

BARTHOLOMEW ENNALLS (1643-1688), the first of
the name to arrive in Maryland, came from York
County, Va., between 1660 and 1669, with his wife
Mary, the widow of Francis Hayward. He purchased
.two thousand acres on Transquaking River, Md.[12]
There is a patent from Charles "the absolute Lord
Proprietor of the province of Maryland and Avalon,
Lord Baron of Baltimore," etc., confirming a grant of
his father, Cecilius, etc., dated June 10, 1671, to Bartholomew Ennalls, East side of the Chesapeake Bay,
in which place he lived and died. He was Commissioner in Dorchester County, Md., 1676, member of the
Maryland Assembly, and "Gentleman Justice" 1682
to 1688. His son:

COLONEL HENRY ENNALLS (1675-1734), his son,
was Burgess for Dorchester County, 1712 to 1713;
Justice 1726. He married *Mary,* the daughter of
Henry and Elizabeth (Denwood) Hooper, and grand-
daughter of LEVIN DENWOOD. She was born 1674,
and died 1745. Their daughter, *Sarah,* married DR.
WILLIAM VANS MURRAY, and their daughter, *Mary
Murray,* married Rev. Daniel Maynadier II.

HOOPER

CAPTAIN HENRY HOOPER, who died 1676, came to

11 Jones' *Dorchester County, Md.,* p. 393.
12 Jones' *History of Dorchester County, Md.*

Maryland 1651, and settled on the Patuxent River, in
what is now Calvert County, with his wife Sarah. He
was Justice 1658, and commissioned Captain June 3,
1658.[13] His son:

HENRY HOOPER II., was born 1645, and came with
his parents to Maryland. He was Justice of Dorchester County, 1669 to 1689, and Burgess for " Old
Kent," 1664. He married, July 4, 1669, *Elizabeth,* the
daughter of LEVIN DENWOOD. Their daughter *Mary,*
married HENRY ENNALLS.

DENWOOD

LIVEINGE DENWOOD (or LEVIN as it is now usually
called) was an early resident of the Eastern shore of
Virginia, first appearing in the records of Northhamp-
ton County, 1633, the name always being given as Liveinge.[13a] There are two traditions concerning this name.
One that his mother was a Huguenot maiden, named
Le Vigue, the other that he was the thirteenth child,
twelve of whom had died, and upon his birth he was
promptly named " Livcinge." He was appointed
Commissioner of Northampton County, Va. 1654. He
married Mary Cutting (?).

Among their children were *Elizabeth,* who married
HENRY HOOPER II., and *Levin II.,* who married Mary,
——, whose daughter *Mary,* married *Henry Hill,* the
son of CAPTAIN RICHARD HILL.

MURRAY (*Continued*)

The son of James and Sarah Ennalls (Maynadier)
Murray, *Daniel Murray* (1778-1842), was educated at

[13] *Md. Arch.* Vol. III, p. 344, 347. Jones' *Dorchester County, Md.,* pp.
320, 321, 322.

[13a] *Ancestry of Rosalie Morris Johnson,* by R. Winder Johnson, p. 57.

St. John's College, Annapolis, and then entered the United States Navy where, in 1797, he received his commission from Thomas Jefferson. He resigned a few years after his marriage, and went to live at Melrose, West River, and in 1822 removed to Rockburn, Howard County, Md., where he passed the remainder of his days. He was the intimate friend of Francis Scott Key, and of Commodore Perry. He married *Mary*, the daughter of Edward and Elizabeth (Dorsey) Dorsey.[14]   Their son was *Francis Key Murray*.

DORSEY

The colonist, Edward Dorsey, of Hockley, Essex County, Eng., came to this country with or before his three sons, JOHN, Edward and Joshua.   It is said that the name was originally D'Arcy, and that they went from Normandy to Ireland, and thence to England.[15]

COLONEL JOHN DORSEY, who died in 1714, was Burgess 1692, 1700, 1703; a Justice of Anne Arundel County, Md. 1694, and a member of the Council, 1710 to 1714.   He married Pleasance Ely.

Their son, *Caleb Dorsey I.,* of Hockley, was born 1685, and married *Eleanor,* the daughter of Richard and Elinor (Browne) Warfield; she was born 1683.

Their son, *Caleb II.,* of Belmont (1710-1772), married 1735-36, *Priscilla,* the daughter of Henry and Mary (Denwood) Hill, granddaughter of CAPTAIN RICHARD HILL.

Their son, *Edward,* of Belmont (1758-1799), married his cousin *Elizabeth,* the daughter of John and Mary (Hammond) Dorsey. Their daughter, *Mary,* married *Daniel Murray*.

14 *Family Recs.*
15 *Ibid.* Md. *Arch.* Md. *Society of Colonial Dames.*

The parents of *John Dorsey,* the father of *Elizabeth,* were Edward and Sarah (Todd) Dorsey, and he was a grandson of COLONEL JOHN DORSEY.

WARFIELD

The family of Warfield had been one of consequence in England from the time of the Norman Conquest. Pageñ de Warfield, a Norman gentleman of the retinue of William the Conqueror, won a knight's fee and the estate of Warfield Walk, at the battle of Hastings, 1066, in consideration of his services to the king on that eventful occasion.[16]

CAPTAIN RICHARD WARFIELD, emigrated from Berkshire, Eng. 1662, and married Elinor Browne (See p. 82.)

Their daughter *Eleanor,* married *Caleb Dorsey* of Hockley.

HILL

CAPTAIN RICHARD HILL, born in 1650, married Milcah ——. He was a member of the House of Burgesses, Anne Arundel County, Md., 1681 to 1689, 1694 to 1699, and Chief Judge of the County Court, 1686. He was also Captain of the Militia 1689.

His son, *Henry Hill,* (1672-1738-39), married, ——, *Mary,* the daughter of Levin Denwood. Their daughter, *Priscilla,* married *Caleb Dorsey II.,* of Belmont, grandson of COLONEL JOHN DORSEY.

HAMMOND

MAJOR-GENERAL JOHN HAMMOND, was born 1643, and died 1707. He was Burgess for Anne Arundel County, Md., 1692; Justice of the Provincial Court, and

16 *Md. Heraldry.*

member of the Council, 1698 to 1707; commissioned
Colonel October 4, 1699; Judge of the Vice-Admiralty
1702, and Major-General of the Western Shore. He
married Mary Howard. Their son:

Colonel William Hammond, was born 1711, and
died 1752. He was the Commissioner appointed to lay
out Baltimore Town, 1729; High Sheriff, 1736, and
Colonel of Militia. He married Mary Todd. Their
daughter, *Mary,* married *John Dorsey.*

MURRAY (*Continued*)

The son of Lieutenant Daniel and Mary (Dorsey)
Murray, *Francis Key Murray,* of Rockburn, was born
in 1820. He entered the navy 1836, and was graduated
1842, serving through the Mexican War, and also the
Florida Indian War. His friend and classmate Gen.
Edward Beale, says of him:

".... During that frightful disaster which resulted
after days of dreadful suspense in the loss of the *San
Francisco,* his cool and even temper enabled him to
control the most disorderly of the soldiers and sailors
of that ill-fated ship, and to calm the wildest terrors of
the helpless women and children—they looked to him and
as long as they could see his calm and cheerful face, they
felt that they were to be saved. Afterwards, when his
own ship seemed sinking under him, and the men were
clamorous to save themselves by the boats, he stood knee
deep in water on the deck, and with the same wonderful
influence his example always carried, without force or
menace, calmed their uneasy fears, and carried his ship
into port, through hazards it seemed impossible to
escape."

He married *Anna Maria,* the daughter of Thomas

Willing and Caroline (Calvert) Morris. Their daughter, JULIA MORRIS, married Henry J. Bowdoin.

MORRIS

The first known member of this family, Anthony Morris I, was born in 1600. He was at one time a resident of Reading, Great Britain, and subsequently of Barbadoes.

His son, Anthony Morris II., married Elizabeth Semoi, about 1653. He was styled "mariner" and made voyages between London and Barbadoes. His only child:

ANTHONY MORRIS III. (1654-1721), removed to Philadelphia 1685 or 1686, and soon became prominent in affairs. He was appointed one of the first six aldermen of that city 1691; commissioned Justice of Peace and Courts, 1692; recommissioned 1693, when he was appointed Presiding Justice of the Court of Common Pleas, and again recommissioned in 1697. During the years, 1694 to 1698, he was Justice of the Supreme Court of the province. Was a member of the Provincial Council of Pennsylvania, and from 1698 to 1704 represented Philadelphia in the Assembly.[17] In the year 1703 he was chosen Mayor of the city. The first of his four marriages occurred January 30, 1676, to Mary Jones, who died 1688. Their son:

ANTHONY MORRIS IV. (1682-1763), was a member of the Council of Philadelphia, 1715, and served for many years; represented that city in the Assembly 1721 to 1726, and was elected Mayor in 1738, serving one year. Some years later, he was again appointed for that

[17] Penn. *Arch.* 2d series, Vol. IX, pp. 625, 630, 701, 728.

office.[18] He married, 1685, Phoebe, the daughter of George and Alice Guest.

Their son, *Anthony Morris V.* (1705-1780), was one of those who established in 1748, the popular social club known as the " Colony on Schuylkill," an organization still in existence. He married, as his second wife, *Elizabeth,* the daughter of William and Jane (Evans) Hudson, (1721-1783). She was a highly esteemed minister in the Society of Friends. Their son:

CAPTAIN LUKE MORRIS (1760-1802), was commissioned Captain in the Fifth Battalion of the Philadelphia militia 1785, and in 1789, Lieutenant of Delaware County.[19] He married, May 9, 1788, *Ann,* the daughter of Charles and Elizabeth H. (Carrington) Willing.

Their son, *Thomas Willing Morris,* married *Caroline Maria,* the daughter of George and Rosalie Eugenia (Stier) Calvert, and their daughter, *Anna Maria,* married *Francs Key Murray.*

HUDSON

The records of the " Friends " in England, show that William Hudson, who died 1713, resided in York, and married three times. His first wife, whom he married ——, was Mary Head (Heads).

WILLIAM HUDSON, JR., their son, was born in England ——, and emigrated to Philadelphia about 1686. He was a member of the Common Council of Philadelphia 1701, and of the Provincial Assembly 1706. In 1715, he became an Alderman and associate Judge of the City Court, and was chosen Mayor of Philadelphia 1725.[20] He married first, 1688, *Mary,* the daughter of Samuel and Ellinor Richardson; she was born 1675, and died 1708.

[18] *Ibid.* pp. 719, 729, 731.   [19] *Ibid,* Vol. XIV, p. 687.
[20] *Ibid,* Vol. IX, pp. 729, 730, 738.

Their son *William Hudson III.*, married Jane Evans, and their daughter, *Elizabeth*, married *Anthony Morris V.*

RICHARDSON

Samuel Richardson, who died 1719, came to Philadelphia from Jamaica 1686, driven from England to the West Indies as is supposed, and thence to Pennsylvania, by the persecution that followed the sect of Friends. He purchased five thousand eight hundred acres of land, also two large lots on High Street (now Market), in the city of Philadelphia, for £340. He was Judge of the County Court 1688 to 1704; a member of the Provincial Council 1691 to 1694, 1695 and 1709; and elected Alderman in 1705, which position he held until his death.[21] He married, Ellinor —— (first wife).

Their daughter, *Mary*, married William Hudson, Jr., whose son, *William Hudson III.*, married Jane Evans. Their daughter, *Elizabeth*, married *Anthony Morris V.*, and their son, Luke Morris, married *Ann Willing*.

WILLING

This well-known colonial family was descended from Michael Willing, through his son, John, and grandson, Joseph Willing I., (who married Mary ——), to great-grandson, Joseph Willing II., who married Ava Lowle.

Their son, Thomas Willing, of Bristol, Eng., (1679-1760), married, 1704, *Ann*, the daughter of Charles Harrison, and granddaughter, of both Major-General Thomas Harrison and Simon Mayne, who are said to have been members of the Court which condemned Charles I.

[21] *Ibid*, pp. 715, 716, 717, 734.

CHARLES WILLING I., (1710-1754), their son, was born in England, and died in Philadelphia. He married, 1730, *Ann,* the daughter of Joseph and Abigail (Gross) Shippen (1710-1791). Charles Willing came to Philadelphia 1728, and was Captain of the Associated Regiment of Foot of Philadelphia 1747, member of the Common Council 1743, Associated Justice of the City Court 1747, Mayor of the city 1748, and again 1754. He died of ship-fever, contracted while in discharge of his official duties.[22]

Their son, *Charles Willing II.,* married Elizabeth Hannah, the daughter of Paul Carrington (1706-1756), (the son of Doctor Paul Carrington, of Barbadoes, and his second wife Henningham Codrington; she died 1744-45).

Their daughter *Ann,* married LUKE MORRIS, whose son *Thomas Willing Morris,* married *Caroline Maria Calvert,* and their daughter, *Anna Maria,* married *Francis Key Murray.*

SHIPPEN

In Yorkshire, Eng., William Shippen, was born, at Hillam, a hamlet in the parish of Monk Fryston, in the West Riding, where the family is said to have been seated since the thirteenth century; he died 1681.[23]   In 1626, he married, Mary, the daughter of John and Effam (Crosfield) Nunes, of Methley, Yorkshire.

EDWARD SHIPPEN (1639-1712), their son, eimgrated from England to Boston, 1668, and was a member of the Ancient and Honorable Artillery Company, of that city. His first wife was Elizabeth Lybrand, of Boston.

---

[22] Martin's *Bench and Bar,* p. 61. *Penn. Arch.,* 2d series, Vol. ix, p. 729.

[23] *Ancestry of R. M. Johnson* by R. Winder Johnson.

It is probable that his marriage to a Quakeress led him to become a " Friend," and as a member of this Society, he experienced severe persecution, being twice "publickly whipped." Subjected to great annoyances in various ways, he finally, about 1693 or 1694, removed to Philadelphia.

In this latter city his wealth, fine personal appearance, and home on Second Street, styled a " Princely Mansion," together with his talent and high character, obtained for him such position and influence that he was elected Speaker of the Assembly, on July 9, 1695. He was chosen one of the Provincial Council [24] by popular vote, in 1696, and was returned every year at the fresh elections. He was also Presiding Justice of the Court of Common Pleas, 1699. William Penn called him to the Council in 1700, and he was named the first Mayor of the city of Philadelphia, under Penn's Charter of 1701, and was the first named in the Commission issued by the Proprietary 1701. Also President of the Council, 1702 to 1704, and upon the death of Penn's Deputy, in 1703, became the head of the government until the arrival of John Evans.

His son, *Joseph Shippen,* was born 1678-79, and died 1741. He removed from Philadelphia to Boston 1704, and later to Germantown. He was among the men of science of his day and in 1727 joined Dr. Franklin in founding the " Junto " which was the forerunner of the "American Philosophical Society." He married first, 1702, Abigail, the daughter of Thomas and Elizabeth Gross.

Their daughter, *Ann,* married CHARLES WILLING, and their son, *Charles Willing II.,* married Elizabeth Hannah Carrington, whose daughter, Ann, married

24 *Provincial Councillors,* p. 47-48.

LUKE MORRIS. Their son, *Thomas Willing Morris,* married *Caroline Maria Calvert,* whose daughter, *Anna Maria,* married *Francis Key Murray.*

CALVERT

In or near the town of Danby Wiske, Yorkshire, Eng., Leonard Calvert, the son of John, was living in the time of Elizabeth. He was a country gentleman, apparently in easy circumstances, who owned land and raised cattle, a fact which, at a later time, gave an enemy of George Calvert an opportunity to sneer at him as the "son of a grazier." [25]

(See p. 562.) His son:

SIR GEORGE CALVERT (1580-1631), at the early age of fourteen entered Trinity College, Oxford, as a Commoner, and took his degree 1597. In 1605 he received his first Master's degree at Oxford, and became Cecil's private secretary, and was appointed by King James I., Clerk of the Crown and of Assize in County Clare, Ireland, an office resembling that of an Attorney-General. In 1617 he received the order of knighthood, and two years later was raised to the office of the principal Secretary of State. On February 18, 1621, the King granted him a manor of twenty-three thousand acres in County Longford, Ireland. The Longford estates were then erected into the Manor of Baltimore, from which he took his title. He had a seat in Parliament 1624, and later announced to the king his conversion to the faith of the church of Rome, and asked to be allowed to resign his secretaryship. The King, however, retained him in the Privy Council, and in 1625 elevated him to the Irish

[25] *Ancestry of Rosalie Morris Johnson,* by R. Winder Johnson, p. 9, who quotes from Wm. Hand Browne's *George & Cecilius Calvert. The Calvert Papers. The Lords Baltimore,* by John G. Morris.

peerage as Baron Baltimore, of Baltimore. Although
Charles I. wished to retain him in the Council, Lord
Baltimore was firm in his resolution to retire from official
life.

As early as 1609, he had been a member of the second
Virginia Company,
and one of the Pro-
visional Council for
that colony, and one
of the eighteen
Councillors of the
New England
Company, 1622,
and in that year he
applied for a pat-
ent and received a
grant for the whole
of Newfoundland.
This was super-
seded by a re-grant
in March, 1623,
conveying to him
the south-east pen-

CALVERT

insula, which was erected into the province of Avalon by
a Royal Charter, in which Lord Baltimore was given a
palatinate or quasi royal authority over the province.
He visited Avalon 1627, but the discomforts of life
there seem to have been too much for Lady Baltimore,
as she sailed to Virginia 1628, remaining for sometime
at Jamestown. Lord Baltimore followed her 1629. The
Virginians received him coldly as it was within the
bounds of possibility, as well as of law, that the king
might give him a charter for the whole of Virginia. He
was tendered the oath of supremacy, which he could not

take, on account of his religious faith, though he offered
to take a modified form of it; but to this they would
not agree, and he departed for England. There he
found that his grant would be delayed, and before the
patent for Maryland had passed the "Great Seal," he
died.

He is ranked among the "Makers of America,"
although the colony he founded was almost a failure,
and he did not live to see the beginnings of the colony
which succeeded. His portrait by Mytens, court painter
to James I., is owned by the present Earl of Verulam.
The late John W. Garrett presented a fine copy of this
portrait to the State of Maryland, and it hangs in the
State House, Annapolis. Lord Baltimore was buried
in the church of St. Dunstan, Fleet Street, London,
which was destroyed by fire. He married first, Anne,
the daughter of John and Elizabeth (Wroth) Mynne,
who died 1613. Elizabeth Wroth was the daughter of
Sir Thomas, of Durance, in Enfield, Middlesex.

Their son, *Cecilius Calvert,* second Lord Baltimore
(1606-1671), entered Trinity College, Oxford, 1621.
The charter for the Province of Maryland, which had
been promised to his father, was issued [26] in 1632 to
Cecilius, and he appointed his brother, Leonard Calvert,
as Governor, and sent out colonists and continued to
promote the interest of that colony until his death. (See
pp. 562-565 for Leonard Calvert.) He married, 1629,
Anne, the daughter of Thomas, Lord Arundel, of
Wardour, and his second wife, Anne Philipson. Their
son:

CHARLES CALVERT, third Lord Baltimore (1630-
1714-15), was appointed Governor of Maryland in

[26] *The Lords Baltimore and Md. Palatinate,* by C. C. Hall, p. 29.
George and Cecilius Calvert, by Wm. Hand Browne, p. 46.

1661, by his father, and continued as such until the boundary disputes with Penn made his presence in England necessary. Embarking in 1684, he appointed his infant son, *Benedict Leonard Calvert*, Governor with a board of Deputies, of which George Talbot was president. Through Talbot's indiscretion, an insurrection was raised and the members of the Council were forced to resign. In 1691, King William appointed the Governor, and thereafter the Governors were appointed by the Crown until 1715. The authority of the Lords Baltimore was thus in abeyance, being no longer absolute Lords as prescribed in the charter of Maryland, but they remained Proprietaries in the sense that they were "Lords of the Soil." After 1684, the third Lord Baltimore did not return to the colony.[27]   Charles Calvert, married first, Jane, the daughter of Vincent Lowe, and the widow of Henry Sewall (who had been Secretary of the Province of Maryland).

Their son, *Benedict Leonard Calvert*, fourth Lord Baltimore, (1678-79-1715), was elected member of Parliament for Harwich in Essex, during the last years of his life, and succeeded to the Baltimore title upon the death of his father, a few weeks before his own decease. In 1713 he had renounced the Catholic faith, and attached himself to the Church of England. This displeased his father, who withdrew his allowance of £450. Benedict applied to Queen Anne, who granted him a pension of £300 during his father's lifetime, and at Benedict's request, appointed John Hart Governor of Maryland. The news of the succession of Benedict Leonard Calvert as Proprietary, had hardly been received in Maryland, before it was followed by the announcement of his death. There is no record of his acts

27 Hall's *Baltimore*, p. 123, etc.

as Proprietary. Hart continued Governor until 1720.[28]

He married, January 2, 1698-99, Lady Charlotte Lee, the daughter of Edward Henry Lee, first Earl of Litchfield, and his wife, Lady Charlotte Fitzroy, the daughter of the Duchess of Cleveland, and Charles II., of England.

Their son, *Charles Calvert*, fifth Lord Baltmore, (1699-1751), succeeded to the title in 1715, and as the Maryland charter still stood firm, the proprietary government being only suspended by the Crown on the pretext that it was unsafe in Catholic hands, the accession of this Protestant Charles Calvert, made the pretext no longer tenable. The government was restored to the Proprietary after twenty-three years abeyance.[29] Charles Calvert was a Fellow of the Royal Society, and a member of Parliament. He was Lord of the Admiralty six years from 1741, Cofferer to the Prince of Wales, and Surveyor-General of his land in Cornwall. His principal residence was at Woodcote. Surrey, and his London residence was Roslyn House, corner of Russell Square and Guilford Street, where he died. He married, July 20, 1730, Mary, the daughter of Sir Theodore Jensen of Wimbleton, Surrey, and his wife, Williamza, the daughter of Sir Robert Henley, of the Grange, in Hampton. Lady Baltimore died 1748. Their son:

BENEDICT CALVERT, of Mt. Airey, Md., died 1788. He was sent to Maryland in charge of Captain Vernon to Dr. George Stuart, of Annapolis, with a private tutor. Through the influence of his father he was appointed Collector of Customs at Patuxent, November 16, 1744. In the Maryland *Gazette,* Annapolis, March 9, 1744-45, appears the following:

[28] *Ibid,* p. 151.   [29] *Ibid,* p. 144.

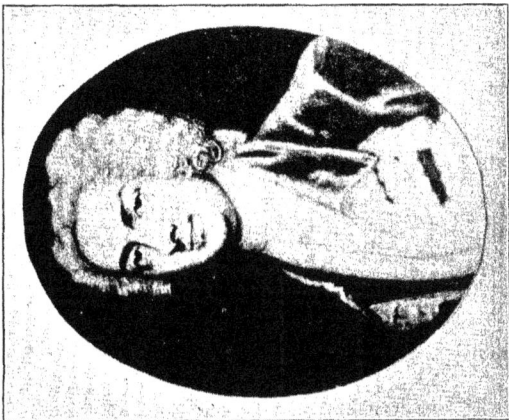

CHARLES, FIFTH LORD BALTIMORE

GEORGE CALVERT

"Yesterday . . . was appointed Benedict Calvert, Esq., Collector of his Majesties Customs for Patuxent, to be one of his Lordship's Honorable Council of the Province."

He married, April 21, 1748, *Elizabeth,* the daughter of Captain Charles and Rebecca (Gerrard) Calvert.

A descendant writes:

"Benedict Calvert was buried under the chancel of St. Thomas Church at Croome, Prince George's County, Md. My great-grandmother, Eleanor Custis Stuart, the daughter of Benedict, was the last person buried under the church. The Vestry had forbidden such burials but the body was carried to the church at night and buried. In digging the grave, after taking up the floor, the gold coffin plate of Benedict Calvert was uncovered."

His death is thus noticed:

"A few days ago in an advanced Age at his Seat in Prince George's County, in this State, Hon. Benedict Calvert, Esq., a Gentleman, whose Benevolence of Heart and many other exalted Virtues, justly endeared him to his Relations, and a numerous and respectable Acquaintance, who have sustained an irreparable Loss by his Death." [30]

His son, *George Calvert,* of Riversdale, Md., married Rosalie Eugenia Stier.

CAPTAIN CHARLES CALVERT, (uncle of Benedict Calvert, of Mt. Airey, and father of *Elizabeth,* his wife) died 1734. In 1720, Lord Guilford, the guardian of Charles, fifth Lord Baltimore, removed John Hart, the Governor of Maryland, and applied to the King and Council for permission to appoint in his stead, CAPTAIN

[30] *Md. Journal and Advertiser,* Tuesday, Jan. 15, 1788.

CHARLES CALVERT, of the First Foot Guards, and uncle of Lord Baltimore. This being acceded, the new Governor at once sailed for Maryland. He continued in office until 1727, when Benedict Leonard Calvert, brother of Lord Baltimore, succeeded him, and Charles was appointed Commissary General.[31] Charles Calvert married, 1722, Rebecca, the daughter of John and Elizabeth Gerrard, of Prince George's County,. Md., and their daughter, *Elizabeth,* married *Benedict Calvert,* of Mt. Airey. Md.

Their son, *George Calvert, Esq.,* of Riversdale, Md., married Rosalie Eugenia, the daughter of Henri Joseph and Marie Louise (Peeters) Stier, and their daughter, *Caroline Maria,* married *Thomas Willing Morris,* whose daughter, *Anna Maria,* married *Francis Key Murray.*

STIER

The Stiers are traced to Albert Stier (1629-1676),

of Amsterdam, who married, 1658, Catherine Ryser, whose son, Henri (1673-1744), married, 1701, Cornelie Nicolette Van Tetz.

Their son, Albert Jean (1701-1759), married, 1736, Isabelle Heléne, the daughter of Jean Baptiste de la Bistrate, Lord of Laer

STIER

and Neerwinde, and his wife, Heléne Francoise, the

31 *Ibid,* p, 151.

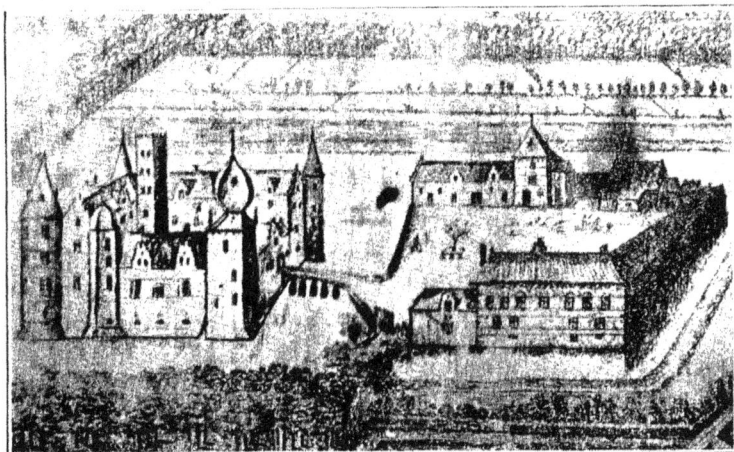

AERTSELAER AND CLEYDAEL

"RIVERSDALE," THE HOME OF GEORGE CALVERT
Built by the Lord of Aertselaer

daughter of Jacques Jean de Mont de Brialmont, descended from the Rubens family.

Their son, Henri Joseph, Lord of Aertselaer and Cleydael, was born 1743, and died 1767. He fled from Antwerp 1749, with his wife and three children, just before the French occupied the city, taking with him what property he could, arriving in Philadelphia October 1, 1794. There he continued to live until December, 1795, when he removed to Alexandria, Va. After the French Revolution he returned to France in order to hasten the settlement of his affairs, and took the oath of fidelity at Versailles, July 19, 1802. Directly after he sailed for America, but in November of that year he once more returned to Antwerp with his family, with the exception of his daughter. He married Marie Louise Peeters, and their daughter Rosalie Eugenia, married *George Calvert, Esq.*

RUBENS

The only child of his parents, John Rubens, who died 1587, was lawyer, sheriff, Councillor and Alderman of Antwerp, Germany.[32] He married, 1561, Marie Pypelinex, a lady of good position, distinguished for beauty, intelligence and elevation of character.

Their son, Peter Paul Rubens (1577-1640), was appointed court painter to Archduke Albert in Antwerp, and shortly after his first marriage in 1609, to Isabella Brandt, he bought a house with spacious grounds, and garden, on the street which now bears his name, and built a palatial abode. A separate compartment for works of art was arranged, which was placed beyond the court-yard in the form of a capacious rotunda, lighted from the top. This residence is still standing.

[32] *Ancestry of Rosalie Morris Johnson*, by R. Windsor Johnson.

Inscribed on the monument in the chapel of the church of St. James, Antwerp, where he is buried, is the following:

"Here lies Peter Paul Rubens, Knight, and Lord of Steen, son of John Rubens a senator of this city. Gifted with marvelous talents, versed in ancient history, a master of the liberal arts, and of the elegancies of life, deserved to be called the ' Apelles of his age ' and of all ages. He won for himself the good will of monarchs and princely men, etc."

Some of his descendants, through his son, Nicholas Rubens, Lord of Ramey, who was born 1618, died 1655, and married, 1640, Constance Hellman, are as follows:

Helène Françoise Rubens, daughter of Nicholas, married, 1660, Jean Baptiste Lunden.

Jeanne Catherine Lunden, married, 1686, Jacques Jean de Mont de Brialmont.

Helène Francoise de Mont de Brialmont, married, 1709, Jean Baptiste de la Bistrate, Lord of Laer and Neerwinde.

Isabelle Helène de la Bistrate, married Albert Jean Stier, whose granddaughter Rosalie Eugenia, married *George Calvert, Esq.,* of Riversdale, Md.

Their daughter, *Caroline Maria Calvert,* married *Thomas Willing Morris,* whose daughter, *Anna Maria,* married *Francis Key Murray.* Their daughter is:

JULIA MORRIS MURRAY BOWDOIN,

Member of Chapter I., The Colonial Dames of America.

VIII

PRICE (Ap Rhys)

The first of the name recorded in this country, William Price, came from Wales early in the seventeenth century, and settled in Kent County, Md., with two sons, William and Thomas.

"The Dividings," a tract of six hundred acres, on the east side of the Elk River, was bought by these three men May 27, 1661. "Price's Venture," on the west side of the Elk, "Price's Forest," and "Woodlawn Neck," were also bought by them.

The eldest son, William II., was born 1626. He married Margaret ——, and sold "Price's Forest."

His son, William III., a church warden of St. Stephen's Church, Cecil County, Md., 1709, married Mary, the daughter of John and Mary (Dorrington) Hyland. Issue: Richard, William, Andrew, Hyland, John and Rebecca.

PRICE

HYLAND

In October, 1677, "John and Mary's Hyland," consisting of ten hundred and fifty acres on the west side of the Elk River, was surveyed for Colonel John Hy-

land, of Labadeen, Eng., who settled at Elk Neck, Cecil
County, Md. He also owned " Arundell," " Triumph,"
a tract of six hundred acres,
and " The Hylands," contain-
ing over two thousand acres.
This and " John and Mary's
Hyland " were part of " St.
John's Manor," Elk Neck.

He married Mary Dorring-
ton, and died January 17, 1695,
leaving two sons, John and
Nicholas, and his daughter
Mary, who married William Price III.

HYLAND CREST

PRICE (*Continued*)

The third son of William III. and Mary (Hyland)
Price, Andrew Price, was born November 17, 1704;
married, in June, 1725, Elizabeth Perry.

Their son, John Hyland Price, born April 22, 1744,
married Rachel, the daughter of Nicholas and Rachel
(Bruff) Benson. Issue: Hyland, Benson, Benjamin,
Isaac, James, Spencer, Elizabeth, Sarah, and Rachel.

The fifth son, James Price, was born in Kent
County, Md., and died in Wilmington, Del., June 10,
1840. He was the first president of the Union Bank,
of Delaware, 1839, and second president of the Philadelphia, Wilmington and Baltimore Railroad (Pennsylvania Railroad), 1837.

He married, June 12, 1802, *Margaret,* the daughter
of Joseph and Elizabeth (Lea) Tatnall. She was born
August 23, 1767, and died March 21, 1841. Issue:
Joseph, John, and *James Edward.*

TATNALL

The widow and five of the seven children of Robert

Tatnall, a native of Leicestershire, Eng., who died there 1715, sailed from Bristol, Eng., 1725, and settled in Darby, Pa. One of the daughters married William Shipley, who came from England with them, and they lived in Chester County and Wilmington.

EDWARD TATNALL, the eldest son, was born in England, 1704, and died January 7, 1790. He came to America, 1725, and was one of the founders of Wilmington, Del., where he went to reside after his marriage, and was Assistant Burgess, 1763 to 1765.[1] He married, April 11, 1735, at London Grove Friends' Meeting House, Chester County,[2] *Elizabeth*, the daughter of Joseph and Mary (Levis) Pennock.

Their son, *Joseph Tatnall,* one of the original owners of the flour mills at Brandywine Village, was born September 6, 1740, and died August 3, 1813, in Brandywine Village.

For nearly a century these mills did a large exporting business to the West Indies and South America, of flour and cornmeal, loading their ships in the Delaware. Oliver Canby's mill was probably the first one of any importance, built in 1742. To that mill, the Swedes and early settlers, on both sides of the Delaware, brought their grist in rowboats. Canby died in 1755, and the mill became the property of Thomas Shipley, who, in 1762, built the "Old Shipley Mill." Other mills were soon after built upon the south side, and attention was then turned to the north side, which had not been im· proved before on account of the masses of rocks jutting out into the stream. In 1770, the Marshalls contracted to make improvements on the north side of the river, and build a mill, which they abandoned, and sold the con-

1 *Hist. of Del.,* by Thomas Scharf, p. 638.
2 *Recs. of New Garden Monthly Meeting.*

tract to Joseph Tatnall, who, with his son-in-law,
Thomas Lea, built on the north side. The old books
show that in 1780 wheat was bought for £24 a bushel,
and that three hundred barrels of flour sold for £21,000.
Several of the mills on the south side were bought by
James Price, from his father-in-law, Joseph Tatnall,
and he left them to his three sons, hereinbefore mentioned. As the war progressed, the demands on the
several States for supplies of all kinds were incessant,
owing to the sufferings and privations the patriots were
compelled to encounter. In the winter of 1779, General Washington wrote Cæsar Rodney as follows:

" The situation of the army with respect to supplies
is beyond description, and we have not more than three
days' bread, at a third allowance, on hand, nor any-
where within reach. . . . We have never experienced a
like extremity at any period of the war. . . . Unless
some extraordinary and immediate exertions be made by
the State from which we draw our supplies, there is
every appearance that the army will infallibly disband
in a fortnight."

Through Mr. Robert Morris, Commissioner of Fi-
nance, and in co-operation with him, Joseph Tatnall
furnished large supplies of flour to be forwarded to the
famishing troops, at the risk of having his valuable
property destroyed by the British commander, should
he appear in the vicinity.

Shortly before the Battle of Brandywine, General
Washington issued a military order, directing that the
several mills in northern Delaware should be dismantled,
from fear that they would fall into the possession of the
British army. The order directed that the utmost
secrecy should be observed in the removal of the " runners or upper millstones." The work was duly accomplished, and the " runners " were dragged by yokes of

EDWARD TATNALL

JAMES EDWARD PRICE

JAMES LEA

JOSEPH TATNALL

oxen over the hills, and secreted in the forest, one account says in Chester County, Pa., from which place of concealment they were ultimately recovered.

The house built by Joseph Tatnall in 1770, near the Brandywine bridge and the mills, now known as No. 1803 Market Street, sheltered General Washington as a guest more than once, and there also General Lafayette was entertained. It was given to the commander-in-chief for his headquarters just before the Battle of Brandywine. At one time General Wayne had his headquarters there, and for many years the front door jamb bore the mark of a missile hurled at him by a Tory, when he was standing in the doorway. On these several occasions the room used as a "council chamber" was the back parlor. British officers took possession of the house and enjoyed its comforts when Wilmington was captured by them.

It is related of Joseph Tatnall, that being in company with the commander-in-chief, the latter, in a spirit of great despondency, alluded to the necessities of his troops, when Mr. Tatnall, observing his distress, and wishing to assure him of his sympathy, said:

"George, I cannot fight for thee, but I will tell thee what I will do. I will feed thee."

When Washington was President, while passing through the village of Brandywine from Philadelphia, then the seat of government, to his home at Mount Vernon, he called at the Tatnall residence, and being told that his friend was at his counting-room, he left his chaise at the door, and walked down the hill to find him at the mill. They then returned to the house, tradition says, arm in arm.

As the first president of the Bank of Delaware, Joseph Tatnall signed the first bank-note issued by it, which is still preserved, bearing date of August 17, 1795. The following letter is of interest:

"Brandywine Bridge, 5th month, 1798.

"Friends and Fellow Citizens:

"Having for years past apprehended a great convenience might derive to the inhabitants of this borough by having a commodious time-piece erected in the central part of the town; in the first place, it would accelerate the punctual meeting of the different religiously disposed, at their several places of worship; secondly, it will be of service to those who think themselves not of ability to purchase time-pieces; and the last but not least consideration is, it would be some ornament to the place of my nativity. Therefore, I have procured from Europe a large and complete town clock of excellent workmanship, which I now present to you for the use of the town, with a sum of money not exceeding two hundred pounds, to be laid out in a large complete and good bell, to serve the clock, as well as the town hall now erecting, which I beg you to accept. Your friend,

"JOSEPH TATNALL." [3]

He died before General Lafayette returned to America, in 1824, but when the General passed through the village and the people showed their respect for the hero by a heart-felt demonstration, the General asked that the procession might be delayed at the Tatnall mansion, while he paid his respects to the family of his deceased friend.

According to the custom among the Friends, before a young man and woman could marry, it was necessary to declare their intention in the public meeting either two or three times. Then some of the elder Friends

---

[3] From the papers of Miss Montgomery, author of *Reminiscences of Wilmington*. The bell remained in place until 1866.

were appointed to examine into the case, to see that they were not too nearly related, etc., and if no good reason was found for objecting, they were "allowed to proceed," and the marriage usually took place soon after they had "passed meeting."

The marriage of *Joseph Tatnall* and *Elizabeth,* the daughter of James and Margaret (Marshall) Lea, occurred in the Friends' Meeting, January 31, 1765. She was born January 15, 1744-45.

Their daughter *Margaret* married, first, Isaac Starr, of Philadelphia, and second, James Price.

PENNOCK

The first military officer of the English army to emigrate to America, according to history, was Christopher Pennock, who had served under William of Orange. After coming to Chester County, Pa., in 1685, where he had a large grant of land, he was ordered to return to England, to join the campaign of William of Orange against James II. After the Battle of Boyne, 1690, Christopher Pennock returned to Chester County, finally removing to Philadelphia, where he died 1701.[4] He married Mary, the daughter of George Collett, of Clonmell, Ire., who died in Chester County, Pa., 1687. Their son:

JOSEPH PENNOCK, was born in Clonmell, Ire. At the age of twenty he had crossed the ocean four times. Once his vessel was captured by a French ship-of-war, and he was taken to France and held a prisoner for nearly a year, suffering great hardships from the French prison officials. He represented the County of Chester for twelve years in the Provincial Assembly;

[4] Authority: Mrs. William H. Miller (née Pennock), Media, Penn.; also *Family Tree,* compiled by Mrs. Caspar Wistar.

first elected 1716. He built a large house, called "Primitive Hall," in West Marlborough. When he first purchased his tract of land in Marlborough, the country was a wilderness and a favorite resort for a band of Lenape Indians. Pennock, by making peaceful negotiations with them, laid out his ground and erected his house without any molestation on their part. The Pennock family, at night, always left plenty of food in an outhouse for the Indians, who never failed to appease their appetites there. He married *Mary,* the daughter of Samuel and Elizabeth (Clator) Levis, before two justices of the court in 1701. She was born August 9, 1685, and died January 2, 1747. Their daughter *Elizabeth* married EDWARD TATNALL.

LEVIS

ARMS: *A chevron ermine between three dolphins, coronet, French viscounty.*

CREST: *A dolphin transfixed by a spear.*[5]

The original name of this family was De Levi, and they were French Protestants. One, Richard Levis, had a son Richard, Jr., who was baptized April 11, 1585, at Beeston, County Nottingham, Eng.

His son, Christopher Levis, was baptized September 20, 1621, at Beeston, and died in England, 1677. He married, 1648, Mary Nede. Their son:

SAMUEL LEVIS, born "7th month, 30th day," 1649, in Harley, Leicestershire, Eng., came to America 1682, and died 1734. He married "3rd month, 4th day," 1680, Elizabeth, the daughter of William Clator, of Elton, Nottinghamshire, Eng., a Friend who suffered for his religion. She came to America 1684.

Their daughter *Mary* married JOSEPH PENNOCK.[6]

5 C. E. Gildersome Dickenson.   6 *Family Records.*

LEA

In Bisley, Gloucester, Eng., Baldwyn Ley was taxed in 1543. Baldwyn Lea, who was church warden of Dauntsey, County Wilts, Eng., in 1609 [7] (1550-1622), may have been his son. The latter married Elynor, the daughter of Thomas and Elizabeth (Knight) Dench, of Longdon, County Worcester.

Two of her brothers were settled at Leigh de la Mere, not far from Dauntsey, at this period. Her sister, Fortune Dench, married, 1586, William Nicholson, of Christian Malford, Gent.

LEA

Baldwyn Lea's widow, Elynor, was buried at Calne, July 10, 1622. Issue: Elynor, Katherine, Thomas, Symon, Joane and George.

The third son, George Lea, of Christian Malford (1599-1640), on October 6, 1625, administered on the estate of his niece, Audrey Hoare, and sealed his bond on that occasion with the arms of the Lion Rampant. He married, February 7, 1621, at Seagry, Wiltshire, Sarah, the daughter of John and Agnes (——) Welden, of that place. He was living May 19, 1640, and his wife was alive in 1642. Issue: John, Samuel, Priscilla, and George.

The eldest son, John Lea, was of Christian Malford, and buried there March 7, 1685. His marriage to Joane —— occurred before 1654. Issue: Sarah, George, John, Daniel, and Lucy.

The third child, John Lea II., was the American colonist, who was baptized July 12, 1674. He removed to Gloucester, became a Quaker, and married February

[7] *Ancestry and Posterity of John Lea*, etc.

1, 1697, at Friends Meeting, Gloucester, Hannah. the widow of Joseph Webb, of Ashleworth, Gloucestershire, and the daughter of Samuel and Mary (Whitcomb) Hopton, of Painswick. They removed to Pennsylvania, receiving from the Nailsworth Quarterly Meeting the usual removal certificate. After a few months' residence in Philadelphia, they settled in Concord, Chester County, on land purchased of the Proprietary, as we learn from a warrant signed and sealed by William Penn, dated "3d Month, 16th, 1701," the tract containing one hundred and thirty-six acres and one hundred and fifty-two perches, lying to the south and west of the Concord Meeting House. Both John and Hannah Lea were noted and valued preachers, "Public Friends," or "Ministering Friends," as they were called. In 1718, "Fifth Month, 28th," John Lea was appointed to revise the book of discipline at Chester Monthly Meeting. He died in Springfield, "10th Month, 27th, 1726." Issue: Isaac, John, Hannah, and Rachel.

The eldest son, Isaac Lea, was born January 15, 1699, in Gloucester, Eng., and accompanied his parents to Pennsylvania. He resided at Darby, Pa., was taxed 1721, his valuation being £9, and again in 1735. He was appointed of Chester County, October 4, 1746, and resigned 1750, to move to Delaware.

He married, at Christ Church, Philadelphia, December 29, 1721, *Sarah,* the daughter of Walter and Rebecca (Fearne) Fawcett, of Chester, born May 10, 1702, and died 1800, at the age of ninety-eight, in Wilmington, Del. Issue: JAMES, Elizabeth, John, Rebecca, Hannah, Susannah, Mary, Ann, George, Sarah, Rachel.

JAMES LEA, was born in Darby, Pa., March 26, 1723. He lived in Wilmington, where he was Assistant Burgess of the Borough, 1757-1762, and 1766; Chief Burgess 1768 and 1769, and Town Treasurer, 1773 to 1775. He had property on Market Street, and was a member in good standing of the Society of Friends. His residence stood next the City Hall, and there he died, October 2, 1798, of yellow fever. His will was dated May 16, 1796, and proved November 19, 1798.

He married, in Darby, June 24, 1741, *Margaret,* the daughter of John and Joanna (Pascall) Marshall of that place. She was born "11th Month, 31st, 1723-24." Issue: Sarah, Frances, *Elizabeth,* who married *Joseph Tatnall,* Isaac, Margaret, Sarah, Abraham, Frances, James, and John.

DENCH

ARMS: *Sable, a chevron between three Towers triple towered argent.*

The Dench family [8] (also spelled Dunch) is traced back to the time of Henry VIII. at Longdon, Worcestershire County, Eng., and there John Dench was buried, March 15, 1542, and his wife Sibbil August 13, 1551. Issue: Jocosa, Ellen, Elizabeth, John, and Thomas.

The will of Thomas Dench, dated August 22, 1593, was probated April 11, 1594. Thomas was buried December 24, 1593. He married Elizabeth Knight, who was buried August 25, 1598. Issue: Giles, Jone, John, Thomas, Thomas, Henry, William, Elynor, who married Baldwyn Lea II., Robert, Fortune, Stephen.

HOPTON

The pedigrees of this ancient English family be-

8 *Ancestry and Posterity of John Lea,* p. 409.

gin with Walter de Hopton, who was living in 1223. There were two principal families of the name; one of Hopton Castle, in Salop, and one of Canon Frome, in Hereford, and the arms of both are similar.

In Bisley, three generations of Hoptons are traced in the sixteenth century, William, Richard, and William.

The connection of the last named William with Richard Hopton, who was buried at Stroud, August 2, 1660, rests on a probability, and it is therefore not assured that Richard was the son of William. His wife was Jane ――, who was buried December 3, 1658.

Their son, Samuel Hopton, baptized at Stroud, February 1, 1628, was of Painswick, Gloucestershire, where he was buried February 25, 1677. He married, at St. Mary's de Crypt, Gloucester, May 25, 1663, Mary, the daughter of William and Mary (Pincke) Whitcomb, of St. Owens, Gloucester, and the granddaughter of Thomas and Elizabeth (Devias) Whitcomb.[9] She was buried at St. John Baptist, Gloucester, December 22, 1679. Issue: Mary, Hannah, Samuel, Richard, Daniel, and William.

The second child, Hannah Hopton (called Anna in her mother's will), married, first, Joseph Webb, of Ashleworth, Gloucester County, when she was nineteen; married, second, John Lea II.

FAWCETT

WALTER FAWCETT, resided in Haverale Park, an extra parochial region, between Hampsthwaite and Fenston, and Orkley, in the County of Yorkshire, West Riding, Eng. The names of his parents have not been ascertained. He emigrated to Chester County, Pa.,

―――――
[9] *Lea Book*, p. 406.

1684, where he was a peace maker that year, and a member of the Pennsylvania Legislature in 1695. He died in Ridley, Pa., January 29, 1704-05. His will, dated " 7th month, 2, 1703," was probated July 8, 1704.

He married, second, June 14, 1694, Rebecca, the daughter of Robert and Elizabeth (Egginton) Fearne. She died November 15, 1756. Issue: Rebecca, Mary, Sarah, *Sarah,* who married Isaac Lea, and Elizabeth.

FEARNE

The widow of Robert Fearne brought his children to America. He was the son of Henry and the grandson of another Henry Fearne, of Pole Hall, in Hartington parish, County Derby, who died before 1617. Henry Fearne II., of Kniveton and Bonsall, County Derby, was a yeoman, and a considerable land-owner.

One of his younger sons, Robert Fearne, was baptized at Hartington, May 2, 1630. When he made his declaration of intention to marry at Bakewell, Derby, he was of Bonsall. He appears to have joined the Quakers, as he was buried in the Friends' Ground at Chesterfield, " 8th month, 10th, 1680."

He married Elizabeth, the daughter of Richard Egginton, of Ible, in Wirksworth. His widow came to Pennsylvania in 1682, with her son Joshua and daughters Elizabeth, Sarah, and Rebecca, bringing a certificate from Derby Quarterly Meeting for herself and children.

Their daughter Rebecca married WALTER FAWCETT, whose daughter *Sarah* married Isaac Lea.

MARSHALL

In the sixteenth century, the family of Marshall appears in records in Youlgrave parish, Eng., but no continuity of descent is shown until Edmund Marshall, of that parish, is reached, who occurs there from 1559 to 1571. Issue: Humphrey, Thomas, John, Edmund, and Margaret.

The eldest son, Humphrey, was baptized October 30, 1559; he was of Gratton, in Youlgrave. Issue: seven children.

One of the sons, John, was baptized February 2, 1603. He married Mary ——. Their son, John II., married Mary ——. Issue: Sarah, Abraham, Ann, Jonathan, and John III.

The youngest child, John Marshall III, baptized at Youlgrave, May 12, 1661, was of Elton, in the parish of Youlgrave, and a cousin of Abraham Marshall, of Pennsylvania, and eight years his senior. John Marshall came to America in the ship *Desire,* James Cock, Master, and landed at Philadelphia, June 23, 1686. He seems to have brought no certificate with him.

He married in Darby, Pa., Monthly Meeting, " the 19th of the 10th month, 1688," Sarah Smith (the sister of Thomas, of Croxton Keyrial, Leicestershire, and also the sister of John, of Darby, in said county, who was in Pennsylvania by 1684). Their wedding was the first solemnized in the Darby Meeting House. Sarah died " 16th of 5th Month, 1749," and John died at Darby, " 13th of 9th Month, 1729." Issue: John, William, and Thomas.

The eldest son, John Marshall IV., was born in Darby, Pa., " 16th of 6th Month, 1690 "; married there, first, 1715, *Joanna,* the daughter of Thomas and Margaret (Jenkins) Paschall; married, second, 1730, Eleanor Shenton. He died " 14th of 8th Month, 1749." Issue, first wife: Thomas, Sarah, Abraham, *Margaret,* who married JAMES LEA, Joanna, John, Susanna, and Elizabeth.

PASCALL, OR PASCHALL

The most notable family of Pascall is that which purchased a manor at Great Baddow, Essex, Eng., in the time of Edward VI., or earlier, in which place they had been yeomen. They were granted arms, and appear in the *Visitations of Essex,* as gentry for a century after.

Before 1634, Thomas Pascall, of Wrington, Somersetshire (occurring there 1609-1622), removed to Churchill. He died January 26, 1638; will probated in the Prerogative Court of Canterbury, November 10, 1639. He married Mary ——, who survived him, and died at the house of her son in the parish of St. John the Baptist, Bristol, and was buried there January 18, 1669. Issue: William, Margaret, Joan, Thomas, John, Mary, Elizabeth, Agnes, Sara.

Their eldest son, William Pascall, married, first, Johanna Collins, at Bath Abbey, June 25, 1632. Issue: Elizabeth, THOMAS, Mary, Joseph. His wife died before 1640, and he married again three times.

THOMAS PASCALL, was born September 3, 1634; died August 13; will proved September 18, 1718. He purchased, before 1682, five hundred acres of land in Pennsylvania from William Penn, and later came to Philadelphia, where he was elected a Member of the Provincial Assembly, 1685 and 1689; a Member of the Philadelphia Common Council, 1701 to 1704, and one of a committee to divide the city into wards, 1705. He married in England, before 1665, Joanna Sloper, who was born November 2, 1634; died at Philadelphia, September 2, 1707. Issue: William, *Thomas,* Elizabeth, Joseph, Mary, Joseph, and Francis.

The second son, *Thomas Pascall,* was born 1668, and came with his parents to Philadelphia; married at Radnor, Pa., in the Monthly Meeting, November 15, 1692, *Margaret,* the daughter of William and Elizabeth (Griffith) Jenkins, of Tenby, County Pembroke, Wales. Issue: Thomas, *Joanna,* William, Joseph, Benjamin, Abigail, John, Benjamin, Samuel, Stephen, Jonathan, Mary.

The second child, *Joanna Pascall,* married John Marshall IV., whose daughter *Margaret* married JAMES LEA.

JENKINS

WILLIAM JENKINS, came to America from Tenby, Pembroke County, Wales, and settled in Haverford township, Delaware County, Pa.; purchased a thousand acres of land before leaving England. Jenkintown, near Philadelphia, bears the name of this family. He was one of the Justices of the Court of Chester County, 1691, and a Member of the Assembly, 1690 to 1695.[10] He is also called a Justice of the Peace, 1691 to 1692, and is said to have been in the Council, 1703.[11]

He married Elizabeth, the daughter of Lewis Griffith, in 1673. Their daughter *Margaret* married *Thomas Pascall.*

GORDON

The first of this family recorded is James Gordon, of Kent County, Del., who died in 1740.

His son, Griffith Gordon, died in Kent County, 1762.

COE GORDON, his son, died in 1789; married, February 19, 1777, Sarah, the daughter of Nimrod and Eliza-

---

[10] *Hist. Delaware Co., Penn.* By George Smith, pp. 475, 524, 525.
[11] *Penn. Arch.,* 2d Series, Vol. ix, Assembly list.

PETRUS TRONBERG

ELIZABETH TRONBERG
Wife of Rev. Olaf Parlin

JAMES PRICE

MARGARET TATNALL
Wife of James Price

beth (Taylor) Maxwell, who was born September 28, 1761. (See p. 489.)

Their son, *John Gordon,* born June 7, 1782, and died in Wilmington, Del., July 10, 1847, married December 20, 1804, when she was but sixteen years of age, Anne Catherine, the daughter of William and Anne Catharine (Parlin) Sharpe, who was descended from the Rudman, Tronberg, and Parlin families. Issue: Sydney Ann, Charles, William, Louisa, Sarah Matilda, Elizabeth, *Catharine,* who married *James Edward Price,* Helen, and George.

RUDMAN

In answer to the requests of the Swedish Colony in America, the King of Sweden, Charles XI., and the Archbishop, as Provost or Bishop of the Colony, sent to them the Rev. Andreas Rudman, Ph. D., of the Upsala University, Gevalia, Province of Gertrickland, Sweden. He was born 1668, and died September 17, 1708. He journeyed to England and thence to America, reaching Annapolis, June 19, 1697, where he remained four days at Governor Nicholson's house, thence to Philadelphia. Holy Trinity Church, Christina (Wilmington), was dedicated Trinity Sunday, 1698, Dr. Rudman preaching. He was the founder of the Gloria Dei Church, in Philadelphia, 1700, and was buried under the chancel. In 1701 he went to New York, and officiated at the Oxford English Church until his death in 1708.[12]

He married Gertrude Mattson. Their daughter, Anna Katrina, married the Rev. Petrus Tronberg.

[12] Clay's *Annals. Records of Eric Bjork. Records of Old Swedes Church, Wilmington.*

TRONBERG

Another clergyman, the Rev. Petrus Tronberg, was sent to America by the King of Sweden, in 1726. He became Rector of the church at Christina (Wilmington), known as "Old Swedes," in 1742. His seal ring, bearing his arms, about two hundred and fifty years old, is owned by the family. He built the first brick house in Wilmington, with bricks imported from England.

TRONBERG

" The workmanship was so superior that people came from New York and Philadelphia to see it, and his descendants occupied it to the fifth generation. . . . A beautiful garden joined one belonging to the parsonage. . . ." [13]

He married Anna Katrina, the daughter of the Rev. Andrea Rudman, and died November 8, 1748. His tomb is in front of the chancel of the church, and has a lengthy inscription. The venerable Bible, presented to the church by Queen Anne in 1712, is still preserved, and the silver chalice and plate, presented by the miners of Sweden, to the Rev. Mr. Byork, are still in use.

Their daughter Elizabeth married the Rev. Olaf Parlin.

PARLIN

Another Rector of Holy Trinity Church, Wilmington, came from Sweden, the Rev. Olaf Parlin. He was born there 1716, ordained 1745, and arrived in America by the *Speedwell*, July 7, 1750. He married, October

[13] *Reminiscences of Wilmington*, by Miss Montgomery.

31, 1751, .Elizabeth, the daughter of Petrus and Anna Katrina (Rudman) Tronberg, who died September 29, 1802. They lived with Mrs. Tronberg (Anna Katrina Rudman) in the house built by her husband, while Olaf Parlin remained Rector of Holy Trinity Church. Afterwards they went to Philadelphia, where he was Rector of Gloria Dei Church. He died December 22, 1757, and was buried in the chancel of Gloria Dei, where a stone with an inscription of some length commemorates his life and service.

One of his daughters married Colonel Benzell, stationed on Lake Champlain in colonial times, and afterwards at Crown Point. His portrait in its scarlet uniform hung on the walls of the Tronberg mansion, and protected the old home during the war, at the time of the British possession, as one of the English colonels, seeing the portrait, ordered his men to protect the house.

The youngest daughter of Olaf and Elizabeth (Tronberg) Parlin, Anne Catharine Parlin, was born about 1752, and died May, 1800; buried in Old Swedes Church Yard. She married, 1782, William Sharpe, from England, who died at New Orleans in 1800, of yellow fever, and the same scourge carried off herself and her mother, leaving of the family only a son and daughter. William Sharpe was engaged in an extensive commercial business which took him to all parts of the world. After the death of his wife, their son settled in Canada.

Their daughter, Anne Catharine Sharpe, was born March 1, 1787, and died May 26, 1869. At the death of her parents she went to live with her guardian, Mr. Lea, of Wilmington. She had inherited the family portraits with the Tronberg house, which remained closed for several years, and when reopened it was found that most of the portraits had been stolen. Fortunately, the portrait of her great-grandfather, Petrus Tronberg, had been sent to the parsonage for safe-keeping, as well as that of his predecessor, Acrelius.

She married *John Gordon*, of Delaware. Their daughter, *Catharine Gordon*, married *James Edward Price*.

PRICE (*Continued*)

The youngest son of James and Margaret (Tatnall) Price, *James Edward Price*, was born August 8, 1809, and died July 25, 1898. He married, November 5, 1833, *Catharine*, the daughter of John and Anne Catharine (Sharpe) Gordon, who was born June 5, 1810, and died July 20, 1885. Issue: Anne Gordon, Margaret, William Gordon, Mary, James, Edward, KATHARINE GORDON, who married William Graham Bowdoin, and SYDNEY.

KATHARINE GORDON PRICE BOWDOIN,

SYDNEY PRICE,

Members of Chapter I., The Colonial Dames of America.

IX

MALLETT

One of the Huguenots of La Rochelle, France, David Mallet, went to England with his family, after the Revocation of the Edict of Nantes.

His son, John Mallet, died in Fairfield, Conn., 1745. He married Johanna Lyon.

Their son, Peter Mallet, born March 31, 1712, and died June 18, 1760, in Fairfield, Conn., married Naomi ——.

PETER MALLETT, their son, born November 14, 1744, and died February 2, 1805, married, 1780, Sarah (1765-1836), the daughter of Robinson and Sarah (Coit) Mumford.

Their son, *Edward Jones Mallett*, born in Fayetteville, N. C., May 1, 1797, and died August 20, 1883, married, September 11, 1820, *Sarah*, the daughter of James and Sarah (Jencks) Fenner; she was born May 13, 1797, and died May 17, 1841. *Sarah Fenner*, their daughter, married Stephen States Lee.

MUMFORD

The Mumfords of Connecticut descend from James Mumford, who was born February 7, 1715, and died 1773. He married *Sarah*, the daughter of Richard and Elizabeth (Saltonstall) Christophers, baptized December 6, 1719.

Their son, *Robinson Mumford*, also of Connecticut, married February, 1761, Sarah Coit. *Sarah*, their daughter, married PETER MALLETT.

CHRISTOPHERS

One of the early colonists, Richard Christophers, born July 15, 1662, and died June 9, 1726, married, June 26, 1681, *Lucretia,* the daughter of Peter and Elizabeth (Brewster) Bradley; she was born August 16, 1661, and died 1691.

Their son, *Richard Christophers II,* born August 18, 1685, and died 1736, married, August 16, 1710, Elizabeth, the daughter of Gurdon and Jerusha (Richards) Saltonstall; she was born May 11, 1690. *Sarah,* their daughter, married James Mumford.

BREWSTER

ELDER WILLIAM BREWSTER, born 1560, and died April 10, 1644, came to America with his wife Mary.

Their son, *Jonathan Brewster,* born in England, August 12, 1593, and died in Connecticut, May 7, 1659, married, April 15, 1624, Lucretia Oldham.

Their daughter *Elizabeth,* born May 1, 1637, and died in 1708, married September 7, 1653, Peter Bradley, who died April 3, 1682; and their daughter, *Lucretia,* married Richard Christophers I, whose son *Richard* married Elizabeth Saltonstall. (See pp. 740-743.)

SALTONSTALL

One of the grantees of the Massachusetts Company, Sir Richard Saltonstall (1586-1658), married Grace Kay.

Their son, Richard Saltonstall, born 1610, and died April 29, 1694, married, 1633, Muriel Gurdon.

Their son, Nathaniel Saltonstall, born 1639, and died May 21, 1707, married, December 28, 1663, Elizabeth Ward.

Their son, Gurdon Saltonstall, born March 27, 1666, and died September 20, 1724, married Jerusha Richards.

Their daughter, Elizabeth Saltonstall, married *Richard Christophers II*, whose daughter *Sarah*, married James Mumford.

FENNER

ARTHUR FENNER I, the son of Thomas Fenner, of Branford, Conn., born in September, 1622, and died October 16, 1703, married *Mehitable*, the daughter of RICHARD WATERMAN (1590-1673); she died 1684.

THOMAS FENNER, their son, born in September 1652, and died February 27, 1718, married, July 26, 1682, *Dinah*, the daughter of Thomas and Mary (Harris) Borden.

Their son, *Arthur Fenner II*, born October 17, 1699, and died February 2, 1788, married, June 2, 1723, *Mary*, the daughter of James and Hallelujah (Brown) Olney; she was born September 30, 1704, and died March 18, 1756. *James*, their son, married *Freelove Whipple*, and *Freelove*, their daughter, married *Silvanus Jenckes*. Another son:

GOVERNOR ARTHUR FENNER III., born December 10, 1745, and died October 15, 1805, married *Amy*, the daughter of *Gideon Comstock;* she died September 2, 1825.

Their son, *James Fenner*, born January 22, 1771, and died April 17, 1840, married, in November, 1792, *Sarah*, the daughter of Silvanus and Freelove (Fenner) Jenckes.

Their daughter, *Sarah Fenner*, married *Edward Jones Mallett*, whose daughter, *Sarah Fenner*, married Stephen States Lee.

BORDEN-HARRIS

Richard Borden, born 1601, and died May 25, 1671, married Joan, who died July 15 1688, aged eighty-four.

Their son, *Thomas Borden,* who died November 25, 1676, married *Mary Harris,* and *Dinah,* their daughter, married Thomas Fenner.

William Harris (1610-1681), married Susannah ——, who died 1682, and their daughter *Mary* married *Thomas Borden.*

JENCKES

Joseph Jenckes, born 1622, and died January 4, 1717, married Esther Ballard, who died 1717.

Governor Joseph Jenckes, their son, who died June 15, 1740, married Martha, the daughter of John Brown (1630-1706), and his wife, Mary Holmes.

Their son, *Obadiah Jenckes,* who died 1763, married, May 21, 1713, Alice, the daughter of Zachariah and Mercy (Baker) Eddy; she was born January 5, 1694, and died 1770. (Her father, Zachariah, the son of Zachariah and the grandson of Samuel Eddy, born April 10, 1664, and died April 12, 1737, married Mercy Baker, February 13, 1683.)

Their son, *Ebenezer Jenckes,* married Alice ——, whose son *Silvanus,* born May 22, 1746, and died May 25, 1781, married, July 7, 1772, *Freelove,* the daughter of James and Freelove (Whipple) Fenner. *Sarah,* their daughter, married *James,* the son of Governor Arthur Fenner.

Sarah Fenner married *Edward Jones Mallett.*

Sarah Fenner Mallett married Stephen States Lee.

OLNEY-BROWN

THOMAS OLNEY (1606-1681), married Mary Small (1605-1679).

Their son, *Epenetus Olney,* born 1634, and died June 3, 1698, married *Mary,* the daughter of John and Sarah Whipple.

Their son, *James Olney,* born November 9, 1670, and died October 6, 1744, married, August 31, 1702, *Hallelujah,* the daughter of *David Brown.*

Their daughter, *Mary Olney,* married *Arthur Fenner II.*

CHAD BROWN, died in 1650. His wife's name was Elizabeth, and their son *David,* who died 1710, married, 1669, Alice, the daughter of Benjamin Hearnden (died 1685), whose wife Elizabeth was the daughter of William White.

Their daughter, *Hallelujah Brown,* married *James Olney,* whose daughter, *Mary,* married *Arthur Fenner II.*

WHIPPLE

JOHN WHIPPLE, born 1617, and died May 16, 1685, married Sarah ——, who was born 1624.

JOSEPH WHIPPLE, their son, was born 1662, and died April 28, 1746, married *Alice,* the daughter of Edward Smith and Amphilis Angel, the daughter of THOMAS ANGEL (1618-1694), whose wife Alice, died in 1695.

Their son, *John Whipple,* born May 18, 1685, and died May 18, 1765, married Abigail, the daughter of Joseph and Sarah (Pray) Brown.

Their daughter, *Freelove Whipple,* born December 24, 1728, and died August 21, 1751, married, January 10, 1750, *James,* the son of Arthur and Mary (Olney)

Fenner (and the brother of GOVERNOR ARTHUR FEN-
NER); he was born February 9, 1730, and died October
25, 1751. *Freelove,* their daughter, married *Silvanus
Jenckes.*

COMSTOCK-PRAY

SAMUEL COMSTOCK, the son of Samuel, who died
1660, was born May 27, 1637; he married, November
23, 1678, *Elizabeth,* the daughter of THOMAS ARNOLD
(1599-1674), and his wife, Phebe Parkhurst, who died
1688.

Their son, *Hazadiah Comstock,* born April 16, 1682,
and died February 21, 1764, married Catherine, the
daughter of John Pray.

Their son, *Gideon Comstock,* born November 4, 1709,
and died 1801, married Amy ——, whose daughter
Amy, married GOVERNOR ARTHUR FENNER III, and
died September 2, 1825.

The colonist, Richard Pray (1630-1695), married
May ——, who died in 1686.

Their son, John Pray, died October 9, 1733; his wife
Sarah, the daughter of John Brown (1630-1706), died
1735; her mother was Mary Holmes. Their daughter,
Catherine Pray, married *Hazadiah Comstock.*

LEE

The descendants of Francis Lee of Barbadoes, and
Mary, his wife, are as follows:

Thomas Lee, born February 6, 1710, and died August 8, 1769, married in Charlestown, S. C., Mary
Giles.

Stephen Lee, born January 21, 1750, in Charleston,
married Dorothea Alison, the widow of Rev. Hugh Alison.

Paul S. H. Lee, born September 22, 1784, and died April 20, 1852, married in Charleston, January 10, 1809, Jane Elizabeth, the daughter of Jacob Martin, of Charleston, and his wife, Rebecca Murray, who was born October 7, 1755, and died May, 1840. The father of Jacob was the Rev. John Nicholas Martin (1725-1795), of Charleston.

Stephen States Lee, of Baltimore, born November 8, 1812, and died August 22, 1892, married, April 30, 1840, *Sarah Fenner Mallett,* born August 14, 1821. Issue, among others:

Hillyard Cameron Lee.

Julian Henry Lee.

Amabel Lee, married John Cowman George.

GEORGE

The pedigree of John Cowman George is as follows:

Samuel Knox George, married —— Findley.

Archibald George, married Henrietta Duckett Cowman.

John Cowman George, married *Amabel Lee.* Issue: Stephen Lee, AMABEL LEE, who married, June 28, 1905, Heyward E. Boyce; Henrietta Cowman and SARAH FENNER.

AMABEL LEE GEORGE BOYCE,

SARAH FENNER GEORGE,

Members of Chapter I., The Colonial Dames of America.

X

BRANDT

ARMS: *D'argent a un brandon de sa, posè sur une terrasse de sin et allume en haut.*

CREST: *Le brandon.*

LAMBREQUIN: *D'argent and sable.*[1]

CAPTAIN RANDOLPH BRANDT, who came to Maryland from the Island of Barbadoes in the year 1674, was a descendant of the Brandts of Hamburg, Ger. He was the son of Marcus Brandt, of London, who was the second son of Daniel Brandt, of Hamburg, Ger. Marcus Brandt was a merchant prince and sea commander, who was twice entrusted by Charles II. with diplomatic commissions in connection with the Dutch treaty in Suri-

[1] Arms of the old Baronial House of Brand-Brandt of Hamburg, Germany, as given by Reiststap in his *Armorial General.* The same arms are shown in the Herald's *Visitation of London,* 1633-34, Vol. xv, Harleian Soc. Pub., p. 99.

nam.[2] He died in the Island of Barbadoes, where he settled. Captain Brandt brought with him to Maryland his wife Mary, daughters Mary and Judith, and son Randolph II. From his will, we learn that a son Marcus remained in Barbadoes, and a son *Charles* was born in Maryland.

In the year 1678 Captain Brandt was commanding a troop of horse in Charles County, Md. He perpetuated the former places of residence of his father and himself in England and Barbadoes, in the names given to his patents of land, which descended for generations; these were, " Hammersmith," " Barbadoes," " Greenwich," etc. He enjoyed the friendship of the third Lord Baltimore, and the confidence of General Thomas Notley. On August 20, 1678, General Notley sent instructions to Randolph Brandt regarding a reconnoitering expedition of great importance to be made by him in connection with the Indian uprisings.[3] From that time until 1681 he was active in Indian warfare.

Lord Baltimore's correspondence with Captain Brandt forms a voluminous part of the official records from 1680 to 1682. Brandt inaugurated the " Post," a public official carrier of letters being ordered the day after the receipt of his letter by Lord Baltimore and the Council, dated May 21, 1680, in which he says:

" If your Lordship thinks fitt to employ a Post for our County it will be much better for the people is much dissatisfied to have their horses pressed from them."

In June, 1681, Brandt is empowered by Lord Baltimore to make a treaty of peace with the Northern In-

2 Annapolis *Land Warrants* Liber xv, fol. 506.   Calendar of State Papers of Great Britain, Col. Series, 1675-76, p. 167.

3 *Archs. of Md.*, Vol. xv, p. 106.

dians, for which a special commission was issued, as follows:[4]

"Whereas, greate Troopes of the Northern Indians have and doe daily make inroads and incursions into this our Province to the greate terror and confusion of the Inhabitants thereof, and highly to be suspected upon noe good designe, we haveing already had some murders lately committed by strange Indians upon severall good people of this Province We doe therefore by and with the advice and consent of our Councill hereby authorize and empower as also strictly Charge and Command you Capt. Randolph Brandt Commander of a troope of horse in our said county (Charles) to range with your troope or such and so many men thereof well mounted and armed as you shall from time to time think necessary for the discovery of the said Indians with whom you are to endeavor by all faire waies and means possible to come to a treaty according to the Instructions from us and our Councill this day to you Directed, And in case you or any of your Troope shall be assaulted by any the said Indians or other enemys, or that they by any waies or means offer to breake peace, by open violence or privately contriving and conspiring to sett upon or betray you or any of you or any English Plantation or people You are to the best of your skill knowledge and endeavour, and to the utmost of your might and power, to fall upon, pursue, fight, take, kill, vanquish and destroy all such enemys, or otherwise if you be at any time overpowered, you are to contrive and make what honble retreate possibly you cann with your Company for such further aid and assistance as shall be Deemed necessary for your Recruite with regard had to the number and power of your Enemy according to the tenor of your said Instructions; ffor all of which this shall be your sufficient power. Given under our hand and seale at Armes this first day of July in the sixth yeare of our Dominion &c Annoq Domini 1681." [5]

The Northern Indians were compelled by Captain Brandt to refrain from exterminating the peaceful tribes in southern Maryland. So constantly were his troopers in the saddle and away from home in the public service, that they could not make crops to feed their families. Most of them got into debt and had to be protected from arrest by the Government.

The strenuous summer of 1681 over, the northern Indians pacified and friendly, Captain Brandt was once more enrolled a Member of Assembly at the September term, 1681 (he having been a member at the October session, 1678), and was a bearer of important messages to the upper house, with others from the lower house. [6] March 10, 1684, Brandt is instructed, as Deputy Surveyor, to lay out towns and ports in Charles County. [7] He was again in the field, March, 1686, an ardent supporter of Lord Baltimore in the Protestant Revolution, in which Coode and Fendall were the conspicuous leaders in Maryland. Brandt was active in quelling the rebellion, and although tempted by his lieutenant to become the leader against his Lordship, he remained faithful, and frustrating the plans of Fendall's party to take him unawares when at church, to tie him and put Fendall in his place, he succeeded in bringing his traitorous lieutenant to justice. [8]

The youngest son, *Charles Brandt,* is mentioned in his father's will, dated 1697:

5 *Ibid,* Vol. xvii, pp. 12, 13, 15, 27 and 28.
6 *Md. Arch.,* Vol. 7, pp. 23, 163, 178, 180, 212, 229, 266.
7 *Ibid,* Vol. xvii, fol. 359.
8 *Ibid,* Vol xv, p. 402 (1688).

"To my son Charles the moiety one half of land where I reside, West side of 'Piccawaxen Creek' containing four hundred and fifty (450) acres, also the moiety of two hundred (200) acres on the Potomac River called 'Green Weigh.' . . . Sons Charles and Jacob to be brought up in the Catholic Faith. . . ."

The absence of any record of the marriage of Charles Brandt in the parish registers of the State can be accounted for by the fact that he was a Catholic. His will was proved March 10, 1714.[9] He married Elizabeth, the daughter of John and the granddaughter of Colonel John Douglas. She married, second, Thomas Howard.[10]

In his will Charles bequeathed "to his son *Jacob*, . . . a gold seal ring, saddle, holsters, pistols, sword, belt and young horse; two silver spoons to daughter Elizabeth; daughter Sarah, leather chairs, pewter, etc.;" no land mentioned, that going by law of entail to his son, Charles Brandt. It is recorded [11] that Thomas Howard and Elizabeth, his wife, executrix of Charles Brandt, late of Prince George County, administered on his estate.

DOUGLAS

One of the leading military figures of Colonial Maryland, Colonel John Douglas, arrived in the Province 1659, as that year he demanded land for transporting himself into the colony. In his will, he bequeathed "Cold Spring Manor," in Charles County, a tract of over a thousand acres; also "Blithwood," and other tracts aggregating fully two thousand acres. Colonel Douglas has not been identified with the earlier and dis-

---

9 Annapolis *Wills, Liber,* W. B. No. 5, p. 692.

10 The Douglasses were doubly related to the Howards, a brother of Elizabeth also marrying one of that family.

11 *Prerogative Court Records, Liber, B.,* xxxvi, fol. 97.

tinguished family of Virginia, or with any branch of the house of Douglas in Great Britain, but his records, both civil and military, are recorded.[12]   John Douglas died in the year 1678, and his wife married twice afterwards.   His son was John, whose daughter Elizabeth, married CHARLES BRANDT.

BRANDT   (Continued)

No record of the marriage of *Jacob Brandt* has been found. His will was probated March 13, 1750.[13]   In this he mentions his wife Mary, sons *Charles* and Edward, and daughter Ann.   Neither Jacob nor his father Charles, held office in the Province, as both lived after Maryland was under the rule of the Protestants, when Catholics were not permitted to hold office.   Jacob was Grand Juror at the November term of court, 1748.[14] This is the only mention of him in the court records. His wife Mary married, second, John Wood.

"The final account filed under the estate of Jacob Brandt by John Wood and Mary, his wife, executrix of Jacob Brandt, deceased," is recorded [15] under date of November 30, 1754.

The eldest son, *Charles Brandt,* a minor at the time of his father's death, was left to the guardianship of his mother.   He lived on the estate which descended to him by law of primogeniture, from his great-grandfather, Captain Randolph Brandt, of Charles County.   The proof of Charles' marriage to Martha Wood, the daughter of James Greenfield Wood, of Charles County, is in the will [16] of that gentleman where he bequeaths her

12 *Archs. of Md.,* Vol. xv, pp. 56, 71, 72, 99, 124, 172.
13 *Annapolis Wills, D. D.,* No. 7, p. 29.
14 *Charles County Records, Annapolis, Liber* 42, p. 509.
15 *Annapolis Land Office, Balances,* No. i, p. 120.
16 *Charles County Wills, Liber,* B, No. i, p. 282.

"three negroes" and directs the balance of the estate to
be divided between wife and daughter, Martha Brandt.
Charles Brandt was joint executor of this will with the
widow Margaret Wood.

One of the sons, *Jacob Brandt II.*, married Ann
Mankin.

Their son, *Jacob Brandt III.*, was born January 22,
1812, and died January 12, 1882. He married, June
26, 1851, *Miriam*, the daughter of Daniel and Letitia
(Mankin) Dodge, born September 7, 1832, and died
November 5, 1894.

Their daughters are: MIRIAM, and LENITA, who married Commander Poundstone, U. S. N.

DODGE

JOHN DODGE,[17] the son of Richard I. and his wife,
Edith Dodge, and the brother of Richard Dodge II.,
was born at East Coker, Somersetshire County, Eng.,
1631, and died 1711. He was Deputy to the General
Court from Beverly, 1676, 1678, 1679; representative
to the General Court at Boston, 1683, 1689, 1690. He
married Sarah ——.

Their son, *Josiah Dodge,* married Sarah Fiske.

Their son, *Josiah Dodge II.,* married *Prudence Fairfield Dodge.*

LIEUTENANT WILLIAM DODGE, was the son of Richard II. and Mary (Eaton) Dodge, and the grandson of
Richard Dodge I. He married Prudence Fairfield.

Their daughter, *Prudence Fairfield,* married *Josiah
Dodge II.*

Their son, *Josiah Dodge III.,* married Susannah
Knowlton.

Their son, *Josiah Dodge IV.,* was born September 8,
1740, and married, November 8, 1761, *Hannah,* the

17 *Recs.* of Beverly, Mass.; Mass. *Recs.,* Vol. v.

RESIDENCE OF JOHN CONANT, B.D.
In close of Salisbury

REV. JOHN CONANT, B.D.

daughter of Ebenezer and Ruth (Pierce) Conant. She
was born February 12, 1740, and died 1810.

Their son, the *Rev. Daniel Dodge,* born December
1, 1775, and died May, 1852, married, February 2,
1831, Letitia Mankin, born 1793, and died in September, 1878.

Their daughter *Miriam* married *Jacob Brandt III.*

EATON

GOVERNOR THEOPHILUS EATON,[18] born 1591, died
January 7, 1657, came to America in the year 1637,
and was a founder of the city of New Haven, 1637 to
1638, and the first Governor of the New Haven Colony,
1638 to 1657. He married the daughter of the Bishop
of Chester.

Their daughter *Mary* married Richard Dodge II.

CONANT

ARMS: *Gules, ten billets, or four, three, two, one.*

CREST: *A stag, holding with the dexter foot an escutcheon of the Arms.*

MOTTO: *Conanti dabitor.*

ROGER CONANT,[19] first Governor of the Cape Anne
Colony, in Massachusetts, was born April 15, 1591, and
died November 19, 1679. He married, November 11,
1618, Sarah Horton.

" He was appointed under the Charter of Lord Sheffield, 1624, and remained at the head of the Colony until
1628, when he was succeeded by John Endicott. During this time he occupied the 'great white house' at
Cape Ann. This was built in 1624 and was afterwards
moved to Salem and occupied by succeeding Governors.

18 Allan's *Biog. Dict.*

19 Authorities: Savage *Gen. Dict. of N. E.;* Allan's *Am. Biog. Dict.;*
Hubbard, pp. 109, 110; *Landing at Cape Ann,* by I. W. Thornton; Felt's
Hist of Mass.

It still stands after nearly three centuries. Governor
Conant discovered the site and founded the town of
Salem and his son was the first child born in Salem.
Soon after the removal of the Colony to Salem there
was danger of its abandonment through an invitation
to their minister, the Rev. John Lyford, to settle in
Virginia, and the decision of most of the colonists to
accompany him. They tried to induce Governor
Conant to go with them, but Felt's *History* says: ' He

CONANT

had taken his position and pledged his faith though
perils from savages and hardships of a new settlement
clustered around him.' The success of the Massachusetts Colony rested on his decision. He was frequently
called to offices of honor and trust by his fellow towns-
men. In 1634 he was chosen as Representative to the
General Court at Boston, May 14. This was the second representative Assembly which met in this country,
that of Virginia being first. He was deputy from

Salem and thus assisted in laying the foundation of that form of Government which remains to-day our noblest heritage. Governor Roger Conant was instrumental in settling a quarrel between Captain Miles Standish and Captain Hewes. This is memorialized by a stained glass window in a church in Dudley Centre, Massachusetts. In Hawthorne's description of Main street, Salem, he speaks of Conant as follows: ' Roger Conant, the first settler of Naumkeag, has built his dwelling on the border of the forest path, and at this moment he comes Eastward through the vista of woods, with his gun over his shoulder, bringing home the choice portions of a deer. Roger Conant is of that class of men who do not merely find but make their place in the system of human affairs. A man of thoughtful strength, he has planted the germ of a city.' "

One of Governor Conant's sons, *Lot,* was born 1624, and died September 29, 1674. He married Elizabeth Walton.

A son, *Roger II.,* was born March 10, 1668-1669, and died 1745; married, April 25, 1698, Mary, the daughter of Captain Thomas and Mary Raymond. Captain Raymond was born ——, in Salem, Mass., and died 1735.[20]

One of the sons of *Roger Conant II.,* was *Ebenezer,* born December 20, 1698, and died October 24, 1794. He married, Ruth, the daughter of John Pierce II., and his wife, Patience Dobson, who died November 19, 1797; their daughter, *Hannah Conant,* married *Josiah Dodge IV.*

PIERCE

CAPTAIN MICHAEL PIERCE,[21] was the son of John

20 *Gen. Dodge Family,* p. 61.
21 Allan's *Am. Biog. Dict.;* Savage's *Hist.,* pp. 431, 630; *Gen. Reg.* Vol. xiii, p. 365.

Pierce I, (who came in the *Mary and John*, 1630-31, and died August 19, 1661). Captain Pierce lived at Hingham, Mass., from the year 1646 until March 26, 1676, when he was killed in the battle of Pawtucket. He was Captain from 1669 to 1675.

His son, John Pierce II., married Patience Dobson, whose daughter, *Ruth*, married *Ebenezer Conant*.

Their daughter, *Hannah Conant*, married *Josiah Dodge IV.*, whose son, the *Rev. Daniel Dodge*, married Letitia Mankin.

Their daughter, *Miriam Dodge*, married *Jacob Brandt III*, whose daughters are:

MIRIAM BRANDT,

LENITA BRANDT POUNDSTONE,

Members of Chapter I., The Colonial Dames of America.

XI

STRONG

ELDER JOHN STRONG,[1] son of Richard Strong (1561-1613), was born in Taunton, Eng., 1605, and died April 14, 1699. He removed to London and afterwards to Plymouth. In 1630 he came to America in the ship *Mary and John,* settling first at Dorchester, Mass. After having assisted in founding and developing the town of Dorchester, in 1635, he removed to Hingham, and took the freeman's oath at Boston, March 9, 1636. His stay at Hingham was short, as December 4, 1638, he was an inhabitant and proprietor of Taunton, Mass., and was made a freeman of Plymouth Colony that year. He remained at Taunton as late as 1645, and was Deputy from that place to the General Court in Plymouth 1641, 1643, and 1644. From Taunton he removed to Windsor, Conn., where he was appointed with four others " to superintend and bring forward the settlement of that place." In 1659, he removed from Windsor to Northampton, Mass., of which town he was one of the first and most active founders. There he lived for forty years and was a leading man in the affairs of the town and church. He was a man of means, a tanner, and a large land owner as appears from the records of the county clerk's office. The church records show that he was the " Ruling Elder," 1663.[2]   He was twice married, his first wife dying on the voyage to America; his second wife was Abigail

---

[1] Matthew's *Am. Armoury and Blue Book, Addenda,* p. 72.
[2] *Hist. of the Strong Family;* Stiles' *Hist. Windsor,* Vol. II, p. 743.

Ford, and they were married December, 1630. She died July 6, 1688, aged about eighty years. Issue, first wife, two children, viz:

John, Jr.

Infant who died 1630.

Issue, second wife, sixteen children, viz:

Thomas, died October 3, 1689, in Northampton, Mass.; married Mary, the daughter of Rev. Ephraim Hewitt of Windsor.

Jedediah, born May 7, 1637, died May 22, 1733; married first, November 18, 1662, Freedom, the daughter of Henry Woodward; second, December 19, 1681, Abigail, the daughter of John Stebbins; third, January 5, 1661-62, Mrs. Mary (Hart) Lee, the daughter of Stephen Hart.

Josiah, born about 1639, died young.

Return, born 1640-41, died April 9, 1726; married May 11, 1664, Sarah, the daughter of Rev. John Warham.

Ebenezer, born 1643, died February 11, 1729; married October 14, 1668, Hannah, the daughter of Nicholas Clapp.

Abigail, born about 1645, died April 15, 1704; married, first, November 12, 1673, Rev. Nathaniel, the son of Rev. Charles Chauncey, President of Harvard University; second, September 8, 1686, Medad, the son of Edward Pomeroy.

Elizabeth, born February 24, 1647, died May 12, 1736; married Joseph, the son of Joseph Parsons.

Experience, born August 4, 1650; married May 27, 1669, Zerubbabel, the son of Lieutenant Walter Filer.

Samuel, born August 5, 1652, died October 29, 1732; married June 19, 1684, Esther, the daughter of Deacon Edward Clapp.

Joseph, twin to Samuel, died young.

Mary, born October 26, 1654, died December 8, 1738; married March 20, 1679, Deacon John, the son of Lieutenant William Clark.

Sarah, born 1656, died February 10, 1733; married December 19, 1675, Joseph, the son of Francis Barnard.

Hannah, born May 30, 1659, died April 23, 1748; married July 15, 1680, Captain William, the son of Lieutenant William Clark.

Hester, born June 7, 1661, died March 4, 1726-27; married October 15, 1678, Thomas, the son of Thomas Bissell.

Thankful, born July 25, 1663, married —— Baldwin, of Milford, Conn.

Jerijah, born December 12, 1665, died April 24, 1754; married July 18, 1700, Thankful, the daughter of John Stebbins.

The eldest child of Elder Strong and his first wife, *John Strong, Jr.,* was born in England, 1626, and died in Windsor, Conn., February 20, 1698, where he spent his life, and was a man of prominence in affairs. He came with his parents to America. He married first, November 26, 1656, Mary, the daughter of Joseph Clark, of Windsor; she was baptized September 30, 1638, and died April 28, 1663; second, 1664, Elizabeth Warriner, who died June 7, 1684. Issue first wife, two children, viz:

Mary, born April 22, 1658, died November 22, 1676; married Timothy Stanley.

Hannah, born August 11, 1660, died November, 1745; married Stephen, the son of Stephen Hopkins.

Issue second wife, four children, viz:

John III.

Jacob, born April 8, 1673, died 1750; married November 10, 1698, Abigail, the daughter of Nathaniel Bissell.

Josiah, born January 11, 1678, died May 29, 1749; married, January 5, 1698, Joanna, the daughter of Josiah Gillett.

Elizabeth, born about 1684, died April 18, 1720; married Thomas, the son of Thomas Burnham.

The eldest son of John and Elizabeth (Warriner) Strong, *John Strong III.*, was born in Windsor, Conn., December 25, 1665, and resided there where he died, May 29, 1749; married November 26, 1686, Hannah, the daughter of Deacon John Trumbull, of Suffield, Conn., who was the immigrant ancestor of Governor Jonathan Trumbull, of Connecticut. There were nine children, viz:

Mary, born May 24, 1688, died December 12, 1718.

Elizabeth, born September 21, 1689, died young.

Jonathan.

Esther, born April 12, 1699.

Abigail, born May 11, 1701; married January 1, 1729, Nathaniel, the son of Sergeant Thomas Ellsworth.

David, born December 15, 1704, died January 25, 1801; married Thankful, the daughter of Moses Loomis.

John Warham, born September 30, 1706, died September 25, 1752; married November 30, 1727, Abigail, the daughter of Captain Timothy Thrall.

John, born July 14, 1707, died October 1, 1793; married Hepzibah, the daughter of Governor Roger Wolcott.

Elizabeth, born August 13, 1708.

The eldest son of John and Hannah (Trumbull)

Strong, *Deacon Jonathan Strong*, was born in Windsor, Conn., April 22, 1694, and died July 16, 1763. He removed to Bolton, Conn., 1721, where he was one of the original proprietors of the town. He married Hannah, the daughter of Captain Job and Mary (Trumbull) Ellsworth, of Windsor; she was born February 10, 1700, and died October 9, 1762. Her father, Captain Job, was the son of Josiah and Elizabeth (Holcombe) Ellsworth, and his maternal grandfather was Thomas Holcombe, who was in Dorchester, Mass., 1634, and went to Windsor 1635. They had three children, viz:

Jonathan, Jr.

Charles, born April 14, 1728, died March 5, 1810; married first, January 16, 1755, Prudence Talcott; second, May 2, 1776, Desire Lyman.

Job, born January 13, 1730, died May 16, 1800; married 176-, Damaris, the daughter of Aaron Strong.

The eldest son of Deacon Jonathan and Mary (Ellsworth) Strong, *Deacon Jonathan Strong, Jr.*, was born in Bolton, Conn., May 19, 1725, and died September 17, 1807. He removed to Orford, N. H. 1772, of which town he was one of the first settlers, and where he was elected deacon May 17, 1799. He married, June 28, 1750, Mary, the daughter of Ebenezer and Mary (Glover) Northam, of Colchester, Conn. She was born March 13, 1725, and died December 20, 1817. Issue, six children, viz.:

Hannah, born July 15, 1751; married Edward Sawyer.

Mary, born November 25, 1752; married Abel Sawyer.

Sarah, born December 29, 1755, died May 21, 1742; married Captain Jonathan Derby.

Esther, born November 3, 1758; married Ichabod Palmer.

Alexander, born January 15, 1761, died November 25, 1836; married October 7, 1784, Amelia, the daughter of Daniel Tillotson.

Jonathan.

The youngest child of Deacon Jonathan and Mary (Northam) Strong, *Rev. Jonathan Strong, D. D.,* was born in Bolton, Conn., September 4, 1764, and died in Randolph, Mass., November 9, 1814. He went with his parents to Orford, N. H., 1772; was graduated from Dartmouth College 1786, and ordained as pastor of the church at Randolph, January 28, 1789. He married, November 3, 1790, *Joanna,* the daughter of Deacon Thomas and Joanna (Gilman) Odiorne, of Exeter, N. H. She was born February 6, 1771, and died in Brookline, Mass., December 23, 1845. Joanna Gilman was the daughter of *Major John Gilman.* Issue, nine children, viz:

George Odiorne, born November 6, 1791, died February 8, 1867; married Sophia, the daughter of John Mann, Jr.

Jonathan, born November 18, 1793, died June 14, 1794.

Eliza Ann, born August 22, 1795, died January 5, 1838; married Luther, the son of Luther Thayer.

Joanna, born April 21, 1797, died March 31, 1857; married November 11, 1818, Rev. William, the son of Dr. William Cogswell.

Mary, born February 13, 1799, died December 17, 1814.

Caroline, born December 2, and died December 23, 1800.

Jonathan, born July 9, 1802, married May 10, 1832,

Salome Saxton, the daughter of Joseph Warren Gilman.

Caroline, born October 21, 1804, died February 18, 1805.

Alexander.

The descendants of Elder John Strong are connected by marriage with the leading families of western New England. Among them, the Dwights, Trumbulls and Lymans. A large number performed important military service in the several wars in which the country has been engaged. There have been several Governors of states, among them Governor Caleb Strong of Massachusetts, several members of the Continental Congress, several United States Senators, many members of Congress, Judges and men of eminence in the academic and literary life of the country.

ODIORNE

The colonist, John Odiorne, of Portsmouth, N. H., was born in England 1627, and came to Newcastle, N. H., 1660. He married Mary Johnson, and their son, Deacon John Odiorne, Jr., was born 1675. His son, Captain Ebenezer Odiorne, (1704-1745), married Catherine, the daughter of Captain John and Hannah (Jackson) Sherburne.

Their son, Deacon Thomas Odiorne, was born December 1, 1733, and died April 29, 1819. He was one of the signers of the protest against the Stamp Act at Exeter, N. H., November 15, 1765, and was also one of a committee December 26, 1774, to see that "the association agreement," or "non-importation agrement," determined on by the Continental Congress, be strictly adhered to. He was the first manufacturer of cotton duck in America, beginning in 1790.[3] He married, January 31, 1762, *Joanna*, the daughter of Major John and Jane (Deane) Gilman, and their daughter *Joanna*, married *Rev. Jonathan Strong, D. D.*

SHERBURNE

In 1632, Henry Sherburne[4] (1612-1680), came to Portsmouth, N. H., in the ship *James*. He was Associate Judge of the Court at Strawberry Bank, 1651 and 1652; Town Clerk and Treasurer 1656; Commissioner 1658; and Deputy to the Massachusetts General Court 1660. He married, November 13, 1637, Rebecca, the daughter of Ambrose Gibbons who came to Portsmouth 1630; was Deputy-Governor of New Hampshire 1640; Selectman, Magistrate, Commissioner 1641, 1642, 1646; Captain of the Portsmouth Alarm 1643, and a factor of the Laconia Company, Piscataqua, 1657.[5]

The son of Henry and Rebecca (Gibbons) Sherburne, Captain John Sherburne, was born April 3, 1647, and died 1702. He was King's Councillor 1699, and signer of test and association papers. He married Mary, the daughter of Edward Cowell.

Their son, Captain John Sherburne II., was born January 19, 1676-77, and died in Newcastle, N. H., 1747. He married Hannah, the daughter of Thomas and Hannah (Johnson) Jackson, and grand-daughter of James Johnson, and their daughter Catharine, married Captain Ebenezer Odiorne.

---

[3] *Hist. of Exeter*, pp. 79, 80; *Mass. Hist. Soc. Coll.* Vol. IV, pp. 94, 339.
[4] Savage's *Geneal. Dict.*, Vol. iv, p. 77.   *Reg. N. H. Soc. Col. Dames*, p. 84.
[5] *Reg. N. H. Soc. Dames*, p. 63; *Reg. Officers and Members Soc. Col. Wars*, N. Y., Jan. 1898. *State Papers*, N. H., Vol. i, Vol. xxix, 1896.

GILMAN

JOHN GILMAN,[6] son of Edward Gilman, the colonist, married Elizabeth, the daughter of James and Elizabeth (Shapleigh) Treworgie, and the grand-daughter of Alexander Shapleigh.

CAPTAIN JOHN GILMAN II., their son, married *Elizabeth*, the daughter of Peter Coffin, whose son:

MAJOR JOHN GILMAN, III.,[7] married *Jane*, the daughter of Dr. Thomas and Deborah (Clarke) Deane; descended from the *Rev. John Clarke*, the *Rev. Benjamin Woodbridge*, and GOVERNOR THOMAS DUDLEY.[8] Their daughter, *Joanna Gilman*, married Deacon Thomas Odiorne. (See pp. 260-275.)

COFFIN

PETER COFFIN,[9] son of Tristram[10] and Dionis (Stevens) Coffin, married Abigail, the daughter of Edward and Catharine (Reynolds) Starbuck. Their daughter *Elizabeth*, married CAPTAIN JOHN GILMAN II. (See pp. 262-264.)

The colonist, Edward Starbuck, born in Derbyshire, Eng., 1604, died December 4, 1690, came to Dover, N. H., with his wife, Catharine Reynolds, of Wales, about 1635.[11] He was representative to the General Court 1643 and 1646, and an elder in the church. He had grants of land at different times, the first June 30, 1643, settling in Nantucket 1659.

6 *Hist. Exeter*, p. 351.

7 *Ibid*, pp. 225, 235, 237, 423.

8 *Year Book Mass. Soc. Col. Dames*, p. 101; *Savage's Gen. Dict.* Vol. II.

9 *Year Book Mass. Soc. Col Dames*, p. 101; *Savage's Gen. Dict.* Vol. I, p. 419.

10 *Early Settlers of Nantucket*, pp. 24, 25; *Year Book Mass. Soc. Col. Dames*, p. 101.

11 Austin's *160 Allied Families*, pp. 220, 222; *N. E. Hist. and Gen. Reg.* Vol. VIII, p. 68; *Early Settlers of Nantucket*, pp. 21, 22.

WOODBRIDGE-DUDLEY-WARD

The colonist, Rev. John Woodbridge,[12] married *Mercy*, the daughter of Governor Thomas and Dorothy (Yorke) Dudley, of Massachusetts. He was the son of Rev. John and Sarah (Parker) Woodbridge of Stanton, Wiltshire, Eng. Sarah Parker was the daughter of Rev. Robert Parker.

Their son, *Rev. Benjamin Woodbridge*, married Mary, the daughter of Rev. John Ward[13] (who was the son of the Rev. Nathaniel Ward),[14] and his wife Alice, the daughter of Nicholas Edmunds. (See pp. 266, 269, 362-365, 366.)

Their daughter, *Elizabeth Woodbridge,* married *Rev. John Clarke,* the son of Nathaniel and Elizabeth (Somerby) Clark. (Elizabeth Somerby was the daughter of Henry Somerby.)

Through their daughter, *Deborah Clark,* who married Dr. Thomas Deane, the son of Thomas and his wife, Jane Scammond (the daughter of Richard), the line descends to the Strong family, as follows:

Jane Deane, married MAJOR JOHN GILMAN III.

Joanna Gilman, married Deacon Thomas Odiorne.

Joanna Odiorne, married *Rev. Jonathan Strong D. D.*

WALDRON

In 1637, William Waldron,[15] the son of William Waldron, of Alcester, Warwick County, Eng., came to America. He was baptized October 18, 1601, and was drowned at Kennebunk, Me., September, 1646. A

[12] *Woodbridge Geneal.* 7 to 9; Savage's *Gen. Dict.; Year Book Mass. Soc. Col. Dames,* p. 154.

[13] Savage's *Gen. Dict.* Vol. IV, p. 408.

[14] Ibid, p. 410.

[15] Savage's *Gen. Dict.* Vol. IV, p. 321

Freeman in Massachusetts, May 19, 1642, he was Representative for Dover, Mass., the same year; made Recorder for the Province of Maine, by Sir Ferdinando Gorges, and Recorder for Dover by the power of the Massachusetts Colony, 1646. His daughter Prudence, married Richard Scammond, and their daughter, Jane married Thomas Deane.

STRONG *(Continued)*

The youngest of the nine children of Rev. Jonathan and Joanna (Odiorne) Strong, *Alexander Strong,* was born in Randolph, Mass., November 25, 1807, and died June 6, 1881. He married first, June 11, 1832, Catherine, the daughter of Jesse and Susanna (Plympton) Goodenow; she was born in Boxford, Mass., February 14, 1809, and died in Boston, May 8, 1864; second, February 11, 1868, Mary Elizabeth, the daughter of Shadrach Robinson. Issue, first wife, two children, viz:

Helen Cornelia, born June 30, 1833, died November 5, 1884, married first, June 2, 1853, John Dorr, the son of Charles Hayward; second, 1874, Lucius J. Knowles. *Edward Alexander.*

GOODENOW-PLYMPTON

The ship *Confidence,* in 1638, brought Captain Edmund Goodenow [16] to America from Dunhead, in Wilts, Eng., when twenty-seven years of age, accompanied by his wife Ann, two sons, John and Thomas, and his servant Richard Sanger. He took the freeman's oath May 13, 1640, and was Deputy to the General Court from Sudbury, Mass., 1645, 1649, 1650, 1660, 1673, 1674, 1679 and 1680. He was appointed Ensign

16 *Year Book Mass. Soc. Col. Dames,* p. 113; Savage's *Gen. Dict.,* Vol. II, p. 271.

August 12, 1645; Captain of Foot Company at Sud-
bury, May 27, 1674, and is mentioned in Johnson's
"Wonder Working Providence" as leader of the militia.
He was also appointed by the General Court to lay out
Sudbury.

One of his sons, Joseph, married Patience ——. Their
son Daniel, married Ruth, whose son, Daniel, Jr., married Catherine Moore. In the fifth generation from
the colonist, was Jesse, who married Susanna, the
daughter of Ebenezer and Susanna (Ruggles) Plympton.

A settler of Sudbury, Mass., 1643, Thomas Plympton
died in the Sudbury fight, April 21, 1676. He married
Abigail, the daughter of Peter Noyes. Their son, Peter,
was born January 4, 1667, and married November 8,
1720, Abigail Thompson, who died September 14, 1743;
whose son, Thomas, born April 17, 1723, served in the
Revolution. His son, Ebenezer, married Susanna Ruggles, and their daughter, Susan (Susanna), married
Jesse Goodenow, whose daughter Catherine, married
Alexander Strong.

STRONG *(Continued)*

The only son of Alexander and Catherine (Goodenow) Strong, *Edward Alexander Strong,* is a retired
merchant living in Boston. He was born in Boston,
Mass., December 10, 1834, and was graduated from
Amherst College in the class of 1855. He married, June
10, 1858, Marion Hubbard, the daughter of Clinton and
Eunice Bradbury (Whitney) Clarke, of Boston. She
was born March 16, 1834, and died April 7, 1909.
(Eunice Bradbury Whitney (1801-1881), was the
daughter of Jesse and Mary (Sawyer) Whitney and
the grand-daughter of David Sawyer, of Saco, Me., the

son of Ephraim Sawyer, whose mother was Prudence Standish, (the great granddaughter of Captain Miles Standish.) They had two children, viz:

George Alexander, born May 23, 1859, married November 22, 1887, Margaret Phillips, the daughter of Dr. John Phillips Reynolds.

ELLEN CLARKE, born in Boston, Mass., June 1, 1863; married, October 12, 1892, William Bullock, the son of Barna Atherton Clark. He is Professor of Geology, Johns Hopkins University. They have four children, viz: Edward Strong, born April 16, 1894; Helen, born August 13, 1896; Atherton, born May 29, 1899, and Marion, born December 14, 1903.

ELLEN CLARKE STRONG CLARK,

Member of Chapter I., The Colonial Dames of America.

XII

JOHNS

ARMS:[1] *Argent, a chevron sable between three ravens proper, a bordure bezanty invected gules.*
CREST: *Two battle axes saltierwise sable.*
MOTTO: *Deus pascit Corvos.*

The colonist, Richard Johnes (Johns) of the Johnes family of Dolau Cothy Hall, Albemarles, Carmarthen, Wales, was born in Bristol, Eng., 1645, and died October 10, 1717. He came to Maryland, about 1660, and settled at The Cliffs, Calvert County. The Friends' records say of Richard Johns that he was a man of integrity and influence in the community, and greatly beloved. The early meetings of the Society of Friends took place at his house, where George Fox staid while first in this country.. Elected a Burgess, September 21, 1694, on account of his membership in the Society of Friends, he refused to take the oath.[2] He married, May 7, 1676, *Elizabeth,* the daughter of Hugh and Margaret Kensey, of England.

JOHNS

Their son, Kensey Johns, a planter, born July 5, 1689, and died February 2, 1729, married *Elizabeth,* the daughter of Benjamin and Elizabeth (Benson) Chew.

[1] Arms of the Johnes family of Dolau Cothy Hall, Albemarles, Carmarthen, Wales, and of Maryland and Delaware, according to Burke's *Landed Gentry.*

[2] *Md. Arch.,* Vol. XIX, p. 29.

ANNE VAN DYKE
Wife of Hon. Kensey Johns III

HON. KENSEY JOHNS III
Chancellor of Delaware

KENSEY JOHNS I

ELIZABETH CHEW
Wife of Kensey Johns I

CHEW

COLONEL JOHN CHEW, baptized 1600, and died about 1668, came to "James citie," Va., and was Burgess 1623, 1624, 1629, 1642 to 1644; Justice of York County, Va., 1634 to 1652; (apparently dead 1668).[3]

COLONEL SAMUEL CHEW, their son, resided in Maryland as early as 1648, and died March 15, 1676. At the date of Truman's impeachment trial in 1676 he is described as " Colonel Samuel Chew, Chancellor and Secretary." He married Anne, the daughter of William Ayres. (See pp. 249, 499-501.)[4]

Their son, *Benjamin Chew* (1671-1700), married Elizabeth Benson.

Their daughter, *Elizabeth Chew*, married Kensey Johns, the son of Richard and Elizabeth (Kensey) Johns.

JOHNS (*Continued*)

The son of Kensey and Elizabeth (Chew) Johns, *Kensey Johns II*, a planter, married Susannah, the daughter of Richard and Mary (Paca) Galloway. Their son was CHANCELLOR KENSEY JOHNS III.

PACA

CAPTAIN AQUILA PACA,[5] the son of John Paca, the brother of the signer of the Declaration of Independence, was Captain of the Second Battalion of Flying Camp in Maryland, 1776. His daughter, *Mary*, married Richard Galloway.

3 Henings *Stats.*, Vol. I, pp. 129, 138, 239.
  Va. Hist. Mag., Vol. I, p. 89.
  Thomas' *Geneal. Notes.*
  William Cary, *Genealogist.*
4 Thomas' *Geneal. Notes.*
5 McSherry's *Hist. of Maryland.*

JOHNS (Continued)

CHANCELLOR KENSEY JOHNS III, the son of Kensey and Susannah (Galloway) Johns, was born June 14, 1749, at West River, and died in New Castle, Del., December 21, 1840. Elected to the State Constitutional Convention 1776 and appointed Associate Judge of the Supreme Court of Delaware 1779, he succeeded in March 1794, U. S. Senator George Read, resigned, but the Senate on a technicality, refused to admit him. He became Chief Justice of Delaware 1798, retaining the office three years, and Chancellor of the state, 1828, holding that post until the change of the constitution in 1832. He married, 1784, *Ann,* the daughter of Nicholas and Elizabeth (Nixon) Van Dyke. *Ann Van Dyke* was a great beauty. General Washington and General Lafayette were both at her wedding, and General Washington told the groom that he should be a very happy man, as he had married one of the most beautiful women in the country. Their son was *Kensey Johns IV.*

VAN DYKE

GOVERNOR NICHOLAS VAN DYKE, born 1738, was a signer of the articles of Confederation and one of the delegates that ratified them. He attained the rank of Major in the Militia; was one of the Committee of Correspondence to communicate with the other colonies, in regard to the Boston Port Bill 1774; a Deputy from his county to the state convention, July 1776, which framed the first constitution of Delaware; elected to the Continental Congress February 22, 1777, serving until 1783; appointed Judge of the Admiralty 1777; one of the Council of Delaware, and Speaker 1779, and Congress appointed him, 1781, one of a committee

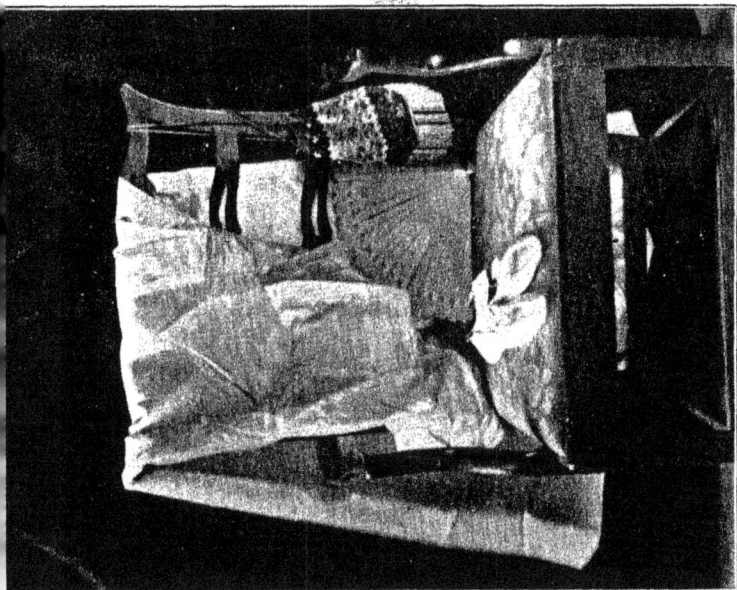

WEDDING GOWN, BEAD BAG, SLIPPERS AND FAN WHICH
BELONGED TO FIDELIA ROGERSON MONTGOMERY

SAMPLER, EMBROIDERED BAG AND TWO FANS WHICH BELONGED TO
LAVINIA MONTGOMERY JOHNS

of five to confer with the people of New Hampshire, relative to the admission of the colony into the Federal Union of these states. He was elected President of the state of Delaware 1783, holding the office until 1786.[6] He married Elizabeth, the daughter of Thomas Nixon II, who was born July 1, 1745, in Dover, Del., and died January 2, 1770. (His son, Nicholas Van Dyke II, was Senator of Delaware, 1815, and went to the United States Senate 1817, holding that office until 1826). Their daughter, *Ann*, married CHANCELLOR KENSEY JOHNS III.

The Nixon family descended from Thomas and his wife Ann (Manlove) Nixon, whose son, Nicholas, married Elizabeth ———, and died 1735. Their son was Thomas Nixon II.

MANLOVE-MOLESTON

HON. GEORGE MANLOVE[7] (the son of Mark Manlove, who married in England, ———, Elizabeth———), was born September 24, 1660, and died February 16, 1695. He was one of the Assembly from Kent County, Del., 1692. He married Anne ———.

Their son, *Jonathan Manlove* (1681-1727), married *Hannah*, the daughter of HENRY MOLESTON, who was one of the Governor's Council of Sussex, Del., in 1700, and the son of ALEXANDER MOLESTON[8] of Sussex, one of the Assembly 1683. Their daughter, *Ann Manlove*, born 1715, married, December 25, 1736, Thomas Nixon I, whose son, Nicholas, was the father of Thomas Nixon

6 Scharf's *Hist. of Del.*, Vol. I, p. 218; Appleton's *Cycl. Am. Biog.*, Vol. VI, p. 246; Penn. *Gazette*, July 6, 1774; Penn. *Jour. of Commercial Advertising*, July 6, 1774.

7 *Penn. Arch.*, 2d series, Vol. IX, p. 660.

8 Proud's *Hist. of Penn.*, Vol. I, pp. 236-375; 406-416.

II, whose daughter, Elizabeth, married NICHOLAS VAN DYKE.

JOHNS (*Continued*)

The son of Kensey and Ann (Van Dyke) Johns, *Kensey Johns IV*, was Chancellor after his father, the two holding the position fifty years.

His son, *Rev. Henry Van Dyke Johns, D. D.*, born October 23, 1803, and died April 22, 1859, was Rector of Old Christ Church, and the first Rector of Emmanuel Church of Baltimore, Md. Ten thousand people attended his funeral on foot,[9] for he was greatly beloved. He married, 1827, *Lavinia*, the daughter of COLONEL WILLIAM MONTGOMERY and his wife Fidelia Rogerson, a niece of John Rogerson Montgomery and Mary Carpenter Reigert, his wife.

MONTGOMERY, OR MONTGOMERIE

ARMS: *Quarterly first and fourth azure, three fleur de lis or for Montgomery second and third gules. Three annulets, or, stoned, azure for Eglinton, all within a border of the second charged with a double tressure of the third.*

CREST: *For Montgomery an arm embowed in armor, the hand grasping a broken spear, head drooping, all ppr.*

MOTTO: *Honeur sans Repos.*

The first Earl of Eglinton, Hugh Montgomerie, third Lord Montgomerie, died 1545, having married Lady Helen, the daughter of Colin, the first Earl of Argyll.

Their third son, Sir Neil Montgomery, married about 1500, Margaret, the daughter and heiress of Quintin Mure, Laird of Skeldon.

Their son, Sir Neil Montgomery II, of Lainshaw,

---

9 Mrs. Charles Ridgely, of Hampton, erected in his memory and that of her brother, the memorial church, corner of Lafayette Avenue and Bolton Street, Baltimore.

married Jean, the daughter of John and Grisel (Betoun) Montgomery.

Their son, Major Hugh Montgomery, was killed in the battle of the Boyne, 1690.

His son, Major John Montgomery, born 1665, and died 1721, fought with his father in the battle of the Boyne, and succeeded him as Major. He married Margaret, the daughter of Sir William Dunbar of Mochrum, County Galloway, Ire.

Their son, Alexander Montgomery, came to this country from Ireland about 1720. He married Mary McCullock of Ardmaugh, Ire.

Their son, Thomas Montgomery, born 1734, and died August 3, 1816, married Miss Nevins.

COLONEL WILLIAM MONTGOMERY, their son, born in Little Britain, Lancaster County, Penn., 1756, and died January 4, 1822, ranked as one of the leading lawyers of the state. He left Princeton College in his senior year to join the army of Washington with a company of students of which he was Captain and his father Major-General. He took part in the battles of Trenton and Princeton, and afterwards served as Colonel of a company of Light Horse. He married, 1791, Fidelia Rogerson, and their daughter *Lavinia*, married *Rev. Henry Van Dyke Johns, D. D.*

The wife of Sir Neil Montgomery II., of Lainshaw, Jean Montgomery, had the following line of descent:

The third Lord Lyle, Robert Montgomery, died 1511. He married Mariot Lindsay, of the House of Dunrod.[10]

The fourth Lord Lyle, John Montgomery (1495-1540), married Grisel, the daughter of Sir David Betoun.

Their daughter, Jean Montgomery, married Sir Neil Montgomery II, of Lainshaw, whose line of descent is hereinbefore given.

JOHNS (Continued)

The son of Rev. Henry Van Dyke Johns, D. D. and his wife, Lavinia Montgomery, *Henry Van Dyke Johns II,* was born in Baltimore, Md., October 22, 1832, and died September 11, 1897. He married, January 3, 1867, *Annie E.,* the daughter of Colonel George and Mary J. (Perkins) Davis; she was born May 16, 1843, and died May 24, 1892. Their daughter, EDYTH, married, first, Jesse Tyson; second, Bruce Cotten.

DAVIS

The Davises descend from Thomas Davis, who married, November, 1670, Judith Bost.

JUDGE JEHU DAVIS, their son, an officer of the Delaware Militia during the Revolutionary War, was also one of the Committee of Public Safety. He afterwards represented the county in the General Assembly, and for many years presided as Speaker of the House, in which capacity he acted as Governor of the State for a time. He also served as Judge of the board of property, and for many years was Judge of the Court of Common Pleas for Kent County, Del.[11]

[10] From here back to Roger de Montgomerie, Count of Montgomerie before the coming of Rollo in 912, see a genealogical *History of the Family of Montgomery,* by Thomas Harrison Montgomery, of Philadelphia, Penn.
[11] *Hist. and Biog. Encycl.* of Del., p. 256; Scharf's *Hist. of Del.,* p. 324.

COL. WILLIAM MONTGOMERY
At the age of 23

HENRY VAN DYKE JOHNS II

COL. WILLIAM MONTGOMERY
At the age of 50

MARY CARPENTER REIGERT
Wife of John Rogerson Montgomery

His son, *Judge Isaac Davis,* born 1765, was elected one of the Assembly 1793, and of the senate 1794; Speaker in 1799, and also Register of Wills. He was appointed Associate Judge 1814, and continued on the bench until the revision of the Constitution in 1831.[12] He married Mary Johnson Killen, the niece of Chancellor Killen of Delaware.

Their son, *Colonel George Davis,* born January 1, 1806, and died April 12, 1877, married Mary J., the daughter of Dr. John Day and Elizabeth (Bradshaw) Perkins, and their daughter, *Annie E.,* married *Henry Van Dyke Johns II.*

PERKINS, OR PEARKINS

A branch of this ancient family of Ufton Court, Berkshire; Eng., begins with George Pearkins [13] of Abbotts Lalford, Warwick County, whose son William, was born January 1, 1579.

A son of the latter, William Pearkins II, of London, Eng., born August 25, 1607, and died May 21, 1682, came to Ipswich, Mass., and with John Winthrop settled that place. In 1640 he represented Weymouth, Mass., in the General Court. A good historian has said of him: "He was probably the most accomplished person of the town; a scholar, a man of business, clergyman, soldier, and legislator, and in each relation bore himself with ability and discretion."

His son, Daniel Perkins, who died 1744, came from Norwich, Conn., to Kent County, Md., in 1700. He married first, 1682, Dolinda, the daughter of Thomas Bliss, and second, Susannah Starton, and their son, Daniel Perkins II, married Susannah ———.

---

12 Scharf's *Hist. of Del. Bar and Bench,* p. 537.
13 *Hist. of Ufton Court,* by A. Mary Sharp.

Their son, Thomas Perkins, born January 14, 1762, and died December 22, 1832, married, July 20, 1786, Mary Kittridge, the daughter of John Thomas and Mary (Fergueson) Maulden; she was born September 18, 1761, and died November 25, 1837. (John Thomas Maulden, came from England and settled at Bohemia Manor, Cecil County, Md. He married Mary Fergueson, who was born 1722, and died 1802.)

Their son, Dr. John Day Perkins, born August 27, 1790, and died August 13, 1860, married, February 22, 1813, Elizabeth (1792-1858), the daughter of James Bradshaw, and the great-great-granddaughter of John Bradshaw (1602-1659), who was President of the High Court of Justice which tried, convicted and condemned Charles I of England; President of the Council of State 1649 to 1652; Chancellor of the Duchy of Lancaster, and Attorney-General of Cheshire and North Wales 1649.[14]

Their daughter, Mary J. Perkins, married *Colonel George Davis,* whose daughter, *Annie E.,* married *Henry Van Dyke Johns II.* Their daughter is:

EDYTH JOHNS COTTEN,

Member of Chapter I., The Colonial Dames of America.

[14] *Cent. Dict.,* p. 177.

XIII
PARKER

ELISHA PARKER I., yeoman of Woodbridge, who died in 1700, received his first grant of land April 19, 1675. In November, 1694, he was appointed High Sheriff of Middlesex County, in the province of East Jersey.[1] He married, July 15, 1657, Elizabeth, the daughter of Samuel Hinckley, of Yenterden, Kent County, Eng., a settler in Scituate, Mass. She was the sister of Thomas Hinckley, Governor of Plymouth, Mass., 1681-1692.

ELISHA PARKER II. (1660-1717), their son, represented Middlesex County in the Provincial Assembly of New Jersey for two years, 1708 to 1710, and was later a member of Governor Hunter's Council, 1713 to 1717. He was also Captain of the Provincial Troops of Middlesex County, 1707.[2] He married Hannah Rolfe.

JOHN PARKER, their son, was born November 10, 1692, and died in September, 1732. He built the stone part of the old Parker house, familiarly called the " Castle," which is still standing, and owned by the family, and until lately the residence of a great-grandson of John. He was Captain of the Provincial Troops of Middlesex County 1715, and one of the Judges in a special Court to try pirates, 1718. Also one of the King's Council of the Province 1718 to 1732. In 1726, he was Mayor of Perth Amboy, N. J. He was chairman of a committee to prepare an ordinance for regulat-

[1] *N. J. Arch.* Vol. IV, p. 326. Whitehead's *Contributions to E. Jersey His.*, pp. 128-129. *N. Y. Gen. and Biog. Recs.* Vol. XXIX, p. 192.

[2] *N. J. Arch.,* Vol. iv, pp. 153, 171, 182, 326; Vol. xiii, pp. 308, 353, 414, 495, 562, 563; Vol. XIV, pp. 1, 7, 29, 70. Whitehead's *Cont. to E. Jersey Hist.* pp, 129, 130. *N. Y. Gen. and Biog. Recs.* Vol. XXIX, 192.

ing the courts of the judicature, and several times chairman of a committee to regulate the expenditures of the
public money.[3] He married, September 16, 1721, *Janet,*
the daughter of Dr. John Johnstone. Their son was
JAMES PARKER.

JOHNSTONE

ARMS: *Argent, a saltire, sa. On a chief, gu., three cushions, ar.*
CREST: *A winged spur, ar.*
MOTTO: *Nuquam non parates.*

DR. JOHN JOHNSTONE came to the province of East
Jersey in 1685, from Scotland, where he had been a
druggist in Edinburgh. The ship, *Henry & Francis,*
on which he sailed, met with many difficulties of storm
and disease. On the death of the captain, George Scot,
Laird of Pittoclive, the direction of the voyage devolved
on Johnstone, who was betrothed to Scot's daughter,
Eupham, whom he married shortly after their arrival in
this country. They were given a grant of land in Monmouth County, N. J., "in consideration of ye great loss
they did suffer by importing ye Sd people upon ye
propre incouragement & wh has contributed very much
to ye good of this province." Doctor Johnstone settled
first in New York, but removed to Perth Amboy sometime prior to 1709. He was a member of the King's
Council in the province of East Jersey, 1686 to 1688,
and 1704 to 1726; a member of the Provincial Assembly,
1709, 1710, 1720-1732, and Speaker 1720 to 1732;
Mayor of New York, 1714 to 1718; member of the Governor's Council, 1716 to 1722; and of the boundary com-

---

[3] *N. J. Arch.* Vol. IV, pp. 333, 334, 363, 373, 374, 394; Vol. V, pp. 3, 34,
155, 301; Vol. XIV, pp. 77, 110, 137, 150, 210, 243, 269, 279, 314, 325,
392, 405, 407, 455, 465. Whitehead's *Cont.,* p. 130. *Rep. of N. Y. State
Hist.* Vol. I, p. 526. *N. Y. Gen. and Biog. Rec.* Vol. XXIX, p. 192.

ELIZABETH PARKER

THE VAN CORTLANDT HOUSE, NEW YORK

mittee for East Jersey, 1719-1720.[4] The following notice of his death appeared in the *Philadelphia Weekly Mercury*:

"Perth Amboy, Sept. 19th, 1732. On the 7th inst. died here in the 71st year of his age, Doctor Johnstone, very much lamented by all who knew him, and to the inexpressible loss of the poor, who were always his particular care, etc."

In writing to Governor Hunter, James Alexander, who was warmly attached to Dr. Johnstone, said:

"Dr. Johnstone died on the 7th of this month, being spent with age and fatigue in going about to serve those who wanted his assistance."

His daughter, *Janet,* married JOHN PARKER.

PARKER *(Continued)*

JAMES PARKER, the son of John and Janet (Johnstone) Parker, was Captain of the Provincial Troops in 1746, and filled a vacancy in Governor Franklin's Council in October, 1764. He was Mayor of Perth Amboy in 1771, and appointed Delegate to the Provincial Congress 1775, but did not serve. During the Revolution, he was neutral. He was invited to be a candidate for Congress in 1789, but withheld his consent until too late. He married, in 1763, *Gertrude,* the daughter of William and Elizabeth (van Cortlandt) Skinner, who was born in 1737, and died in 1811. Their son was *James Parker II.*

SKINNER

The colonist of this name, the Rev. William Skinner

---

[4] Whitehead's *Cont.* p. 69. *Record of Governor's Council of E. Jersey,* pp. 134, 144, 394; *N. J. Arch.,* Vol. III, pp. 51, 335; IV, pp. 56, 68, 119. 129, 132, 394; V, pp. 55, 62, 263; XIII, pp. 161, 174, 185.

(1687-1758), was said to be a Scotchman named Mc-
Gregor who, being compromised in Scotland during the
rebellion of 1715, fled to this country under the name
of Skinner, and settled first in Philadelphia. Later, he
went to London and took orders, and on his return to
the colonies settled in Perth Amboy, N. J., where he
became the first pastor of St. Peter's Church. He married, June 8, 1726, *Elizabeth,* the daughter of Stephanus
and Gertrude (Schuyler) van Cortlandt, whose daughter, *Gertrude,* married JAMES PARKER I.

VAN CORTLANDT

ARMS: *Argent the four wings of a windmill conjoined saltireine sable
voided gules, between five mullets placed crosswise of the last.*

CREST: *A star gules between two wings displayed the dexter argent,
the sinister sable.*

MOTTO: *Virtus sit meum.*

OLOFF STEVENSE VAN CORTLANDT, was born in 1600,
at Wisk, near Ultrect, in Holland. He came to New

Amsterdam, New Nether-
lands, in 1637, attached to a
military company of the West
India Company. He was a
man of good education, and
his seal, bearing the van
Cortlandt arms, still in the
possession of his descendants,
and articles of Dutch plate,
marked with the same arms,
also preserved, indicate that

VAN CORTLANDT

his position was that of a gentleman. In the summer
of 1637 he was transferred to the civil service, as a
commissary of cargoes, and in 1643 was made keeper
of the stores of the West India Company. In 1648
he resigned from the company and became a Freeman

of the city, a merchant and brewer, and died April 4, 1684, leaving a very large fortune for that time.

His public career began in 1645, when he was chosen one of the "Eight Men," a body representative of the citizens at large; became president of the "Nine Men" in 1650, and while holding that position was one of the signers of the remonstrance transmitted to Holland against the maladministration of Director Kieft, and the obnoxious measures of Director Stuyvesant. The latter retaliated by turning the "Nine Men" out of their pews in the church and tearing up the seats. In 1654, he was elected a Schepen of the city of New Amsterdam, and was appointed Burgomeister 1655, which office he held almost uninterruptedly until the close of the Dutch government, covering the years 1655-1656, 1658-1660 and 1662-1663. He was a special Commissioner of Indian Affairs 1645, Colonel of the Burgher Corps 1649, Commissioner of boundaries 1663, and one of the Governor's Council of New York, 1674.[5]

A portion of his property was a plot on the west side of Broadway, extending to the North River, and adjacent to the present Cortlandt Street. His place of residence was the Brouwer Straat, now Stone Street. He married Annatje Loockermans, February 26, 1642.

STEPHANUS VAN CORTLANDT, their eldest son, was born in New Netherlands, May 7, 1643. In the public service, under the English rule, he filled every prominent office in the province, except that of Governor. At the early age of thirty-four he became the first native

5 Bolton's *Hist. of Westchester Co., N. Y.* Vol. I, p. 99.
   N. Y. *Civil List*, pp. 59, 61, 62.
   O'Callaghan's *New Netherland Reg.*, pp. 14, 54, 56, 59, 60.
   O'Callaghan's *Dutch Mss.*, pp. 254, 304.
   Appleton's *Biog. Enc.* Vol. VI, p. 236.
   Schuyler's *Colonial New York*, Vol. I, p. 190.
   Albany Recs., Vol. II, pp. 57, 61, 83, 99, 132.

American Mayor of the city of New York, and held that position from the year 1677, when he was Lord of Cortlandt Manor, until his death, November 25, 1700. In 1678 he was first Judge of the Court of Admiralty; member of the Governor's Council, Province of New York, 1680 to 1688, and 1691 to 1700; Secretary of the Province, 1688; Chancellor of the Province, 1696; Receiver-General, 1687 to 1698, and Chief-Justice of the Province, 1700. He began his military career in 1668, as an Ensign in the King's County regiment, then became Captain, and later Colonel of the regiment.

On the death of the husband of his sister Maria, Jeremias van Rensselaer, in 1675, Stephanus assisted in the administration of the affairs of Rensselaerwyck, during the minority of Kiliaen van Rensselaer, the son, who was but twelve years of age at the death of his father.

In the present counties of Westchester, Putnam and Dutchess, Stephanus van Cortlandt purchased, in 1683, large tracts of land from the Indians, and obtained for them a patent from Governor Dongan, two years later. This was afterwards called the Manor of Cortlandt, and Stephanus was the first and only Lord of the Manor.[6] He married, September 10, 1671, *Gertrude,* the daughter of Philip Pieterse and Margaritta (van Slichtenhorst) Schuyler, and their daughter, *Elizabeth,* married Rev. William Skinner.

SCHUYLER

ARMS: *Vert issuing from a cloud proper, a cubit arm in fess, vested, az., holding on the hand a falcon, close; all ppr.*
CREST: *A hawk close; ppr.*

PHILIP PIETERSE SCHUYLER was born 1625 or 1628,

[6] N. Y. *Civil List,* pp. 173, 180, 327, 330, 343, 363, 560.
Scharf's *Hist. Westchester Co.,* Vol. I, p. 24.
Bolton's *Hist. Westchester Co.,* Vol. I, pp. 9-78, 101.
Albany *Recs.* Vol. II, pp. 57, 61, 83, 99, 132.

and emigrated from Holland to America. Nothing is
known of his life previous to his marriage, December
12, 1650, with *Margaritta,* the daughter of Brand
Arentse Slichtenhorst. She appears to have been a
woman of unusual strength of character and business
ability.

For seven years, Philip Pieterse Schuyler held the
position of Vice-Director at Fort Orange, appointed
thereto in 1655, by Governor Stuyvesant. He was reappointed by Governor Nicholls, and retained the place
almost without interruption until near the close of his
life. November 1, 1667, he was commissioned Captain
of a "Company of Ffoote" at Albany, and two years
later was Captain of a company at Schenectady, thus
being in command of all the militia of Albany and vicinity. He was acting Indian Commissioner from 1655
to 1658, 1659 to 1662, and 1666 to 1679.[7] His arms
are painted on a window of the Dutch church in Albany. His daughter, *Gertrude,* married STEPHANUS
VAN CORTLANDT, whose daughter *Elizabeth,* married
William Skinner; their daughter *Gertrude,* married
JAMES PARKER.

VAN SLICHTENHORST

BRANT ARENTSE VAN SLICHTENHORST was the owner
of an estate in Holland called the Gijse Westphalinx
estate on de Slichtenhorst, and came to Beverwyck,
from Nykerk in Gelduland. In 1648, after the resig-
nation of van Curler, he was appointed Resident Di-

---

7 O'Callaghan's *Eng. Mss.,* p. 5.
N. Y. *Civil List,* p. 220.
New Netherland *Reg.,* pp. 68, 69, 70.
Report N. Y. State Historian, Vol. I, p. 377.
Schuyler's *Colonial New York,* Vol. I, pp. 108-109.

rector of the colony of Rensselaerwyck, also Chief Magistrate and Superintendent, as the Patroon was a minor. As principal officer of the West India Company, his authority extended over the whole province, including the manors. He opposed Stuyvesant's attempts to interfere in certain colonial matters at Rensselaerwyck, on the ground that the property belonged to the minor Patroon, and was not under the company's jurisdiction. Finally, Stuyvesant had him arrested, and taken to New Amsterdam, where he was detained until he made his escape and forfeited his bond. He spent his time in the New Netherlands entirely in the interest of his principals, making no attempt to acquire a private fortune through his position. The only other office he held was that of acting Indian Commissioner, under Dutch rule, in New Netherlands. After his death, the company confessed that he was right in the Stuyvesant affair.

His wife had died before he left Holland, and he returned there alone pror to 1660, his son, and daughter *Margaritta,* who married PHILIP PIETERSE SCHUYLER, having settled in the colony.[8]

PARKER (*Continued*)

The son of James and Gertrude (Skinner) Parker, *James Parker II.,* was a Commissioner to settle the boundary line between New York and New Jersey, and was also a member of the State Legislature, and later of Congress. He married Penelope, the daughter of Anthony Butler, of Philadelphia.

Their son, *Judge James Parker,* married, 1831, *Anna,* the daughter of Cleaveland Alexander and Su-

[8] *Documents relating to Col. Hist., N. Y.,* Vol. I, p. 456.
Schuyler's *Col. N. Y.,* Vol. VII, pp. 171-176.

san (Foster) Forbes. After their marriage they went West, and James Parker became a Judge in Cincinnati, dying in July, 1861. The family then returned to the East, and lived in Bay Ridge, L. I.

Their daughter, *Anna Forbes,* married *Cleaveland Forbes Dunderdale.*

FORBES

ARMS: *Azure three bears' heads couped argent, muzzled gules.*
CREST: *A stag's head attired proper.*
SUPPORTERS: *Two greyhounds argent, collared gules.*
MOTTO: *Grace me guide.*

The fourth Lord of Forbes, Alexander Forbes, of Pitslogo County, Aberdeen, Scotland, was the founder of the present family of Forbes, Earls of Granard.

His son, Timothy Forbes, of Dublin, Ireland, was the father of Captain Alexander Forbes, an officer in the British army, who married *Abigail,* the daughter of Joseph and Mary (Townley) Lawrence and descended from RICHARD SMITH.

Their son, *Captain Alexander Forbes II.,* also of the British army, married Susan Gifford, of Newark, N. J., and had many children. The descendants of a son and daughter of this family, *Cleaveland Alexander,* and *Maria Susannah* (see Dunderdale), united the two family lines in marriage.

The son, *Captain Cleaveland Alexander Forbes,* was a captain in the American mercantile marines. He settled in Perth Amboy, N. J., and married Susan Foster, of Piscataway, N. J. Their daughter, *Anna,* married *Judge James Parker,* whose daughter, *Anna Forbes,* married, in 1868, *Cleaveland Forbes Dunderdale.*

DUNDERDALE

The daughter of Captain Alexander and Susan (Gifford) Forbes, *Maria Susannah Forbes,* married Joseph Dunderdale, of Leeds, Yorkshire, England.

Their son, *John Dunderdale,* was born in Leeds, 1805, and came to America at the age of twenty-one. He married in New York, 1833, Emily, the daughter of Thomas Hewitt, of Thorpe Hall, Chester, near Liverpool, also of New York City, and Philadelphia, in which latter city he is buried.

Their son, *Cleaveland Forbes Dunderdale,* married *Anna Forbes,* the daughter of Judge James and Anna (Forbes) Parker.

BEATRICE, their youngest daughter, was born in Kingston, N. Y. She married, October, 1900, at St. Peter's Church, Perth Amboy, N. J., Dr. George W. Dobbin, of Baltimore.

LAWRENCE

ARMS: *Argent a cross raguly gules.*
CREST: *A demi-turbot in pale gules, the tail upwards.*
MOTTOS: (1) *In cruce salus.* (2) *Quaero invenio.*

WILLIAM LAWRENCE came to New Netherlands in 1645, having emigrated from England some years earlier with his brother John and sister Maria, coming from Great St. Albans in Hertfordshire. Political troubles prior to the death of Charles I., caused them to leave England, and they settled at first in New England. They claimed to be descendants of Sir Robert Lawrence, of Ashton Hall, in Lancastershire, who was a Crusader with Richard Cœur-de-Lion, by whom he was knighted. The wills of both William and John have the Laurens coat-of-arms on the seals, and it also appears on some of the old plate still possessed by some of their descendants. William Lawrence resided in

Flushing, L. I., where he was one of the patentees, and where he served as magistrate, 1655, 1658, and 1661, under the Dutch. Under the English, he held both civil and military offices on Long Island, being a Captain of the Burgher Corps 1655, and Commander of the Flushing troops 1673. Energy and decision of character, as well as a liberal education and a superior mind, are shown in a letter to Stuyvesant and his Council, written 1662-1663. His death occurred in 1680, and the inventory on file in New York shows that his personal estate, which included a sword and some plate, amounted to £4,432 sterling.[10]

He married, 1664, *Elizabeth,* the daughter of Richard and Sarah (Folger) Smith, and their son, *Joseph Lawrence,* married Mary Townley, of Elizabethtown, Essex County, N. J. (now Union County), whose daughter *Abigail* married Captain Alexander Forbes I.

SMITH

RICHARD SMITH, for whom Smithtown, L. I., is named, was the son of Richard Smith, of Gloucestershire, England, with whom he came to Boston, Mass., in 1630. The younger Richard purchased a tract of about thirty thousand acres of land from the Narragansett Sachems, in 1641. He erected a house for trade, and gave free entertainment to travellers, it being the great road of the country. Smith's was the first house built in what is now North Kingston, and was

---

10 O'Callaghan's *Eng. Mss.*, p. 68.
Documents rel. to Col. Hist. of N. Y., Vol. XIV, pp. 653, 697.
Walter's *Hist. of Flushing, N. Y.*, pp. 16, 55, 56.
Riker's *Annals of Newtown*, pp. 281-290.
Thompson's *Hist. of Long Island*, Vol. II, pp. 362, 367.
N. Y. Gen. & Biog. Rec., Vol. III, p. 125; Vol. VII, p. 89.
The Thomes Book, p. 413.

probably a block house. In 1659, he leased an enormous tract from the Indians for a thousand years, which gave rise to so many disputes, that it was the final cause of his leaving Narragansett and settling Smithtown. Richard Smith became very influential with the Indians. He negotiated and signed the treaty for Connecticut, and several times made peace between the Narragansetts and the Massachusetts colonies. His eastern neighbors became jealous of his power, had him indicted in their court, and carried to Newport for trial. They tried to prevent his release, which caused Roger Williams to interfere in his behalf, and to write a very complimentary letter concerning him to King Charles II. Smith became so incensed with his neighbors' behavior that he purchased land on Long Island from Lion Gardiner, removed there, and left his Narragansett property with his relatives. The Long Island property was given to Lion Gardiner by an Indian chief, Wyandauch, as a ransom for the chief's daughter, who was taken captive during the war between the Ninigrets and the Long Island Indians. The princess spent her captivity at Smith's house, which was the rendezvous of the whites during all the Indian wars. The patents for Smithtown were dated March 25, 1677. He had been one of the "Eight Men," 1645, and was a member of the Governor's Council, Province of New York, in 1688. His wife, whom he married in England, was Sarah Folger. He died 1691, leaving his town on Long Island to his seven children, in equal shares.

His daughter, *Elizabeth,* married, first, WILLIAM LAWRENCE; and, second, Sir Philip Carteret, the first Governor of New Jersey, who named the town Elizabeth, for her. A son of her first marriage, *Joseph Lawrence,* married Mary Townley, and their daughter, *Abi-*

gail, married Captain Alexander Forbes I., whose descendant, *Anna Forbes Parker,* married *Cleaveland Forbes Dunderdale.* Their daughter is:

BEATRICE DUNDERDALE DOBBIN,

Member of Chapter I., The Colonial Dames of America.

XIV

MONTGOMERY

COLONEL JOHN MONTGOMERY, the first of the Scotch-Irish branch of this powerful Normandy family to come to America, was born at the Manor House, near Londonderry, which is still owned and lived in by his family. He brought with him a young nephew, Charles Montgomery, and settled in Cumberland Valley, Pa., 1718. The valley was called Kittecktinny, at that time, by the Indians, who ranged from the Potomac to the Susquehanna. They were the six tribes who, in 1736, ceded their claim to the Proprietory Government, but continued savagely hostile to the settlers. To insure safety, a stockade fort, two acres square, was built by the settlers, with a block house in each corner, to which they fled in times of danger. Many massacres and horrible atrocities are recorded, together with deeds of heroism, by these brave men and women. The settlers were men of prayer and action, who loved their Bibles, hated tyranny, and at the first collision between the Royal and Colonial governments, made ready to maintain the right, and were one in spirit with the men

of the "Mechlenburg Convention." From the first con-
stant vigilance was necessary, and men worked, ate and
worshipped with guns in their hands. The first pastor
in the log church, built on the lands of the Conodo-
guinet, commonly called the "fighting parson," was the
Rev. John Steele, captain of the Provincial troops, who
preached with a gun at his side.[1] Through John Montgomery, who in 1757 was one of the founders of Carlisle, Penn., Dickinson College and the First Presbyterian Church of Carlisle, Penn., were established. He
was Colonel of the third Battalion against the Indians
and Fort Duquesne, 1758; a member of the Assembly
of Pennsylvania, 1763 to 1775; in the Provincial Council, held in Philadelphia, January 23-28, 1775; a' member of the Convention, held in Philadelphia, July 15,
and continued until September, 1776, and was continuously re-elected to the Committee of Safety, of which
Dr. Benjamin Franklin was president. From 1767 to
1776 he served as Treasurer of Cumberland County,
and in the latter year Congress sent him to treat with
the Indians at Fort Pitt. The next year, 1777, he became a member of the Continental Congress, and served
until 1784. At the time of his death, which occurred
in Carlisle, 1806, he was Judge of the County. From
the beginning of the resistance to Great Britain, he devoted his energy, ability and money to the cause of
liberty.

The first wife of Colonel Montgomery was Sidney,
the daughter of Samuel and Sidney (Gamble) Smith.[2]
(Her father emigrated to America 1728, and settled in
Pennsylvania.) He married, second, 1778, Sarah, the
daughter of James Diemer, and the widow of Hon.

[1] *Family Mss.* verified.
[2] *Family Bible.*

James Ralph. Issue, first wife, seven children, viz.:

William, an officer in the Continental army.

Samuel Smith, a captain in the Revolutionary army and member of the Society of the Cincinnati.

John, Jr., was member of Congress and second Mayor of Baltimore. Married, first, Mary Harris, and second, Maria Nicholson.

Esther, married Colonel James Morrison, of the Continental army.

Jane, married Colonel Edmiston, of the Continental army.

Mary, died unmarried.

Sidney, knew intimately many of the men who made history before and after the Revolution.

Issue, second wife, four children, viz.:

Sarah, married David Harris.

Margaret (1781-1807) ; married the Rev. Dr. Davidson II., President of Dickinson College, Penn., and pastor of the First Presbyterian Church of Carlisle.

Thomas, was a Major in the United States army, in the War of 1812; in command at Fort Stephen, Mobile, 1819; died unmarried.

James, married Eliza Virginia Smoot, of Washington, D. C., and had one son, John James, of Mobile.

DIEMER

An officer in the British army, James Diemer, of Huguenot descent, served through the horrors of the French and Indian wars. He was born 1713, and died a Tory, having settled in Lancaster, Penn. He was a linguist, speaking French, English and German; was highly musical, and his portrait, in scarlet and gold, is that of a handsome man. He educated his sons and daughters equally, to the unusual advantage of the latter, in those days. He married Rachel ———, and died many years before her, who lived to a great age. Issue, three children: James (1733-1820), for many years a practicing physician in Reading, Penn.; Mary and Sarah.

Mary, married Judge Bard, of Bardstown, Ky.; their daughter married Judge Buchanan.

Sarah, born 1744, married, first, 1762, Hon. James Ralph, a Captain in the British army, and son of a younger daughter of the Duke of Bedford; second, COLONEL JOHN MONTGOMERY. In 1769, James Ralph was commissioned Major in command at Carlisle, commission signed by John Penn. A year or two later he went to England and died. Issue, first husband: Mary and Anne, to whom gifts were sent on their birth from the Earl of Aylesbury, god-father of Captain Ralph, and from his son, Lord Bruce, an intimate friend. The second daughter, Anne, married James Somerville, a wealthy Scotchman (a cousin of Colonel Montgomery), who did a large importing business between Baltimore and foreign countries. Issue, second husband: *Sarah Montgomery,* who married David Harris.

HARRIS

The father of William Harris, who was born near Belfast, Ireland, was a landed proprietor, and the family still lives in and around the old home.[3] William came to America 1768, and bought a house on Market Street, Baltimore, and a tract of land on Federal Hill, the direction in which the city was expected to grow. Shortly after this he left Baltimore, and bought land near Germantown, Penn. An agent, whom he trusted, advised the sale of the Federal Hill property, as being

3 *Family letters and Bibles.*

a poor investment. The purchaser afterward proved to be the agent himself, who paid a trifling sum for the property, and laid the foundation for a fortune now enjoyed by his descendants. In the struggle with Great Britain, William Harris became deeply involved, and his house was burnt by the British. He then moved near York, Penn., and bought another place, to which he gave the name of "Springfield," which was that of his last home. Here he lived many years, and afterward in a house which is now the German Theological Seminary. He was an author, a poet of wit and versatility, and possessed of great patriotism, giving large sums to the country in its hour of need. He married in Ireland (where his daughters were born), Sarah McKillup, and brought his family to America in his own vessel. Issue, eight children, viz.:

Jane, who married (third wife) Robert Davidson, D. D., President of Dickinson College, Penn., and Professor of Belles-Lettres. He became President of the college at the death of its first President, Dr. Nesbit, and also pastor of the First Presbyterian Church. He was master of eight languages, an astronomer, inventor of the cohmosphere, and very musical. His second wife was Margaret Montgomery, and they had a son Robert, whose descendants live in New York.

Sarah, died 1842, unmarried.

David, married *Sarah Montgomery.*

Esther Montgomery, 1808-1877, was unmarried.

John Montgomery, married and died without issue.

George W., married Ellen Reed McIlvaine, of Philadelphia, widow of a physician of Berkley, Va.; issue, six children.

David Caldwell, married Ellen George.

Thomas, died an infant.

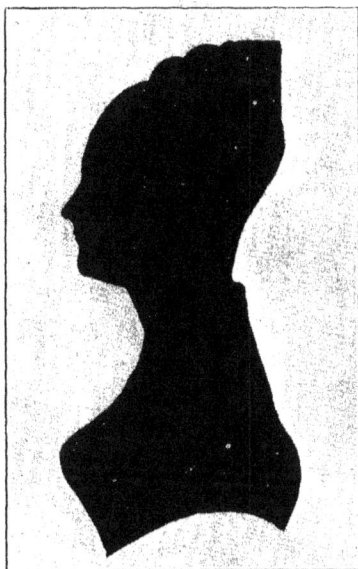

SARAH MONTGOMERY
Wife of David Harris

THE SOMERVILLE SILVER

James Morrison (1815-1898), a lawyer and a man of rare attainment, was one of the founders of the Maryland Historical Society. He was the inspirer and one of the founders of the Mercantile Library of Baltimore, starting it with books from his father's library. He served three terms in Congress, 1855 to 1859, from which he resigned after making an impassioned speech against the declaration of war. He married, in October, 1852, Sidney Calhoun, the daughter of Benedict William Hall, of Baltimore; issue, William, who married Alice, the daughter of Henry Patterson, of Baltimore, and has four children.

MONTGOMERY (*Continued*)

The eldest daughter of John and Sarah (Diemer) Montgomery, *Sarah Montgomery,* was born 1779, and married, 1803, David, son of William Harris, who was born 1770. David Harris was one of the volunteers to put down the Whiskey Rebellion in the West, 1794, and as Colonel in the War of 1812 he behaved with great bravery, both during the campaigns, and in putting down the mob in Baltimore, 1812. He declined the rank of General after the war. He met with serious business reverses, and never fully recovered from an attack of cholera in 1832. His death occurred in Virginia, 1844, when he was seventy-four years of age. Issue, eight children, of whom:

The second daughter, *Anne Somerville* (1806-1880), was adopted by her aunt and uncle, Anne and James Somerville. She married, first, Stephen Stewart Wilson, who died after two years, leaving no issue; second, John Barnett Hammond, the son of Robert and Margaret Templeman (Browne) Fulton, who was born July 14, 1808, and died in July, 1876.

The ancestor of the Browne family, Sir Edwin Browne, came to America with Captain John Smith, and settled in present Westmoreland County, Va. William Browne (1737-1818), in the sixth generation from Sir Edwin, married, 1768, Margaret Templeman. Their daughter, Margaret Templeman (1783-1836), married Robert Fulton (1781-1839). Their son, John Barnett Hammond Fulton, and his wife, *Anne Somerville Harris*, had issue, seven children, viz.:

Sarah Montgomery.

Somerville, died 1860, unmarried.

Margaret Templeman, died an infant.

William and Jane Purviance, also died in infancy.

MARY ESTHER.

George Harris, died 1897.

MARY ESTHER FULTON,

Member of Chapter I., The Colonial Dames of America.

XV
GAITHER

The colonist, John Gaither, was born in England, February 16, 1604, and died 1652. He married, 1631, Jane Morley, and emigrated to America, where he was one of the founders of the First Parish Church at Sewall's Point, Md., 1640.

His son, John Gaither II. (1635-1703), settled on South River, Anne Arundel County, Md., and maried, 1675, *Ruth,* the daughter of Richard and Rachel (Robins) Beard. Their son was *Benjamin Gaither.*

BEARD

RICHARD BEARD, of South River, Md., Anne Arundel County, came up from Virginia, with his brother-in-law, Edward Burgess. He took up "Beard's Habitation," on Beard's Creek, and built a mill, which also bore his name. He was a member of the Provincial Assembly of Maryland,[1] 1662 and 1663. His death occurred in 1675. He married Rachel, the daughter of Edward Robins, of Northampton County, Va. Their daughter, *Ruth,* married John Gaither II.

GAITHER (*Continued*)

The son of John and Ruth (Beard) Gaither, *Benjamin Gaither,* was born February 2, 1681, and died 1741. He settled upon the Patuxent River, on "Gaither's Fancy," and became a large land owner. He was most active in establishing Queen Caroline

---

[1] Warfield's *Anne Arundel County,* p. 69.

Parish, in 1728. He married, 1709, *Sarah,* the daughter of Edward and Sarah (Chew) Burgess, who died 1750. A son was *Henry Gaither.*

BURGESS

COLONEL WILLIAM BURGESS (1622-1686), settled first in Northampton County, Va., but followed Governor William Stone to Maryland, and settled on South River, bringing there a company of one hundred and fifty "adventurers." In 1661, he was in command of the South River Rangers; in 1664, he was High Sheriff of Anne Arundel County, and in 1665 he was Commander-in-chief of all the forces of the five western shore counties. He was a member of the Council of the State of Maryland, a Justice of the Provincial Court, and a Deputy-Governor from 1678 to 1683.[2] He married Elizabeth, the daughter of Edward Robins, who was born in England 1602, and came to Virginia 1615, in the bark *Thomas;* he lived in Northampton and Accomac Counties, and built "Newport House," now Eyreville.

EDWARD BURGESS (1651-1703), went to Maryland with his father, Colonel William, and was a Justice of the Provincial Court of Anne Arundel County, and one of the Quorum 1685; also "Captain of the Foote." He married *Sarah,* the daughter of Samuel and Anne (Ayres) Chew. Their daughter, *Sarah,* married *Benjamin Gaither.*

CHEW

JOHN CHEW, of "Chewtown," Somersetshire, Eng., came to America, and settled at James City, Va., where

2 *Arch.* of Md.

he built a house, and was a merchant until 1649, when he moved to Maryland with his wife Sarah and two sons, SAMUEL and Joseph. He was Burgess from James City.

COLONEL SAMUEL CHEW, was born 1625, and died 1676. He laid out Herrington, on Herring Creek, Anne Arundel County, Md., a grant being issued to him 1650. He was Keeper of the Seal, a Justice of Chancery of the Provincial Courts of Maryland; member of the Council of State, 1669 to 1676, and Delegate to the General Assembly 1660; Chancellor [3] and Colonel in 1675. He married, Anne, "the Quakeress daughter" of William Ayres, of Nansemond, Va. Their daughter, *Sarah,* married EDWARD BURGESS.

GAITHER. (*Continued*)

A son of Benjamin and Sarah (Burgess) Gaither, Henry Gaither (1724-1773), married, 1746, *Martha,* the daughter of William and Elizabeth (Duvall) Ridgely. Their only son was *Daniel Gaither.*

RIDGELY

ROBERT RIDGELY, of St. Inigoes, emigrated early to Maryland and died 1681. He was Keeper of the Great Seal, June 16, 1674, and Secretary of the Province of Maryland under Lord Baltimore.[4] He married Martha ——. His only daughter, *Martha,* married Lewis Duvall, whose daughter, *Elizabeth,* married her cousin, *William Ridgely.*

The second son, *Charles Ridgely I.,* who died 1705, married *Deborah,* the daughter of JOHN DORSEY. Two of their sons were *William* and CHARLES II.

[3] *Ibid.*   [4] *Ibid.*

The elder of these, *William Ridgely,* married *Elizabeth,* the daughter of Lewis and Martha (Ridgely) Duvall. Issue, among others, *Martha,* who married *Henry Gaither.*

COLONEL CHARLES RIDGELY II., a younger son of Charles Ridgely I., died 1772. He was a Colonel of the Colonial Militia, a Commissioner of his county, a member of the Assembly from 1751 to 1754, etc. He married Rachel Howard in 1721.

Their daughter, *Achsah,* married John Carnan. By the will of his uncle, Captain Charles Ridgely, of " Hampton," he took the name of " Ridgely," and was placed at the head of the entail of " Hampton."

Their son, *Governor Charles Ridgely,* was born December 6, 1762, and died July 17, 1829. From 1815 to 1818, he was Governor of Maryland. He married, October 7, 1787, *Priscilla,* the daughter of Caleb and Priscilla (Hill) Dorsey (1762-1814). One of their daughters, *Mary Pue,* married *Charles S. W. Dorsey,* whose daughter, *Rebecca Hanson,* married *George Riggs Gaither II.*

DORSEY

HON. JOHN DORSEY, of Hockley, a son of the emigrant, Edward Dorsey, died 1714. He was a member of the Provincial Assembly of Maryland for several terms, and a member of the Council 1710-1714. He married Pleasance Ely in 1683.

His daughter, *Deborah,* married *Charles Ridgely I.*

Through a son of John Dorsey are the two following lines of descent:

FIRST LINE.

Caleb Dorsey I., of Hockley, born 1686, married in

1704, *Eleanor*, the daughter of ~~Benjamin, the son~~ of
CAPTAIN RICHARD WARFIELD.

Caleb Dorsey II., of Belmont, born July 18, 1710,
died June 28, 1772; married *Priscilla*, the daughter of
Henry and Mary (Denwood) Hill, the granddaughter
of CAPTAIN RICHARD HILL, and the great-granddaughter of LEVIN DENWOOD I.

Priscilla Dorsey, born July 12, 1762, died April 30,
1814; married *Governor Charles Ridgely.*

Mary Pue Ridgely married *Charles S. W. Dorsey.*

Rebecca Hanson Dorsey, married *George Riggs
Gaither II.*

SECOND LINE.

Caleb Dorsey I., of Hockley, married *Eleanor Warfield.*

Thomas Beale Dorsey, married Anne Worthington.

COLONEL JOHN WORTHINGTON DORSEY, married
Comfort, the daughter of Samuel and Mary (Tolley)
Worthington.

Charles S. W. Dorsey, married *Mary Pue Ridgely.*

Rebecca Hanson Dorsey, married *George Riggs
Gaither II.*

A third line descends through another son of Edward, the emigrant, viz.:

COLONEL EDWARD DORSEY, of Anne Arundel
County, Md., who married Sarah, the daughter of
Nicholas Wyatt. (See pp. 150, 568.)

Their son, *Joshua Dorsey*, married *Ann*, the daughter of Henry and Catherine (Greenberry) Ridgely.

Their son, *Philemon Dorsey* (1713-1755), married
Catherine, the daughter of Henry and Elizabeth
(Warfield) Ridgely, whose daughter, *Amelia* (1749-
1807), married SAMUEL RIGGS; their daughter, *Henrietta Riggs*, married *Daniel Gaither.*

DUVALL

A celebrated Huguenot, Mareen Duvall, emigrated from Nantes, under Colonel William Burgess, in the middle of the seventeenth century, settling in Anne Arundel County, Md., where he became a prosperous merchant and planter. His name is found in Colonel Greenberry's letter to Governor Copley, as one of the Jacobin party, whose mysterious meetings he could not solve. His will was probated 1694. He was married three times, and one of his wives was Elizabeth.

A son, Lewis Duvall, married, 1699, *Martha,* the only daughter of Robert Ridgely, the colonist of St. Inigoes, and their daughter, *Elizabeth,* married her cousin, *William Ridgely,* whose daughter, *Martha,* married *Henry Gaither.* Their son, *Daniel,* married *Henrietta Riggs.*

Captain John Duvall, another son of Mareen Duvall, died 1711. He was Captain in the Maryland militia 1696. He married, 1686, Elizabeth, the daughter of William Jones, Sr., a Justice of Anne Arundel County, Md., 1676.

Their daughter, *Elizabeth,* married *Benjamin,* the youngest son of Captain Richard Warfield, and their daughter, *Eleanor,* married *Caleb Dorsey I.*

WORTHINGTON

Captain John Worthington, was born 1650, and died April 6, 1701. As early as 1675 he was living on the Severn River, near Annapolis, and in 1686 he bought "Greenberry Forest," from Colonel Nicholas Greenberry. He was Justice from 1692 to 1696, Captain of the Horse, 1694, and member of the Assembly 1699. He married, 1688, Sarah, the daughter of Matthew Howard.

A son, *John Worthington,* was born 1689. He in- herited from his father the home plantation of four hun- dred acres on the Severn River, and became a prosper- ous merchant and planter. In his will he left to his children sixteen different plantations, besides several thousand acres. He married *Helen,* the daughter of Thomas and Mary (Heath) Hammond.

Their son, *Samuel Worthington,* married, 1759, *Mary,* the daughter of Walter and Mary (Garretson) Tolley, and their daughter, *Comfort,* married JOHN WORTHINGTON DORSEY.

GAITHER (*Continued*)

The son of Henry and Martha (Ridgely) Gaither, *Daniel Gaither* (1769-1804), married, 1791, *Henrietta,* the daughter of Samuel and Amelia (Dorsey) Riggs. She was born December 22, 1769, and died April, 1854. Their son was *George Riggs Gaither I.*

RIGGS-DAVIS

The colonist, John Riggs, was born 1687, and died August 17, 1762, the son of John Riggs, born in Lon- don, and Jane Warden, his wife. The home of John Riggs II. was "Rigg's Hills," east of Laurel, Md. He married, 1721, Mary, the daughter of Thomas Davis.

SAMUEL RIGGS, their son, was born October 6, 1740, and died May 25, 1814. During the Revolution, he was Second-Lieutenant in the Montgomery County Militia, under Colonel Zadock Magruder.[5] On his mar- riage to *Amelia,* the daughter of Philemon and Cather- ine (Ridgely) Dorsey, he moved to "Bordley's Choice," in Montgomery County, and built the homestead which still stands on a hill near Brookeville. His wife was

5 Md. *Arch.*

254 ANCESTRAL RECORDS AND PORTRAITS

born August 23, 1749, and died August 6, 1807. Their
daughter, *Henrietta,* married *Daniel Gaither.*

The father of Mary Davis, the wife of John Riggs
II., was Thomas Davis. He was one of the Virginia
settlers of Herring Creek. He is supposed to have
been the grandson of Sir Thomas Davis, one of the
London Company, who came to James City in 1619,
on *The Margaret,* and that same year was in the Virginia Assembly from " Martin's Brandon." His wife
was Mary, the daughter of Henry Pierpont.

HAMMOND

MAJOR-GENERAL JOHN HAMMOND, was born 1643,
and died November 29, 1707. He lived near Annapolis, on the Severn River, and was for many years one
of the vestry of St. Ann's Church, and one of the Commissioners to lay out the town of Annapolis. He married Mary Howard. (See pp. 151-152.)

A son, *Thomas Hammond,* inherited the plantation
called Mt. Airey Neck, as well as a house in Annapolis.
He married Mary, the daughter of Thomas Heath,
and their daughter, *Helen,* married *John Worthington.*

TOLLEY

THOMAS TOLLEY, was Burgess for Baltimore County
1721-1731; Justice of the Provincial Court; Commissioner to lay out Joppa 1724, and Commissioner to lay
out Baltimore 1729. He died 1732.

COLONEL WALTER TOLLEY, his son, was Burgess for
Baltimore County and Justice, 1754; a member of the
Maryland Convention 1774 to 1776, and a Colonel in
the Revolution 1776, dying in 1782. He married
Mary Garretson. Their daughter, *Mary,* married *Sam-*

uel Worthington, whose daughter, *Comfort,* married JOHN WORTHINGTON DORSEY.

RIDGELY

COLONEL HENRY RIDGLEY, was born in England 1645, and died 1710. He was a member of the Provincial Assembly of Maryland, 1692 to 1695; Justice of Anne Arundel County, Md., 1676 to 1695; Colonel in the Militia 1669. He married, second, Sarah Warner.

Their son, *Henry Ridgely II.,* married *Catherine,* the daughter of COLONEL NICHOLAS GREENBERRY. Issue, among others: *Ann* and HENRY III. Ann married *Joshua Dorsey,* whose son, *Philemon,* married his cousin, *Catherine,* the daughter of Henry and Elizabeth (Warfield) Ridgely.

COLONEL HENRY RIDGELY III. (1690-1750), married, 1702, Elizabeth Warfield. He was a Colonel in the Militia from 1726 to 1740. *Catherine,* their daughter, married *Philemon Dorsey,* whose daughter, *Amelia,* married SAMUEL RIGGS, and their daughter, *Henrietta,* married *Daniel Gaither.*

GREENBERRY

COLONEL NICHOLAS GREENBERRY (1627-1699), emigrated from England in 1674, with his wife Anne. He was commissioned Justice of the Provincial Court, April 16, 1691. Upon the death of Colonel Lionel Copley, he became Acting-Governor from September 9 to September 25, 1693. Prior to this he was Keeper of the Great Seal, May 17, 1693. He was sworn in as Judge of the Vice-Admiralty Court, and was Judge of the Provincial Court of Maryland, Judge of the High Court of Chancery, December 17, 1697, and

President of the Provincial Court, 1693. His daughter, *Catherine,* married *Henry Ridgely II.*

GAITHER *(Continued)*

The son of Daniel and Henrietta (Riggs) Gaither, *George Riggs Gaither,* was born in Baltimore, April 28, 1796, and died September 13, 1875. He married, 1822, *Hannah,* the daughter of Abraham and Hannah (Smith) Bradley. She was born in Georgetown, D. C., May 1, 1800, and died June 27, 1873. Their eldest son was *George Riggs Gaither, II.*

BRADLEY

LIEUTENANT STEPHEN BRADLEY, was born 1642. He was a Delegate from Guilford, Conn., to the General Assembly of Connecticut, 1692, until his death, which occurred January 20, 1701. He married Hannah Smith in 1663.

LIEUTENANT ABRAHAM BRADLEY, their son, was born 1674, and died April 20, 1721. He was a Lieutenant in the Militia from 1714 to 1721. He married, 1697, Jane Leaming.

Their son, *Abraham Bradley II.* (1702-1771), married Reliance Howe, who died 1757.

CAPTAIN ABRAHAM BRADLEY III., their son, was born December 11, 1731. He was a Captain in the Connecticut line of the Revolutionary Army. He married Hannah Baldwin (1737-1804).

Their son, *Abraham Bradley IV.,* was born February 21, 1767, and died May 8, 1838. He married Hannah Smith, and their daughter, *Hannah Bradley,* married *George Riggs Gaither.*

GAITHER (*Continued*)

The son of George Riggs and Hannah (Bradley) Gaither, *George Riggs Gaither II.*, was born in Baltimore, Md., January 25, 1831, and died May 10, 1899. He was Captain in the Maryland line C. S. A., and served during the war. He married, August 6, 1851, *Rebecca Hanson,* the daughter of Charles S. W. and Mary Pue (Ridgely) Dorsey, born May 15, 1833.

Their son, *Charles Dorsey Gaither,* was born November 27, 1860. He married, April 25, 1885, *Alice Stockton Williams,* the daughter of John Witherspoon and Augusta Rebecca (Howell) Williams, who was born December 18, 1861. Their daughter is NINA WILLIAMS GAITHER.

HOWELL

HON. RICHARD HOWELL (1752-1802), was Captain and later Major in the New Jersey Continental line, in the Revolution. After the war, he was Governor of New Jersey for thirteen years. His father, Ebenezer Howell, founded Newark, Del. He married Keziah Burr.

Their son, *Major Richard Lewis Howell* (1793-1815), married *Rebecca Augusta,* the daughter of Lucius Witham and Elizabeth Augusta (Coxe) Stockton, born 1798, died 1877.

Their daughter, *Augusta Rebecca,* married *John Witherspoon,* the son of John Nicholas and Sarah Cantey (Witherspoon) Williams. (See pp. 6-55 for the Williams family and its connections).

STOCKTON

HON. JOHN STOCKTON, was born 1701. He was the son of Richard and Susannah, and the grandson of

Richard and Abigail Stockton. The first Richard was
born 1606, and the second Richard died 1709. John
Stockton was Presiding Judge of the Court of Common
Pleas of New Jersey, from 1734 to 1739. His wife
was Abigail Phillips. They had several sons, one of
whom, Richard, was a Signer of the Declaration of Independence.

Another son, *Rev. Philip Stockton* (1746-1792), married Catherine Cummings.

Their son, *Lucius Witham Stockton,* married Elizabeth Augusta Coxe.

Their daughter, *Rebecca Augusta Stockton* (1798-
1877), married *Major Richard Lewis,* the son of RICH-
ARD HOWELL, and their daughter, *Augusta Rebecca,*
married *John Witherspoon Williams,* whose daughter,
Alice Stockton, married *Charles Dorsey Gaither.*

WITHERSPOON

In 1734, John, the son of David Witherspoon, emigrated to South Carolina, where he had a grant of
twenty-nine miles square from the king. The land was
called Williamsburg, in honor of the king, and they
founded a town called King's Tree. He married his
cousin Janet, the aunt of Dr. John Witherspoon, later
President of Princeton College, and a Signer of the
Declaration of Independence.

Their son, Gavin Witherspoon (1712-1773), married Jane James. Their son:

GAVIN WITHERSPOON (1748-1834), married Elizabeth Dick, of Sumter. He was Captain in General
Francis Marion's Brigade in the Revolution and was
a notable scout, of whose bravery many tales are told in
Simms' "Life of Marion."

Their son, *John Dick Witherspoon,* was born March

17, 1778, and died April 2, 1860. He married, 1808, *Elizabeth,* the daughter of SAMUEL BOYKIN, whose wife was Elizabeth Inman.

Their daughter, *Sarah Cantey,* married *John Nicholas,* the son of David Rogerson and Sarah (Power) Williams, of Society Hill, S. C. (See pp. 6-55 for Williams, Boykin, Miller, Cantey, Chesnut, Cox, Power, and connecting lines.) Their son, *John Witherspoon,* married *Augusta Rebecca Howell,* and their daughter, *Alice Stockton,* married *Charles Dorsey Gaither,* whose daughter is:

NINA WILLIAMS GAITHER,

Member of Chapter I., The Colonial Dames of America.

XVI
GILMAN

ARMS: *Sable, a man's leg couped at the thigh in pale argent.*
MOTTO: *Si Deus quis contra.*

The Gilmans[1] of America trace their lineage back directly only to Edward Gilman, of Caston, Norfolk, Eng. Church records were not kept at Caston before 1539, but there are earlier Gilmans in Norfolk and other parts of England who bear the same coat of arms. The name was variously spelt, Gylmyn, Gilmyn or Gilman. Edward was married at Caston June 26, 1550 to Rose Rysse. She survived him, and his will was proved by her, July 7, 1573.

[1] The authorities used in the preparation of these sketches were: *The Gilman Family*, by Arthur Gilman (Albany, N. Y., 1869); *The Gillman or Gilman Family*, by Alexander W. Gilman (London, 1895); *Noyes-Gilman Ancestry*, by Charles P. Noyes (St. Paul, Minn., 1907); *American Armory and Blue Book*, by John Matthews.

Their third son, Robert, was baptized July 10, 1559. He married Mary ——, and they both died at Caston, she in 1618, and he March 6, 1631.

Their son Edward was born 1587; married, June 3, 1614, Mary Clark, at Hingham, a small market town about five and a half miles from Caston, and near Norwich. The English branch of the family continued to live there until 1860, and have frequently been visited by the American Gilmans. The rector of the parish at Hingham, the Rev. Robert Peck, "a man of very violent schimatic spirit," having provoked his Bishop to prosecution, sailed from Gravesend, April 26, 1638, in the ship *Diligent,* with a party of one hundred and thirty-three persons, some of whom had sold their estates for half their value, and arrived at Boston, August 10, 1638. In the company were Edward Gilman, his wife, three sons, two daughters and three servants. They settled with their companions, at Hingham, Mass., and he was admitted Freeman there, December 16, 1638. In 1641 the Plymouth Colony granted him a tract of land eight miles square called "Seekonk," and he is later at Ipswich, and then at Exeter, N. H., which became the family home for generations. He died June 22, 1681. One of his sons:

JOHN GILMAN, was baptized at Hingham, Eng., May 23, 1626; died July 24, 1708. He was engaged in the lumber and milling business, and his name is on the records as Selectman and as receiving grants of land. When New Hampshire was separated from Massachusetts in 1680, he was made Councillor and held that office three years; was Judge of the Court of Pleas 1682; member of the Provincial Assembly of New Hampshire from 1693 to 1697; elected Speaker 1693.

He married, June 20, 1657, Elizabeth, the daughter

of James Treworgye, born 1639, and died September
8, 1719. One of her chairs is still in the possession of
her descendants. The genealogist quaintly says that
John Gilman lived to see his family circle very greatly
increased, fourteen having been added by marriage to
the original sixteen. Two of the sons, *John,* and
Nicholas, continue this Gilman line.

The eleventh child, *John Gilman II.,* was born January 19, 1676, and died between 1738 and 1742. The
government of New Hampshire sent out scouting expeditions against the Indians 1703-04, and Captain
John Gilman commanded one of the two Exeter companies. They went on snow shoes in quest of the savages, but, though they did not find them, the Council
declared it to be honorable service and ordered gratuities
to the officers. He went on similar service in 1710 to
pursue the Indians who had killed Colonel Hilton. In
1709 the town voted to give "all the right the town
have in the stream and island to Captain John Gilman,
where the said Gilman's cornmill now stands, with
privilege for a bridge to go on the island; and the above
said John Gilman doth oblige himself to grind the inhabitants' corn when wanted for two quarts in every
bushel." He was one of the grantees of Gilmanton,
N. H., and was mentioned in the Charter as chairman
of the first Board of Selectmen. He was Moderator
of the first meeting of the Proprietors and was called
both Major and Colonel.

He married, June 5, 1698, *Elizabeth,* daughter of
Peter Coffin, born January 27, 1680, and died July 4,
1720. Their fifth child was JOHN GILMAN III.

COFFIN

The residence of Nicholas Coffin was in Brixton,

1587 *Edward Gilman* 1681

1626 *John Gilman* 1708

1676 *John Gilman* 1738

1752 *John Gilman*

1763 *Benj: C, Gilman* 1835

1795 *Saml Gilman* 1863

1831 *Daniel C. Gilman* 1908

AUTOGRAPHS OF SEVEN GENERATIONS OF THE
GILMAN FAMILY

Devon, Eng., and he was buried there October 8, 1613; his will being proved the following third of November.[2] He married Joan ——.

His eldest son, Peter Coffin, evidently succeeded to his father's estate. He was Church Warden at Brixton, and in 1604, married Joan Thember.

,His will was proved March 13, 1628, providing that his wife should have a life tenure of his land, and that it should then go to his son Tristram, "who is to be provided for according to his degree and calling."

TRISTRAM COFFIN, of Brixton Parish, was baptized there March 11, 1609-10. He married Dioris, the daughter of Robert Stevens. He was a Church Warden. At the beginning of the Civil War in 1642, he left his property and friends in England, and, accompanied by his mother, wife, five little children, and two unmarried sisters came to America.

He lived at various places in Massachusetts and went to Nantucket, 1659, on a tour of observation, having with him as interpreter, Peter Folger, a grandfather of Benjamin Franklin. July 2, 1659, he and eight other men bought the Island of Nantucket, from Governor Mayhew, who retained one-twentieth interest himself; the consideration was "thirty pounds and also two Beaver Hatts, one for myself and one for my wife."

Tristram moved his family to Nantucket and in 1671 was appointed Chief Magistrate of the island. He and the Chief Magistrate of Martha's Vineyard, with two assistants, constituted the General Court over both islands. This court at its first sitting "enacted a law prohibiting the sale of intoxicating drinks to Indians," probably the first prohibitory liquor law

[2] A copy of the Coffin Coat of Arms and Crest can be found in Matthews' *American Armoury and Blue Book, Armorial Addenda*, p. 22.

on record. He died in Nantucket 1681. The eldest son:

PETER COFFIN, was baptized in Brixton, Eng., July 18, 1630, and died March 21, 1715. He emigrated with his father, and was Chief Justice of the Superior Court of New Hampshire, and Councilor of the State.

He married Abigail, the daughter of Edward Starbuck, and their daughter, *Elizabeth,* married *John Gilman II.*

Their daughter, *Elizabeth,* married *John Gilman II.*

GILMAN (*Continued*)

MAJOR JOHN GILMAN III, son of John and Elizabeth (Coffin) Gilman, was born October 25, 1712. He was a Major at Fort Edward, and in 1757 was sent to Fort William Henry with reinforcements, arrived just after the capitulation, was captured by Montcalm's Indian allies, stripped, and with great difficulty escaped. He married, 1738, Jane, the daughter of Dr. Thomas and Deborah (Clarke) Deane, born June 20, 1721, and died 1786, and their son was *Benjamin Clarke Gilman.*

The daughter of John and Elizabeth (Woodbridge) Clarke, *Deborah Clarke* (1696-1735), was descended on her father's side, from EDMUND GREENLEAF, and on her mother's side, from GOVERNOR THOMAS DUDLEY.

One of the proprietors of Gilmanton, N. H., Dr. Thomas Deane (1694-1768), was a physician, and also a captain in the militia.

GREENLEAF

EDMUND GREENLEAF, a silk dyer, was the son of John and Margaret Greenleaf of the Parish of Ipswich, Suf-

DANIEL COIT GILMAN

THE HOME OF MAJOR JOHN GILMAN
At Exeter, N. H., photographed in 1891

folkshire, Eng., where he was baptized at St. Mary's-La-Tour, January 2, 1573-74, and died in Massachusetts, March 24, 1671. The name Greenleaf is only found in this Parish.

He must have come to America by 1638, when according to the records, he was appointed, with three other men, to direct the defence of the church in Newbury, Mass., against the Indians, during worship. Edmund Greenleaf's name is found in the first division of home lots, and his house was near the old "Towne Bridge." He was freeman and ensign 1639, and Lieutenant of the Massachusetts Provincial Forces, 1642; he was said in 1644, to be "an ancient and experienced lieutenant and head of the Militia," under Captain William Gerrish. He applied for and was granted his discharge from military service, 1647, when he was seventy-three years old. In 1639, he was permitted to keep a house of entertainment, but removed to Boston in 1650.

He married Sarah Dole, and the baptisms of his nine children are recorded at the Parish church in Ipswich. Sarah, died in 1663, and he married, second, Mrs. Hill, who had been twice widowed. Edmund Greenleaf, in his will, tried to rectify the troubles arising from a complicated family relationship, as follows:

"When I married my wife, I kept her Grand Child as I best remember, 3 yeare to scooling Dyet & apparell, and William Hill, her son had a bond of six pound a yeare whereof I receiued no more than a barrell of porke of £3. 0. 0., of that £6. 0. 0. a yere to pay mee & I sent to her son Ignatius Hill, to the Barbadoes, in Mackrell, Sider & bred & pease, as much as come to twenty pound I neuer receaued one penny of itt; his Aunt gaue to the three Brothers £50 apiece—I know not whether they receaued it or noe but I haue not receaued any pt of it. Witness my hand Edmund Greenleaf. Beside—when I married my wife, she brought mee a siluer bowle a siluer porringer a siluer spon—she lent or gaue them to her son James Hill without my consent."[3]

The daughter of Edmund Greenleaf, *Judith Greenleaf*, (1625-1705), married Henry Somerby (1612-1652), who was from little Bytham, Lincolnshire; having come to Boston in the ship *Jonathan* 1639. He went at once to Newbury; was admitted Freeman 1642, established himself as a merchant-tailor, and was licensed 1650 "to keep an ordinary instead of Mr. Greenleaf," his father-in-law.

Their daughter, *Elizabeth Somerby*, was born November 1, 1646, and died March 15, 1716. She married, November 23, 1663, Nathaniel Clarke, a merchant of Newbury (1644-1690). He was Constable 1667 and 1668, Selectman 1682 and 1688; made Naval Officer for the ports of Newbury and Salisbury 1684, and was promoted from Sergeant to Ensign 1685. His will was probated September 30, 1690, and his estate was inventoried at £714, 9s.

Their son, the *Rev. John Clarke* (1670-1705), was graduated from Harvard College 1690, and became the third minister of Exeter 1698. He married *Elizabeth*, the daughter of the Rev. Benjamin and Mary (Ward) Woodbridge (1673-1729).

Their daughter, *Deborah*, married Thomas Dean, whose daughter *Jane* married JOHN GILMAN III.

DUDLEY-WOODBRIDGE

GOVERNOR THOMAS DUDLEY, son of Captain Roger

[3] The Greenleaf *Genealogy* says that he came from Brixon, Devon, England.

and —— (Nicolls) Dudley, was born in Northampton, Eng., 1576. His education was gained in a Latin school. Toward the close of the sixteenth century, he was the leader of a company of volunteers, to aid Henry of Navarre, in France, but was not called into active service. After his return, he studied law under Judge Augustine Nicholls, a Faxton kinsman. Having been appointed Deputy-Governor of Massachusetts in 1630, he came to New England on the ship *Arbella,* with Governor John Winthrop, and others, who were to play an important part in the history of

DUDLEY

the colony. Dudley was Governor 1634, 1640, 1645 and 1650. He was Deputy-Governor thirteen years, and Assistant five years in the Colony of Massachusetts Bay. In March, 1644, he became Sergeant Major-General. Dudley was a member of the Court which condemned Anne Hutchinson, in 1637, ex-communicating and banishing her from the colony, and was one of the signers of the Charter of Harvard College. Among his descendants are to be noted, William Ellery Channing, Richard Henry Dana, Wendell Phillips, Oliver Wendell Holmes and Donald G. Mitchell. In 1639, Dudley purchased land. at Roxbury and lived there until his death, July 31, 1652-53. His wife was

Dorothy ——, and their daughters were *Mercy,* and Anne the poetess, who married Governor Bradstreet.

The elder daughter, *Mercy Dudley,* married 1639, the Rev. John Woodbridge, of Andover, Mass., the son of the Rev. John and Sarah (Parker) Woodbridge, his father being the Rector of Stanton, Wiltshire, Eng. He had studied at Oxford, and came to New England in 1643, with his uncle, the Rev. Thomas Parker, and from 1634 to 1638 was Town Clerk of Newbury; Surveyor of Arms, 1637; and taught school in Boston 1643. He was one who negotiated the purchase of the land on which Andover, N. H., is built, from the Indians; was first minister of that place, being one of the earliest ministers ordained in New England. He returned to England in 1647, but came back and served as assistant to his uncle Thomas Parker; in consequence of dissensions in the church, however, he was dismissed from that office. Later he held local offices, and 1683 to 1684 was an Assistant of Massachusetts Colony. Cotton Mather mentions him in the *Magnalia,* and Woodbridge Island, near the mouth of the Merrimac river, was named for him. John Woodbridge died in Newbury July 1, 1691.

His son, the *Rev. Benjamin Woodbridge,* (1645-1710), of Bristol and Kittery, Me., wrote the ingenious lines for Cotton Mather's tomb. He married, 1672, Mary, the daughter of the Rev. John Ward (1649-1685).

Their daughter, *Elizabeth Woodbridge,* married the *Rev. John Clarke,* whose granddaughter, *Jane Deane,* married JOHN GILMAN III.[4]

---

[4] Authorities: Appleton's *Cycl. of Am. Biog.;* Lamb's *Biog. Dict. of the U. S.;* Noyes-Gilman *Ancestry.*

WARD

A famous Puritan minister, the Rev. John Ward, was of Haverhill and Bury St. Edmonds.

His son, the Rev. Nathaniel Ward, was graduated from Cambridge 1603, educated for the law, and admitted an outer barrister. He travelled extensively abroad, and during his travels was induced by the celebrated writer, David Pareus, to leave the profession of the law, and enter that of the ministry. On returning to England he lectured in London, and became the rector of Stondon, Massey. Brought before Laud, and deprived of his living in 1633, on account of his Puritan faith, he sailed for America in 1634. He returned to England, and was the minister of the church at Shenfield, where he died in 1652.

In America he was assistant to the Rev. Thomas Parker, in Ipswich, Mass.; compiled the first code of laws established in New England, and was the author of the well known work, *The Simple Cobler of Aggawan in America.*

His son, the Rev. John Ward, Rector of Hadleigh, Essex, Eng., settled in Haverhill; his daughter Mary, married the *Rev. Benjamin Woodbridge.*

GILMAN (*Continued*)

The ninth child of John and Elizabeth (Treworgye) Gilman, *Judge Nicholas Gilman,* was born at Exeter, N. H., December 26, 1672. He was a member of the church and subscribed to the Confession of Faith and Covenant with his father, September 21, 1698. The Indians were very hostile at this period and the Exeter men formed a militia and in 1695 Nicholas was among the men trained for service. He was Captain of one of the scouting parties 1710, also in command of part of the garrison, and went with his brother John in pursuit of the murderer of Colonel Hilton. When the province of New Hampshire issued £15,000 sterling of paper money in 1717, to be lent to the people in small sums on land, he was one of a committee of five for Exeter to superintend the loan there, and to appraise the land offered as security. When a new meeting-house was built 1730, eleven of the thirty-two pews were bought by Gilmans, Nicholas paying £21 for his pew. The town of Gilmanton was granted to one hundred and seventy-seven persons in 1727, as compensation for serv-ices rendered in defence of the country. Nicholas is first on the list, and there were twenty-three other Gil-mans among the number. He became Justice of the Court of Common Pleas in Exeter for one year 1729, and Judge of the Superior Court 1732 to 1740, when he retired. Judge Gilman died at Exeter in 1749. His estate was valued at £33,931, 7s, 10d. The inven-tory includes, "the Pew in the old meating house, £100 —— th Genelogy in the Parler 100, —— one Negro man named Tom, £260, and a Melater woman named Jenee and her child, £280." He married, June 10, 1697, Sarah, the daughter of Nathaniel Clarke.

Their fifth son, *Nicholas Gilman II,* was born in Ex-eter, January 18, 1707, and died April 13, 1748. He went to the Latin school at Newburyport at the age of eight, and was graduated at Harvard College, class of 1724, when but seventeen years old, and began immedi-ately to teach school at Stratham. He preached his first sermon at Kingston, N. H., October 30, 1727, but did not accept a permanent pastorate until March 3, 1742, when he was ordained at Durham, N. H. Among his papers is a "Carnal Scheme," giving the details of his salary: —

"Pork 500 lbs. . . . Beef 600 lbs. that is well fatted . . . Candles, Winter Rye and other grains, Molasses, Malt for Beer . . . Cyder 10 Barrells . . . Rum . . . gallons or Wine . . . Apples and Turnips . . . Pasturing & Wintering 4 cows & an horse, etc. . . . Wood 40 Cord, If I should need so much for firewood, to be hauled to my door in 4 foot length . . . 110 pounds pr. year for this first year and then the additions of 10 pounds per year for four years & yn 150£ per year to be paid in payable Bills of Credit in this province, &c."

In the extracts from the Rev. Nicholas Gilman's diary, kept from 1722 to 1738, we have varying entries, for instance:

"1723, March 17. Came to Cambridge.

March 27. Analyzed Matthew 21st in the hall.

June 18. Being grieviously exercised with the headache, I cut off my hair.

1725, May 3. I began to keep school at Exeter.

June 11. Took a violent emetic.

1726, June 9. Exercised with the mumps."

In the controversy about Whitefield, Nicholas Gilman, who was his friend, wrote in his defence to the ministers who were opposed to Whitefield's mission to New England. His books were inventoried at the time of his death at £392. In the library of Harvard University there is preserved an early catalogue of that institution, once the property of Nicholas, interleaved with brief annotations about the early graduates, now very valuable. The Master's address at the Harvard Commencement of 1727, was delivered by him.

He married, October 22, 1730, Mary, daughter of Bartholomew Thing. She was born January 11, 1713,

and died February 22, 1789.   A son was Judge Joseph
Gilman (1738-1806), and his commission as Judge of
the Northwest Territory, signed by George Washington, is own by Benjamin Ives Gilman of Boston.

Their fifth child *Josiah Gilman,* was born September
2, 1740, and died February 8, 1801.   He was commissioned by Governor John Wentworth, January 31,
1771, as " Captain of the Third Company of Foot in the
Fourth Regiment of Militia in the Province of New
Hampshire aforesaid."[5]   In 1800 Josiah was commissioned Justice of the Peace for the County of Rocking-
ham, N. H., by Governor John Taylor Gilman, for the
"term of five years from the date hereof, provided you
are of good behavior during said term."[5]   Josiah was
town clerk of Exeter.   A patriotic document printed
in an Exeter paper, dated November 15, 1765, two
weeks after the Stamp Act had gone into effect, is
signed by nine Gilmans, including Josiah:

"It has often been remarked that the success of our
Revolutionary contest is to be attributed, in some meas-
ure, to the excellent government prevailing throughout the towns in New England—a government at times
altogether voluntary, and neither imposed or sustained
by any superior authority.   The following is an
example of this species of *social compact:*

WHEREAS, many Evil minded Persons Have, on account of the Stamp Act, Concluded that All the Laws
of this Province, and the Execution of the same, Are
at an End: and that Crimes against the Publick Peace
and Private Property May be Committed with Impu-
nity, Which opinion will render it unsafe for the Peace
Officers to Exert themselves in the Execution of their
Offices.

[5] These commissions are in the possession of the family.

Therefore, We the Subscribers, Inhabitants of the Town of Exeter, to prevent, as much as in us lies, The Evils Naturally Consequent Upon Such an opinion, And for preserving the Peace and Good Order of the Community and of our own Properties, Do Hereby Combine, Promise and Engage to Assemble ourselves together when and Where Need requires, In aid of the Peace Officers, and to Stand by and Defend them in the Execution of their respective offices, And Each other In our respective Properties and Persons, to the utmost, Against all Disturbers of the Publick Peace and Invaders of Private Property."

The wife of *Josiah Gilman* was Sarah, the daughter of Samuel Gilman. She was born June 17, 1745, and died July 26, 1785.

Their third child, *Mary Thing Gilman,* born May 10, 1768, and died December 7, 1841, married *Benjamin Clarke Gilman,* a merchant of Exeter, N. H., born July 8, 1763, and died there October 13, 1835. Two lines of Gilman, descended from Edward and Rose (Rhysse) Gilman, were united by this marriage.

Their third son, *William Charles,* was born May 2, 1795. He was educated at Phillips Academy, Exeter. When thirteen years of age, however, he went to Boston as a clerk, and at his majority engaged in business at Norwich. In 1844 he moved to New York, and died there June 6, 1863.

He married, at Norwich, May 2, 1820, *Eliza,* the daughter of Daniel Lathrop and Elizabeth (Bill) Coit. She was born August 23, 1796, and died March 16, 1868. Her mother, *Elizabeth Bill,* was descended from SIMON HUNTINGTON II. William Charles and Eliza (Coit) Gilman had issue nine children, the fifth being *Daniel Coit Gilman.*

HUNTINGTON

The colonist, Simon Huntington, of Norwich, Eng., died of smallpox on the voyage to America, in 1633. His wife was Margaret, the daughter of Christopher Baret, Mayor of Norwich, 1634 and 1648. Their son:

DEACON SIMON HUNTINGTON, was born in England, 1629, and died at Norwich, Conn., 1706, where he was one of the founders. He came there from Massachusetts, with his mother, in 1659-60, and his home lot is described in the first book of records of Norwich. He was Constable, Townsman, Deputy, and deacon in Mr. Fitch's church. In 1695 he was appointed by the town "to keep an ordinary or house of publique entertaynement." The inventory of his books is dreary reading; among them Thomas Hooker's *Doubting Christian,* the *Bound Book* of Mr. Fitch and John Rogers, and the *Day of Doom.* He married Sarah Clarke. The gravestones of Simon and his wife are in the Norwich town burying-ground. His estate was valued at £275.

Their son, *Simon II,* (1659-1736), came to Norwich from Saybrook when he was a year old. He married, 1683, Lydia Gager (1663-1736), both are buried in Norwich.

Their son, *Joshua,* was born 1698, and died 1745. He was a noted merchant and married 1718, Hannah Perkins (1701-1789).

Their daughter, *Lydia* (1727-1798), married Captain Ephraim Bill, in 1746, who had served in the battery at Waterman's Point, was also on the ship-of-war *Defence,* and a member of an association to protest against illicit traffic with the enemy.

Their daughter, *Elizabeth Bill* (1767-1846), married Daniel Lathrop Coit, who was born September 20, 1754, and died November 27, 1833. His diary (1783), kept when he went to Europe on business, is most interesting. In Paris he saw the first successful balloon ascension. He became an original subscriber of the Connecticut Land Company for the Western Reserve in Ohio, 1796, but never resided there, although he made five journeys thither, the first on horseback. He lived in New York, but spent his last years at Norwich.

Their daughter, *Eliza Coit,* married *William Charles Gilman.*

GILMAN (*Continued*)

The fifth son of William Charles and Eliza (Coit) Gilman, *Daniel Coit Gilman,* was born in Norwich, Conn., July 6, 1831. He was graduated from Yale College 1852, and served his alma mater as librarian and professor until 1872, when he became President of the University of California, until 1875. The first President of Johns Hopkins University, and first director of the Johns Hopkins Hospital, he served as President of the University for twenty-five years. He then became first President of the Carnegie Institution of Washington, for three years.

He married, 1861, Mary, daughter of Tredwell Ketcham. She died October 25, 1869. In 1877 he married Elizabeth Dwight Woolsey. His death occurred October 13, 1908.[6] Issue, first wife:

ELIZABETH GILMAN,

ALICE GILMAN WHEELER, wife of Everett P. Wheeler,

Members of Chapter I., The Colonial Dames of America.

6 Authorities: Perkins; Old House of the Ancient Town of Norwich; Memoir of Daniel Lathrop Coit (privately printed, Norwich, 1907).

XVII

EPPES

LIEUTENANT-COLONEL FRANCIS EPPES obtained a grant of land August 26, 1636, for the transportation of himself, his three sons, and some thirty servants into the Virginia Colony, and in 1635 settled there on the south shore of the James River, near the mouth of the Appomattox. This river formed the boundary line between the southern halves of the counties of Henrico and Charles City, which then lay on both sides of the James River; and as Colonel Eppes subsequently acquired very extensive estates in both counties, he was returned to the House of Burgesses indifferently from either. Some time previous to his death, which occurred 1655, he became a member of the Colonial Council. Four of his descendants in lineal succession, each bearing the name of "Francis" and three of them distinguished by the title of "Colonel," all county officials and members of the House of Burgesses, enjoyed in tail male the large landed estates the first Francis had secured in that part of the County of Henrico, which was subsequently erected into Chester-

EPPES

THE EPPES FAMILY RESIDENCE NEAR CITY POINT, VA.

Know all men by these presents that we Thomas Jefferson and Francis
Eppes are held and firmly bound to our sovereign lord the king, his heirs
and successors in the sum of fifty pounds current money of Virginia, to the
payment of which, well and truly to be made we bind ourselves jointly and seve-
rally, our joint and several heirs executors and administrators, in witness
whereof we have hereto set our hands and seals this twenty third day of
December in the year of our lord one thousand seven hundred and seventy one.

The condition of the above obligation is such that if there be no lawful
cause to obstruct a marriage intended to be had and solemnised between
the abovebound Thomas Jefferson and Martha Skelton of the county
of Charles city, widow, for which a license is desired, then this obligation is to be null and void; otherwise to remain in full force.

Th: Jefferson

Francis Eppes

BOND SIGNED BY FRANCIS EPPES AND THOMAS JEFFERSON

field.[1] The lands in and around City Point, which were granted in 1636, are still owned by the Eppes family, after a lapse of over two hundred and seventy years. It is said that no other tract of land in America has been so long in unbroken possession of one family. Francis Eppes was Lieutenant-Colonel of the county, member of the House of Burgesses, 1625 to 1632, Commissioner, 1631 to 1639, Member of the Council, April 30, 1652.[2] His son:

LIEUTENANT COLONEL FRANCIS EPPES II of Henrico County, Va., was born 1628 and died 1678. He was Lieutenant-Colonel of the County Militia[3] and in 1677 was Commissioner. He married Elizabeth the widow of William Worsham. Issue, among others: Francis III, Mary, who married Lieutenant Colonel John Hardiman, and LITTLEBURY.

LIEUTENANT-COLONEL LITTLEBURY EPPES was of Charles City County, Va., and died in 1743. He was Lieutenant-Colonel of the County Militia, a Commissioner 1699, Member of the House of Burgesses 1710 and 1714, and Clerk of the County, 1710.[4] He married —— Llewellyn.

LLEWELLYN EPPES, their son, was of Charles City County, and died 1758. He was Justice High Sheriff 1721, and Clerk of the County, 1731 to 1752.[5] He married Angelica ——.

Their son, *Peter Eppes,* who died in 1773, married *Elizabeth,* the daughter of Lieutenant-Colonel John Hardiman.

1 *Scribner's Mag.,* November, 1904. By W. M. Cary, of Batimore.

2 Charles City Co. *Reg.; Virginia Mag. of Hist. & Biog.,* Vol. iii, p. 281.

3 Henrico Co. *Recs.; Virginia Mag. of Hist. & Biog.,* Vol. iii, p. 393.

4 Charles City County *Recs.; Va. Mag. of Hist. & Biog.,* Vol. iii, p. 394.

5 *Ibid. Ibid,* p. 397.

Their daughter, *Elizabeth Eppes,* married *Littlebury Hardiman. Jr.*

COLLATERAL LINE OF FRANCIS EPPES III

The grandfather of Martha Eppes, who married John Wayles, was Francis Eppes III, and their daughter, Martha Wayles, as the widow of Bathurst Skelton, became the second wife of Thomas Jefferson. Their daughter, Maria Jefferson, married her first cousin, John Wayles Eppes, Jefferson's favorite son-in-law, and a Member of the House of Representatives and Senate of the United States. After her death, he married Martha, daughter of Honorable Wylie Jones of North Carolina, from whose family the naval hero, John Paul Jones, took his name.

" One of the interesting features in tracing genealogy is to note how often the lines diverge to come together again in succeeding generations. Colonel Francis Eppes III, brother to Colonel Littlebury Eppes, married Anne Isham, and their daughter Elizabeth married Henry Randolph, both being collateral branches of Elizabeth Southall Clarke (the Colonial Dame of this paper), and her husband, Douglas H. Gordon, Jr., the lines uniting in their children."

HARDYMAN, OR HARDIMAN

LIEUTENANT COLONEL JOHN HARDIMAN of Charles City County, Va., died before 1713. He was Commissioner (justice) of the county, 1699 to 1702, also lieutenant-Colonel of the County Militia.[6] He married *Mary,* the daughter of Colonel Francis II and Mary Worsham Eppes. Their son:

LIEUTENANT-COLONEL FRANCIS HARDIMAN of Charles City County, died 1741. He was Burgess for that county 1718, Justice 1737 to 1738, also Lieutenant-

[6] *Ibid,* p. 293.

Colonel for the County Militia.[7]   He married *Sarah*, the daughter of CAPTAIN JOHN TAYLOR, of Charles City County, who was Burgess for that county, 1692 to 1693, and Captain in the County Militia.[8]   Two of their sons were John and LITTLEBURY.

CAPTAIN LITTLEBURY HARDIMAN, the younger of these two sons of Francis Hardiman, was of Westover Parish, Charles City County, and died in 1771.   He was Captain in the County Militia 1762; Commissioner (justice), 1753, 1760 and 1762.[9]   He married Susanna, the daughter of Richard Bassett Lightfoot.

Their son, *Littlebury Hardiman II,* married *Elizabeth,* the daughter of Peter and Elizabeth (Hardiman) Eppes.

Their daughter *Susan* married *John Southall,* whose son *Norborne* married a descendant of the Bland family.

A COLLATERAL INTERMARRIAGE

The elder of the two sons of Francis Hardiman, Lieutenant-Colonel John Hardiman, died in 1771.   He was Commissioner (justice) of Charles City County, 1742, 1747, 1748 and 1750; High Sheriff, 1747, and Lieutenant-Colonel of the County Militia, 1756.[10]

His daughter, Elizabeth Hardiman, married *Peter,* the son of Llewellin Eppes.   As shown by these records, the two families frequently intermarried.

BLAND

The Blands are descended from William de Bland who lived in the reign of Edward III.   Roger Bland, time of Henry VIII, lived in Devon County, Westmoreland, and his son, Adam Bland, was Sergeant Pellectier of Queen Elizabeth in 1563.   His wife was Joan, daughter of William Altryus of St. Gregory's London.[11]

7 *Col. Va. Reg.,* p. 101; *Charles Co. Recs.*

8 *Ibid; Virginia Mag. of Hist. & Biog.,* Vol. v, p. 138.

9 Charles City Co. *Recs.*   10 *Ibid.*

11 Appendix to the *Bland papers,* published in Petersburg, Va., 1840.

JOHN BLAND, of Sythe Lane, a Hamburg merchant, their son, was a Captain of St. Gregory's, 1572,[12] and came to America, where he was granted four shares of land in the Colony of Virginia, September 16, 1618. He was a leading member of Sir Edwin Sandys' party during 1620 to 1624;[13] and a Member of the Council of Virginia, 1623. He returned to England where many honors were conferred upon him, and died there suddenly 1632, being buried in St. Antholius. His personal estate was large. He married Susanna, and they had issue, nine sons and seven daughters. Two of the sons were *Edward* and Theodorick. Both were merchants in Spain, and both removed to Virginia.

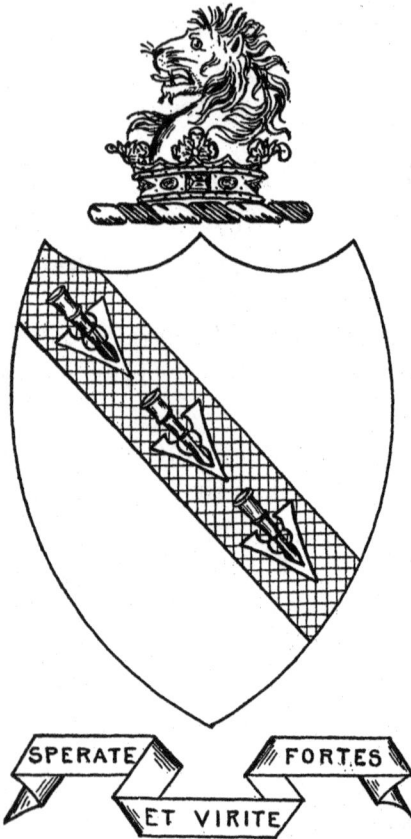

BLAND

The colonist, *Edward Bland,* settled in Charles City County, died in 1653, and was buried at "Westover," the family estate on the James River. His wife Jane, was a daughter of Gregory, who was a brother of John Bland of Sythe Lane, London, and of Virginia.

12 *Familiæ Memorium Gentium,* Harleian Soc. Pub., Vol. ii, p. 421.
13 Brown's *Genesis,* p. 829.

Their only son, *Edward Bland II*, of "Kymages," is also buried at "Westover." He married Margaret ——, and their daughter *Sarah Bland*, married Edmund New II.

OTHER BLAND DESCENDANTS

The other brother, Theodorick Bland, married Ann, the daughter of Richard Bennet, a former Governor of the colony, and he was one of the King's Council for Virginia. After living seventeen years at "Westover," on the James River, he was buried there in April, 1671. Colonel William Byrd was a later owner of "Westover."

Among the Bland descendants in Virginia are the Lees, beginning with "Light-Horse Harry," whose mother was descended from John Bland; thus the beloved General Robert E. Lee was also a descendant.

NEW

The colonist, R i c h a r d New, settled in James City County, Va., receiving a grant of land April 6, 1655, of seven hundred and fifty acres.

A resident of St. James Parish, H e n r i c o County, Va., Edmund New mentions in his will, dated July 4, 1726, a wife Mary and a son Edmund, also a grandson John ("son to my son Edmund").

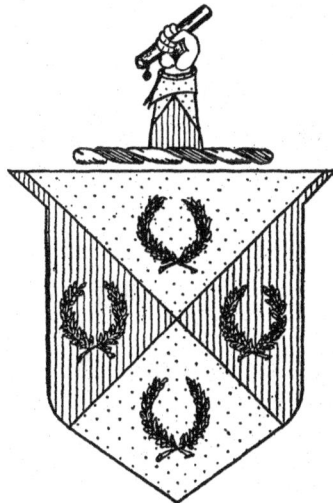

NEW

Their son Edmund II. married *Sarah*, the daughter of Edward and Margaret Bland.

Their son *John* had a son *William,* whose daughter
Tabitha married Chislen Morris.

Their daughter *Mary* married *Norborne Southall.*

SOUTHALL

HENRY SOUTHALL, of Charles City County, Va., died
in 1795. He was a member of the Committee of Observation [14] of that county, December 17, 1774.

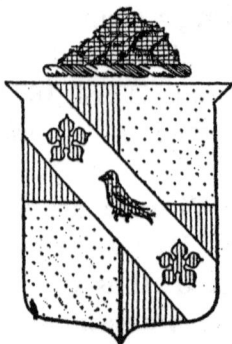

His son *John* married *Susan
Hardyman,* the daughter of Littlebury and Elizabeth (Eppes) Hardiman. She was the ward of the first
Governor Tyler, of Virginia, and
lived at the executive mansion in
Richmond during his administration. She is said to have been a most
beautiful and brilliant woman, and
the tradition that Governor Tyler wooed and lost her, is
sustained by a poem which he wrote, an acrostic to her
name. Her brother, Colonel Stith Hardyman, married Rachel Tyler, a sister of the Governor. John and
Susan (Hardyman) Southall died a few years after
their marriage, leaving two sons, *Norborne* and Albert.
They were adopted and reared by Governor Tyler's
son, John Tyler, who was President of the United
States.

SOUTHALL

The elder son, *Norborne,* married *Mary,* the daughter of Chislen and Tabitha (New) Morris.

Their daughter *Anastia* married John Eldridge
Clarke, whose daughter, *Elizabeth Southall,* married
Douglas H. Gordon, Jr.

ELIZABETH SOUTHALL CLARKE GORDON,

Member of Chapter I., The Colonial Dames of
America.

[14] *William & Mary Quar.,* Vol. v, p. 253.

JACOB HITE

AMBROSE ROBERT HITE RANSON

JAMES LACKLAND RANSON

ROBERT RUTHERFORD

XVIII

HITE

As early as 1710, Hans Jost Hite came to New York with his wife, Anna Maria DuBois, and their children, from Alsace, Germany.[1] He settled in the Valley of the Shenandoah in 1730, on a tract of land which became known as " Hite's Grant."

The second son, Jacob Hite, came to the Valley of Virginia with his father. He was sent to Ireland to secure settlers for their lands, and while there married Catherine O'Bannon. She died, leaving two sons, and he married, second, Fannie, the daughter of Colonel Ambrose and Frances (Taylor) Madison, and the widow of Colonel Taverner Beale. Jacob Hite owned several handsome estates in Berkely and Jefferson Counties, on which he resided. He was involved, however, in a dispute as to the seat of justice, for the county, with Stephan, who advocated Martinsburg, while Hite contended for Leetown. Stephan prevailed, and Hite became so dissatisfied that he gave up five of his estates to his son Thomas, and to his daughter, and leaving his son George at William and Mary College, moved with wife and younger children to a new home in North Carolina in 1786. Establishing a trading station, he was soon very popular with the Cherokee Indians. Later they became offended, and massacred the family, except one little girl, Eleanor, who was rescued by a squaw. The Indians burned the house, and escaped to Florida, taking the negro servants with them.

[1] There is still in the family a soup ladle which belonged to Jacob Hite, with a crest, a sheaf of wheat on it. Also a grant of land on the original parchment from George III to Jacob Hite in 1760.

Compiled from article written by Miss Jane G. Keys, *Baltimore Sun*.

The son, George Hite, went at once to the ruined home, and found the charred remains of all the family except his little sister, for whom he searched many years, finding her at last in Pensacola. The Indians had sold her to the wife of an English army officer, and the child refused to be separated from her foster parents. George Hite married, February 4, 1780, in Charles Town, Jefferson County, Va., *Deborah,* the daughter of Robert and Mary (Howe) Rutherford.

Their daughter was *Frances Madison Hite,* who married James Lackland Ranson.

RUTHERFORD

ROBERT RUTHERFORD, born in Scotland, October 20, 1728, was the son of Hugh and Sarah (de Montargis) Rutherford. [He was educated at the Royal College of Edinburgh. With his brother Thomas he settled in Berks County, Tenn., but soon removed to the Valley of Virginia. Thomas was the first High Sheriff of Frederick County, Va., 1743 to 1744, and both were trustees of Bath and Berkely Springs, 1786. Robert entered actively into the cause of independence. A delegate to the convention held in Richmond, Colony of Virginia, December 1, 1775, afterwards held at Williamsburg, Va., he was the first member, from beyond the Blue Ridge, elected to Congress, where he represented Berkely from 1793 to 1797. His patriotism was never better shown than in his speeches in Congress, in the early days of the new government. He was one of General Washington's devoted friends. His large estate, near Charles Town, Jefferson County, in the picturesque valley of the Shenandoah, called "Flowing Spring," commanded a full view of the beautiful Blue Mountains. In this lovely place he was laid to rest beside his wife, in October, 1803.

He married Mary, the daughter of William and Deborah Daubine, or Dobbin, and widow of John Augustus Howe, "who was killed at Ticonderoga in the war with the Indians." His only son died at the age of eighteen. His daughters' descendants are to be found in the families of Peyton, Hite, Briscoe, Brown, etc.

His daughter *Deborah* married *George Hite*,[2] whose daughter, *Frances Madison*, married *James Lackland Ranson*.

RANSON

The daughter of George and Deborah (Rutherford) Hite, *Frances Madison Hite*, married in Charlestown, Jefferson County, Va., May 16, 1820, James Lackland Ranson. He was the son of Ambrose and Rachel (Lackland) Ranson, of Buckingham County, Va.

Their son, *Ambrose Robert Hite Ranson*, born in Charles Town, April 12, 1831; married, October 12, 1854, in Jefferson County, *Frances Elizabeth Beverly*, daughter of John James and Frances Perrin (Lowndes) Frame, born February 17, 1834, descended from WILLIAM BLADEN. Her early married life was spent in Virginia, but after the Civil War they moved to Maryland, living in Catonsville, where she died August 4, 1876, and was buried in the graveyard of Zion Church, Charles Town. Issue:

FRANCES LOWNDES, married Nathaniel James.

ELIZABETH ANNE, married Harry Prescott Hall.

MARY TASKER, married Charles James.

BLADEN

HONORABLE WILLIAM BLADEN, came to Maryland in 1690 at the early age of nineteen. He was the son of Nathaniel and Isabella (Fairfax) Bladen, the grand-

---

2 Compiled from an article by Miss Richardson in the *Baltimore Sun*.

son of the Rev. Thomas and the great-grandson
of William Bladen, Lord Mayor of London, 1647. In
1698, William Bladen, the colonist, was Surveyor and
Deputy Collector of the port, was appointed Secretary
of the Province by Nathaniel Blackistone, the Royal
Governor, 1701; commissioned Attorney-General May
8, 1702; served as Clerk of the Council, 1704, and
was a Vestryman of old St. Anne's Church, Annapolis.
William Bladen's name is associated with the important
work of compiling the first laws of Maryland in one
volume.

His first residence in this country was in St. Mary's
County, and there he married Anne, the daughter of
Gerret Van Swearingen, of St. Mary's, a native of
Holland. They removed to Annapolis. Issue:

Anne, who married BENJAMIN TASKER.

Thomas.

Christopher.

TASKER

HON. BENJAMIN TASKER, son of Thomas Tasker
(see pp. 671-672), born in 1690, and died June 19, 1768,
was President of the Council of Maryland at the time
of his death, an office he had held for thirty-two years,
and a Delegate to the Colonial Congress, which as-
sembled in Albany, 1754. He married *Anne,* the
daughter of William and Anne (Van Swearingen)
Bladen. Issue:

Benjamin, who died at the age of thirty-nine, being
Secretary of the Colony.

Anne.

Elizabeth, who married Christopher Lowndes.

Frances.

FRANCES PERRIN LOWNDES
Wife of John James Frame

FRANCES ELIZABETH BEVERLY FRAME
Wife of Ambrose R. H. Ranson

LOWNDES-FRAME

The ninth child of Richard and Margaret (Poole) Lowndes, of Bostic House and Hassall Hall, Chester, Eng., Christopher Lowndes, was baptized June 19, 1713. He came to Maryland, settling at Bladensburg, and married *Elizabeth,* daughter of Hon. Benjamin and Anne (Bladen) Tasker.

Their son, *Charles Lowndes,* died in Jefferson County, Va., April 16, 1846. He married, first, Eleanor Lloyd, of Wye House, Talbot County, Md. (see Lloyd) and had issue, six children; married, second, Frances Whiting, of Virginia, who died September 3, 1841, aged seventy-two years, and had issue, four children, viz.:

Two daughters, died young.

Beverly Bladen, was drowned while bathing, in 1835, in the Shenandoah River.

The surviving daughter, *Frances Perrin,* was born October 11, 1810, and died January 23, 1901. She married, July 24, 1828, John James Frame, of Charles Town, Jefferson County, Va., who died October 17, 1834. They lived at the home place called "Beverly," a large farm situated about three miles from Charles Town, which had been in the Whiting family for many years. After the Civil War the place was sold and Mrs. Frame moved to Maryland. Issue:

Frances Elizabeth Beverly Frame, who married *Ambrose Robert Hite Ranson.* Their daughters are:

ELIZABETH ANNE RANSON HALL,

FRANCES LOWNDES RANSON JAMES,

MARY TASKER RANSON JAMES,

Members of Chapter I., The Colonial Dames of America.

XIX
GILMOR

In 1767, Robert Gilmor, the son of Gavin and Janet (Spier) Gilmor, made a voyage to the shores of the Chesapeake, where he disposed of a cargo of merchandise advantageously. He was born at Paisley, Scotland, in November, 1748, and married, in 1771, Louisa Airey. They were living in St. Mary's County, at the time of the outbreak of the war of the Revolution. Afterwards, he formed a business partnership with Thomas Williams and Robert Morris, the well-known financier.

Their son, William Gilmor, married *Mary Ann,* the daughter of Isaac and Elizabeth Custis (Teackle) Smith, and the widow of ―― De Drisdale. Issue, five children, one being *Robert.*

SMITH

The first of this line, John Smith, married Ioane, the daughter of LIEUTENANT-COLONEL JOHN SHEPPARD.

Their son, *Isaac Smith I.,* married *Sarah,* the daughter of MAJOR JOHN WEST, and his wife, *Frances Yeardley.*

ISAAC SMITH II., their son, married *Elizabeth Custis,* the daughter of Thomas and Elizabeth (Custis) Teackle. Issue, among others, two daughters, *Mary Ann* and *Ann Teackle.*

The elder, *Mary Ann,* married, first, ―― De Drisdale; second, William Gilmor.

The younger, *Ann Teackle,* married John Donnell,

ROBERT GILMOR
Painted by Sir Thomas Lawrence

WASHINGTON SQUARE, BALTIMORE, SHOWING THE GILMOR HOUSE AT LEFT.
From an old print

ISAAC SMITH II

ELIZABETH CUSTIS TEACKLE
Wife of Isaac Smith II

ROBERT GILMOR
Taken in 1780

and one of their daughters, *Elizabeth,* married *James Swan;* another, Frances, married Gustav W. Lürman.

TEACKLE

REV. THOMAS TEACKLE, of "Craddock," Accomac County, Va., married, first, Isabella Douglas, and second, Margaret, the daughter of Robert and Mary (Temple) Nelson.

JOHN TEACKLE, of "Craddock," their son, married *Susannah,* the daughter of Arthur and Sarah (Browne) Upshur.

Their son, *Thomas Teackle II.,* married *Elizabeth,* the daughter of JOHN CUSTIS IV., and his wife, Ann Upshur.

Their daughter, *Elizabeth Custis Teackle,* married ISAAC SMITH II.

BROWNE

JOHN BROWNE, grantee of large tracts of land in Virginia, married Ursula ——.

Their son, *Thomas Brown,* married *Susannah,* the daughter of LEVIN DENWOOD.

Their daughter, *Sarah,* married ARTHUR UPSHUR II., whose daughter, *Susannah,* married JOHN TEACKLE. Their son, *Thomas Teackle,* married *Elizabeth Custis.*

WEST-SCARBOROUGH-YEARDLEY

The emigrant was Anthony West.

LIEUTENANT-COLONEL JOHN WEST (1638-1705), his son, married *Matilda,* the daughter of COLONEL EDMUND SCARBOROUGH and his wife, *Mary,* the daughter of STEPHEN CHARLTON. The Scarborough line in America began with CAPTAIN EDMUND SCARBOROUGH I.

MAJOR JOHN WEST, son of John I., married *Frances,* the daughter of Captain Argall and Sarah (Michael) Yeardley, and their daughter, *Sarah,* married *Isaac Smith I.*

The Yeardley line in America is as follows:

SIR GEORGE YEARDLEY married Temperance West.

COLONEL ARGALL YEARDLEY married Anne Custis.

CAPTAIN ARGALL YEARDLEY married *Sarah Michael,* the daughter of John and Elizabeth (Thoroughgood) Michael. *Elizabeth* was the daughter of CAPTAIN ADAM THOROUGHGOOD.

Frances Yeardley married MAJOR JOHN WEST.

CUSTIS

A son of John and Ioane Custis, of Rotterdam, Germany, Thomas Custis, lived in Baltimore, Ireland.

EDMUND CUSTIS, his son, married *Tabitha,* the daughter of Colonel William and Tabitha (Smart) Whittington.

Their son, *Thomas Custis,* married his cousin, *Elizabeth,* the daughter of COLONEL JOHN CUSTIS III. and his wife, Margaret Michael.

JUDGE JOHN CUSTIS IV., their son, married Ann Upshur, and their daughter, *Elizabeth,* married *Thomas Teackle II.* (See pp. 336-350 for Smith, West, Yeardley, Scarborough, Teackle, Brown, Thoroughgood, and Custis lines.)

GILMOR (*Continued*)

A son of William and Mary Ann (Smith) Gilmor, *Robert Gilmor,* was graduated at Harvard University in 1828. He was appointed attaché of the American legation in Paris, William C. Rives being the American minister. It was his good fortune to spend several days

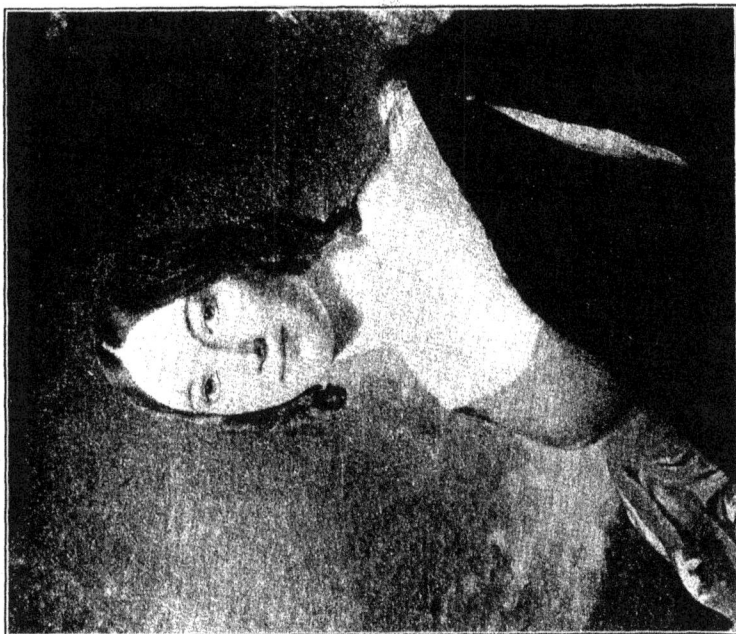

ELLEN WARD, WIFE OF ROBERT GILMOR, JR.
From a painting by Benjamin West

ROBERT GILMOR
Taken in Paris, 1828

at Abbotsford, upon the invitation, and as the guest, of
Sir Walter Scott. Robert Gilmor married, 1832,
Ellen, the daughter of *Judge William H. Ward,* of
Maryland. She was celebrated for her beauty. Issue,
several sons and daughters, among them *Robert* and
William.

WARD

WILLIAM WARD I. was Justice of Cecil County
Court, Md., 1689-1692.

COLONEL JOHN WARD was Burgess of Cecil County,
1708 to 1736.

JOHN WARD, JR., was Justice of Cecil County Court,
1726 to 1730.

WILLIAM WARD II. was in the Provincial Assembly
of Maryland, 1762 to 1769, and Burgess, 1770 to 1774.

GILMOR (*Continued*)

The second son of Robert and Ellen (Ward) Gilmor, *William Gilmor* (now deceased), married MARY,
the daughter of Philip Barton and Ellen (Swan) Key.
(See Key.)

The elder son of Robert and Ellen (Ward) Gilmor,
Judge Robert Gilmor, Jr., was born in 1833. He was
Judge of the Supreme Bench of Maryland, from 1867
to 1882, and a man of literary attainments. He married, first, Casilda Hodges; second, Josephine Albert,
and was survived by eight children. A daughter of
the second marriage, JOSEPHINE GILMOR, married Wallace Harvey.

JOSEPHINE GILMOR HARVEY,

Member of Chapter I., The Colonial Dames of
America.

XX
HULL

ARMS: *Sable, a chevron engrailed eminois between three talbots' heads erased argent.*[1]

The Hull family [2] are recorded in the Heralds Distinctions of Devonshire, but the original name, De La Hulle, in Shropshire, in the reign of Edward II., indicates that they went from the Continent to England, probably from Normandy. (The family is to be found as early as the fourteenth century in Somerset County.[3]) Shortly after the Pilgrims landed at Plymouth, five brothers came to Massachusetts from England: John, George, Richard, JOSEPH, and Robert Hull.[4]

HULL

REVEREND JOSEPH HULL, was born in Somersetshire, Eng., 1594. He was of Weymouth, Mass., 1635, and of York, Me., 1642 to 1643. He matriculated at St. Mary Magdalen Hall, Oxford, May 12, 1612, aged seventeen, and was instituted Rector of Northleigh,

[1] Old Hull Seals. The seals of Edward Hull of London were a Bear, ar., on a chevron az., between 3 demi-lions passant gu.

[2] Authorities: *Rev. Joseph Hull and Some of His Descendants*, by A. E. E. Hull, Cong. Lib.; *Data*, published by the Hull Family Assn., 1905; Austin's *R. I. Gen.*; Freeman's *Hist. of Cape Cod*, p. 269; *Am. Ancestry*, Vol. 2, p. 63; *Cotton Mather's Hist. of N. E. Ministers; Family papers.*

[3] See List of Incumbents of Somerset named Hulle, Instituted at Wells from the Earliest Records in the *Register* to 1734. Collinson in his *History of Somersetshire* gives certain Hulls in his list of those in Parliament from that County.

[4] Todd's *Hist. of Redding.*

diocese of Exeter, Devonshire, April 14, 1621. He sailed March 20, 1635, with his family, consisting of his second wife, Agnes, aged twenty-five years, two sons, five daughters and three servants, from Weymouth, bound for New England, with a company composed of sixteen families, and numbering one hundred and four (six) persons, chiefly west country people. They reached Boston Harbor, May 6, 1635.[5] On their arrival, a grant was obtained to establish a plantation at Wessaguscus, and here, with others from Boston and Dorchester, they soon gathered into a church organization, with Joseph Hull as their pastor. In September of the same year, Joseph Hull, with other prominent members of his community, took the freeman's oath, and their plantation was erected into a township and decreed hereafter to be called Weymouth.

The new church did not meet with favor from its Puritan neighbors. Dissension quickly arose within the church itself, instigated by the authorities outside, and in less than a year the Separatists had called the Rev. Thomas Jenner, of Roxbury, to be their pastor, and Joseph Hull relinquished his charge and withdrew. He obtained a grant of land in Hingham, the adjoining town, and after a brief season of preaching at Bass River, now Beverly, he gave up his ministerial labor, and turned his attention to civic affairs. He evidently possessed the confidence of his fellow-townsmen, for he was twice elected Deputy to the General Court, and in 1638 was appointed one of the local magistrates of

---

5 From *data* published by the Hull Assn. of New York in 1905. " This company of adventurers, numbering 106 people, is known in New England history as ' Hull's Colony.' 1, JOSEPH HALL of Somerset, a Minister aged 40 year. . . . 5, TRISTRAM his son aged . . . 11 Yeare.' " From Camden Hotten's *Original Lists*. *N. E. Hist. Gen. Reg.*, Vol. iv, p. 326.

Hingham. In June, 1639, the Plymouth Court granted
authority to Joseph Hull and Thomas Dimoc to erect
a plantation at Barnstable, on Cape Cod, and the former
was elected Freeman, and Deputy for Barnstable at the
first General Court held at Plymouth. For a time he
supported his family by agriculture and the raising of
cattle and horses.

Turning once more to the ministry, he preached for
a time at the Isle of Shoals. Returning to Barnstable
he accepted a call at Yarmouth, and moved his family
there; but as the call was not for a recognized church
organization, it aroused the hostility of the authorities,
and Joseph Hull was excommunicated by the Barnstable church in 1641. He withdrew to the more
friendly association of the Maine Colony. For a time
he was settled at the Isle of Shoals, and in 1643 was
called to York, Me., as minister. In 1652, Joseph Hull
returned to England, and was given the living at St.
Burian, in Cornwall, where he remained until after the
Restoration. In 1662, he returned to America, and
was settled as minister at Oyster River, now Dover,
N. H. Here, among his old friends, he passed the clos-
ing years of his life in quietness and esteem. He died
at the Isles, November 19, 1665, in his seventy-first
year.[6]

THE HULL BROTHERS

Of the four immigrant brothers of the REV. JOSEPH
HULL, George Hull married, at or near Krewkerne,
Somerset, Eng., Thamzen Michell, of Stockland, August 27, 1614, and sailed from Plymouth, March 30,
1629-30, in the ship *Mary and John,* with a notable

6 *Barnstable papers,* by Hon. Amos Otis.

company. He settled at Dorchester; was made Freeman of Massachusetts, March 4, 1632; was Representative to the General Court, May, 1634, and one of the first Selectmen of Dorchester. Removed to Windsor, Conn., 1636, where he surveyed that place, also Weathersfield; and held various offices from 1637 to 1654. He married, second, Sarah, the widow of David Phippen, of Boston. His will was admitted to probate, November 20, 1659.

Among his descendants were Josiah Hull, a Deputy of the General Court, between 1659 and 1674, and Cornelius, a Deputy between 1658 and 1667, a Lieutenant of Fairfield County, and in King Philip's War.

The third brother, Richard Hull, of New Haven, Conn., came from Derbyshire, Eng. The name was originally spelled "Hulls," and the final "s" was dropped by his descendants. He is on the list of Freemen in the Massachusetts Colony prior to 1639; also in the list of those who took the oath of fidelity to the Colonies. Resided in Dorchester, Mass., 1634, but moved to New Haven, Conn., 1639, of which town he was one of the founders. Was admitted to the General Court of Connecticut, 1639, and died December 3, 1662. He was a member of the church, but not a believer in Puritanism.

Among his descendants are Commodore Isaac Hull, the hero of the *Constitution;* Captain Joseph Hull; General William Hull; Admiral Andrew Hull Foote, commander at Fort Donelson and Island No. 10; General Elias Hull, of Georgia, who was in the War of 1812; General Joseph Wheeler, who was in the Spanish War; Judge Andrew Hull; Doctors Titus and Amos Hull, Mrs. Richmond P. Hobson, and many others.

Another brother, Robert Hull, was the father of John

Hull, the "Mint Master," of Boston. Point Judith was named for his daughter, Judith Quincy.

A sixth brother, William Hull, was Vicar of Colyton, in Devon, 1611, and died without issue, 1627.[7]

THE LINE OF REV. JOSEPH HULL (*Continued*)

TRISTRAM HULL, the second son of the Rev. Joseph Hull, was a man of prominence in Barnstable, where he was chosen Selectman, and served on numerous committees, being empowered to buy land from the Indians, for the improvement of the town, etc. Captain Hull was a "chip of the old block," and cared for neither King nor Kaiser, when either interfered with what he wished to do. Colonel Hull, in his pamphlet, gives an interesting account of the manner in which Tristram aided an old church member, who had been fined and banished for "raising his voice" against Quaker persecution. He picked him up bodily, and carried him off in his own ship as far as Sandwich, on the Cape, in direct violation of the law and contempt of the magistrates. When Captain Hull died he left, besides two fine ships, land, etc., £1150, 5s, 2d. Tristram Hull and his wife Blanche had issue:

Mary, born in Yarmouth, September 16, 1645, and married Joseph Holley, of Sandwich.

Sarah, born in Barnstable (as were the remaining three children), in March, 1650, married Robert Burgess.

Joseph, born June, 1652, married, October, 1676, Experience, the daughter of Robert Harper, who was one of the first Quakers to suffer in body and estate, and was banished from Boston in 1660; he removed to South Kingston, R. I., where he died about 1709.

[7] Compiled from the *Pamphlet* of the Col. Robert Hull.

JOHN.

Hannah, born February, 1656; married, September 15, 1674, Joseph Blish; died November 15, 1733.

CAPTAIN JOHN HULL, fourth child and second son of Tristram and Blanche Hull, was born in Barnstable, March, 1654. He held various public offices at Jamestown, R. I., and was Assessor, Town Clerk, for seven years, in the Town Council, and Deputy, 1698, 1703, 1706, 1707, 1709. He was also on the important committee to hire out ferries, belonging to the Colonies. Admiral Sir Charles Wager was his apprentice when a boy, and a sincere friendship always existed between them.

He brought over from London an English wife, having been married there October 23, 1684, to Alice, the daughter of Captain Edmund Teddeman, of St. Magdalens, London. Their marriage certificate is in the possession of the family, and is a most interesting document, bearing the names of a great number of those who witnessed the ceremony. · Their son:

JOHN HULL II., lived at Canonicut, and married *Damaris*, the daughter of John and Damaris (Arnold) Cary. He held various offices, among others that of Representative, in 1757. Their son was *Oliver Hull*.

CARY

"The ancient family of Cary derives its name from the manor of Cary, or Karri, in the Parish of St. Giles, in the Heath, near Launceston, 1198.[8] . . . The intermediate descents of Cary from Adam (de Karry), are given in the visitations of Devon, 1620." This line

[8] Burke. For history of John Cary's line of 1198, see *Cary Memorials*.

of John Cary, the colonist, from Alfred the Great, has recently been traced.[9]

JOHN CARY, founder of Duxbury and Bridgewater, came to Plymouth in 1630, and settled at Duxbury. He taught the first Latin school in the Colony and was the first Town Clerk at Bridgewater, 1651 to his death in 1681. He was Selectman in 1667-8-9. He married Elizabeth, daughter of Francis Godfrey. Their son:

HON. JOHN CARY, was one of the two first deacons of the first church of Bristol, and is recorded as Sergeant; one of the raters in the town; first Recording Officer of the county, and Clerk of the Peace; Selectman, sometimes Magistrate, appointed to solemnize marriages; on many committees, and sent as Representative to the General Court, 1694, after the Plymouth Colony had united with Massachusetts. He married, 1670, Abigail, the daughter of Samuel Allen.

CARY 10

Their son, *John Cary III.,* married *Damaris,* the daughter of Oliver and Phoebe (Cook) Arnold.

Their daughter *Damaris* married JOHN HULL II.

ALLEN

The colonist, Samuel Allen, came in 1630 from Bridgewater, Eng., to Braintree, Mass., and with Myles

---

[9] A. E. E. Hull; *English Hist.; Jour. of Am. Hist.,* Vol. i, No. 3, p. 520; Ripley's *Ancestors of Lieut. Thomas Tracy;* Burke's *Commmoners,* Vol. ii, p. 33; *Landed Gentry,* Vol. i, p. 194, etc. *Plymouth Records,* Vol. iv, p. 14; *R. I. Genealogies,* Arnold; Munroe's *History of Bristol, R. I.,* for American Carys.

[10] " The three White Roses and the Motto of the Coat of Arms were bestowed upon Sir Robert Cary on account of his defeat of the Knight of Aragon, at Smithfield, London, by King Henry Fifth (1413-1422,) in the early years of his reign."

Standish became one of the proprietors and settlers of East Bridgewater, Mass. Samuel Allen took the oath of allegiance 1635, and was Town Clerk, Selectman, Surveyor of Highways, Constable, and Deputy three

ALLEN

times. His second wife was Margaret, the widow of Edward Lamb. One of his daughters married a son of Myles Standish.

His daughter Abigail married JOHN CARY II.

OLIVER ARNOLD

OLIVER ARNOLD, the son of Governor Benedict and Damaris (Westcott) Arnold,[11] lived at Canonicut, where he was Deputy, 1682, and held other important offices. He married Phoebe, daughter of Captain Thomas and Mary (Havens) Cook. Captain Cook (descended from Thomas, who was a Deputy in 1666), was Commissioned to run the west line of the Colony. Mary Havens was the daughter of William Havens, one of the original settlers of Aquidneck.

Their daughter *Damaris* married *John Cary III*.

11 For Arnold and Westcott families, see pp. 15-16, 112-113.

HULL (*Continued*)

Though a Friend, *Oliver Hull,* the son of John and Damaris (Cary) Hull, took an active, if quiet, part in the Revolution. He married Penelope Ffones (Fones), whose great-grandfather had been one of the most important men of the Colony, and with her he moved to New York a few years before the war. She has been especially honored because of her great kindness to the prisoners during the Revolution. The late Robert Hull, in his pamphlet of the Hull family, gives a very interesting account of the efforts the Quakers made to mitigate the suffering of the American prisoners during the time the British had possession of New York. "Among the most active of these was Oliver Hull, Robert Murray and his son John. The Long Island Quakers furnished the beef, vegetables, etc., and in the garden of Oliver Hull's house, corner of Beekman and William Streets, these were put into a huge caldron and under Mrs. Hull's directions speedily converted into soup, was soon brought to the famishing prisoners. One day Mrs. Hull, with her daughter Penelope, was passing the old Sugar House in Liberty Street when a prisoner called out from a grated window, 'I hope you won't be discouraged, dear ladies; the rebels are not discouraged; they'll never give up.' When the British took possession of the town, several people were billeted at Oliver Hull's house, one a young officer, Count Saint Leger, of whom they became exceedingly fond, who presented Mr. Hull at parting with a tall staff made of some curious wood and mounted in gold, as a souvenir of his gratitude and friendship. . . ."

The son of Oliver and Penelope (Fones) Hull was *John Hull III.*

FONES, OR FFONES

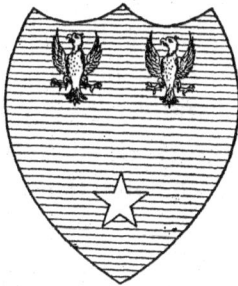

ARMS: *Azure, two eagles displayed in chief and a mullet in base argent.*

CAPTAIN AND HONORABLE JOHN FONES,[12] of Westerly, R. I., was the son of Thomas and Anna (Winthrop) Fones. Anna Winthrop was the daughter of Adam and Anna (Brown) Winthrop, and the sister of Governor Winthrop, of Massachusetts. Captain Fones was a lineal descendant of "William Fowns, of Saxby, Esq.," and his wife, daughter of Robert Hyelton, Knight.[13]

A member of the court martial at Newport, for the trial of Indians charged with taking part with King Philip in 1676, with the title of Captain, John Fones was also Deputy, from 1679 to 1681, and later was respectively Justice, Clerk of the Court of Commissioners, Permanent Clerk of the Court of Records, and in 1698 was Assistant and Deputy. His sister Elizabeth married, first, Henry Winthrop, and second, Robert Feake. His wife was Margaret ——.

Their son, *Jeremiah Fones,* married Elizabeth ——.

12 Authorities: *N. E. Hist. & Gen. Reg.,* Vol. xviii, p. 185; *Records* at Newport; Hist. Soc. *Records* at Jamestown, R. I.; Austin's *R. I. Gen.; Family Papers.*

13 " The Fones pedigree is one of the oldest manuscript pedigrees extant, found among the old Winthrop papers." *N. E. Hist & Gen. Reg.,* Vol. xviii, p. 185.

Their son, *Joseph Fones,* had the distinction of being the oldest Ensign, so far recorded, in the Revolutionary War. He was born May 11, 1699; responding to an alarm call, July 30, 1778, in his seventy-ninth year, he was created Ensign and served seven days, for which he received sixteen shillings. He lived in Canonicut, R. I., and married there Penelope Remington, of the Rhode Island family.

Their daughter, *Penelope Fones,* married *Oliver Hull.*

Their son was *John Hull III.*

WINTHROP

ARMS: *Argent, three chevrons crenellé gules, over all a Lion rampant, sable, armed and langued, azure.*

CREST: *A hare proper, running on a mount vert.*

MOTTO: *Spes vincit thronum.*

An early ancestor of Governor Winthrop, and his sister Anna, was Adam Winthrop, whose wife was Joane Burton (or Burwell).

Adam Winthrop II. married, second, Agnes, the daughter of Robert Sharp, of Islington.

Adam Winthrop III. was of Groton, and married, second, Anna, the daughter of Henry Brown. Two of their children were:

John, the first Governor of Massachusetts.

Anna,[14] the wife of Thomas Fones, of London, and the mother of CAPTAIN JOHN FONES.

HULL (*Continued*)

A son of Oliver and Penelope (Fones) Hull, *John Hull III.,* was born in Canonicut, August 11, 1762. He came to New York with his father, and married, 1781, Mary Avery. She died 1802, in Dutchess County, where they had moved in 1800. On November 23, 1803, he married Amy, the daughter of Quinby and Hannah (Underhill) Cornell. Issue, seven children, viz.:

Hannah.

William.

Edward, married Edwina Willett Coles. From them is descended Sarah Coles Hull, wife of Henry Trowbridge, of New Haven, Conn.

Ann, married Edward Dibble, Esq.

Rebecca, married —— Haviland.

Robert.

Henrietta, married —— Cowdrey.

14 Cape Ann was named for Anna Winthrop Fones.

UNDERHILL

Underbill

Underbill

ARMS: *Argent on a chevron sable between three trefoils slipped, vert, as many bazants.*

CREST: *On a mount vert, a hind, lodged or.*

CAPTAIN JOHN UNDERHILL, believed to be descended from a Warwickshire family, served as a soldier in the Netherlands, under the Earl of Leicester, and in Spain

CAPT. UNDER-
HILL'S SEAL

and Ireland, under the Earl of Essex. When that nobleman was executed, Captain Underhill went to Holland, and finally to America in Winthrop's company. Soon after he was training the militia in Boston, wh·ch he represented at the first Court of Deputies. Being too liberal in his ideas of religious toleration, he was disfranchised, November 20, 1637, and banished from Massachusetts. He retreated to New Hampshire, where, in 1638, he was chosen Governor. Again his liberal views and possibly his Boston enemies compelled him to flee, and he was soon found in Albany, where he became a favorite with the Dutch of that place, who called him " Captain Hans Van Vanderhill," and gave him a command of one hundred and twenty men. He became a noted fighter and slayer of Indians. In 1643 he was a Delegate from Stamford, Conn., to the General Court at New Haven, and appointed Assistant Justice. Settling at Oyster Bay, he was a Delegate from that place, 1665, and made Lord High Sheriff of North Riding on Long Island, by Governor Nicholl. The Matinecock Indians conveyed to him a large tract of land in 1667. Part of it, named Killingworth (originally Kenilworth, from the place in Warwickshire, Eng., of that name), remained in his family nearly two hundred years. In the Pequot War he was Captain of all the New England troops and so vanquished the Indians as to make it possible for the white settlers to live in that region.[15]

His will was dated September 18, 1671, and he died at " Killingworth " at an advanced age. He married *Elizabeth,* daughter of Robert and Elizabeth (Fones) Feake.

Their son, *Nathaniel Underhill,* was one of the trustees of the town of Westchester 1720. He married Mary, daughter of John Ferris, Esq., of Leicestershire, Eng., who was one of the purchasers of Stamford, Conn., in 1640, and in 1654 removed to Westchester, and became one of the first patentees of the town and one of the ten proprietors. The family of Ferris came from Normandy. Henri de Ferrers is written on the famous " Battle Roll," and received large grants of land from William the Conqueror in Straffordshire,

15 Bolton's *Hist. of Westchester, N. Y.*

Derbyshire and Leicestershire. James, a grandson of the colonist, lived on his grandfather's estate when Lord Howe took it for his headquarters, and James was made prisoner by the Queen's Rangers, dying from hardship.

FERRIS

Their son, *Abraham Underhill,* of White Plains, N. Y., married Hannah Cromwell, "a descendant of that family of Cromwells who at a very early period possessed estates in Westchester County, N. Y. The several branches of the family in America claim descent from the same parent stock as that of the Protector."

Their son, *Jacob Underhill,* married, 1747, Amy, the daughter of John and Hannah Hallock, the granddaughter of John and Abigail (Sweezey) Hallock, the great-granddaughter of William and Margaret Hallock; and descended from Peter

CROMWELL

Hallock, who married a widow, Mrs. Howell, in England, and was in New Haven by 1640.

Their daughter, *Hannah Underhill,* married *Quinby,* the son of William and Mary (Quinby) Cornell.

FEAKE

LIEUTENANT ROBERT FEAKE, was born in England, and died in Watertown, Mass., 1662. He was the son of James and Judith (Thomas) Feake, and the grandson of William and Mary Wetherell Feake, of London (will 1595), and great-grandson of James Feake of County Wighton, Eng. He came to Massachusetts Bay with Governor Winthrop,[16] 1630, and subsequently held many public offices of trust. In 1632 he was appointed Lieutenant to Captain Patrick, chief military officer at Watertown. In 1634, when the first Court of Delegates was held, his name appears fourth on the list, which is given by Winthrop in his *History*. Again, 1635 and 1636, he was Representative from Watertown, and 1639 to 1640 he united with Captain Patrick in the purchase of land, now the town of Greenwich. He married Elizabeth, the widow of Henry Winthrop (the son of Governor Winthrop) and the daughter of Thomas and Anna (Winthrop) Fones.

[16] Winthrop's *Hist. of N. E.*, Vol. i, pp. 69, 101; Harleian *Surrey Visitations, etc.*

Their daughter *Elizabeth* married CAPTAIN JOHN
UNDERHILL.

QUINBY

One of the first settlers of Stratford, Conn., Colonel
William Quinby,[17] came from England, and settled near

QUINBY

New York City, while under Dutch
occupancy. He signed allegiance to
England in 1664. His son:

JOHN QUINBY, was Justice, Deputy and Member of the first New
York Assembly. He was one of the
five patentees of Westchester, and
took out the first patent of land there.
He married, 1686, Deborah (or
Charity) Haight.

Their son, *Josiah Quinby,* married Mary Mullineux.
Their son, *Josiah Quinby II.,* of Mamaroneck,
N. Y., married Hannah, the daughter of Richard
Cornell, of Scarsdale, the owner there of a large
amount of property. *Mary Quinby,* their daughter,
married *William Cornell.*

The town of Scarsdale, near Mamaroneck, joins New
Rochelle on the Cornell property, the farm thus being
in three towns. Some of Richard Cornell's descendants
still live on the place. He held various offices of trust,
and in 1703 was foreman of the Grand Jury which ig-
nored the bill against Bownas, the Quaker.[18]

CORNELL

The family of Cornell traces through the Barons of
Burford to Richard de Cornewall, son of Richard, Earl

---

[17] Authorities: Bolton's *Hist. of Westchester; N. E. Hist. & Gen.
Reg.,* Vol. xvii, p. 62; *Family Papers.*

[18] *Cornell Gen.,* by Rev. John Cornell.

of Cornwall, second son of King John, younger brother
of Richard Coeur de Lion. The name is written variously: Cornel, Cornwall, Coornell, etc.

THOMAS CORNELL,[19] arrived in Boston, with wife and
family in 1638. In 1641 he removed to Portsmouth,
R. I., and from there, in 1643, to Throgg's Neck, N. Y.,
where, after a brief period, as Gov-
ernor Winthrop records:

" The Indians set upon the English that dwelt under the Dutch and
killed such of Mr. Throckmorton's
and Mr. Cornhill's families as were
at home. These people," he adds,
" have cast off ordinances and
churches and for larger accommoda-
tions had subjected themselves to the Dutch and dwelt
scattering near a mile apart."

CORNELL

Among those who escaped was Thomas Cornell, who,
with the remainder of his household, went back to Portsmouth, where, in 1646, he was granted about two hundred acres of land. The same year he received a grant
of land in Westchester County, N. Y.,[20] known to this
day as " Cornell's Neck."[20] He died in 1673, having
been closely associated with Roger Williams in his colonization of Rhode Island, and having held many positions of trust, among others that of Commissioner, 1643.
The place at Portsmouth is still owned by the family.
The old house was burnt in 1889. From the windows of
the modern house, built in colonial style, can be seen the
old burying-ground of the family, where Thomas Cor-

[19] Authorities: Austin's *R. I. Gen.*; *Cornell Gen.*, by Rev. John Cornell; Arnold's *R. I. Gen.*; *Family Papers.*

[20] " Thomas was the second grantee receiving one half Dutch mile.
Refer to Bolton's *Westchester* for interesting account of grant. Cornell's Neck is now within the limits of Greater New York."

nell, the first of his name in this country, was interred. He married Rebecca Briggs, of Portsmouth, R. I., a sister of the Hon. John Briggs. His son:

HON. JOHN CORNELL, married *Mary*, daughter of Hon. John Russell and his wife Dorothy. Their son: *Joshua Cornell*, married *Sarah*, the daughter of John and Mary (Pearsall) Thorne. The line descends as follows:

Joshua Cornell II., married Charity Haight.

William Cornell, married *Mary Quinby*.

Quinby Cornell, married *Hannah Underhill*.

Amy Cornell, married *John Hull III.*

RUSSELL

One of the first settlers of Dartmouth, Ralph Russell, of Pontipool, Eng., died in 1676. He was the ancestor of the Russell family of New Bedford, which received its name from one of Ralph's descendants in the fourth generation. His son:

HON. JOHN RUSSELL, was Deputy 1646 to 1648, represented Dartmouth 1665, and was again Deputy, 1680 to 1683. He was in the earliest list of Freemen, 1644; was sent out to fight the Indians, 1645, and in 1677 was one of the important committee for distributing charity coming from Ireland. His wife was Dorothy, the widow of the Rev. Henry Smith.

Their daughter *Mary* married HON. JOHN CORNELL.

THORNE

ARMS: *Argent, a fess gules between three lions rampant sable.*
CREST: *A lion, rampant, sable.*
MOTTO: *Principes Obsta.*

WILLIAM THORNE,[21] was one of the first settlers of Long Island, and with seventeen others became a pat-

[21] Authorities: Bunker's *L. I. Gen.;* Bolton's *Westchester; Family Papers*, etc.

entee of Flushing, in 1645, granted by the Dutch governor, Kieft. He was also granted a plantation lot in Gravesend, of which Lady Moody, and three others, had received a general patent; about ten years later he became one of the proprietors of Jamaica. He and thirty-one others signed a remonstrance to Governor Stuyvesant, in 1657, against the severe treatment of the Quakers.[22]

His son, *John Thorne,* married *Mary,* daughter of Nicholas and Sarah Pearsall.

Their daughter, *Sarah Thorne,* married *Joshua Cornell I.*

The name Pearsall is given " Parcell, of Flushing," in the will of Nicholas Pearsall, 1689, recorded at Jamaica, L. I. In some records the name of his wife is given as Mary Van Dam. He was one of the patentees of Flushing, L. I.

HULL (*Continued*)

A son of John and Amy (Cornell) Hull was *Robert Hull,* who married, first, Hannah Anne Janney, and second, Susanna Rebecca, the daughter of Judge Lucas Powell and Susanna Caroline (Tapscott) Thompson. Issue, first wife:

Elizabeth.

Joseph J., married Mary Delafield; issue, Cornelius DuBois and Marion.

Julia, married John Newport; issue, Elizabeth (who married Charles L. Hepburn).

Alice.

John.

William J., married Amelia B. Murphy, of Wood-

22 For detailed account of Thorne family, refer to *N. Y. Gen. & Biog. Rec.*

stock, Va.; issue, John, Harry (who married Louise Peckham), and William Buchanan.

Issue, second wife:

Henry Powell, married Lelia Gordon Taylor; issue, Elizabeth, who married Francis M. McKey, and had Francis.

Caroline Tapscott.

AMY ELEANOR E. HULL.

John Baker Thompson, married Louise Gertrude M. Ranstead.

Robert Carter, married Susan Boush Johnston; issue, Elizabeth Carter.

POWELL

LUCAS POWELL, of Amherst County, Va., was a lineal descendant " of those Powells whose first representative, Nathaniel, came to America with John Smith." Lucas Powell married, 1754-55, *Elizabeth,* the daughter of *John Edwards.*

Their daughter, *Rebecca Edwards,* married John Thompson.

EDWARDS

EDWARDS

The family [23] descended from the ancient Welsh kings of Powysland. The first to assume the name of Edwards was Robert, the son of Edward ap Thomas, ap Llewellyn, lineally descended from Elnon Efell, Lord of Cynllaeth. He married Ann, the daughter and heir of Robert Ryffin, and was succeeded by his son John, who purchased Ness

[23] Authorities: *Va. Mag.,* Vol. v, p. 185; *William & Mary Quar.,* Vol. iii, p. 123; *Va. Carolorum.*

Strange, Salop, which is still owned by the Edwards family. The branch of the family that emigrated to Virginia, early in the seventeenth century, came from near Cardiff, Wales, where the ruins of an old castle, known as " Edwards Hall," are still to be seen.

WILLIAM EDWARDS, held among other offices, that of Burgess for Surry, 1652 to 1653, 1658 to 1659. His son:

WILLIAM EDWARDS II., was Justice, 1714. He married Ann, the daughter of Colonel Benjamin Harrison, ancestor of Benjamin Harrison, who signed the Declaration of Independence, father and great-grandfather, respectively, of General William Henry Harrison and Benjamin Harrison, ex-Presidents of the United States.

Their son, *John Edwards*, was the father of *Elizabeth*, who married LUCAS POWELL.

Rebecca Edwards Powell, married John Thompson.

TAPSCOTT

The Tapscotts (who married into the Thompson family), came to America with John and Lawrence Washington, and settled in the Northern Neck of Virginia.

HENRY TAPSCOTT, of Lancaster County, Va., a son of Edward, of Northumberland County, Va., was on the Committee of Safety for Lancaster, 1775. He married *Mary*, the daughter of Martin Sherman and Ann Chinn, his wife (descended from COLONEL WILLIAM BALL).

Their son *James* married Susanna Howard, the daughter of John and Judith (Wood) Baker, and the widow of Dr. John Wood.

Their daughter, *Susanna Caroline,* married *Judge Lucas Powell Thompson.*

BALL

COLONEL WILLIAM BALL, of Lancaster County, Va., was the progenitor of the Virginia Balls (see pp. 134-137).

His granddaughter *Esther,* the daughter of COLONEL JOSEPH and Elizabeth (Rogers or Romney) BALL, married Rawleigh Chinn, and was the mother of *Ann Chinn,* who married Martin Sherman, whose daughter *Mary* married HENRY TAPSCOTT.

ROMNEY

BAKER

A descendant of the house of Norfolk, through the Howard family, Judith Wood, who married John Baker, was the daughter of Peter Wood and Susanna Howard, his wife, who was the daughter of Sir William and Lady Judith Howard, of Howard Hall, Eng.

Their daughter, Susanna Howard Baker, married, first, John Wood, and second, *James Tapscott.*

THOMPSON

In 1774, at the age of eighteen, John Thompson came to America. He joined the Revolutionary army, serving in Captain Watson's company in a Pennsylvania regiment, fought in the battles of Long Island and Trenton, and crossed the Delaware with Washington. He settled after the war in Nelson County, Va., where he died in 1828. He married *Rebecca Edwards,* the daughter of LUCAS POWELL, and his wife, *Rebecca Edwards.*

The sixth of his seven children was *Judge Lucas*

JUDGE LUCAS POWELL THOMPSON

JUDITH WOOD
Wife of John Baker

SARAH COLES HULL
Wife of Henry Trowbridge

Powell Thompson. At the age of eighteen, after a walking tour through Spain, he returned to Virginia, where he studied and graduated in law, his license bearing the names of three of the most eminent men of that State, Archibald Stuart, Hugh Holmes, and Briscoe Baldwin, Judges of the Supreme Court of Virginia, and by a coincidence all cousins of his wife. In a few years he was elected Judge of the Circuit Court of Augusta, Albemarle, Nelson, Amherst, and Rockbridge counties, succeeding Chief Justice Marshall, being the youngest man who had ever held this position, and after Chief Justice Marshall, admitted to be the most learned jurist in Virginia. He held his position during the Civil War, and was still kept in it by the Federal government during the stormy reconstruction days. By the advice of General Robert E. Lee, he took the oath of allegiance, and after the war, though refusing to "soil the ermine of the office" by running for the position he had held before, was elected to it again, one vote only being cast against him. Judge Thompson was the originator of the idea of sending a commission, during the Civil War, to meet Mr. Lincoln in the interests of peace, a suggestion which was accepted, Hon. Alexander H. H. Stuart, of Staunton, one of President Fillmore's cabinet, being chosen to represent Virginia. Judge Thompson married *Susanna Caroline,* the daughter of James and Susanna Howard (Baker) Tapscott. Issue: two sons and six daughters.

The sons, as follows:

The eldest, Lucas Powell, died s. p.

The second, John Baker, became professor at Kenyon College, Cambria, Ohio, before he was twenty-one, and President of St. John's College, Arkansas, when only twenty-three years old. When the Civil War broke out he commanded a regiment of boys from his college, officered by their professors. As Lieutenant-Colonel, on his twenty-seventh birthday, he led a charge at the Battle of Shiloh, and the spot where he fell, mortally wounded, is one of the cycloramic features of the battle. Wounded unto death he was carried from the field still shouting encouragement to his men. His name is on a tablet in the rotunda at the University of Virginia, erected to the memory of the alumni who fought in the Civil War.

The daughters were known as the "Six lovely Virginia sisters."

Margaret, married Dr. Paul J. Carrington, of Virginia.

Caroline, Eleanor Stuart, and Mary Carter, married, respectively, three brothers, Charles, Robert Harper Goodloe, and John Lee Carroll (the latter then governor, lineal descendants of Charles Carroll, the signer).

Alice Louise.

The second daughter, *Susanna Rebecca,* married *Robert Hull,* of New York and Baltimore. Their daughter is:

AMY ELEANOR E. HULL,

Member of Chapter I., The Colonial Dames of America.

ROBERT HULL
From a miniature

SUSANNA REBECCA THOMPSON
Wife of Robert Hull

d clock with picture of the Indians
meeting Gov. Winthrop

Old pitcher with portrait of Capt.
Isaac Hull and frigate *Constitution*

XXI

KUHN

Among the eighteenth century families that were swept into Pennsylvania, on the flood tide of the remarkable German emigration, were the Kuhns, whose ancestor, John Kuhn, was a magistrate of Berwangen, near the Black Forest, Germany, and died previous to November 30, 1676. His son, George Martin Kuhn, was assistant jurat of the Court of Furfield, a village on the Neckar, in the province of Würtemburg. He married Barbara, the daughter of Friedrich Ponmes, a Justice of the Peace, and had six children.

Their second child, John Christopher Kuhn, was born December 16, 1684, and died in 1754. He continued to reside in Furfeld, in the beautiful valley of the Neckar, until 1719, when he removed to Hutten. He had married Margaret, the daughter of the late Marx Reichss, a citizen of Sernum. The Kuhn family embarked on the ship *Hope* of London, Rotterdam being the port of departure, Daniel Reed, Master. They arrived in Philadelphia, August 28, 1733, with their three children, ADAM SIMON, aged nineteen; Eva Barbara, aged thirteen, and Anna Maria, aged nine. The list of passengers of the *Hope* is preserved at Harrisburg, Pa. The family settled in the present Berks County, Pa., and the father was naturalized March 28, 1747. He was living in that section, in Maiden Creek township, when he died.

ADAM SIMON KUHN, the eldest child and only son, was born in Furfeld, Germany, December 26, 1713, and died January 23, 1780. He was naturalized, April 8, 1744, in Lancaster County, Pa. A man of bright natural parts, liberally educated, he became a physician and settled in Lancaster, where he was considered a very skillful, attentive and successful practitioner. He also became conspicuous in public affairs in his new home. From 1749 to 1753 he was Chief Burgess of Lancaster. During the French and Indian War he took an active part in the defence of his neighborhood. He was commissioned a Justice of the Lancaster County Courts 1752, 1761, 1764 and 1770; a member of the committee of Observation and Correspondence, December 15, 1774, and served as a delegate to the Provincial Convention held at Philadelphia, January 23, 1775. A memorial tablet was erected to him in Trinity Church, Lancaster. Of him it has been said, "He was the principal and almost the only person who was concerned for the promotion of classical learning amongst the youth of that community." He married, December 11, 1740, Anna Maria Sabina, the daughter of John Jacob and Eva Rosina Schrack. She was born at sea October 26, 1717, and died in Lancaster, Pa., 1799. They had eight children, viz.: *Adam John,* Johann Frederick, Daniel, Peter, Maria Sabina, John Jacob, Hannah, Eve.

The eldest son, *Adam John Kuhn,* was born November 17, 1741. He decided upon the medical profession as his life work, in which he eventually gained worldwide distinction. Having sailed for Europe 1761, he began the study of medicine and botany in January, 1762, at the University of Upsala, Sweden, under the celebrated Linnaeus. He continued there until 1764, when he entered the University of Edinburgh, graduating in 1767. While at Upsala he was a member of the family of Professor Linnaeus, who, in a letter still preserved in the family said: "Your son of great promise, and endowed with most engaging manners, arrived

here," and writing a year later, said, "You have ven-
tured to send your beloved son to a foreign country, he
is unwearied in his studies, lives in a most temperated
and correct manner—he long since began to taste the
sweets of science, therefore I congratulate you and myself on this your son, and I have never known any one
more correct in his deportment or superior in applica-
tion."

After taking his degree in Edinburgh 1767, Dr.
Adam Kuhn made a tour of France, Holland and Germany, returning to Philadelphia 1768, when he was at
once appointed professor of Materia Medica and Botany in the College of Philadelphia. He was chosen
one of the physicians of the newly organized society for
inoculating the poor for small-pox in 1774, and May,
1775, was named as one of the physicians to the Pennsylvania Hospital, resigning in 1798. Upon the establishment of the Philadelphia Dispensary, 1786, for the
relief of the poor, Dr. Kuhn was selected as consultant
physician. In 1787, the College of Physicians was
founded and he was one of its charter members, becoming its president 1808, holding the office at the time
of his death. In 1789 he was called to the Chair of
Theory and Practice in the University of Pennsylvania,
and when the college and university were united 1792,
was chosen to the professorship of Physic. At the outbreak of the Revolution he was commissioned surgeon
and physician of the continental service July 8, 1776,
and served until 1777. He resided for some time in
St. Croix, West Indies, where he married, May 14,
1780, Elizabeth, the daughter of Isaac and Mary Carroll (Nanton) Hartman, and the widow of Franie Mar-
koe. She was born August 20, 1755, and died February 25, 1791. Dr. Kuhn died intestate, leaving a

large fortune to his three children, Hartman, *Charles* and William.

The second son, *Charles Kuhn,* was born April 12, 1785, and died September 22, 1842. He was graduated from the University of Pennsylvania 1802. He married, July 28, 1808, Elizabeth Hestia, the daughter of Benjamin and Elizabeth (Kortright) Yard. She was born January 24, 1788, and died March 12, 1870.[1] Issue, eight children, viz.: Cornelius, Elizabeth, Hartman (who married his cousin, Mary Kuhn), *Emily,* William, Edward, and a second Edward.

HARRISON

Their fifth child, *Emily Kuhn,* married *Samuel Thompson Harrison,* of the Maryland Harrisons.

Their son, *Charles Kuhn Harrison,* married *Louisa Triplett,* the daughter of Bolling Walker and Ann (Triplett) Haxall, and their daughter, ANN TRIPLETT HARRISON, married George Somerville Jackson.

HARRISON-CAILE

JOHN CAILE HARRISON, son of Christopher and

---

[1] Authentic *Family Papers.*

Mary (Caile) Harrison, married his cousin, *Mary*, the daughter of HALL CAILE and his wife, *Elizabeth Haskins*, the granddaughter of GOVERT LOOCKERMAN II.

Their son, *Hall Harrison*, married Elizabeth, the daughter of Robert and Elizabeth (Thompson) Galt.

Their son, *Samuel Thompson Harrison*, married *Emily*, the daughter of *Charles Kuhn*, whose son, *Charles Kuhn Harrison*, married *Louisa Triplett Haxall*.

LOOCKERMAN-WOOLFORD-DENWOOD

GOVERT LOOCKERMANS I., married, second, Marritje Jansen.

JACOB LOOCKERMAN, married Helen Ketin.

GOVERT LOOCKERMAN II., married *Sarah*, the daughter of ROGER WOOLFORD, and his wife *Mary*, the daughter of LEVIN DENWOOD I. Their youngest daughter, *Mary Loockerman*, married Thomas Haskins, whose daughter, *Elizabeth*, married HALL CAILE. (See pp. 56-79 for Harrison, Caile, Loockerman, Woolford and Denwood families.)

HAXALL

The first known ancestor of the Haxall family of Virginia, John Haxall, of Exning, England, was born 1681 and died September 17, 1751.

His son, William Haxall, born 1724, and died March, 1787, was one of the leading men of Exning, being churchwarden and collector of the vicar's tithes, and overseer of the poor. He married Catherine Newton, of Bristol, England, who died at "Whitehall," a large house still standing in Exning. Issue, six children, viz.: George, William, Joseph, Henry, John, Philip.

The youngest son, Philip Haxall, was born April

10, 1770, and died December 26, 1831. He emigrated to Petersburg, Va., 1786, where he was vestryman of Old Bristol Parish.[2] He moved to Richmond, Va., in June, 1809, and established the Haxall Mills. He married, July 20, 1801, *Clara*, the daughter of Robert and Elizabeth (Starke) Walker, of Kingston, Dinwiddie County, Va. She was born July 9, 1780, and died March 29, 1857. Issue, nine children, viz.: Robert Walker, Richard Barton, Elizabeth, Harriet, William, Henry, Mary Bell, Philip Augustus, *Bolling Walker*, David Walker, Elizabeth.

HAXALL

The seventh child of the colonist, *Bolling Walker Haxall*,[3] born July 13, 1815, and died June 26, 1885, married, December 30, 1845, Anne, the daughter of John Richards and Louisa (Stone) Triplett, and their daughter, *Louisa Triplett*, married *Charles Kuhn Harrison*.

TRIPLETT [4]

The first of this name to settle in Virginia, Francis Triplett, who died 1700, went to Richmond County. He patented one thousand and fifty acres of land in Rappahannock County 1666. He was a nephew of

[2] *Bristol Parish Records.* Hayden's *Genealogies.*

[3] The name of Haxall is believed to be extinct in England, and it only exists in this country in the descendants of Philip and Clara (Walker) Haxall.

[4] A genealogy of this family will be   published in the *Virginia Hist. Mag.* by Rev. Arnold Harris Hord, of Germantown, Penn.

Rev. Thomas Triplett, Dean of Westminster Abbey, whose monument is in the Poets' Corner of the Abbey. The Dean is described in some very old books as of London and the son of a gentleman.

A son of Francis, the colonist, William Triplett, was a resident of King George's County, and a land deed bearing date November 6, 1733, is on record in Spottsylvania County; his will was dated December 3, 1738. He married Isabella, the daughter of Captain Lyman Miller, whose will was proved in Rappahannock County May 22, 1684. Captain Miller was a noted shipbuilder and a large landowner.[5]

Their son, Francis Triplett II., owned estates in Westmoreland and King George's Counties; his will was proved March 5, 1767. His wife's name was Mildred ———.

Their fifth and youngest son, Daniel Triplett, was born May 8, 1753, and married, January 1, 1777, Elizabeth, the daughter of John and Susannah (Coleman) Richards. She was born May 22, 1760.

Their son, John Richards Triplett, was born January 29, 1785, and died October 2, 1843. He married, May 19, 1813, his cousin, Louisa Richards Stone, and resided in Norfolk, Va. Their daughter, Anne, married *Bolling Walker Haxall.*

RICHARDS

ARMS: *Sable a chevron between three fleur-de-lis or.*

The son of William Byrd Richards, John Richards, was born in England, January 27, 1734, and died September 13, 1785.[6] He married, January 1, 1754, Susannah, the daughter of Robert Coleman, of Goochland

⁵ Bruce's *Economic Hist. of Va.* Vol. II, p. 439.
⁵ *Family Papers.*

County. She died April 15, 1778. Had twelve children, viz.: Patty, James, Elizabeth, Triplett, Susannah, Payne, Sarah, John, William, Mildred, who married William Scandreth Stone November 10, 1787; Fanny, Catherine.

The third child, Elizabeth, was born May 22, 1760, and married, January 1, 1777, Daniel Triplett, whose son, John Richards, married Louisa Richards, the daughter of Mildred and William Scandreth Stone.

WALKER

The first of the name in Virginia, Captain David Walker, lived in Dinwiddie County. Family records say that "he was a man of large means, for years Presiding Magistrate, a position that was only held by men of the highest education and wealth. He was Senior Warden of Bristol Parish, later a Warden of Bath Parish.[7]

His son, Robert Walker, of Kingston, Va., was born October 10, 1729, and married, 1745, *Elizabeth,* the daughter of William and Mary (Bolling) Starke. Had ten children, viz.: Robert, Richard, David, Bolling, Freeman, Starke, Louisa, Martha, Mary, and *Clara,* who married Philip Haxall. Their son, *Bolling Walker Haxall,* married Anne Triplett.

STARKE

ARMS: *Azure, a chevron between three acorns in chief or.*
CREST: *A bull's head erased or, distilling drops of blood proper.*
MOTTO: *Fortiorum Fortia Facta.*

The Starkes came to America from Scotland, the first mentioned being Dr. Richard Starke, of York County, Va. It becomes a matter of interest to identify this gentleman, of whom very little is remembered, beyond

[7] *Ibid.*

his interesting connection with our earliest American law books. In the records of York County is mentioned a Dr. Richard Starke, who died in 1704, leaving a wife Rebecca, and the following children: WILLIAM, Richard, James, Catrine, and Mary Harris. In 1774, there was printed, at Williamsburg, by Alexander Purdie and John Dixson, a book entitled " The Office and Authority of a Justice of the Peace, explained and digested under proper titles," to which are added full and correct precedents of all kinds of process necessary to be used by magistrates, in which also the duties of sheriffs and other public officers are properly discussed. The greater part of the book was written by Dr. Richard Starke, whose death prevented its completion. His friends prevailed upon some benevolent gentlemen of the law to finish the work.

COLONEL WILLIAM STARKE, his eldest son, was a prominent man in York County, Va. He was Justice of the Peace in 1730 and other years, and Colonel of the County Militia. He built and gave Starke's Free School. He married *Mary,* the daughter of Robert and Anne (Cocke) Bolling, and there is a marriage contract on record between William and Mary, 1713. Their daughter, *Elizabeth,* married Robert Walker.[8]

BOLLING

The Bollings are of very ancient origin. Robert Bolling, Esq., in the reign of Edward IV., resided at Bolling Hall, near Bradford, in Yorkshire, England, where many generations of his ancestors in the enjoyment of private life had lived, and where he died 1485. He was buried in the family vault of the church at Bradford. It is probable that his family had been bene-

8 *William and Mary Quar.*

factors of that church, or had even built it, since their
coat-of-arms alone are engraved upon it. Bolling Hall
passed in succession to the families of Tristram Bolling
and Sir Richard Tempest, the latter marrying Rosa-
mond, the daughter and heiress of Tristram.

ROBERT BOLLING, son of John and Mary, of the Bollings of "Bolling Hall," near Bradford, of All Hallows, Barking Parish, Tower Street, London,
was the first of the name who settled in Virginia, arriving there October 2, 1660. He was born December 26,
1646, and died July 17, 1709. He lived at " Kippax,"
sometimes called " Farmingdate," served as a Burgess
1704, and took a prominent part in the affairs of the
colony. The Bolling family were deeply interested in
the church in Virginia, and have been represented in the
Vestry of Old Bristol Parish in every generation.[9]
Robert Bolling married, first, 1675, Jane, the daughter
of Thomas Rolfe and the granddaughter of Pocahon-
tas; second, 1681, *Anne,* the daughter of Colonel John
Stith. Issue, second wife, seven children, viz.: ROBERT,
Stith, Edward, Anne, Doury, Thomas, and Agnes.

ROBERT BOLLING II. was born January 25, 1682, and
died 1749. He was also prominent in the affairs of his
county; Surveyor of Charles City County 1714; Justice
of the Peace, and a member of the House of Burgesses
1723, 1726 and 1730. He married, January 27, 1706,
Anne, the daughter of Richard and Anne (Bowler)
Cocke. They had eight children, viz.: Elizabeth, Anne,
Lucy, Jane, Martha, Susanna, Robert, and *Mary,* who
married WILLIAM STARKE.

STITH

COLONEL JOHN STITH was the first of this family in

[9] *Bristol Parish; Va. Hist. Mag.,* and *William and Mary Quar.*

Virginia. He had a grant of land in Charles City County 1663; was a practicing lawyer 1680; member of the House of Burgesses 1685 to 1692 and 1693, and Sheriff 1691. His known children are: Drury, John, and *Anne,* who married Robert Bolling I.

Their son, ROBERT BOLLING II., married *Anne Cocke,* whose daughter, *Mary,* married WILLIAM STARKE.

COCKE

ARMS: *Argent two lions passant sable crowned or a fesse sable between two talbots passant.*

RICHARD COCKE (1600-1665), the original ancestor of the Cockes of Virginia, emigrated from Leeds, England, about 1630, and settled at Milvert Hills. With him, came Captain Francis West, his sister having married Robert West, son of Lord de la Warr, and settled in Henrico County, Va. Richard Cocke was a prominent merchant in London, and several of his family were connected with the Royal households of Mary, Elizabeth, and James I., and the Cocke family was connected with the Wests, Percy Lord Chandos, the Berkeley family, Sir Hugh Poynty, and Lord Wentworth. In the Committee of Safety of Surry County, Va., 1776, there were five Cockes: Colonel Allen, Colonel John, John Jr., J. H., and Colonel Lemuel Cocke. The Cocke family sat in nearly every session of the Virginia House of Burgesses. Richard Cocke took a leading part in the affairs of the colony, serving as a Burgess 1632, 1644, and 1654. He was also a member of the "Grand Assembly of Virginia." His nephew, Captain Cocke, of London, is well known by his intimacy with Samuel Pepys, and is often mentioned in his celebrated diary. Richard Cocke married *Mary*, the daughter of Walter Aston, and had a large family.

RICHARD COCKE II., third son of the colonist, was born 1639, and died 1705. He took an active part in the affairs of Virginia, being a civil officer of Henrico County 1680; Justice of the Peace 1714, and Burgess. He married, 1675, Ann Bowler, and their daughter, *Anne Cocke,* married ROBERT BOLLING, JR., whose 'daughter, *Mary Bolling,* married WILLIAM STARKE.

ASTON

ARMS: *Argent a fesse sable in chief three lozenges of the last.*
CREST: *A bull's head, couped sable.*

WALTER ASTON (the grandson of Sir Walter Aston, of Longdon, Stafford County, England, who was knighted 1560), was born July 9, 1584, and died August 13, 1639, and is buried at "Westover." The family came to America 1626, and August 12 of that year Walter Aston patented one thousand and forty acres of land near Shirley Hundred, two hundred acres of which were known as "Causey's Care," purchased in 1634 from John Causey (being the same land patented by Nathaniel Causey, who came in with the first supply, 1608. All of this property became part of William Byrd's celebrated "Westover"). Walter Aston represented Shirley Hundred in the House of Burgesses 1629 to 1630 and Causey's Care 1632 to 1633. He was a Justice of the Peace, and Lieutenant-Colonel of the Militia.[10] His first wife's name is mentioned in land patents as being Warboe or Narboe, and his second wife's name was Hannah, who married after his death Colonel Edward Hill. Children: Susannah, Walter,

[10] *William and Mary Quar.*

Elizabeth, and *Mary,* who married RICHARD COCKE.
From them the line descends as follows:

RICHARD COCKE II., married Ann Bowler.

Anne Cocke, married ROBERT BOLLING II.

Mary Bolling, married WILLIAM STARKE.

Elizabeth Starke, married Robert Walker.

Clara Walker, married Philip Haxall.

Bolling Walker Haxall, married Anne Triplett.

Louisa Triplett Haxall, married Charles Kuhn Harrison, whose daughter is:

ANNE TRIPLETT HARRISON JACKSON,

Member of Chapter I., The Colonial Dames of America.

XXII

SWAN

Scottish records, of the year 1599, contain the name of William Swan, a Burgess of Dumfries, who died in January, 1603, leaving a widow, Helen Anderson, and four children, viz.: Andrew, William, Alison, and Helen.

The eldest child, Andrew Swan, married, before 1607, Janet, who was a daughter of Herbert Ranyng (who died in 1601), and Janet Davidson, his wife, and a granddaughter of another Herbert Ranyng (who died 1587), and Malie Kirkpatrick, his wife.

The elder Ranyng was Provost of Dumfries, 1572; member of the Parliament of Scotland the same year, and Commissioner for Dumfries, in the Convention of Royal Burghs, 1578. The younger Ranyng, was Provost of Dumfries, 1586, 1591 to 1592, and was frequently Bailie.

A son of Andrew and Janet (Ranyng) Swan, was John, living in the year 1626. Of the same family was James Swan, a merchant of Dumfries, who died May 24, 1760. His son Robert, born 1720, a partner in the house of Nelson, Carlyle & Company, of Glasgow, resided at Annapolis, Md., as the American representative of the firm, and died there unmarried May 4, 1764. The larger part of his estate he left by will to his nephew, John Swan, the eldest son of his brother John, of Cocketfield, viz.:

MAJOR JOHN SWAN, who was baptized in Torthorwald Parish, November 27, 1750, and came to Maryland in the year 1766, as the heir of his uncle's estate.

ELIZABETH MAXWELL
Wife of Maj. John Swan

MAJ. JOHN SWAN

JAMES SWAN

ELIZABETH DONNELL
Wife of James Swan

He settled first in Annapolis, soon removed to Frederick County, and later to the growing town of Baltimore, where he resided until his death, August 21, 1824. He early entered the army of the Revolution, and was made Captain of the 3d Continental Dragoons, April 26, 1777, at that time being recruited in Fredericksburg, Va., by Colonel George Baylor. He was commissioned Major of the 1st Continental Dragoons, October 21, 1780, and served with gallantry until the close of the war. In 1777 he was wounded during an engagement near Morristown, Penn., and taken to Philadelphia for treatment. While there, General Washington wrote the following letter to Colonel George Baylor, who was then recruiting a regiment in Fredericksburg, Va.

"Morristown, April 25, 1777. To George Baylor, Esq., Colonel of a Reg. of Dragoons to be formed, Fredericksburg.

Dear Sir:—The Captaincy becoming vacant in your Regiment is to be filled by Mr. John Swan of Frederick, Md., a gentleman strongly recommended to me by some members of Congress and whom (from other accounts) you will find fully qualified to give great satisfaction in the execution of his duty. He is at present under confinement in Philadelphia occasioned by a wound received in an action near this place some time ago. I have written for him to join you with all convenient expedition, and to receive your instructions how he is to proceed. I repeat my request that you send in your Regiment, troop by troop, as fast as you can equip them.

I am, dear sir, your most obedient servant, G. Washington." [1]

With his command, Major Swan was present with

[1] *Va. Hist. Register.* By Maxwell, 1848-49. Vol. I, p. 145.

General Lafayette, at the surrender of Lord Cornwallis at Yorktown. The Bible, carried by him throughout the war, was bequeathed by his granddaughter, Miss Willie Swan, to her kinswoman, Mrs. Robert A. Dobbin. On the title page is written, evidently by himself: "John Swan, His Book 1765."

On a blank page between the Old and New Testaments is written:

"John Swan's book, arrived at Annapolis in Maryland from Scotland on the 30th of August 1766"

Pasted in front of the book is the following:

"This Book once the property of General John Swan of the Revolution was by him given to his eldest son Robert Swan, who gave it on his deathbed to his eldest son John, Willie's father."

With the Bible was also sent General Swan's watch.

At the close of the war he was made General of the Maryland State Militia. Generals Washington and Lafayette were his warm personal friends. He was one of the original members of the Society of the Cincinnati, and the membership has passed regularly through his family, being now held by his great-grandson, James Swan Frick, of Baltimore. The Society of the Cincinnati was the only patriotic society in the United States until the formation of the Society of The Colonial Dames of America. Major Swan married, July 12, 1787, *Elizabeth,* daughter of George and Elizabeth (Trippe) Maxwell, born 1757. Their son was *James Swan.*

MAXWELL

Prior to 1676, James Maxwell settled in Anne Arundel County, Md. He died that year, leaving one child, and a widow who afterwards married Patrick Hall.[2]

[2] *Testamentary Proceedings,* Ann Arundel Co., Md. Vol. X, fol. 326.

GEORGE MAXWELL

THOROUGHGOOD SMITH
Second Mayor of Baltimore

DR. CHARLES SLOAN

JOHN FRICK

COLONEL JAMES MAXWELL, the only child of James Maxwell, was born 1661, and died January 5, 1728, leaving a will, dated that year.[3] He was a Ranger 1692, and his district was from the Falls of the Patapsco to the Susquehannah; Sheriff, 1693; and Member of the General Assembly, 1694.[4]

He married, first, Mary ——; second, —— ——. "William Savary of Baltimore County, married the widow of Colonel James Maxwell, and administered d.b.n. on his estate, and on that of his son James."[5]

Issue by first marriage, several children, including a son James; by second marriage, several children also, one being referred to as James the younger. In the *Records* of St. James Parish, Baltimore County, page 41, is the following entry:

"Phillisyanna Maxwell, daughter of James Maxwell and Mary his wife, he being the eldest son of Colonel James Maxwell deceased, was born 3rd March, 1723; Mary Maxwell, daughter of said persons born 6 April, 1724; Elizabeth Maxwell daughter of said persons was born 3rd June, 1727; Eleanor Maxwell daughter of said persons was born 12th Feb. 1729."

GEORGE MAXWELL, one of this family of children, was born 1725, but there is no entry of his birth in these records, doubtless because he moved to Benedict in Charles County. He married, May 27, 1756, *Elizabeth,* daughter of Major Henry and Elizabeth (Emerson) Trippe. George Maxwell died in Charles County, leaving a will dated 1777, by which he appointed his wife Elizabeth executrix, and names his son James. He refers to his daughters, but does not name them. They

3 *Office of the Reg. of Wills,* Baltimore Co., *Liber* No. 1, fol. 215.
4 *Arch. of Md.* Vols. XIX, p. 205; XX, p. 580; XXII, p. 80.
5 Adm. No. 3, fol. 137, of Baltimore County; passed Nov. 19, 1733.

were: *Elizabeth,* Mary, Ann and Eleanor. Mary left
a will dated December 18, 1816,[6] in which she gives
certain moneys to Robert, John, James and Robert
Maxwell Swan, " sons of my very affectionate brother-
in-law John Swan." At the foot of this will is an
agreement signed by " A Maxwell and E. Maxwell,
only sisters of Elizabeth Maxwell, that letters may be
granted to a stranger in blood." *Elizabeth Maxwell*
married MAJOR JOHN SWAN.

TRIPPE

MAJOR HENRY TRIPPE came to Maryland before
1663 and settled in Dorchester County. His birthplace
is said to have been Canterbury, England, 1632. He
was Justice and County Commissioner, 1669 to 1681,
and 1685 to 1694; Captain of Foot in the Dorchester
County Militia 1676, and commissioned Major of
Horse 1689. He represented his county in the Maryland Assembly 1671 to 1675, 1681 to 1682, and 1692
to 1693; member of the Committee of Twenty in whose
hands the government of the Province was placed 1690.
He married Elizabeth, widow of Michael Brooke, an
early colonist. He died 1698 and left a large landed
estate to his children. His eldest son:

CAPTAIN HENRY TRIPPE, who died in 1724, was a
member of the Assembly 1712 to 1715. He married
Susanna Heron, and had with other issue:

MAJOR HENRY TRIPPE, who died in 1744. He was
High Sheriff of Dorchester County, 1731 to 1734, and
Justice and member of the Assembly, 1735-1744. He
married *Elizabeth,* daughter of MAJOR THOMAS EMER-
SON, of Talbot County, who was a member of the As-

---

[6] *Office of the Reg. of Wills* of Baltimore City, *Liber* No. 11, fol. 546.
[7] *Arch. of Md.* Vol. v.

Ann Teackle Smith
Wife of John Donnell

John Donnell

sembly 1716 to 1719 and died 1720.   Issue, with other
children: *Elizabeth,* who married GEORGE MAXWELL.

SWAN *(Continued)*

In 1796, *James,* the son of Major John and Elizabeth (Maxwell) Swan, was born, and his death occurred
in 1859.   He married, 1818, *Elizabeth,* the daughter of
John and Ann Teackle (Smith) Donnell, who was born
in January, 1801, and died 1838.   They had three children:
John, married Isabel Davies.
Ellen, married PHILIP BARTON KEY.
Anne Elizabeth, married William Frederick Frick.

DONNELL

About the year 1800, John Donnell, an Irish gentle-
man, came to America.   He married, October 10, 1798,[8]
Ann Teackle, the daughter of Isaac and Eliazbeth Cus-
tis (Teackle) Smith; she was born October 15, 1781,
and died 1858.   Two of their daughters were:
Elizabeth, married *James Swan.*
Frances, married Gustav Lürman.   (See Lürman-
Powel line.)

SHEPPARD

THOMAS SHEPPARD was a member of the House of
Burgesses, for Elizabeth City County, 1632 to 1633.[9]
LIEUTENANT-COLONEL JOHN SHEPPARD, his son, was
a member [10] for James City County, in 1644.   His
wife's name was Jean.   Their daughter, *Ioane,* married John Smith.

8 *Marriage Bond,* Clerk's Office, Northampton Co., Va.
9 Hening's *Statutes,* Vol. I, pp. 202, 213.
10 *Ibid,* Vol. I, pp. 213,. 283.

SMITH

A son of John and Ioane (Sheppard) Smith, *Isaac Smith I.*, came from Scotland prior to 1760, according to family tradition, and taught school in Pungoteague, Accomac County, Va. There he lived and died. He was an educated man, and a vestryman of St. George's Parish, in lower Accomac County.

He married *Sarah,* the daughter of Major John and Frances (Yeardley) West, and died in 1760.

Isaac Smith II., their son, was born November 4, 1734, and died March 23, 1813.[11] He succeeded his father in the office of vestryman of St. George's Parish, and was on the Committee of Safety for Accomac County, Va., 1774, and a delegate to the Virginia Convention of June, 1774, and those of 1775 and 1776.[12]

He married, March 14, 1759, *Elizabeth Custis,* the daughter of Thomas and Elizabeth (Custis) Teackle, who was born December 13, 1742, and died August 19, 1829.

A daughter, *Mary Ann Smith,* married, first, —— De Drisdale, and second, William Gilmor.

Their son, *Robert Gilmor,* married *Ellen Ward,* whose son, *Judge Robert Gilmor,* married Josephine Albert.

Their daughter is Josephine, who married Wallace Harvey.

Another daughter, *Ann Teackle Smith,* married John Donnell. Of their daughters, *Elizabeth* married *James Swan,* and *Frances* married Gustav W. Lürman. (See Lürman-Powel line.)

---

11 Tombstone at Selma, Northampton Co., Va.
12 *Principles and Acts of the Revolution,* pp. 89, 261.

MAJOR JOHN SWAN'S CERTIFICATE OF MEMBERSHIP IN THE SOCIETY OF THE
CINCINNATI

WEST

ARMS: *Argent, a fesse dancetty between three leopards' heads sable.*
CREST: *Out of a mural coronet a griffin's head argent, charged with a fesse dancetty sable.*

The immigrant, Anthony West, who came to America in the ship *James* in 1622,[13] died 1652.

LIEUTENANT-COLONEL JOHN WEST, his son, was born 1638, and died 1703. He was High Sheriff of Accomac County, 1664 and 1667, one of the Council,[14] and Captain of Militia, 1663, Major 1675, and Lieutenant-Colonel 1679. He married *Matilda* (born 1644), the daughter of Colonel Edmund and Mary (Charlton) Scarborough.

MAJOR JOHN WEST, their son, who died 1718, was Major of Militia of Northampton County, Va.[15] He married *Frances*, the daughter of Captain Argall and Sarah (Michael) Yeardley. Their daughter, *Sarah*, married *Isaac Smith I*.

13 Hotten's *Lists*.
14 Northampton Co. *Recs.*, No. 4, p. 136.
15 Accomac County *Recs.* Vol. X, p. 107.

YEARDLEY

ARMS: *Argent on a chevron azure three barbs or, on a canton gules a fret of the third.*

CREST: *A buck courant gules, attired, or.*

SIR GEORGE YEARDLEY came to the Virginia Colony 1609, in the ship *Deliverance.* He was descended from a Staffordshire family, known as the "Lords of Yeardley," and had fought with distinction in Holland in the war against Spain. He was commissioned Captain upon his arrival in Virginia, and given command of a stockade, near the present site of Fortress Monroe. Sir Thomas Dale, then Governor of the Colony, sailed for England 1616, and Captain George Yeardley was made Deputy-Governor in his absence, and served until the arrival of Governor Argall, 1617. Sometime during 1618, Captain Yeardley married Temperance West, going the same year to London in the interest of the Colony. The Virginia company had been for some years divided by political discord into two parties. The Court party looked upon the colonists as men-servants of the Company, giving them no voice in the settlement of their affairs. The Virginia party sought and demanded more rights and privileges. When Captain Samuel Argall was appointed Governor to succeed Deputy-Governor Yeardley, who had grown greatly in favor with the people, it was considered a great calamity. It proved in the end, however, to be much to their advantage. Captain Yeardley had now lived for a number of years in Virginia, had learned the needs of the settlers, and had wit-

YEARDLEY

nessed their oppression. The representations he made
to the London Company created a great conflict in the
management of its affairs. The Court party was de-
feated, Governor Argall was recalled, Yeardley was
knighted and made Governor-General in Argall's stead.
He returned to Jamestown in 1619, with his Commission. Among its provisions was one granting to the colonists the right to have a share in governing themselves,
and to that end it was provided that they should hold an
Assembly once every year, "whereat were to be present the Governor and Council and two Burgesses from
each plantation, said Burgesses to be elected by the
inhabitants thereof, the Assembly to have power to
make and ordain whatever laws and orders were necessary and good for the Colony." The Commission
was issued in London on the 28th day of November,
1618. That night a flaming comet appeared in the
heavens and was considered an ill omen. It was vis-
ible until the 26th day of December, and the supersti-
tion of the times prevented the sailing of the expedition until the comet had disappeared. Yeardley set
sail on the 29th of January, 1619, more than a year
before the sailing of the *Mayflower*. Acting under the
authority of his commission he called an Assembly to
meet on the 30th day of July of that year at Jamestown. This was the first Legislative Assembly held
in America and ante-dated all others by some fifteen
years. The largest building in Jamestown was the
Episcopal Church, a wooden structure about sixty feet
long, and twenty-four feet wide, and it was there that
the Assembly was held. On this day the Governor,
accompanied by the members of the Council of State
and escorted by a guard dressed in the Governor's
livery, went to the meeting. The Assembly was form-

ally organized, and at once entered upon the performance of the work.[16]

In 1627 Sir George Yeardley died, leaving a will by which he bequeathed one-third of his estate to his widow, Lady Temperance Yeardley, one-third to his son Argall Yeardley, and one-third to his daughters, Elizabeth and Frances Yeardley.

COLONEL ARGALL YEARDLEY, his son, sailed for Rotterdam in his own vessel in 1649, carrying a cargo of tobacco raised by himself. After transacting his business, he returned to his Virginia home bringing with him a bride, who was Ann, the daughter of John and Ioane Custis of Rotterdam. His boat dropped anchor before his house, where it is said Argall and his new wife entertained lavishly. He was a member of the Council 1644, and also a Colonel of Militia of the Eastern Shore of Virginia. He died intestate.

CAPTAIN ARGALL YEARDLEY, II., his son, was Captain of Militia of Virginia, and High Sheriff of Northampton County.[17]   He married, 1678, *Sarah,* the daughter of John and Elizabeth (Thoroughgood) Michael. Their daughter, *Frances,* married MAJOR JOHN WEST, whose daughter, *Sarah West,* married *Isaac Smith I.*

SCARBOROUGH

ARMS: *Or, a chevron, between three towers gules.*

CREST: *Out of a mural coronet gules, a demi-lion or, holding upon the point of a lance of the first, a Saracen's head, ppr., wreathed azure.*

[16] See Account of the meeting of the first legislative Assembly held in America, in *Report of American Hist. Association.* By W. W. Henry, of Richmond, Va.

[17] Northampton Co., Va. *Recs.* Vol. VI.

Va. Carolorum, pp. 180-225.

Palmer's *Va. State Papers.* Vol. I, p. 13.

Hening's *Statutes,* Vol. I, p. 179.

CAPTAIN EDMUND SCARBOROUGH, the son of Henry
Scarborough of North Walsham, Norfolk County,
came to this country, bringing his wife Hannah, and
his son Edmund. He was Commissioner of Accomac
County, Va., and a member of
the Board of Justices, 1632,
and of the House of Burgesses
from 1628 to 1630.[18] He died
1634, leaving two sons, Charles
and Edmund Scarborough. Sir
Charles was educated at Caiu's
College, Cambridge, and was
physician to Charles II., James
II. and William I. He was
knighted 1669, a member of Par-
liament, and died 1639; buried at Cranford, Middlesex.

SCARBOROUGH

COLONEL EDMUND SCARBOROUGH, was of Northampton County, and for many years one of the most useful
men in Virginia.[19]   He was Burgess 1642 to 1671, the
year of his death; Surveyor-General of the colony from
1655 to 1671, and Speaker of the House, 1645; High
Sheriff 1660 to 1661, and frequently Justice.   He
gave to Hungars Church one thousand acres of land.[20]
This church, the third erected in Northampton County,
was built in 1680, of brick made and burnt just behind
the church, where are still the remains of the old kiln.
He married *Mary*, the daughter of STEPHEN CHARL-
TON, who was a member of the House of Burgesses
1644, 1645, and 1647,[21] and they had several children,

---

18 Hening's *Statutes*, pp. 203-289.
   County *Recs.* Vol. I, 1632-1640.
19 Hayden's *Va. Genealogies*, p. 439.
   Va. Carolorum, p. 301.
20 *Va. Carolorum*, pp. 186-198.
21 Hening's *Statutes*, Vol. I, pp. 289-340.

among them *Matilda,* who married JOHN WEST I., and *Tabitha,* who married first, William Smart, and third, JOHN CUSTIS II.

NELSON

ARMS: *Per pale argent and sable a chevron between three fleur-de-lis countercharged.*

CREST: *A cubit arm quarterly, argent and sable, holding in the hand proper a fleur-de-lis per pale of the first and second.*

An ancestor of the Teackle family, Thomas Nelson, or Neylson, of York, Merchant of the Staple, was Lord Mayor of York, 1454 to 1465. His will was proved March 22, 1484-85.

NELSON

One of the Lord Mayor's direct descendants, by Ioane his wife, was William Nelson of the city of York, whose son, William Nelson, of Belfast, County York, married Elinor Oglethorpe of that place. Their son, William Nelson, was of Bedale, County York, and his son, Robert Nelson, of Barnard's Inn, London, was buried at St. Dunstan's on the West, December 21, 1641; will proved 1642. He married Helen ——.

Their son, Robert Nelson, admitted to Gray's Inn March 11, 1630, will proved August 4, 1698, married Mary, the daughter of Sir John Temple, of Staunton Bury, Knt., and sister of Sir Thomas Temple, Bart., Governor of Nova Scotia. Their only daughter Margaret, heiress by will to her brother, married the REV. THOMAS TEACKLE.

ARMS OF TEMPLE

ARMS: *Quarterly, first and fourth or, an eagle displayed sable; second and third argent two bars sable, each charged with three martlets, or.*
CREST: *On a ducal coronet or, a martlet gold.*

TEACKLE

THE REVEREND THOMAS TEACKLE, was born in Gloucestershire, Eng., 1624, and came to America in 1656, on account of persecution by Cromwell. On the restoration of Charles II. he received from the Crown a grant of a large tract of land in Accomac County, Va., called "Craddock." It remained in his family until sold in 1810. He was an Episcopal clergyman, and founded a church in this county, of which he was the rector for many years. He married first, Isabella Douglas, in 1658;[22] married second, Margaret, the

[22] County *Recs.* 1657-1685, p. 111.

daughter of Robert and Mary (Temple) Nelson of London. He died January 25, 1695, at his country seat, "Craddock." A son of the second marriage:

JOHN TEACKLE, of "Craddock," was born September 2, 1693, and died at Yorktown, Va., December 3, 1721, in which year he was a member of the House of Burgesses. He married, November 2, 1710, *Susannah*, the daughter of Arthur and Sarah (Browne) Upshur.[23]

Their son, *Thomas Teackle II.*, was born November 11, 1711, and died July 20, 1769, at "Craddock." He had a grant of three thousand acres of land. He married *Elizabeth*, the daughter of JUDGE JOHN CUSTIS IV., and Ann Upshur, his wife. Their daughter, *Elizabeth Custis Teackle*, married ISAAC SMITH II.

DENWOOD

LEVIN (LIVING) DENWOOD,[24] the colonist, married Mary ——. (See pp. 149, 481-482.)

Their daughter *Susannah*, married *Thomas*, the son of John and Ursula Brown.

Their daughter *Sarah Brown*, married ARTHUR UPSHUR II.

Their daughter *Susannah Upshur*, married JOHN TEACKLE.

Their son, *Thomas Teackle II.*, married *Elizabeth Custis*.

BROWN-UPSHUR

JOHN BROWN appears first in the records of Northampton County, Va., in 1633. He is mentioned in

[23] Henings *Statutes*.
[24] *Recs. Northampton County.*, Vols. I and VII; Vol. XVI, p. 16.
Keith's Provincial Councillors of Va., pp. 128, 129.

Hotten's list as living on Hog Island, February 10, 1623. He owned large tracts of land, and was highly respected in the colony. November 14, 1645, he received a grant of one hundred and fifty acres of land, and another grant September 15, 1647, and one of six hundred and fifty acres on July 4, 1652.[25] He also owned one thousand two hundred and sixty-two acres in addition. John Brown died in 1655. His will was written August 26, 1654, and recorded March 15, 1655.[26] His wife, believed to have been Ursula —— (although no evidence has been found[27]), survived him. Issue: John, *Thomas*, Stephen, Elizabeth, Sarah, Mary. John and Stephen died without issue.

The second son, *Thomas Brown,* married *Susannah,* the daughter of LEVIN DENWOOD I.

Their daughter *Sarah,* married ARTHUR UPSHUR II. the son of Arthur and Mary (Clark) Upshur, who had a grant of three thousand acres of land.

Their daughter, *Susannah Upshur,* married JOHN TEACKLE.

Their son, *Thomas Teackle II.,* married *Elizabeth Custis.*

CUSTIS

In Rotterdam, Germany, in the middle of the seventeenth century, lived John Custis and his wife Ioane. Of their seven children, four came to America, viz.: Ann, John, William, Joseph. Ann came to Virginia as the wife of COLONEL ARGALL YEARDLEY, and her three brothers followed. The elder:

25 Northampton Co. *Recs.* Vol. iii, p. 102; Vol. iv, p. 86.
   Virginia Carolrum.
26 *Northampton Co. Recs.* Vol. V, p. 86.
27 Northampton Co. *Recs.* Vol. Vii, p. 69, May 29, 1656.

MAJOR-GENERAL JOHN CUSTIS II. (1630-1696), called "of Arlington," was Surveyor-General of Virginia 1662; Major-General of Militia 1675, and a member of the Council the same year.[28] The inscription on his tombstone at "Arlington," near Cape Charles, Northampton County, on the eastern shore of Virginia (from which place "Arlington" on the Potomac derived its name), reads as follows:

CUSTIS

Here lies the Body of
JOHN CUSTIS, ESQ., one of the
Councill and Major Genarall of
Virginia who departed this life ye
29th of January 1696 aged 66 years
And by his side a son and daugter
Of his Grandson John Custis whom
He had by the daughter of
Daniel Parke Esq. Capt. Generall
And Chief Governor of the Leeward
Islands.
Virtus Post Funera.

He married second, Tabitha (Scarborough) Smart, the widow of William Smart. (She was married four times: First to William Smart, second to —— Brown, third to John Custis II., and fourth to Edward Hill.) Their son:

COLONEL JOHN CUSTIS III., of "Wilsonia" (1653-1713), married first, *Margaret,* the daughter of John and Elizabeth (Thoroughgood) Michael, and second, Sarah Littleton. The inscription on his tombstone reads as follows:

28 Hening's *Statutes;* Northampton Co. *Recs.*

Beneath this Marble Tomb lies ye body
of the Honorable John Custis, Esq.,
of the City of Williamsburg and Parish of Bruton
Formerly of Hungars Parish on the Eastern Shore of
Virginia and the County of Northampton the
place of his nativity.
Aged 71 years and yet lived but seven years
Which was the space of time he kept
A Bachelor's House at Arlington
On the Eastern Shore of Virginia.
This information put on this tomb was by his
own positive order.
Wm. Colley, Mason, in Fenchurch Street
London. Fecit.

A daughter of the first marriage, *Elizabeth Custis,*
married her cousin *Thomas,* the son of Edmund and
Tabitha (Whittington) Custis.

JUDGE JOHN CUSTIS IV., their son, married Ann
Upshur, whose daughter, *Elizabeth,* married *Thomas
Teackle II.*

This second Custis line was descended from another
son of John and Ioane Custis, of Rotterdam, Ger.,
viz.: Thomas Custis of Baltimore, Ire., whose son:

EDMUND CUSTIS, married Tabitha, the daughter of
William and Tabitha (Smart) Whittington, their son
Thomas Custis, marrying his cousin *Elizabeth,* Colonel
John Custis' daughter. They thus united two of the
American Custis' lines in their son, JUDGE JOHN CUS-
TIS IV., whose daughter *Elizabeth* married *Thomas
Teackle II.*

THOROUGHGOOD-MICHAEL

CAPTAIN ADAM THOROUGHGOOD (1603-1640), was
the son of William and Ann (Edwards) Thoroughgood of Norfolk, County, Eng., and brother of Sir
John Thoroughgood of Kensington. He married, at
St. Anne's, Blackfriars, London, July 18, 1627, Sarah,
the daughter of Robert and Anne (Osborne) Offley.
Sarah Offley was baptized at St. Benet's, London,

April 16, 1609, and died in Virginia, 1675. She married second, Captain John Gooking, and upon his decease she married Colonel Francis Yeardley; but had no issue by second or third marriages. Adam Thoroughgood was Burgess for Elizabeth City County, 1629 to 1632, and a member of the Council of Virginia, and Presiding Justice, in 1637.[29]

Their daughter, *Elizabeth*, married JOHN MICHAEL, a Commissioner of Northampton County, Va.,[30] and Captain of Militia in Virginia. Among others, they had two daughters: *Sarah*, who married CAPTAIN ARGALL YEARDLEY, and *Margaret*, who married COLONEL JOHN CUSTIS III.

OFFLEY

ARMS: *Argent on a cross pattée flory azure, a lion passant or, between four Cornish choughs ppr., beaks and legs, gules.*

CREST: *A demi-lion rampant, per pale or and sable collared gules, holding in his paw an olive branch stalked and leaved vert, fructed or.*

In Stafford, Eng., lived John Offley and Margery, his wife, who were the parents of William Offley, twice Mayor of Stafford, who removed to Chester and was alderman of that city, 1517. He had issue by two marriages. His second wife was Elizabeth, the daughter of William Rogerson (who died 1519), an alderman of Chester. He had seven children.

OFFLEY

The eldest child, Robert Offley, removed to London and established himself in Grace-church street as a Mer-

[29] Hening's *Statutes*, Vol. I, pp. 149-187.
[30] *Recs.* of Accomac Co. Vol. IX, p. 3.

MARY SLOAN
Wife of Judge William Frick

JUDGE WILLIAM FRICK

PETER FRICK

BARBARA BREIDENHART
Wife of Peter Frick

chant of the Staple. He was the executor of his half-brother, Sir Thomas Offley, Knt. Robert was buried April 29, 1596, and his wife, the widow of Nicholas Rose, of London, was buried October 8, 1572.

Their eldest son, Robert Offley, was a Turkey Merchant, residing in Grace-church street. He married, February 3, 1588-89, Anne, the daughter of Sir Edward Osborne, Knt., who died 1591, Lord Mayor of London, 1583, and of Anne, his wife, the daughter of Sir William Hewitt, Knt., also Lord Mayor of London. Anne Osborne's brother, Sir Hewitt Osborne, was the grandfather of the first Duke of Leeds. She was baptized March 25, 1570, and was buried, January 14, 1653-54, and her husband, Robert Offley, was buried May 16, 1625. They had six sons and as many daughters.

One of the daughters, Sarah Offley, married CAPTAIN ADAM THOROUGHGOOD, and their daughter *Elizabeth*, married CAPTAIN JOHN MICHAEL, whose daughters, *Sarah* and *Margaret*, by their marriages, connected the Thoroughgood and Michael families with those of Yeardley and Custis.

WHITTINGTON-SMART

CAPTAIN WILLIAM WHITTINGTON, was a member of the board of County Commissioners 1654, Northampton County, Va., and Captain of the Militia the same year.[31] He was Judge of the Orphan's Court of Northampton County, 1655. His wife was Elizabeth Weston. Their second son:

LIEUTENANT-COLONEL WILLIAM WHITTINGTON, was a Major of Militia of Accomac County, Va., 1693,

31 County *Recs.* Vol. II, p. 84, 94; 1692-1715, p. 431; Vol. III, p. 223. *Arch.* of Md. Vol. XX, p. 138.

and Lieutenant-Colonel, 1711. He married *Tabitha,* the daughter of William and Tabitha (Scarborough) Smart, and their daughter *Tabitha,* married EDMUND CUSTIS.

The colonist, William Smart, was born in Bristol, Eng., and his wife was *Tabitha,* the daughter of Colonel Edmund and Mary (Charlton) Scarborough.[32]

FRICK

ARMS: *Argent, a tree in three tiers vert, terraced of the same.*
CREST: *A garb or, two doves argent.*

A Huguenot refugee from the Palatinate, John Conrad Frick, sailed with his wife, Barbara Enten, from Rotterdam in the ship *Pennsylvania,* landed in Philadelphia September 11, 1732, and became one of the original settlers and founders of Germantown, Penn.

Their son, Peter Frick, born in Germantown, November 9, 1743, moved to Baltimore town during the heat of the Revolution, and soon took an active part in its affairs. In 1797, agreeably to an Act of Assembly incorporating the city of Baltimore, an election was held by the inhabitants for the purpose of electing councilmen and Mayor. At this election Mr. Frick was elected to represent the fourth ward of the city. He married Barbara, the daughter of Doctor John Christopher Breidenhart.

Their second son, William Frick, was born in Baltimore November 2, 1790. His first public position after several years' successful practice of the law in the Courts of Maryland, was as State Senator from Baltimore City, that being succeeded by the office of Collec-

32 Northampton County Recs. Vol. IV, p. 152.
Accomac County, Va. *Recs.,* 1682-1715.

WILLIAM FREDERICK FRICK

ANNE ELIZABETH SWAN
Wife of William Frederick Frick

tor of the Port for the District of Maryland, by appointment of the President, Andrew Jackson, in 1837. He was subsequently appointed Judge of the Baltimore County Courts, by ex-Governor Francis Thomas, which place he held until he was chosen by his fellow-citizens as the first Judge of the Superior Court of Baltimore City, and this post he honorably filled until his death in 1855. He married in 1816, Mary, the daughter of James Sloan, a merchant of Baltimore City.

SLOAN

ARMS: *Gules, a sword in pale point downwards, blade argent, hilt or, between two boars' heads, couped at the neck of the third. On a chief erminois a lion's passant of the first, between two mascles, sable.*

CREST: *A lion's head erased or.*

The eldest son of William and Mary (Sloan) Frick, William Frederick Frick, was born in 1817. He married, February 10, 1848, *Anne Elizabeth,* the daughter of James and Elizabeth (Donnell) Swan. Their children were: James Swan, MARY SLOAN and Elizabeth Donnell. (See Swan Continued.)

KEY

PHILIP KEY was a member of the Lower House of Assembly for St. Mary's County, 1728 to 1732, 1735 to 1738, 1745 and 1754, and a member of its Council 1763 to 1764.[33] His wife was Susannah, daughter of John Gardiner and his wife Mary Boarman. John Gardiner was the son of Richard Gardiner, Judge of the Circuit Court for St. Mary's County, 1681, and Elizabeth Weire his wife, daughter of Major John Weire.[34] Richard Gardiner was the son of Luke Gardiner, and was Captain of the Militia of Maryland 1674.[35] Mary Boarman was the daughter of William Boarman, Major of Militia of Maryland, and Justice of the Circuit Court for St. Mary's County 1681, who married Mary, daughter of John Jarboe, Lieutenant-Colonel of Militia 1670.[36]

FRANCIS KEY, son of Philip, was a member of the Lower House of Assembly of Maryland, 1753. He married Ann Arnold, the daughter of John and Alicia (Arnold) Ross. John Ross was the son of Henry and Jane Ross, and his wife, Alicia, was the daughter of Michael and Ann (Knippe) Arnold.

JOHN ROSS KEY, son of Francis, was second Lieutenant of the Rifle Battalion of Maryland Troops, which formed part of General Lafayette's command at Yorktown, when Lord Cornwallis surrendered.[37] He married Ann Phoebe Dagworthy Charlton.

[33] Book of *Col. Wars*, p. 148.
　　Arch. of Md., Vol. XIV, p. 107, etc.
[34]*Arch.* of Md. Vol. XVII, p. 379.
　　Hening's *Statutes*, pp. 55, 250.
[35] *Arch.* of Md. 1660-75, p. 514.
[36] *Ibid*, Vol. XVII, p. 379; 1661-73, p. 504.
[37] Schaff's *Hist.* of Md.
　　Book of *Col. Wars*, p. 40.

FRANCIS KEY

JOHN ROSS

HON. JOHN TAYLOE I

ELIZABETH GWYN
Wife of John Tayloe I

FRANCIS SCOTT KEY, their son, the author of "The Star Spangled Banner,"[38] lived in Georgetown, D. C., in 1814, and practiced law before the Supreme Court, the Courts of Maryland, and the District of Columbia. When the British troops retired from Washington, a squadron of their ships, the fleet then lying at the mouth of the Potomac River, went up the river as far as Alexandria, compelled the place to surrender and plundered it of tobacco and of whatever they wished. Returning to their ships, the army passed through Upper Marlboro, and encamped some miles below the town. At midnight a detachment of troops was sent back there to the house of Doctor Beanes, a prominent physician of the place and an intimate friend of Francis Scott Key, took him prisoner and hurried him to the British camp. Hastening to Georgetown, some of the Doctor's friends requested Mr. Key to obtain permission of the Government to go under a flag of truce to the Admiral's ship and seek the release of Doctor Beanes before the fleet sailed. This mission was readily undertaken; the President promptly gave his sanction, and ordered a vessel to be made ready without delay, and also directed that John S. Skinner, agent for the Government for flags of truce and exchange of prisoners, should accompany Mr. Key. They found the British fleet at the mouth of the Potomac preparing for an expedition against Baltimore.

After considerable negotiation the release of Doctor Beanes was effected. Mr. Key was informed, however, that none of the party would be allowed to leave the fleet for some days, until the attack on Baltimore was over. He and Mr. Skinner were then transferred

[38] See volume of Key's *Poem,* with introductory chapter by Chief-Justice Taney, of the Supreme Court of the United States.

to the British frigate *Surprise,* on which vessel they were detained until the fleet reached the Patapsco, and until preparations were completed for landing the troops. They were then transferred to their own vessel and kept under a guard. By chance their boat was anchored in a position which enabled them to see the flag at Fort McHenry. The bombardment soon began and lasted until late into the night. Mr. Key anxiously paced the deck, watching each shell, for while the bombardment continued it was proof that the fort had not surrendered. Suddenly, before daylight, the firing ceased, and his suspense and anxiety was intense, waiting for the coming day. When light did come, he saw to his great delight that " Our flag was still there." When the British troops had reëmbarked he and Mr. Skinner were permitted to return to Baltimore.

During the bombardment, he made notes of the poem on the back of an old letter that happened to be in his pocket. On reaching his hotel in Baltimore, he wrote it out as it now stands. In less than an hour after it was placed in the printer's hands, the poem was being universally read, and took the place of a national song.[39]

FRANCIS SCOTT KEY married *Mary Tayloe,* the daughter of Edward and Elizabeth (Tayloe) Lloyd.

PHILIP BARTON KEY, their son, married *Ellen,* the daughter of James and Elizabeth (Donnell) Swan. Children: *Elizabeth Swan,* and MARY. (See Swan Continued.)

LLOYD

EDWARD LLOYD I., of Wye House, was born in Wales, and came to America, where he resided in Vir-

[39] Schaff's *Hist. of Md.*

"WYE HOUSE," TALBOT CO., MD.
The homestead of the Lloyd family

"MT. AIRY," RICHMOND CO., VA.
The homestead of the Tayloe family

ginia, from 1637 to 1649, and in Maryland from 1649 until 1668, when he returned to London, and died there 1695.[40] He was Burgess in the Virginia Assembly from 1637 to 1649, and appointed Commander of the Militia of Anne Arundel County, Md., by Governor Stone, July 30, 1650, and on the 29th of the same month was commissioned to grant patents for land. September 26, 1651, he was made Councillor of the Commonwealth of England; 1658 to 1666, a member of the Upper House of Assembly of Maryland; a Justice of the Peace for Talbot County, 1663, in which capacity he continued to act until his return to England in 1668.[41] He married Alice Crouch. Their son:

PHILEMON LLOYD was elected a member of the House of Delegates of Maryland, and made Speaker, holding that position from 1671 to 1674; was first Captain and then Colonel of Militia from 1671 to 1685. He married *Henrietta Maria,* the daughter of JAMES NEALE[42] (and his wife Ann Gill), and the widow of —— Bennett. She was Maid of Honor to Queen Henrietta Maria. (See pp. 548-549 for Neale line.) Their son:

GOVERNOR EDWARD LLOYD II., was born at Wye House, February 7, 1670, and resided in Maryland until his death, March 20, 1718, at Wye House, where he is buried. He was commissioned January 16, 1697 by Sir Francis Nicholson, (one of the Royal Gover-

[40] Hening's *Statutes,* at large.
[41] Hening's *1st Statutes.*
   Bazman's *Hist. of Md.*
   Biog. Enc. Hist. of Md. & Dist. of Col.
   McMahon's *Hist. of Md.*
   Annals of Annapolis.
[42] *Arch. of Md.*
   1st Hening's *Statutes,* pp. 286, 289.
   Arch. of Md., Vol. I, p. 441; Vol. II, pp. 10, 124, 126.

nors), as "One of the worshipful Commissioners and
Justices of the Peace," and made one of the Quorum,
which position he retained until August 19, 1701. A
member of the Upper House of Assembly January
11, 1698; President of the Council 1701; A member of
the Governor's Council 1702, and Royal Governor of
Maryland 1701 to 1704, and 1709 to 1714.[43] He married Sarah, the daughter of Nehemier and Rebecca
(Denwood) Covington.

EDWARD LLOYD III., their son, was born May 8,
1711, and resided in Maryland until January 27, 1770,
when he died. He is buried at Wye House. He was
a member of the Lower House of the General Assembly of Maryland, December 15, 1737, and continued
a member until 1740; was Councillor of the State of
the Commonwealth of England for thirty-two years.
The *Harrison Papers* say:

"To relate the parts taken by the Honorable Colonel Edward Lloyd (III. of the Wye House), in the
public affairs of the colony from the time he entered
the House of Delegates until he resigned his seat as
Councillor on account of ill health, would be to relate
the history of Maryland for thirty-two years."

He was one of the originally appointed Commissioners on the part of Maryland to decide the boundary
line between Maryland and Pennsylvania. The Commissioners met at New Castle November 19, 1760, for
the beginning of their operations.[44] He married *Ann,*
the daughter of John and Barbara (Morgan) Rousby.

EDWARD LLOYD IV., their son, was a member of the

---

[43] McMahon's *Hist. of Md.*
Harrison *Papers.*
[44] McMahon's *Hist. of Md.*
Bazman's *Hist. of Md.*
Annals of Annapolis.

Maryland Assembly 1771 to 1791.[45] He married
Elizabeth, the daughter of John and Rebecca (Plater)
Tayloe, and their daughter, *Mary Tayloe,* married
FRANCIS SCOTT KEY.

ROUSBY

JOHN ROUSBY was born in England, and emigrated
to America, living at Rousby Hall from 1650 to 1685,
when he died. He was Clerk of the Upper House of
Assembly March 27, 1671, and again October 27, 1671;
also member of the Lower House from 1681 to 1683.[46]
He married Barbara, the daughter of Judge Henry
Morgan.

Their daughter *Ann,* married EDWARD LLOYD III.
In 1645 Judge Henry Morgan came to America from
England and lived in Maryland until his death. He was
High Sheriff of Kent County 1648; one of the County
Commissioners 1654; Judge of the County Court 1650
to 1656;[47] Burgess for Lancaster County 1658 to 1659,
and a member of the Council 1663 to 1667.

BROOKE-ADDISON-PLATER

GOVERNOR ROBERT BROOKE (1602-1655), the colonist
of 1650, was Acting-Governor of Maryland, 1652.
(See pp. 553-554.) He married first Mary, the daughter
of Thomas Baker, Esq., and second, Mary, the daughter of Roger Mainwaring, Bishop of St. David's Eng.

MAJOR THOMAS BROOKE, (1632-1676), a son of the
first marriage, was a member of the Legislature from
Calvert County, 1663-1676, and High Sheriff, 1666-

45 *Arch.* of Md.
46 *Arch.* of Md. Vol. VII, pp. 154, 611.
47 *Old Kent.*

1673.[48]　He married *Eleanor,* the daughter of Richard Hatton, and Margaret, his wife.

Colonel Thomas Brooke (1660-1730), their son,
was a member of the Council 1691 to 1707, and Acting-Governor in 1720.[49]　He married *Barbara* (1676-
1754), the daughter of Thomas Dent, a Burgess from
St. Mary's County 1669 to 1674.! Their daughter,
Eleanor, married Captain Thomas Tasker, a member of
the Maryland Legislature 1692.

One of their daughters, *Elizabeth Tasker,* married
Colonel Thomas Addison.　He was the son of Colo-
nel John Addison.[50]　(See pp. 671-672 for Addison-
Tasker lines.)

One of the daughters of this marriage, *Rebecca Addison,* married first, —— Bowles, and second, George
Plater II.

George Plater I., married Ann, the daughter of
Thomas Burford, one of the Justices of Charles
County Court, and a member of the Quorum, 1681.[51]
Their son:

George Plater II., was a member of the Council
of Maryland, 1732.　He married *Rebecca Addison,*
and their daughter, *Rebecca Plater,* married John
Tayloe II.

TAYLOE

One of the Burgesses of Virginia in 1710, was William Tayloe, who married Ann, the daughter of Henry
Corbin, who was a member of the Virginia House of
Burgesses 1658 to 1659, and one of the Council from
1663 to 1667.[52]

[48] *Arch.* of Md.
[49] *Ibid.* Vol. XX.
[50] *Ibid,* Vol. XX, p. 15 and 16.
　Life and Times of Col. Dulany Addison.
[51] Arch of Md. 1681, p. 30.
[52] Hayden, p. 86.

Hon. Henry Corbin

Elizabeth Tayloe
Wife of Hon. Richard Corbin

JOHN TAYLOE, son of William, was a member of the Council of Virginia, 1756. He married *Elizabeth (Gwyn) Lyde,* the daughter of MAJOR HUGH GWYN, of Essex County, and Catherine Griffith his wife. Major Gwyn was a Justice and County Commissioner in 1699, and a Burgess of Richmond County, 1712. He was the son of Hugh Gwyn, a Justice of York County 1641, and of Gloucester County 1652.[53]

JOHN TAYLOE II., the son of John I., was a member of the House of Burgesses of Virginia 1774. He married *Rebecca,* the daughter of George and Rebecca (Addison) Bowles Plater, and their daughter *Elizabeth,* married EDWARD LLOYD IV.

DOBBIN

On account of political troubles in Ireland, George Dobbin, of Monagan, Ire., came to America in the latter part of the eighteenth century. He was the son of Archibald Dobbin (Archibald, Robert). He married in Ireland, Mary Commings, September 25, 1759, and died in Baltimore, May 19, 1808.

Their son, George W. Dobbin, practiced law in Maryland and before the United States Supreme Court until 1867, when he was elected one of the Judges of the Supreme Bench of Baltimore City. He died in 1891. His wife was *Rebecca,* the daughter of Edward and Sarah (Rutter) Pue. (Rebecca Pue was descended from the Hill, Denwood and Dorsey families.)

Their son *Robert A. Dobbin,* was born March 17, 1839. He attended school in Baltimore, and later went to the University of Virginia, remaining until the beginning of the war between the states. In 1862,

[53] *Ibid.*

he joined the Confederate army, and was a private in Company A, of the 3d Virginia regiment of Local Defense Troops, commanded by General Custis Lee. In February, 1870, he married *Elizabeth Swan*, the daughter of Philip Barton and Ellen (Swan) Key. Their daughter is ELLEN SWAN DOBBIN, who married, in 1901, Frederick Hoppin Howland, of Providence, R. I.

HILL-DENWOOD-DORSEY

CAPTAIN RICHARD HILL, had emigrated to America before August 12, 1673, for on that date a patent of one hundred and fifty acres was issued to him. He was a Naval Officer for Anne Arundel Town, 1694 to 1696.[54]

His son, *Henry Hill*, married *Mary*, granddaughter of LEVIN DENWOOD. Their daughter, *Priscilla*, was born May 9, 1718, and married, February 10, 1735, *Caleb Dorsey II*, born July 18, 1710, and descended from COLONEL JOHN DORSEY. See pp. 149, 150, 250, 251.)

Their daughter, *Mary Dorsey*, married Dr. Michael Pue, whose son *Edward*, married *Sarah Rutter*.

PUE-RUTTER

In 1770, Dr. Michael Pue, an Irish physician, came to America, and practiced his profession in and around Baltimore, dying in 1799. He married *Mary*, the daughter of Caleb and Priscilla (Hill) Dorsey.

Their son, *Edward Pue*, married *Sarah*, the daughter of *Solomon*, and the granddaughter of LIEUTENANT THOMAS RUTTER, who was of the Baltimore County Battalion of Infantry. Their daughter, *Re-*

[54] *Arch.* of Md. Vol. II, pp. 407, 448, 485.

becca, married George W. Dobbin, whose son *Robert A.,* married *Elizabeth Swan Key.*

SWAN *(Continued)*

A daughter of James and Elizabeth (Donnell) Swan, *Anne Elizabeth Swan,* married, February 10, 1848, William, the son of William and Mary (Sloan) Frick. Children:

James, married Elise Dana, of Boston.

MARY SLOAN, married first, Robert Garrett, President of the Baltimore & Ohio Railroad Company; second, Dr. Henry Barton Jacobs.

Elizabeth Donnell, married Frank Foster, an Englishman.

Another daughter of James and Elizabeth (Donnell) Swan, *Ellen Swan,* married PHILIP BARTON KEY. Children:

MARY, married William Gilmor (deceased).

Elizabeth Swan, married *Robert A. Dobbin;* their daughter is ELLEN SWAN, wife of Frederick Hoppin Howland.

MARY SLOAN FRICK JACOBS,

MARY KEY GILMOR,

ELLEN SWAN DOBBIN HOWLAND,

JOSEPHINE GILMOR HARVEY,

Members of Chapter I., The Colonial Dames of America.

XXIII

WOODBRIDGE

REV. JOHN WOODBRIDGE II. (1613-1691), of Oxford and Newbury, Mass., the son of Rev. John (died 1637) and Sarah (Parker) Woodbridge, of Stanton, Eng., was elected Deputy from Newbury to the General Court of Massachusetts 1637, 1638, 1640, 1641; Associate Magistrate, County Court of Essex, 1678 to 1679.[1]   He was Chaplain to the Parliamentary Commission treating with King Charles I. at Carisbrooke Castle, Isle of Wight, 1647.   He married, 1639, *Mercy,* the daughter of GOVERNOR THOMAS DUDLEY (1576-1653[2]), the son of Captain Roger Dudley. (See pp. 214, 266-269.)

Their son, *Rev. Benjamin Woodbridge,* married *Mary,* the daughter of John, and the granddaughter of Rev. Nathaniel Ward.

Their son, *Rev. Samuel Woodbridge,* married, in 1707, *Mabel,* the daughter of Rev. Daniel and Mabel (Wyllys) Russell.

WYLLYS

GOVERNOR GEORGE WYLLYS (1590-1644) was the son of Richard Wyllys, born in the town of Fenny Compton, Warwickshire, England.   His biographer says:

" Famed for his social and domestic virtues, his simplicity and his love for civil and religious liberty, a distinguished Englishman of means, he had abundance of

[1] *Reg. Conn. Soc. Col. Dames.*
[2] Appleton's *Cyclopaedia Am. Biog.*
  Geneal. Dict. of N. E.

HOME OF GOV. GEORGE WYLLYS, HARTFORD, CONN.
Showing the historic Charter Oak

MABEL HARLEKENDEN
Wife of Gov. John Haynes

ARMS OF GOV. GEORGE WYLLYS
Hartford, Conn.

time to notice the trend of public affairs, and becoming interested in the Puritan cause he decided to leave England and to settle amongst the Puritan Colony in America. In 1636 he sent his steward, William Gibbons, with twenty men to find an estate in Hartford, Conn., and to erect a suitable mansion for himself and family. This was situated on an eminence overlooking the 'Greate River' (Connecticut), and laid out with flowers, ornamental shrubberies, a miniature lake and orchards planted with imported fruit trees. Here lived successive generations of distinguished patriots, and their unbroken line of honorable public service is an example of ability and loyalty that Connecticut may well be proud of."

It was not until two years later that Wyllys himself came to Hartford. One of the original planters of the town, it was on his farm that the famous " Charter Oak " stood, spared, as the legend goes, by the entreaties of a party of Indians when " Gibbons " would have it cut down. George Wyllys was chosen magistrate 1639 and held the position until his death; Deputy-Governor 1641 and Governor 1642. He married Mary Smith. Their son:

SAMUEL WYLLYS, was born in England 1632, and died 1709. He was graduated from Harvard College 1653; was elected one of the Magistrates of Connecticut 1654 under the charter of Charles II. In this office and the corresponding one of Assistant Governor, he was retained by annual election for more than thirty years. The office of Secretary of State was filled by his son, Hezekiah, grandson George II., and great-grandson Samuel Wyllys II.[3] I. W. Stuart remarks, in his " Lives of the Early Governors of Connecticut ":

3 *Register of Conn. Society, C. D. A.*

"It is believed that this instance of the perpetuation of high office in the same family for so long a term of years (nearly a century) is without parallel in this country.

He married, 1654, *Ruth,* the daughter of John and Mabel (Harlakenden) Haynes, and their daughter, *Mabel,* married Rev. Daniel Russell, whose daughter, *Mabel,* married *Rev. Samuel Woodbridge.*

HAYNES

GOVERNOR JOHN HAYNES, of Copford Hall, Essex, Eng. (1594-1653), emigrated to Massachusetts 1633, and was made Governor of the Bay Colony 1635. In 1636 he removed to Connecticut, and became its first Governor 1639, serving every alternate year until his death.[4] On the Haynes memorial gateway at the old burying ground, Hartford, are two tablets. One records in usual form the birth and death of John Haynes, first Governor of the Colony of Connecticut, and the other bears the following tribute:

"John Haynes, one of the three illustrous Framers of the first written Constitution creating a government upon which were based the principles of American constitutional liberty.[5]

His second wife was Mabel, the daughter of Richard Harlakenden of Earlscomb Priory, Essex, Eng., "whose descent from the whole line of English Norman kings is well known to genealogists." Their daughter, *Ruth,* married SAMUEL WYLLYS, whose daughter, *Mabel,* married Rev. Daniel Russell, and their daughter *Mabel,* married *Rev. Samuel Woodbridge.*

[4] Appleton's *Cycl. Am. Biog.; Gen. Dict.* of N. E.
[5] *Reg. Conn. Soc. Col. Dames.*

WOODBRIDGE (*Continued*)

The son of Rev. Samuel and Mabel (Russell) Woodbridge, *Russell Woodbridge,* married, in 1741, Anna Olmsted, whose son *Deodatus,* married, in 1780, *Esther Wells.*

WELLS, OR WELLES

THOMAS WELLS (1598-1660), the son of Thomas, (a zealous Puritan of London, Eng.), was born in England. He came to this country before 1638, and settled in Hartford,[6] Conn., where he was a Magistrate from 1637 until his death. He was Treasurer of the Connecticut Colony 1639 to 1651; Secretary 1646 to 1648; Moderator of the General Court 1654, and Deputy-Governor the same year; was elected Governor 1655, and again 1658. A writer says:

" Many of the most important early laws and papers pertaining to the founding of the Colony were drafted by Governor Welles," and he also states that he " possessed the full confidence of the people."[7]

Historians do not agree as to the exact spot where Governor Welles was buried, but one of the best authorities says that he lies " in the rear of the Meeting House in Wethersfield, where the Welles family for many generations are buried." He married Elizabeth Street. They are connected with the Woodbridge family as follows:

Thomas Wells, Jr., married Hannah Little.

Samuel, married Ruth Judson.

Captain Samuel, married Esther Ellsworth.

Colonel Jonathan, married Esther Hills.

Esther, married *Deodatus Woodbridge,* whose daughter was *Electra.*

6 Appleton's *Cycl. Am. Biog.,* etc.
7 *Family Recs.*

WOODBRIDGE (*Continued*)

The daughter of Deodatus and Esther (Wells) Woodbridge, *Electra Woodbridge,* married George Cheney.

Their son, *George Wells Cheney,* married Mary Cheney, and their daughter, *Mary E.,* married John Henry Platt, whose daughter, ELIZABETH, married Francis M. Jencks.

ELIZABETH PLATT JENCKS,

Member of Chapter I., The Colonial Dames of America.

XXIV
JOHNSTONE

ARMS:[1] *Argent, a saltire sable; on a chief gules, three cushions or.*
CREST: *A winged spur or.*
MOTTO: *Nunquam non paratus.*

ARCHIBALD JOHNSTON, the first of his family in this country of whom we have record, came to America before 1734 and obtained many grants of land in South Carolina, one of these being one thousand acres in Prince George's Winyah, March 27, 1756.[2] The *South Carolina Gazette*, 1763, notices his death, stating that as a planter of indigo he was "one of the first best and most considerable" in the Province. He was appointed by special act of the Legislature one of the Commissioners of Roads in the Peedee and Waccamaw regions, 1756,[3] and was attorney for Sir Nathaniel Tragagle, 1760, as shown by an old deed signed by the latter. He married

[1] Arms used by William Johnston, born 1776.
[2] *Book of Grants* in State House, Columbia, S. C.
[3] *Stats. of S. C.*, p. 182.

Esther, daughter of William Alston and Esther La
Bruce de Marboeuf (Huguenot), and died December
13, 1763, leaving issue: ANDREW, William, Esther, and
Archibald.

ALSTON

The founder of this South Carolina family, John
Alston, the ancestor of a long line of lawyers and
statesmen, was the son of William Alston, Gentleman, of Hammersmith, Middlesex,
Eng., and came to America in 1682.
He had grants of land,[4] 1734, 1736,
1739, 1769, in Colleton County.[5]
Among the descendants of John
Alston are, Governor R. F. W. Alston; Governor Joseph Alston, who
married Theodosia Burr; the artist,
Washington Alston; Captain Joseph Blythe Alston, of the Confederate army, lawyer, poet, and war-
rior; and others, whose names are prominent in the
history of the nation. He married, 1695, Elizabeth
(Turgis) Harris, the sister of Francis Turgis, Esq., of
Ringwood, Hampshire, Eng., who was a Member
of the Carolina Commons House of Assembly,
1695.

ALSTON

Their eldest son, William Alston, who died 1744,
married, in June, 1721, the beautiful Esther Margaret
(born October 12, 1702), daughter of Dr. Joseph La

----

[4] *S. C. Hist. Mag.; Pedigree* from Bible owned by Benjamin Allston,
Esq.

[5] *Book of Grants*, State House, Columbia, S. C., and Colonial *Records of North Carolina*, Vol. iv, p. 767. Land in Edgecomb 1250 acres,
in Chowan 1745, 400 acres.

WILLIAM JOHNSTONE
At the age of 19

ANDREW JOHNSTONE
From a miniature by Charles Fraser

COL. WILLIAM RHETT
From a pastel probably by Henrietta Johnson

JOHN RUTLEDGE

Bruce Marboeuf, son of Julian la Bruce de Marboeuf [6] (Huguenot) and his wife, Esther Robin, of Bretagne, France.

Their daughter Esther, born July 7, 1726, at Waccamaw, her father's plantation in Carolina, was married by Rev. E. C. Keith, to ARCHIBALD JOHNSTON.[7]

JOHNSTONE (Continued)

ANDREW JOHNSTON, born 1748, was the eldest son of Archibald and Esther (Alston) Johnston. May 2, 1770, he received a grant of a thousand acres, Craven County, S. C. His death occurred January 19, 1795, and he appointed in his will, dated February 28, 1792, his "esteemed friend William Washington" (cousin of the President) one of his executors. He married, February 25, 1773, in Charleston, Sarah Elliott, daughter of Robert and Mary (Elliott) McKewn, who was born February 26, 1756, and died July, 1817. Issue:

Esther Ainslee, born September 25, 1774; married R. F. Withers.

William.

Robert McKewn, died aged two years.

Archibald, died in infancy.

The eldest son, *William Johnston,* born September 22, 1776, and died August 9, 1840, married, December 5, 1797, *Anna Maria,* daughter of Hopson and Eliza (Cannon) Pinckney, born November 3, 1778, and died August 25, 1853. They are said to have been the first couple married in this country by a Bishop—

[6] Mrs. E. C. La Bruce of Georgetown, S. C., has among her old papers a grant of land to Joseph P. La Bruce by George II, with seal attached. There was also a grant of 600 acres to the same Joseph, in Waccamaw, June 16, 1733. Also another grant August 25, 1733. Vol. A. A., p. 178, *Book of Grants,* State House, Columbia, S. C.

[7] From *S. C. Hist. Mag.* and *Bible* of McKewn Johnstone, May 20, 1789.

Bishop Robert Smith performing the ceremony and presenting the bride with a ring (a hoop of diamonds) in commemoration of the event. The year of her marriage, Anna Maria Pinckney received a grant of land in South Carolina.[8]   Issue:

Andrew.

Anna Maria, married William Maxwell.

McKewn, married Martha Webb.

Pinckney, married Harriet Pringle.

Francis Withers, married Eleanor Simons.

Emma, married Simon Lucas.

Eliza, unmarried.

McKEWN

The first of the name in Carolina, Robert McKewn, married Elizabeth Lewis, born in Worcestershire, Eng., 1672.

Their son, Robert McKewn II, was born 1698; married Susannah Hackett, a Scotch girl, and died October 1, 1767.

Their son, Robert McKewn III, born November 30, 1726, was appointed one of the Committee for building a new church "to be the Parish Church of St. Pauls."[9]   There is a record of a grant of five hundred and fifty acres to him, Colleton County, S. C., June 20, 1754.[10]   He died December 16, 1764, and in his will, dated December 13, he bequeaths among other things "a wax doll." He married, March 1, 1753, Mary Elliott, born February 28, 1735, and died June 25, 1769; a daughter of Thomas and Susanna (Wright) Elliott of Stono.

---

[8] *State House Recs.*

[9] Dalcho's *Church Hist.*

[10] *State Recs.*, Columbia, S. C., Book vi, p. 7.

Their daughter, Sarah Elliott McKewn, married *Andrew Johnstone.*

The father of Mary (Elliott) McKewn, Thomas Elliott, was born January 15, 1699, and died 1760; his wife, Susannah Wright, was born 1711, and died 1742, and they were married 1727. This marriage was traced through the Wright arms on an old snuff-box, belonging to Thomas Elliott of Stono.

PINCKNEY

ARMS: *Or five lozenges in fesse gules.*
CREST: *Out of a ducal coronet or, a Griffin's Head ppr.*
MOTTO: *Non nobis solum.*

These are the arms of the Pinckneys of Rushall, Wiltshire, Eng., and of the Roger Pinckney family of South Carolina whose line descends from William Pinckney, of Rushall, Wiltshire; born 1519, died 1591, and married Agnes Page.

Their son, William Pinckney II., was born 1552; married Catherine ——.

Their son, William Pinckney III., was born 1591, died 1658; married Joan ——, who died 1672.

Their son, Roger Pinckney, was born 1631, and died 1705; married Barbara ——, who died 1680.

PINCKNEY

Their son, Roger Pinckney II, was born 1664, and died 1730; married Ann ——, who died 1743; both are buried in Sarum Cathedral, Eng.

Their son, Roger Pinckney III, was born 1696; died September 22, 1774; married Anna Maria Loake; they are buried in Peterborough Cathedral, Eng.

The colonist, Roger Pinckney IV, came to America, and was followed by his brother:

HOPSON PINCKNEY,[11] born in England 1749, and died February 4, 1794, was a Deputy from St. Thomas, S. C., 1777.[12] He married second, January 21, 1777, *Elizabeth,* the daughter of Daniel and Martha (Winn) Cannon; born 1752, and died January 13, 1787.

Their daughter, *Anna Maria,* married *William Johnston.*

CANNON

DANIEL CANNON,[13] born July 10, 1726, married first March 8, 1749, Martha Winn. He resided in Charleston for sixty years, and was a Member of the first Provincial Congress of South Carolina 1775, Captain of "Cannon's Volunteers" and one of the signers against the Stamp Act, at the "Liberty Tree," Charleston, 1776. The *Carolina Gazette,* October 7, 1802, contains a lengthy eulogy on Daniel Cannon. He was a Vestryman of St. Philip's church for thirty years and upwards.

His daughter, *Elizabeth,* married HOPSON PINCKNEY.

JOHNSTONE *(Continued)*

The eldest son of William and Anna Maria (Pinck-

[11] This pedigree from William Pinckney, of Rushall, born 1519, to Hopson, born 1749, is taken from the family record of the late Lady Henry Brudenell Bruce, Marchioness of Aylesbury, nèe Georgiana Pinckney, and from papers in possession of the family of Henry Pinckney Walker, Esq., for fifty years Her Majesty's Consul in Charleston, S. C., and whose sister, Sarah, married Judge Winslow of Crake Hall, Eng., whose mother was a Pinckney, Mary, also Lady Roxburgh, both dead. From Mrs. H. P. Walker. Letter dated 1894.

[12] *State House Recs.*

[13] The Cannons were originally from Wales, and their crest was a "Cannon."

ney) Johnston, *Andrew Johnstone,* was born March 17, 1805. He inherited large plantations on the Santee River, South Carolina, his home " Annandale " being the centre of hospitality in that vicinity. He had also a home in the mountains of North Carolina, "Beaumont" near Asheville, and a house on the seashore at South Island. He married first, Sophia Clarkson, issue: one son, William; married, second, Mary Barnwell, daughter of William and Ann Hutchinson (Smith) Elliott, of Beaufort, S. C. She was born August 27, 1824, in the old house at Beaufort, and was married at the age of twenty-four.

"When but fifteen she accompanied her father and older sister Ann, to Philadelphia, where their portraits were painted, in 1839, by Sully then in the zenith of his fame, who had just completed a picture of Queen Victoria. His ' Kit-Kat,' or three-quarter length portrait of Mary Barnwell Elliott, represents a young girl of a distinctly Southern type. Sully had earlier painted the portraits of her father and his two sisters—Mrs. Charles Coatsworth Pinckney, and Miss Mary Elliott —the two latter being in possession of Miss Pinckney, of Charleston, S. C. Mrs. Johnstone died in Baltimore, Md., March 4, 1909." Issue:

William Elliott, married Sarah Lenox Mills.

Annie, died young.

Mary, married Edward Livingston Thompson, of Maryland.

EMMA ELLIOTT.

Frances, married William Dent, of Maryland.

Edith, married Robert Habersham Coleman, of Lebanon, Penn.

ELLIOTT

ARMS: [14] *Azure, a fesse or.*
CREST: *A griffin's head couped, wings endorsed sable.*
MOTTO: *Virtute spernit victa.*

THOMAS ELLIOTT son of Joseph Elliott, who died 1697, came to America with his brothers John and William. He acquired large possessions in Carolina, numerous grants being recorded in the *Book of Grants,* State House, Columbia, and left estates to his children. He was a Member of the Assembly of Carolina 1696, at which time he had grants on the Stono River, and was one of the Governor's Council, 1720, dying 1731. He was twice married, first to *Mary,* the daughter of Gov. ROBERT GIBBES. Issue, first wife:

Thomas.

William.

Joseph.

Ann, married —— Saunders.

Elizabeth, married —— Butler.

Martha, married, March 14, 1726, —— Fairchild.

The second child, *William Elliott,* was born May 31, 1703, and died before 1731, the date of his father's death. He married Elizabeth ——. Issue:

WILLIAM II.

Stephen, died in Jamaica.

Elizabeth, married George Parsons.

Mary, married —— Clay, of Georgia.

WILLIAM ELLIOTT II, was born in Charleston, S. C., and died in Beaufort, S. C., 1774.

[14] From Bookplate of Lt. Col. Barnard Elliott, died 1778. *Letter* of J. B. Heyward.

MARY RUTLEDGE AND HER SON EDWARD
Wife of Roger Moore Smith. From a painting
by Romney

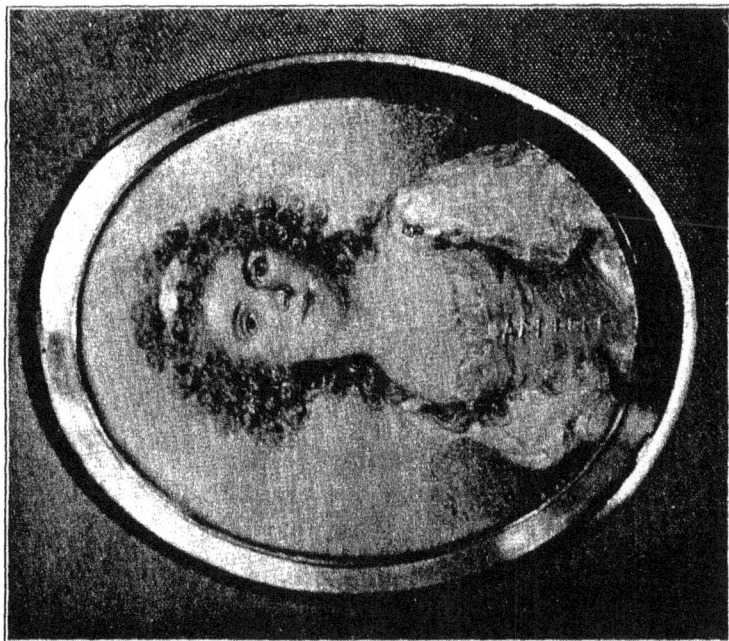

PHOEBE WAIGHT
Wife of William Elliott. Reproduced from a
miniature

He had grants on the Ogeechee River in Georgia 1751, which are still held in the family. Was a Member of the Assembly of Carolina [15] 1739, to fill the place of Nathaniel Barnwell, who went to Ireland for a short time. He married, first, Miss Mulryne, no issue; second, 1760, Mary Gibbes, the daughter of Nathaniel and Mary (Gibbes) Barnwell; born April 11, 1745; third, Mrs. Savage, née Clay, of Georgia. Issue, second wife: *William III.*

Stephen, married Esther Habersham.

Ralph Emms, married Miss Clay, and was the ancestor of the following notable people: Stephen Elliott, Bishop of Georgia; Robert W. Eliott, Bishop of Texas; R. W. Barnwell, Bishop of Alabama; William Boone, Jr., Bishop of China; Rev. John H. Elliott of Washington, a parliamentarian in the Episcopal church; Rev. Stephen Barnwell; Rev. W. H. Barnwell; Gen. Stephen Elliott, Commander of Fort Sumter during the Civil War; Hon. William Elliott, Senator from South Carolina, and many leading men of that State.

The eldest son, *William Elliott III,* was born in Beaufort, S. C., 1761, and died 1808. When very young he fought in the Revolutionary war as an officer, and at the surprise on John's Island was dangerously wounded, taken prisoner and immured in the prison ship *The Pack Horse.* After the war he served in both branches of the State Legislature.[16] He introduced Sea Island cotton in America after the Revolution. He married 1787, *Phoebe,* the daughter of William and Phoebe (Jenkins) Waight, of John's Island, who was born in 1771. Her miniature was painted by Malbone

---

15 *State Recs.* Col., S. C.; *Papers* of Mrs. Frank Hampton, Miss Isabel Johnstone and Miss Elliott.

16 *Dict. of Am. Biog.* Was in the Convention of 1788, St. Helena.

in 1799. She was descended from JOHN LADSON.
Issue:

William IV.

Carolina, married C. C. Pinckney.

Mary.

Ralph, married Miss Mackay.

Stephen, married Miss Habersham; second, the widow Barnwell, née DeSaussure.

George Parsons, married Bower Barnwell.

The eldest son, *William Elliott IV,* was born April 27, 1788, and died in 1863. He was educated at Harvard College, where he formed friendships that withstood all the bitterness of the Civil War, and became a planter, a statesman, owned a fine library and travelled extensively. He represented the United States, as commissioner, at the Paris Expositon of 1855. He was the author of many poems, political articles, and volumes of interest, his *Carolina Sports,* being much read in England as well as in this country. He was Intendant of Beaufort at the time of Lafayette's visit to Carolina (1824), and entertained him. Later he was a member of the State Senate.

May 23, 1817, he married *Anne Hutchinson,* the daughter of Thomas Rhett and Anna Rebecca (Skirving) Smith. She was an heiress, born April 5, 1802, and died February 23, 1877. They passed the summers in Beaufort, and the winters at their plantations. Mrs. Elliott, after her husband's death, lived at her plantation, "Oak Lawn," in Colleton County, until the historic homestead was burned by Sherman, during the Civil War. In William Elliott's will he leaves his "own miniature to daughter Mary, and the miniature of my mother, by Malbone, and bequeathed to me by her, I give to my daughter Anne." Issue:

William, died young.

Thomas Rhett Smith, married Mary Cuthbert.

Anne Hutchinson.

Mary Barnwell, married *Andrew Johnstone.*

William.

Caroline.

Emily.

Ralph Emms.

Harriet Rutledge, married General Ambrose Jose Gongales.

Of the eight heroines of the Revolution, three were Elliotts by birth, viz.: Mrs. Parsons, Mrs. Savage and Mrs. Ferguson; and two by marriage, viz.: Mrs. Charles and Mrs. Barnard Elliott.[17]

The brother of *William Elliott III.,* Ralph Elliott, built a beautiful house at Beaufort, about 1788, leaving it at his death to his eldest nephew, *William Elliott IV.* The northern army, occupying Beaufort after the Civil War, used this old homestead as a Club House, and it was later bought by Admiral Beardsley, of the U. S. Navy, whose widow now occupies it."

LADSON

JOHN LADSON came to Carolina from the Barbadoes 1679, in company with Sir John Yeamans. He was a Member of the Assembly 1683, and concerned in the affairs of the colony from 1691 to 1697. He received a grant of land from the lords proprietors, September 14, 1682. His wife was *Mary,* the daughter of COLONEL JAMES STANYARNE, a member of the Carolina Assembly of 1692, and the Governor's Council of 1693.[18]

Their daughter, *Phoebe Ladson,* (1691-1764), mar-

---

[17] McCrady's *Hist. of S. C.,* Vol. ii, p. 359.
[18] *Journal of Grand Council.*

ried John Chaplin, who had a grant on the Stono River, S. C., 1682.[19]

Their daughter, *Phoebe Chaplin,* (1718-1794), married, 1785, Joseph Jenkins, the son of Joseph Ap Jankin, and Martha, his wife. Joseph Jenkins, the younger, founded the first Episcopal church on Edisto Island, 1760, giving large sums to its establishment. Joseph, Sr., always signed his name "Ap Jankin." His two grants of land called " Sea Cloud," and "Bleak Hall," descended to the Townsends, through their mother, Phoebe Waight Jenkins. (*Mrs. Frank Hampton's Records.*)

A daughter of Joseph, Jr., *Phoebe Jenkins,* (1748-1816), married William Waight.

Their daughter, *Phoebe Waight,* married *William Elliott III.*

BARNWELL

ARMS: *Ermine, a bordure engrailed, gules.*
CREST: *From a plume of five ostrich feathers or, gules, argent, vert and argent, a falcon rising of the last.*
MOTTO: *Malo mori quam foedari.*

" These arms are copied from the seal of Colonel John Barnwell, the emigrant, and are the same as those of the Barnwell family of Crickston, County Meath, Ireland, the parent stock from which the noble houses of Kingsland and Trimklestom branched and which was established in Ireland by Sir Michael de Barnwell, one of the companions in arms of Strongbow." [20]

COLONEL JOHN BARNWELL came to South Carolina

---

[19] *Book of Grants,* State House, Columbia, S. C.

[20] Burke's *Gen'l Armory,* 3d Ed. From *Chart* compiled by B. R. Heyward, and *S. C. Hist. Mag.* These arms are on a silver bowl owned by Miss Elliott.

from Dublin, Ire., 1701. A letter from John Page, Alderman, and subsequently Lord Mayor of Dublin, to John Harleston, in South Carolina, dated Dublin, December 1, 1708, contains the following postscript:

"Cosson, pray in your next let me know wither there will be any such man liveing neare Charlestowne which they call Mr. John Barnwell he went from hence about seven years agon; out of a humor to goe to travel, but for no other reasson, he is the son of a verry good gentleman and Gentlewoman and hath extriordinary friends and Relashons in this Kingdome and therefore let me know [21] how he lives and in what condition."

BARNWELL

The answer to this represents Colonel Barnwell in Carolina, as having taken sides with the Dissenters in the Church Act troubles of 1704, thereby losing many of his offices. He had been Deputy-Secretary of the Colony and Clerk of the Council, and had distinguished himself as a volunteer under Colonel William Rhett against the French and Spaniards. In 1707, however, he was recalled, made Comptroller of the Colony and later became Member of the Commons House of Assembly, Member of the Governor's Council of South Carolina, and a Deputy Surveyor-General. He was "Colonel-Commander" of the first expedition 1712, against the Tuscarora Indians, in North Carolina, and was agent for the Province in London, during the Rev-

[21] From *S. C. Hist. Mag.*

olution of 1719.[22] His commission from King George I. is very complimentary, and his deeds in behalf of his adopted Province of Carolina fill almost an entire volume of the *London State Papers*, 1719 to 1722.[23] Colonel Barnwell married Anne Berners, and died in Beaufort, S. C., in June, 1724, leaving issue:

Margaret, married, first, John Whitmarsh; second, Richard Stephens.

NATHANIEL.

Anne, married four times; first, Thomas Stanyarne, second, Dr. Ambrose Reeve, third, Colonel Thomas Wigg, and fourth, COLONEL JOHN GIBBES.

Mary.

Bridget, married Robert Sams.

Catherine, married Hugh Bryan.

John, was one of the gentlemen volunteers in Oglethorpe's expedition to Florida, 1740; he married Martha Chaplin, and their daughter, Catherine Barnwell, married Andrea de Veaux I. (See De Veaux, etc.)

Elizabeth, married Thomas Tattnall, ancestor of Governor Tattnall of Georgia, and of Commodore Tattnall.

COLONEL NATHANIEL BARNWELL, the eldest son, was born in Charleston, S. C., March 3, 1705. He was named for his father's friend, Sir Nathaniel Johnson, Governor of Carolina, who was also his God-father. During the Spanish Invasion, he was a Colonel, and Aide to General Oglethorpe, in the Florida Expedition of 1740; also a Member of the South Carolina Assembly, from St. Helena, 1739 to 1740, at which date he went to Ireland on family matters. In 1734 he was Judge of Berkely County.[24] He married, April 7,

---

[22] *S. C. Hist. Mag.*
[23] Mrs. Frank Hampton's *Records.*
[24] *State Recs.*, Book 39.

1735, *Mary,* daughter of Colonel John and Mary
(Woodward) Gibbes.[25] Issue:
Nathaniel.
John.
Anne married first, Colonel Thomas Middleton,
second, Colonel Stephen Bull.
Mary Gibbes, married *William Elliott II.*
Nathaniel, John, Robert, Bridget, Robert.
Elizabeth, married, in London, Richard Gough.
Richard, Edward, Robert Gibbes.
Sarah, married James Hazzard Cuthbert.

GIBBES

ARMS: *Shield argent quartered. In first and fourth three Danish
axes sable for Gibbes. In second and third two fusil gules for Champney.*[26]
CREST: *An arm embowed in armour holding a Danish axe.*
MOTTO: *Tenax propositi.*

These are the Arms of the Gibbes of Elmonstone
Court in Kent, England, and of the Gibbes family of
South Carolina, quartered with Champney, whose line
descends from:
Thomas Gybbes, temp Richard II.
John, temp Edward IV.
Jenking, married Ann Eden.
Thomas, married Ann Treuwall.
John, married Margaret Champney.
William, married Jane Gason.
Stephen, married Jane Forney.
The son of Stephen, Robert Gibbes, born November
17, 1594, married February 26, 1630, Mary Coventry,

25 Ped. Ref.: Old *Bible* of Mr. Hampton Gibbes, Columbia; S. C.
Hist. Mag. Hist. Ref.: *S. C. Hist. Mag.;* all *Histories* of the State of
Carolina.
26 From *Chart* prepared by Rev. Robert Wilson of Charleston, S. C.

born 1616.[27]   They removed from Kent to the Barbadoes, 1648, had ten children and soon came to Carolina
with six or seven of them. In the *State Papers*, London, 1692-3, March 1, we find
the following: "Lords, Proprietors to the Governor and Council of Ashley River: John
Gibbes, Esqr., a Kinsman of the
Duke of Albemarle designing
to settle in Carolina every attention and respect is to be
shown him and those accompanying him, three thousand acres of
land granted him rent free."
Issue:

GIBBES

Basil, born 1640.

Thomas, born 1642.

Alice, born 1643; married John Daniel, who became
Governor of the Province.

ROBERT.

Stephen, born 1648.

John, born 1649.

Mary.

Jane, born 1654.

Nicholas, born 1655.

GOVERNOR ROBERT GIBBES, born 1644, and died
1715, held many important positions in the Province
of Carolina and was Governor from 1710 to 1712. He
was Chief-Justice 1709 to 1713; chosen Governor by
the Council 1709 and 1712;[28] in the Assembly from Colleton County, 1671; also high sheriff of Berkeley

[27] *Pedigree* from Gibbes family Bible belonging to Major W. Hampton Gibbes of Columbia, S. C. Johnson in his *Reminiscences* says: "The
name Gibbes belonged to an old distinguished Cavalier family."

[28] McCrady's *Hist. of S. C.*

MARY WOODWARD
Wife of Col. John Gibbes

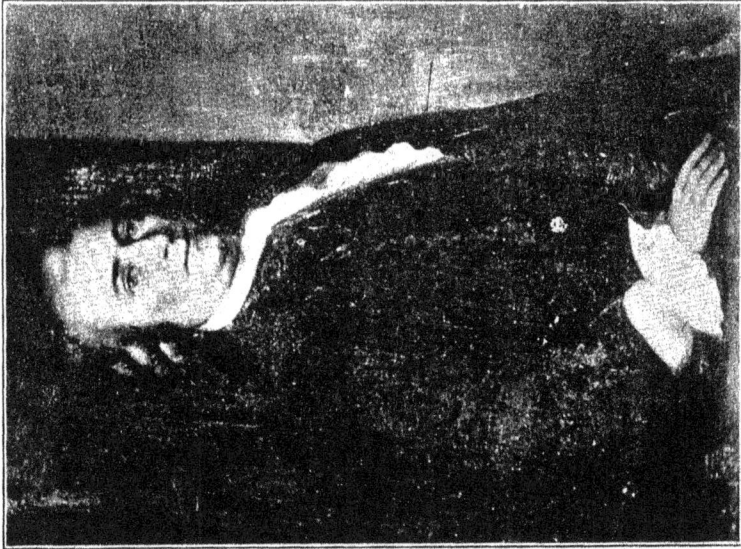

COL. JOHN GIBBES

County, S. C.[29] Robert Gibbes was thrice married;
second to Mary ——,[30] and third, 1710-1711, to Elizabeth (Donne) Neale Godfrey; the daughter of Robert
and Jane Donne, and the widow first, of William Neale
and second, of John Godfrey II.[31]

Robert Gibbes had issue by two wives[32] as follows,
order of birth not known:

Robert.

Mary, married Thomas Elliott.

Issue, second wife:

Elizabeth, married John Fenwick, whose granddaughter, Elizabeth Fenwick, married Henry Scott,
third of Earl of Deloraine.

William, married Alice Culchett. Their third child
was William.

COLONEL JOHN GIBBES was born January 21, 1696,[33]
and died 1764. He had large grants of land on the
Ashley River and is given the title of "Colonel," in all
records. He married in St. Andrew's Church, S. C.,
Mary, daughter of Colonel John and Elizabeth
(Stanyarne) Woodward. Issue:

John, born 1721.

Susannah.

Elizabeth, died young.

Mary, married NATHANIEL BARNWELL.

Elizabeth, married, first, —— Carson; second, John
Ladson.

Sarah.

29 *Journal of the Grand Council of So. Carolina.*

30 Family *Records.*

31 *So. Carolina Genealogies,* by A. S. Salley, Jr., in *The State; Colls.,*
S. C. Hist. Soc.; v. 229; and Probate Court, Charleston, 1751-54, 68.

32 It is evident from the period of Robert Gibbes' third marriage
(1710-11), that Colonel John Gibbes was the son of the second wife.

33 *So. Car. Hist. Mag.* (Dr. Wilson's *Records* say "1664"). Mrs.
Frank Hampton's *Records.*

Anne, married William Ladson.

John, born 1732, married Mary Anne Stevens.

Jane.

Robert, married, first, Ann Stanyarne; second, Sarah Reeve.

WOODWARD

ARMS: *Azure, a pale between two eagles displayed argent.*

DOCTOR HENRY WOODWARD, conspicuous in all histories of South Carolina, was the first English settler of that Colony. He came as Lord Shaftesbury's friend and acted as his Deputy from 1672 to 1677, his name appearing on numberless old records. He made treaties with the Indians, acted as their friend and interpreter, made extended expeditions into the interior of the country, "the Proprietors soon realizing his value and commending the discoveries made by his industries and hazard." He was given a grant of two thousand acres of land.[34]

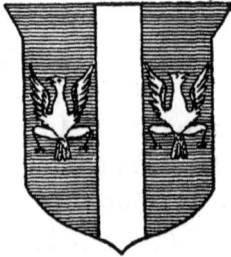

WOODWARD

He married *Mary*, daughter of Colonel John Godfrey and widow of Robert Browne. (After Dr. Woodward's death she married William Davis). Issue:

Richard, married Sarah Stanyarne.

JOHN, married *Elizabeth Stanyarne*.

They were the daughters of COLONEL JAMES STANYARNE, who was a Member of the Carolina Assembly 1671 to 1695, and of the Governor's Council, 1671.[35]

[34] From *Sketch of Dr. Henry Woodward and Some of His Descendants*, by Hon. Joseph W. Barnwell in Vol. viii, S. C. Hist. Mag., p. 29.

[35] *State Papers* in London; *Jour. of the Grand Council of the Prov. of Carolina.*

COLONEL JOHN WOODWARD was a Member of the House of Commons of Carolina, 1706 to 1717, and of the Board of Commissioners 1706 and 1720. He married *Elizabeth,* daughter of Colonel James Stanyarne. Their daughter *Mary,* married JOHN GIBBES.

GODFREY

"The Godfreys are descended from Godfrey de Bouillon. One of the three men appointed by the King of England to lay out the city of Charleston, was William Godfrey, of South Carolina. Another of the family was one of the Deputies for the Proprietors and consequently sat in the Upper House under the Proprietary Government." [36]

Another member of this family, Sir Richard Godfrey, was the father of:

COLONEL JOHN GODFREY, who was among those coming to South Carolina in 1670, "Subsequently to the arrival of the first fleet of settlers." From the time of his arrival, he had shown great interest in the development of the Province.

"He was one of those 'Gentlemen and Merchants of the Island of Barbadoes' who had contributed to the fund raised to send 'William Hilton, Commander, and Commissioner with Captain Anthony Long, and Peter Fabian, in the ship *Adventure,* which set Sayle from Spikes Bay, Aug. 10. 1663,' on a voyage of discovery to the coasts of Carolina. On account of that contribution, the Governor, Sir John Yeamans, of South Carolina, 'by and with the advice and consent of the Councill,' on May 21, 1672, directed John Culpeper, the Suryevor General of South Carolina, 'to cause to be admeasured and layd out for Capt: John Godfrey

[36] Dr. Bullock of the Nat. Genealog. Soc., Washington, D. C.

·five hundred acres of land being the proporcon allowed to him by the lords proprietors, concessions (for his disbursmts in the discovery of this Province by Capt. Hilton)."

"The Governor, Joseph West, and the Council, on April 27, 1675, directed Stephen Wheelewright, a surveyor, to lay out 'For Lieut: Col: Godfrey three hundred acres of land for himselfe, his Wife and one Servt namely John Ferrington arriveing in the yeare 1670 and 1671." At the same time direction was given to John Yeamans, a surveyor, to lay off to him four hundred and forty acres of land ' due him for John Godfrey Junr: Richard Godfrey, selfe, his Wife and one Servt namely Mathew English Thomas Ellis and George 'Jerman arriving in the yeare 1670.'"[37]

"On the *John and Thomas* came Captain Godfrey, who had been a deputy in the Council in Barbadoes, and who went out upon the persuasion of Sir John Yeamans. He took with him five men,—hands—as they were called."[38]

He was soon Captain of Militia, after his arrival, and subsequently became Lieutenant-Colonel of Militia. In 1675, during the absence of Governor West, from June to October, he, as senior Deputy, acted as Governor. He was one of the Deputies of the Proprietors under the government, and was appointed a Deputy for the Duke of Albemarle, under the propriietary government, June 3, 1684.

He married Mary ——. Issue:[39]

John, married Mrs. Elizabeth (Donne) Neale, and died about 1705. He had seven children. His widow married GOVERNOR ROBERT GIBBES, 1710-1711.

[37] *So. Carolina Genealogies*, by A. S. Salley, Jr.
[38] McCrady's *Hist. of So. Carolina*, Vol. i, p. 148 (or 3).
[39] Record given in *So. Carolina Genealogies*, by A. S. Salley, Jr.

Mary, married first, Robert Browne (had a daughter Mary); second, DR. HENRY WOODWARD; third, William Davis.

Richard, had at least one son, John.

Benjamin.

SMITH

ARMS: *Sable, a fesse cottised between three martlets, or.*
CREST: *A greyhound sejant gules collared and lined or.*
MOTTO: *Semper fidelis.*

"Copy of original coat of arms brought from England by Thomas Smith, Landgrave and Governor of Carolina. Same arms were on his ring with date, 1671, and the second Landgrave's will was sealed with this ring."

"THOMAS SMITH, the first Landgrave of that name, was a cousin of the two lords' proprietors, the Duke of Albemarle and the Earl of Bath, all three being descendants of Sir George Smith, the sheriff of County Devon, in 1516. He was not a mere adventurer, but came out to take possession of large estates which he had purchased, and he brought with him ample means to improve them after his arrival." *

SMITH

He was born 1648, and came to America in 1684, with his wife Barbara,[40] two sons Thomas and George, two maids and five men servants. He settled in the Province of Carolina. In a patent dated May 1691,

* From an article by R. R. Heyward in the *Sunday News* of Charleston, S. C., July 10, 1898.
40 *S. C. Hist. Mag.*

he was created Landgrave and four Baronies of forty-
eight thousand acres were granted to him. November
29, 1693, he was made Governor and Commander-in-
chief of·Carolina and died 1694. To him is attributed
the idea of drawing the names of jurors indiscriminately
from a box. He also planted the first rice grown in this
country.

He married second, March 27, 1687, Sabina de
Vignon, Dowager d'Arsens, the widow of John
D'Arsens, Sieur de Vernhaut. No children. His
eldest son, by first wife:

THOMAS SMITH, the second Landgrave, was always
called the "Little Englishman," having been born in
England 1664, and according to the laws of entail received both the title and estates of his father. He made
his mark in the Carolina Assembly, was Speaker 1700,
Judge of Berkeley Court, Member of the Governor's
Council 1693, and held many other offices between 1693
and 1730. He received a grant of five thousand acres
of land November 17, 1730. He married twice and
died May, 1738, being buried on his plantation at Goose
Creek, S. C. Issue, first wife:

Thomas, George, Joseph Blake, Anne, *Sabina,* Rebecca, Rebecca, Justina, Sarah, Barbara.

His fifth child, *Sabina Smith,* was born May 10, 1699,
and married, 1715, THOMAS SMITH III., the son of:

WILLIAM SMITH, who was of the Council of 1695.
He married 1690, *Elizabeth,* the daughter of Bernard
Schencking. She died 1751. Their son:

COLONEL THOMAS SMITH III., was born April 28,
1691, and died March 3, 1724. He was a Major in
the Berkeley County Regiment, S. C., and Lieutenant-
Colonel, 1719 to 1724. He held large grants of land

on Cape Fear River, when eighteen years of age.[41] He married *Sabina Smith,* daughter of the second Landgrave.

Issue, two sons:

The elder, Benjamin, was Speaker of the Commons House of Assembly, 1755 to 1762, and Judge, 1766; married first, Ann, the daughter of William Loughton; and second, Mary Wragg. (See p. 639.)   The second son:

THOMAS SMITH IV., was born November 7, 1719. He was a Member of the South Carolina Assembly 1764, and had a grant of three thousand acres, in Craven County, and a grant on Buffalo River 1763, and one thousand acres in Colleton County, May 25, 1774.[42] Thomas Smith was a wealthy merchant.   In the numerous branches of the family he was called "Long Tom Smith" for distinction, being a tall man.[43]

He married August 2, 1744, *Sarah,* the daughter of Roger and Catherine (Rhett) Moore, who was born September 7, 1728 and died February 14, 1774.   Issue:

ROGER MOORE.

Thomas, Benjamin and William, died young.

Sarah, married first, Chancellor Hugh Rutledge; second, —— Huger.

Peter, married Mary Middleton.

Benjamin, a Major-General and Governor of North Carolina, and on General Washington's staff; married Sarah Dey.

Rhett, died young.

James, married Marianna Gough.

Mary, married John Faucheraud Grimké.

[41] *State Records,* Vol. xxxix, p. 263.
[42] *State House Records,* Columbia, S. C., Vol. B 28, p. 349; Vol. xxx, p. 421.
[43] Johnson in his *Reminiscences.*

Ann, was the second wife of Thomas Bee.

Rhett, died young.

ROGER MOORE SMITH, was born[44] in Charleston August 4, 1745, and died July 29, 1805. He was a member of the first naval board of Carolina and of the Council of Intelligence 1775, and of the First Provincial Congress. He was one of the signers of the old paper money, and lived in handsome style.[45]   Josiah Quincy wrote in enthusiastic terms of the dinner[46] which he attended at Roger Smith's house in Charleston in 1773.

He married, April 7, 1768, *Mary,* daughter of Doctor John and Sarah (Hext) Rutledge. She was born in Charleston December 5, 1747, and was baptized in St. Philip's church there by Rev. Alexander Garden. "On a visit to London in 1786, her lifesize portrait was painted by Romney as a gift to her husband from her father-in-law, who accompanied them to England. In 1888, this beautiful picture (representing Mrs. Roger Smith standing beside a pedestal on which her child, born in London, is seated), was sent from Charleston to England and there sold to the late Duke of Buckingham for £4000. It remained in his gallery until his death, and is owned now by his nephew, Lord Masham." The following list of the children of Roger Moore and Mary (Rutledge) Smith was "Copied from the family Bible owned by Miss Elliott Oak Lawn, Colleton County. Unfortunately the leaves are much torn, many of the dates being lost. . . ."

Thomas Rhett.

[44] "October 4, 1745, Rodger, the son of Thomas and Sarah Smith, was baptized." St. Philip's *Reg.*

[45] Johnson's *Traditions.*

[46] *Records* of Mrs. Hampton; State House *Recs.; S. C. Hist. Mag.; Chart* of B. R. Heyward; *Bibles* of Miss Elliott.

Roger Moore, born August 2, 1770.
Sarah Rutledge, born September 27, 1771.
Mary, born December, 1772.
Caroline, born November 25, 1773.
John Rutledge, born October 17, 1775.
Benjamin Burgh, born October 15, 1776.
Hugh Rutledge, born April 10, 1778.
Andrew Doria, born October 11, 1779.
Infant son.
Mary Sabina, born September 16, 1782.
Edward Nutt, born in London, 1785.
Anna Maria, born July 26, 1785.

The eldest son, *Thomas Rhett Smith,* was born December 20 (or 3) 1768, and died March 28, 1829. He was educated in England. Together with De-Saussure, he led in the movement of forcing South Carolina to establish the Columbia University, and to promote the higher education. He served in the Legislature until 1802; was Intendant of Charleston, during the war of 1812, and lived in that city, and on his plantation, at "Chehaw," where amid his "Ten acres of roses, he found his greatest happiness outside of Paris."

He married, May 28, 1795, *Anna Rebecca,* born in 1778, daughter of Colonel William and Anne Holland (Hutchinson) Skirving. Issue:

William Skirving, Mary, Bethia.
Anne Hutchinson, married *William Elliott IV.*
Thomas Rhett, Caroline and Edward.

SCHENCKING

COLONEL BERNARD SCHENCKING, came from the Barbadoes about 1685, and settled in Carolina, becoming Sheriff of Berkeley County, a Proprietor's Deputy and a Member of the Grand Council. The Lords Proprietors in England wrote to their representatives in America as follows:

"We are alsoe informed that you have put Mr. Schencking out from being Chief Judge or Sheriff of Berkley County and have commissioned Mr. Quary for· the said place . . . We have heard no complaints of Mr. Schencking for injustice or oppression and we think it is not for the King's service or our own honor to have a man turned out of employment who hath behaved himself faithfully therein and it being the Proprietors in general that are responsible to the King for any failure of justice in Carolina, wee have thought fit to exercise to ourselves the power of appointeing Judges or Sheriffs of Countys and have now sent a Commission, under our great seale to Mr. Schencking, to be Chief Judge or Sheriff of Berkley County whom wee require you to permitt quietly to execute that office.
. . .   We rest Yor affectionate Friends, Craven, Palatine, Ashley, Carteret." [47]

In 1687 Bernard Schencking was chosen one of a committee of seven to frame a new code of laws for the colony.[48]   He married Elizabeth ——, and their daughter *Elizabeth,* married, 1690, WILLIAM SMITH, and died 1751.   Their son THOMAS, married *Sabina,* the daughter of THOMAS SMITH II.

SKIRVING

JAMES SKIRVING, ESQ., was the son of William Skirving, of St. Margaret's Westminister, Eng., and was born in Devonshire, Eng., 1715.   He was a surgeon in the British Army, came to America, and was Jus-

[47] River's *Hist. Sketches of So. Car.*
[48] Hewett, pp. 100 and 151.

tice in Colleton County, S. C., 1747.* He had a grant
of one thousand acres of land June 3, 1763, signed by
Governor Bull, and the land is still in possession of the
family. He had also five hundred and eighty acres,
November 5, 1755.[49]

He married, 1744, Mary, daughter of Henry and
Elizabeth Jackson. John Jackson, Mrs. Skirving's
grandfather, was granted in 1700 "The land upon
which was built the town of Jacksonboro,[50] at one time
the seat of the Legislature of South Carolina during
the Revolutionary war."

COLONEL WILLIAM SKIRVING, son of James, was
born 1745, in Charleston. "He owned very large
estates, (eleven plantations in South Carolina), and his
wife, manned with her own negroes, the important ferry
over the Ponpon River by which all the troops, messages
and artillery were transferred during the many years of
the Revolution. Colonel William Skirving left £200
to the Church at Ashepoo for plate, also £500 to his
cousin William Skirving of England. Colonel Skirving's grants of land in 1769 show the very rare signature
of Governor Bull.[51] He and his brother Charles were
commissioned Captains in the First Regiment of Con-
tinentals, the latter being one of Marion's favorite officers. William was Colonel of the American forces
during the Revolution,[52] and was a Member of the second Provincial Congress of South Carolina November
1, 1775, from St. Bartholomews County.[53]

* CREST: "*A stag's head on a wreath,*" *found engraved on forks and
spoons.*

[49] *Papers* of Mrs. Frank Hampton and *Book of Grants*, B. 11, p. 160,
in State House, Columbia, S. C.

[50] Founded by order of the Lords Proprietors in 1711.

[51] Mrs. Frank Hampton's *Papers.*

[52] Moultrie's *Memoirs.*

[53] *S. C. Hist. Mag.*, Vol. vii, p. 105.

He married first, Mary Sacheverell (of the same family as the famous Doctor Henry Sacheverell of Great Britain) and second, January 28, 1769, her cousin *Anne Holland,* daughter of Colonel Thomas and Rebecca (Holman) Hutchinson, born in Charleston 1751, and died 1804. Anne Holland Hutchinson lived in Charleston, on her plantations of Ashepoo and Hutchinson's Island, before her marriage, and afterwards she lived at "Chehaw," in Charleston, or at "Oak Lawn," Colleton County, where the old avenue of live oaks was laid out, and labelled with great care by a Surveyor, in 1767, the trees being ten years old when set out. "A manuscript by one of the Sacheverell's giving an account of 'Oak Lawn' the present home of the Elliotts (with the story of the Angola war in 1739, when the Sacheverell children were massacred there by the negroes) was burned, with the old house in 1865 by Sherman's troops, also Thomas Sacheverell's *Diary.*"

Their daughter, *Anne Rebecca,* married *Thomas Rhett Smith.*

HUTCHINSON

ARMS: *Per pale gules and azure, a lion rampant between eight cross-crosslets argent.*

CREST: *Out of a ducal coronet or, a cockatrice azure, combed, beaked and wattled gules.*

"These arms represent the seal of John Hutchinson,[54] the first to come to America, which seal was inherited by Thomas 'of Chehaw,' his son, and from which the bookplate was made for Thomas Leger Hutchinson," a nephew of Anne Holland Hutchinson (Mrs. William Skirving). The age of this bookplate antedates "the publication of *The Memoirs of Lucy Hutchinson* 1808,

[54] Pedigree Papers of Miss Elliott.

in which the same arms are given to the Nottingham branch. The fact aids in verifying the abiding tradition in the South Carolina family that the Hutchinsons in that State are directly descended from Colonel John Hutchinson, Governor of Nottingham Castle and his wife Lucy Apsley, daughter of Sir Allan Apsley. Another proof of this claim, is the fact that Anne Holland Hutchinson (daughter of Thomas Hutchinson and wife of Colonel Skirving), always addressed as 'Cousin' Polly Sacheverell, who was Colonel Skirving's first wife."

HUTCHINSON

JOHN HUTCHINSON is the first of the name known in Carolina, where he had large grants of land.[55] He married Anne ——, who died November 26, 1723. Their son:

COLONEL THOMAS HUTCHINSON, was born November 16, 1722. He was Justice for Charleston, in March, 1776.[56] He was the owner of large plantations in Carolina, and of land in Georgia, granted originally to Thomas Sacheverell and himself. The will of "one Postel" leaves to his heirs, land in Georgia, originally granted to Thomas Hutchinson and Thomas Sacheverell, whose brother John was attorney for Thomas Hutchinson. These Hutchinsons had cousins in Jamaica, one of whom wrote, 1774, to Thomas, of South Carolina, begging his cousin " To be circumspect in re-

[55] From *Book of Grants*, State House, S. C., Vol. ii, K, p. 3; ix, p. 197.

[56] *Journal of Assn.*, March 13, 1776.

gard to the threatened uprising, as their family had
suffered enough from rebellions." Thomas Hutchinson signed many papers for Sacheverell in 1759, and a
strong tie of friendship and intimacy always existed between the two families. He signed as bondsman for
Charles Pinckney, and Edmund Bellinger, for £25,000
in 1750. He was a member from St. Bartholomew's
to the General Convention, 1774, and died at March's,
South Carolina, 1789.

He married, 1750, *Rebecca,* the daughter of *William,*
and the granddaughter of Thomas and Leah Holman.

"THOMAS HOLMAN came to America in 1700, and
had a grant of seventeen hundred acres on the Ashley
River, S. C., March, 1704, and died, October 27, 1730."

Anne Holland Hutchinson, married WILLIAM SKIRV-
ING.

MOORE

ARMS: *Sable, a swan with wings expansed argent, membered or, within
a bordure engrailed of the same.*[57]

The Moores,[58] of South Carolina, are said, by many

[57] From seal of Governor James Moore.
[58] References: *Bibles; Letters; S. C. Hist. Mag.; Wills,* etc.

authorities, to be of Irish descent, but according to all available records they belong to the Devonshire family of that name. They came to Carolina via the Barbadoes, arriving with Sir John Yeamans, Bart.

GOVERNOR JAMES MOORE, was born 1641, and died in Charleston, 1706. He was Chief Justice of Carolina, 1700 to 1701, and Governor of the Province, 1700 to 1703. While in office he was accused of selling Indians as slaves in Jamaica and Barbadoes, but Johnson (an old authority) says, page 228: "That Governor Moore's measures were known and approved in England is evidenced from his being retained in office about three years, and when superseded by Nathaniel Johnson, was appointed attorney-general. On page 229, Governor Bull said he had investigated the matter, and that the Indians being a terrible scourge to the Colony, Moore had them captured and shipped to the West Indies, but that the proceeds of sales were always placed in the publick Treasury." James Moore married *Margaret,* only daughter of Sir John and Margaret (Gibbes) Yeamans. "Governor Moore afterwards married his mother-in-law. The latter seems to have had a tender heart, as it is recorded concerning two criminals that 'upon the earnest solicitation of Margaret, Lady Yeamans, and the rest of the Ladyes and Gentlemen of this County, it is resolved that the execution of the said persons be suspended.'" Issue, first wife:

James, the second Governor.

Maurice, founder of Brunswick, N. C.

ROGER.

Nathaniel.

John.

—— (Mrs. Clifford), who afterwards married Job Howe, and was the grandmother of General Robert

Howe, of Revolutionary fame, who fought the Dutch with General Gadsden.

Rebecca, married —— Dey.

—— (Mrs. Schencking).

ROGER MOORE, called " King Roger," from the state in which he lived; born August 24, 1694, and died October 20, 1759, was the owner of the beautiful " Orton " plantation near Brunswick, N. C. In the old records he is called " The Honorable Roger Moore, Esq., Member of ye council," where he served continuously from 1734 to 1749. He had a grant of land in North Hanover County, Carolina, 1745.[59]

He married, October 10, 1721, *Catherine,* the daughter of Colonel William and Sarah (Cooke) Rhett; born December 14, 1705, and died June 11, 1745. Issue:

George.

Roger.

Sarah, married *Thomas Smith IV.*

William, married Parris (Mary) Davis.

Mary, married Edward Harleston.

Ann, married, first, John Swann; second, Peter Taylor.

YEAMANS

On August 22, 1651, Sir Robert Yeamans, Baronet, of Bristol, Eng., a Lieutenant-Colonel of His Majesty's forces in England, obtained a warrant for a private man-of-war, being bound to Virginia. In the *Edinburgh Annual Register,* March 16, 1814, a statement is given, regarding the disinterment of his body, which was found " In a coffin of great antiquity," in St. Maryport Church, Bristol. He was executed for his devotion to the King, being Prince Rupert's main stay in the

[59] *Col. Rec.,* Vol. iv, p. 767.

defence of the city. "He was High Sheriff and his body was handsomely accoutred in the costume of the day (1643), embalmed, and in the highest state of preservation, with gloves similar to those worn by the High Sheriff of the present day." His son:

GOVERNOR SIR JOHN YEAMANS, BART, held for some time the office of Governor of the Barbadoes, and came to Carolina in 1665, bringing many Englishmen as colonists; and the first slaves introduced into the Province. He was made Landgrave, 1671, and was Governor of Carolina from 1671 to 1674,[60] after which time he retired to the Barbadoes and died 1676. His home in Carolina, at Goose Creek, "Yeamans Hall," was built prior to 1680, and remains in the possession of the Landgrave's descendants. "The house was surrounded by earthworks as a defence against the Indians and had portholes in the walls. In the cellar was a deep well for supplying the garrison with water in case of a siege, and a subterranean passage, whose entrance can still be seen, led out under the garden to the creek where boats were kept securely concealed. Within, the walls were painted in landscapes, little gilded cherubs spread their wings over the arches. The guest chamber was hung with Gobelin tapestry; the floors tessellated and the apartments adorned with statues. Old Yeaman's Hall has its ghost-story, and its secret chamber where, during the Revolution, and also during the Civil War, the silver and family valuables were concealed."[61] The *Colonial Records of North Carolina* state that Sir John Yeamans had governed the Cape Fear Colony from 1665 to 1690. Charleston, in 1680, was laid out by him.

He married Margaret, the daughter of Sir Philip

60 McCrady's *Hist. of Carolina.*
61 From *Harper's Mag.,* 1875.

Gibbes, of Barbadoes.   In his will, dated 1671, Sir John
leaves a large settlement, cattle, jewels, plate, private
ship, coach and four, and entire guardianship of his
children to his "dear and well-beloved wife, ye ladye
Margaret."

Their daughter *Margaret,* who was not of age when
her father died, had a dowry of three hundred thousand
pounds of sugar, besides land, etc.   She married Gov-
ERNOR JAMES MOORE.   Their son, ROGER MOORE, married *Catherine,* the daughter of William and Sarah
(Cooke) Rhett.

RHETT

ARMS: *Or, a cross engrailed sable.*
CREST: *A dexter arm embowed in armor holding a broken spear.*
MOTTO: *Aut faciam aut periam.*

These arms are taken from the tombstone of Colonel

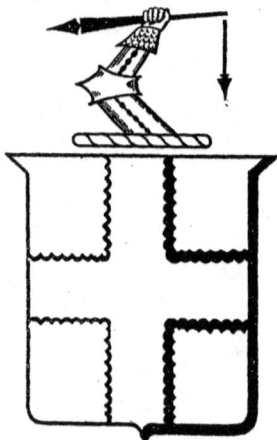

RHETT

William Rhett in St. Philip's
churchyard (Western),
Charleston, S. C.*

COLONEL WILLIAM RHETT,
born September 4, 1666, and
died January 12, 1722, was
the son of Sir Gaulter de
Rhaedt, of Flanders.[62]   He
came to Carolina in 1694, with
his wife Sarah and one child.
His father's family came from
Holland, under William of
Orange, and the original spelling of the name (Rhaedt) was
changed to suit the English mode of pronouncing it.[63]

* *S. C. Hist. Mag.*
[62] Ramsey's *Hist. of S. C.*
[63] Johnson's *Traditions.*

He was Colonel of the Provincial Militia of Carolina,
Receiver-General of the Lords Proprietors of Carolina
1722; Vice-Admiral of the colonial navy; Surveyor and
Comptroller of His Majesty's customs for Carolina
and the Bahama Islands; Lieutenant-General and con-
structor of fortifications.[64] These offices he held until
appointed Governor of the Barbadoes, for which place
he was preparing to start when seized with an attack
of apoplexy, from which he died in Charleston. A
monument was erected in that city to his memory over
the family vault in the Western cemetery of St.
Philip's near the front door of that building. William
Rhett was a follower of Sacheverall's doctrines and
"used to pay a great deal of respect to Sacheverall's
picture, which hung in the colonel's hall in 1715."[65]
Dalcho's Church History mentions one Tankard, one
Chalice and Paten and one large Alms Plate on
which is engraved: "The gift of Colonel William
Rhett to the Church of St. Philip's, Charles Town,
South Carolina." The plate is intact and in use at
the present day. When the pirates had become for-
midable to the trade of the West Indies and Carolina,
Colonel William Rhett proved his courage and skill in
naval warfare. In command of two vessels he pursued
Steede Bonnet into Cape Fear River, captured the sloop
and thirty pirates, the latter being tried, condemned
and hanged at Charleston, for which service Colonel
Rhett received the thanks of the Proprietors.[66] Charleston at this time was "fortified more for beauty than
strength. There are several fair streets in the town and
some very handsome buildings, as Mr. Landgrave

[64] *S. C. Hist. Mag.*; Johnson's *Reminiscences.*
[65] *Collections* of S. C. Hist. Soc., Vol. ii, p. 233.
[66] R. R. Heyward's *Records.*

Smith's house on the Key with a drawbridge and wharf before it, Colonel Rhett's on the Key, also Mr. Rivers', Mr. Boone's, Mr. Schinkings' and ten or twelve more which deserve to be taken notice of." [67]

He married Sarah Cooke, who was born 1665, and died December, 1745. They were the ancestors of many noted men and women of Great Britain and America. Chief Justice Trott, at the age of seventy-one, married William Rhett's widow, aged sixty-three. As Mrs. Rhett, she lived on the west side of East Bay, Charleston. Issue:

Christiana, died young.

William, married Mary, only daughter of Chief Justice Trott.

Sarah, married Eleazer Allen.

Rebecca, died young.

Catherine, married ROGER MOORE; their daughter *Sarah* married *Thomas Smith IV.*, whose son, ROGER MOORE SMITH, married *Mary Rutledge*.

Robert, died young.

Mary, married Richard Wright.

[67] Old Mixon.

RUTLEDGE

ARMS: *Argent, on a chevron azure between three crescents, two lozenges gules.*[68]
CREST: *A Crescent.*
MOTTO: *Progredi non regredi.*

"On March 26, 1776, the Provincial Congress of South Carolina set up an independent government with John Rutledge as president. On Tuesday, April 2, 1776, the General Assembly passed the following: *Resolved* that his Excellency the President and Commander-in-Chief, by and with the advice and consent of the Privy Council may and he is hereby authorized to design and cause to be made a Great Seal of South Carolina and until such an one can be made, to fix a temporary Public Seal. For a temporary seal, President Rutledge used his private seal bearing his family Coat of Arms. . . ."[69]

The Rutledge family, of English origin, settled in Ireland, in the time of Oliver Cromwell, and owned land

[68] From an old Book Plate of Edward Rutledge, Signer of the Declaration of Independence.
[69] *S. C. Hist. Mag.,* Vol. vii, p. 266.

of Ballymagiel, near Baroulog, County Cavan, Ireland, for several generations.[70]

The American family descends from two brothers, Andrew and JOHN, who came to this country from Ireland (some historians say from the north of England), 1735. They were men of the highest education, Andrew a lawyer, and John a physician. Andrew became Speaker of the House of Assembly of Carolina, 1749-1752, and was complimented by both King and Governor on his learning and capacity. The two brothers settled in Charleston, S. C.

DOCTOR JOHN RUTLEDGE was acting surgeon in the 1st South Carolina Regiment, 1738. The records give the following:

" The repeated advices we have received of the designs of Spain against this Province . . . have determined several Gentlemen of Worth and Distinction in Charleston to accept commissions in the Militia and to make themselves Masters in the best manner they could of the Military Discipline, that they might be the better enabled to act vigorously in defence of the province. . . . To this end His Honor the President of the Council (William Bull) has been pleased to form the Town Militia (which for six years consisted only of two Companies and since of four) into the First Regiment of this Province. The Regiment is divided into six companies of which the following are officers. . . . (24 names) and Mr. John Rutledge surgeon to the regiment. The regiment of 600 men exclusive of Officers and Monday last His Majesty's Birthday, appeared for the first time under arms and made a very gallant and genteel appearance."[71]

[70] From Burke's *Colonial Gentry*. Ref. for Rutledge pedigree: Mrs.· C. C. Pinckney; *Bible* of Roger Smith owned by Miss Elliott; *Papers of* the late Mrs. Frank Hampton.

[71] *S. C. Hist. Mag.*, Vol. ii, p. 134.

"Annandale," the Plantation Home of Andrew Johnstone
On the No. Santee River, S. C.

Water Front, Beaufort, S. C.

Dr. John Rutledge married, December 25, 1738, *Sarah,* daughter of Hugh and Sarah (Boone) Hext, who was born 1724. Washington was entertained at breakfast by Mrs. Rutledge in 1791, then a very old lady. She had grants of two thousand four hundred and thirty-three acres in Colleton County, August 20, 1767, and sixteen hundred acres in Berkeley County, February 22, 1768.[72] Dr. Rutledge died December 27, 1750.[73] Issue, seven children, five of whom lived to maturity, viz.:

John and Edward, the Governors.
Hugh, the Chancellor.
Andrew.
Sarah (Mrs. Mathewes).
Mary, married ROGER MOORE SMITH.

HEXT

ARMS: *Or, a tower embattled between three battle-axes, erect sable. A crescent for difference.*

CREST: *Out of a tower embattled a demi-lion holding in dexter paw a battle-axe sable.*

The arms of Hext (or Hicks) of Somersetshire, Great Britain, as given in the " Visitation of Somersetshire ":

HUGH HEXT,[74] came with his family to the province of Carolina from Dorsetshire, Eng., and was related to the Hexts of Somersetshire. He was elected a member of the Commons House of Assembly, 1707, and he was one of the Commissioners appointed under the "Church Acts" of November, 1704, and

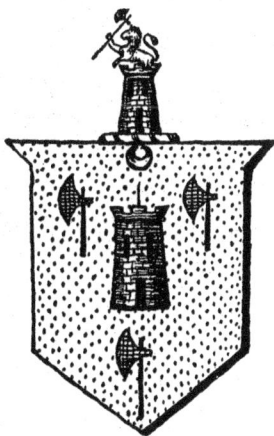

HEXT

72 State House *Records,* B. 16, p. 259.
73 St. Philip's *Register.*   74 *S. C. Hist. Mag.,* Vol. vi, p. 29.

November 30, 1706. Ramsay says, on page 10, Vol. II: "Two of the twenty laymen who were vested 'with these extraordinary powers,' and highly esteemed by the people, were John Woodward and Hugh Hext. They formed a 'board of Commissioners to superintend the temporal concerns of all the parishes and exercise ecclesiastical jurisdiction, with full powers to deprive ministers of their livings at pleasure, etc.'" Surviving issue:

Alexander.

Edward, of Charleston, S. C., in whose will, dated October 6, 1739, bequests are made to "Kinsman Philip Hext of Froome, in Somersetshire, Great Britain."[75]

Francis, David, Thomas, and Amias.

HUGH II.

Amelia, married —— Godfrey.

Katharine, married —— Still.

Martha, married, first, William Bowen; second, John Bee.

HUGH HEXT II., was a member of the South Carolina Assembly, 1717 to 1720,[76] and died in November, 1732. He married, November, 1723, Sarah, the daughter of John and Elizabeth (Fenwick) Boone.

Their daughter *Sarah* married JOHN RUTLEDGE.

Mary Rutledge married ROGER MOORE SMITH.

Thomas Rhett Smith, married *Anne Rebecca Skirving.*

Anne Hutchinson Smith, married *William Elliott IV.*

Mary Barnwell Elliott, married *Andrew Johnstone.* Their daughter is:

EMMA ELLIOTT JOHNSTONE,

Member of Chapter I., The Colonial Dames of America.

[75] *Ibid,* Vol. vi, p. 40.
[76] River's *Hist. of S. C.,* p. 465, Appendix.

www.ingramcontent.com/pod-product-compliance
Lightning Source LLC
Chambersburg PA
CBHW072039020426
42334CB00017B/1324